Database Management
Principles and Products

Charles J. Bontempo
IBM Corporation and Polytechnic University

Cynthia Maro Saracco
IBM Corporation, Santa Teresa Laboratory

For book and bookstore information

http://www.prenhall.com

Prentice Hall PTR
Upper Saddle River, New Jersey 07458

Bontempo, Charles J.
    Database management: principles and products / Charles
  J. Bontempo, Cynthia Maro Saracco.
        p.   cm.
    Includes bibliographical references and index.
    ISBN 0-13-380189-6
    1. Database management.   2. Saracco, Cynthia Maro.   II. Title.
  QA76.9.D3B666 1996
  005.75--dc20   95-16652
                                                  CIP

Editorial/production supervision: **Ann Sullivan**
Cover designer: **Jack Robol**
Cover manager: **Jerry Votta**
Manufacturing manager: **Alexis R. Heydt**
Acquisitions editor: **Paul Becker**
Editorial assistant: **Maureen Diana**

Published by Prentice Hall PTR
Prentice-Hall, Inc.
A Simon and Schuster Company
Upper Saddle River, NJ 07458

The publisher offers discounts on this book when ordered in bulk quantities.
For more information, contact:

    Corporate Sales Department
    Prentice Hall PTR
    One Lake Street
    Upper Saddle River, NJ 07458

    Phone: 800-382-3419   Fax: 201-236-7141
    email: corpsales@prenhall.com

Printed in the United States of America

10 9 8 7 6 5 4 3

ISBN: 0-13-380189-6

Prentice-Hall International (UK) Limited, *London*
Prentice-Hall of Australia Pty. Limited, *Sydney*
Prentice-Hall Canada Inc., *Toronto*
Prentice-Hall Hispanoamericana, S.A., *Mexico*
Prentice-Hall of India Private Limited, *New Delhi*
Prentice-Hall of Japan, Inc., *Tokyo*
Simon & Schuster Asia Pte. Ltd., *Singapore*
Editora Prentice-Hall do Brasil, Ltda., *Rio de Janeiro*

Contents

Preface

Database management has emerged as one of the key areas of software technology in the industry today. Dozens of products are offered in this arena, and many firms throughout the world rely on database management systems (DBMSs) to run their business. As can be expected, DBMS technology has grown increasingly complex over the past several years as researchers and vendors have sought to accommodate new user requirements. Different types of DBMS products have emerged, as well as various extensions and complementary offerings to existing products. It's not uncommon for programmers, database administrators, information systems managers, and students of database management to be expected to understand not only fundamental DBMS concepts but also newer technologies, such as:

- Parallelism
- Replication and copy management services
- Distributed databases
- Data access middleware and connectivity support
- Client/server architectures
- Object-oriented support

Obtaining such information can be a daunting task, requiring perusal of numerous research papers, journal articles, and texts, many of which are highly theoretical in nature and difficult for those without considerable expertise to understand. Furthermore, understanding how commercial products are actually supporting these technologies can be even more elusive, often requiring the purchase of multiple product manuals and possibly installation and testing of multiple products.

This book is designed to provide readers with any easy-to-read, detailed discussion of these and other DBMS technologies. Considerable attention is paid to how these technologies are implemented in five popular commercial DBMSs: IBM's DB2, Oracle's Oracle, Sybase's SQL Server, Tandem's NonStop SQL/MP, and Computer Associate's CA-OpenIngres. It is expected that software professionals interested in understanding commercial DBMS products will find such discussion particularly helpful. And, although vendors ship new releases of their products on a periodic bases, they seldom remove existing functions or alter their fundamental product architecture. Therefore, this book can serve as a useful starting point for understanding these products for years to come.

In addition, the book is designed to serve as a tutorial on key DBMS concepts as they relate to practical issues. This tutorial will facilitate and enhance the reader's understanding of the capabilities and features of each product described.

The intended audiences for this book are technical professionals—both managers and key staff personnel—who are responsible for the evaluation and selection of DBMSs, as well as those seeking to enhance their technical vitality by understanding important activities in the DBMS field. Since the book is highly tutorial, it is also a useful text for database management courses in academic and industrial education programs. A basic understanding of computers and programming concepts is presumed.

For the DBMS student, this book includes tutorials on the advantages of database management systems, an overview of the various types of DBMSs that have been developed, and an explanation of many of the practical aspects of the relational DBMS approach (which is extremely popular in the industry and accounts for a very large revenue base). In addition, this book provides an introduction to the Structured Query Language (SQL), the industry-standard language for interacting with relational DBMSs. Also included are discussions of more recent DBMS approaches, including object DBMSs and hybrid or object/relational DBMSs.

For the DBMS professional, this book offers insight into contemporary technologies and detailed descriptions of the features and functions of popular products. The reader will learn how different products support critical database management features, such as concurrency control, integrity enforcement, recovery, security, optimization, and other functions. More recent topics—such as parallelism, distributed database, and replication—are also discussed for each product.

This book is organized into four major parts:

- Part One discusses fundamental DBMS concepts and principles. This includes chapters on industry trends, and overview of popular database models, and introduction to major DBMS components and functions, a tutorial on the relational DBMS approach, and an introduction to SQL.
- Part Two discusses contemporary DBMS technologies. These include support for client/server environments, distributed databases, replication or

copy management services, data access middleware or connectivity offerings, and parallelism

- Part Three profiles popular relational DBMSs offered by IBM, Tandem, Oracle, Sybase, and Computer Associates (after its recent acquisition of ASK/Ingres). One chapter per product is provided, and topics discussed in the previous parts are discussed.
- Part Four describes object-oriented technology and its impact on the DBMS industry. It discusses both the object DBMS approach as well as hybrid or object/relational DBMSs.

Included at the end of each chapter are detailed references to additional literature on the subject, should the reader desire further information. For ease of reference, a substantial index is also provided.

ABOUT THE AUTHORS

Charles J. Bontempo consults on database topics for IBM and is an adjunct professor at Polytechnic University. He has developed and presented courses on many relational DBMSs, as well as on prerelational and object DBMSs. He was a staff member of the IBM Systems Research Institute, an original member of the ANS Relational Task Group, lectures often for DB2 user groups (including International DB2 Users Group (IDUG)), and has delivered courses nationwide via satellite television. He has also published a number of articles in DBMS publications and has more than 20 years of experience in database management systems as a developer and a user.

Cynthia Maro Saracco has worked on database issues at IBM's Santa Teresa Laboratory for more than 10 years. She has hands-on experience using and/or administering a variety of DBMS products, including DB2, SQL Server, Oracle, Ingres, and ObjectStore. She has published more than 25 technical reports and trade journal articles on a variety of topics, including object-oriented technologies, middleware, and relational DBMSs. In addition, she has presented on numerous database issues at conferences and symposiums throughout North America, South America, and Europe.

ACKNOWLEDGMENTS

The authors are indebted to a number of people for their assistance in reviewing portions of this book and/or supplying source material for information presented in this book. In alphabetical order, these people (and their professional affiliation as of this writing) are: Bernard Antonuk (Computer Associates International Inc.), Paul Bass (Sybase, Inc.), Susanne Englert (Tandem Computers Incorporated), Rob Goldring (IBM Corporation), Ken Jacobs (Oracle Corporation), Jim Lyon (Tandem Computers Incorporated), Roger Miller (IBM Corporation), Ken Paris (Forecross Corporation), Don Weil (IBM Corporation), and Robb Williams (Sybase, Inc.).

PART 1
Concepts and Principles of Database Management Systems

CHAPTER 1
The Industry Today

Database management systems (DBMSs) are a critical element of today's software industry. Many of the world's leading software vendors—including the IBM Corporation, Computer Associates, Microsoft Corporation, Oracle Corporation, Sybase, Inc., and others—offer one or more DBMS products. Major corporations often rely on DBMSs to perform critical business functions (such as processing their payrolls, tracking sales, and managing inventories), and some people even employ DBMSs for their personal use (such as monitoring their financial investments). This versatile software generates worldwide revenues of more than $5 billion annually, and that figure is continuing to increase each year.

CHAPTER OBJECTIVES

This chapter introduces the reader to database management systems, explaining why this software is used, the type of function it provides above and beyond what is found in file systems, and what types of applications often make use of DBMSs. It also introduces the reader to a number of important technology trends that are impacting the DBMS industry—trends that are discussed in greater detail in subsequent chapters of this book.

AN INTRODUCTION TO DATABASE MANAGEMENT SYSTEMS

Just what are DBMSs? Simply put, they are products that—as their name implies—manage data as a shared resource. They enable users to group related

1

data together to form a base of data (or a *database*) and to share this data with others. To enable people to do this effectively, DBMSs must provide mechanisms for storing the data, accessing the data, securing the data (so that people can "see" only what they're supposed to), ensuring that the quality (or integrity) of the data is preserved, and recovering from errors. Supporting such tasks often involves a considerable amount of code and expertise; for this reason, most companies purchase a general-purpose DBMS rather than build their own.

DBMS offerings today are available on a wide variety of computing platforms, ranging from personal computers to massively parallel processing systems. Products are available for such diverse environments as DOS, Windows, Netware, OS/2, Macintosh, Unix, VMS, OS/400, and MVS. In many cases, DBMSs can be configured to run on a single system (in a centralized computing fashion) or to span systems (in a client/server or distributed fashion).

DBMS technology has had a far-reaching impact on the software industry. After DBMSs were first developed and released, customers gradually began seeking "tools" or ready-made programs that would make using the DBMS and accessing its data easier. Popular tools now include query/report writers (which retrieve data stored in the DBMS and summarize key points of interest), application development facilities (which can simplify the task of writing programs to access the data), utilities (which administrators can use to monitor the system's performance or to load the database with data), and graphics packages (which can create bar charts and presentation materials based on information in the database). In addition, some vendors also offer "vertical" or industry-specific applications that make use of a DBMS; such applications, which include accounting, personnel, sales, and health care applications, have also helped drive the sales of DBMSs and further their use in the market. While it's more difficult to quantify the revenue generated from such DBMS-related tools and applications, analysts agree that these revenues far surpass those of the DBMS products themselves. Figure 1–1 illustrates a sample DBMS configuration.

The DBMS industry has impacted not only the number and types of software offerings available today but also the employment opportunities at commercial firms outside the computer industry. Many medium- to large-sized companies now employ individuals to administer or manage DBMSs, write applications for these DBMSs, and support nontechnical users who seek access to the data contained in these DBMSs. Furthermore, many consulting agencies employ specialists to help companies fine-tune their DBMSs for better performance, assist with installation and configuration of these systems, and perform other functions.

Query/report writer	Programming Tools	User-written programs	Purchased programs
Database Management System (DBMS)			
Operating System			

Figure 1–1. Sample DBMS configuration

As a result, many thousands of software professionals now work in positions that require modest to extensive knowledge of at least one DBMS.

All of this may have caused the reader to wonder just *why* DBMSs are so popular. After all, file systems have been around since the early days of the computing industry. They enable people to store and retrieve data. They are a part of all modern operating systems, so they're readily available for free. Why not just use them?

THE NEED FOR DBMSS

DBMSs offer several advantages over file systems. Chief among these are the ability to minimize or eliminate redundant data, the ability to reduce the amount of code required to write applications (by incorporating certain functions into the DBMS), and the ability to enable multiple applications to use the same data in different ways.

Before DBMSs were widely deployed, programmers typically stored their data in files. These files were usually structured to suit the needs of *one* particular application. Other applications, which might be interested in much of the same data, either found the structure of the files unsuitable, the data incomplete or the files inaccessible. Therefore, these applications created their own files, duplicating much of the same data. As the reader might imagine, it gradually became more difficult for companies to keep the data in all these different files in sync or to pinpoint all the files that needed to be changed when a common piece of data needed to be altered. Thus, the quality of the data frequently became suspect, and the effort required to resolve the inconsistencies often became quite costly. Furthermore, gathering information that was spread across multiple files was often quite time-consuming, requiring an in-depth knowledge of the existence, structure, and content of each file.

DBMSs—particularly those that employ a *relational* architecture (which is discussed in Chapter 4, "The Relational Database Approach")—help resolve these problems by enabling customers to apply a common design or structure to their data and make this data readily available to those programs that need it. Thus, redundancy is reduced, and programmers are not required to design their own file systems in order to build their applications. In addition, many DBMSs even provide certain error-checking mechanisms (such as the ability to verify that values describing the "sex" of an employee are either "M" for male or "F" for female), freeing programmers from coding such mechanisms themselves (perhaps multiple times).

Therefore, the overall benefits of DBMSs over file systems typically include reduced costs and shorter application development time. The systems tend to be more readily adaptable to change, as the data is more consolidated and is usually designed to be independent of any given application. And, while DBMSs often use file systems as their underlying storage mechanism, they shield programmers from much of the low-level coding required to work effectively with these file systems. For example, DBMSs may maintain and scan indexes to improve data access, or they may embed addresses with certain data to speed access to related data. Such helpful facilities can be—and usually are—kept hidden from the programmer, freeing him or her from writing what would otherwise be considerable code to improve the data access portions of the application. Programmers who rely strictly on file systems for data storage are likely to find themselves forced to worry about such things in order to effectively implement robust, high-performing applications; in doing so, their time is taken away from the immediate job at hand—writing the code to solve a particular business problem.

TYPES OF DBMS APPLICATIONS

While applications that use DBMSs can be quite varied, most can be grouped into three categories: batch applications, decision support applications, and online transaction-processing (or OLTP) applications.

Batch processing has its roots in the early days of the computer industry, when programs were not executed in real time but were instead submitted to the system (often in the form of a deck or batch of punched cards) for later processing. These applications (sometimes called *jobs*) were scheduled according to their priority, time of submission, and other factors, and then run at some later point. Today, a number of DBMS applications—particularly those executing in large, centralized computing environments—are still batch-oriented. These applications may be either read- or update-intensive but they are well suited toward executing during off-hours when computing resources are more readily available. For example, a firm may choose to write a batch-oriented DBMS application to process its payroll. Every Saturday evening, the application may be scheduled to execute, reading data from the DBMS about employees' wages and the number of hours each employee worked, and using this data to calculate and issue their paychecks. This makes efficient use of computing resources, freeing up the system to handle other work during peak times.

Decision support applications, as their name implies, help businesses use existing data to spot trends, pinpoint problems, and make more intelligent decisions. By making data more accessible and more easily shared than in file-processing environments, DBMSs helped popularize this type of application, which has now become the cornerstone of many businesses. Decision support applications tend to be read-intensive and may be ad hoc or unpredictable in nature. For example, unusually high sales at a particular retail outlet may prompt a district manager to request a report of the most rapidly selling items and the quantities of these currently in stock at the store. If the stock of these critical items is low, the manager may want to know the inventory available at all distribution centers within a certain distance of the store. Finally, the manager may want to understand the number of available cargo trucks in the region, their capacities, and their current schedules in case one or more need to be diverted to help restock the store. Such requests may be difficult to anticipate, may involve a great deal of information (which traditionally would have been spread across multiple files), and often need to be satisfied quickly if the business is to maintain its competitive edge. These types of applications were the initial emphasis of DBMSs that emerged in the commercial arena in the 1980s, and they continue to form the basis for many of today's critical business applications.

Online transaction-processing applications, by contrast, tend to be update-intensive. The type of work involved tends to be more predictable than in a decision support environment, although the data itself is often unknown when the application is written. A typical OLTP application might involve processing deposits and withdrawals at a bank. If all the customer account information is consolidated in a single database, it's quite likely that many people will be trying to deposit and withdraw money from their accounts at the same time. In some cases, two or more people might be trying to withdraw or deposit money into the same account at the same time. DBMSs that seek to satisfy OLTP applications often must be able to handle many logical units of work (or *transactions*) concurrently, must be available around the clock—for example, to support transactions at automated teller machines (or ATMs)—and must offer high performance.

Each of these types of applications places different demands on the DBMS and may require different kinds of functions. Although a single DBMS can be (and often is) used to support two or more of these kinds of applications simultaneously, some products do this more effectively than others. Depending on its particular requirements, a firm may employ multiple DBMSs (using each in primarily one environment and/or for one application type) or a single DBMS to handle mixed workloads.

While batch, decision support, and OLTP work represent the bulk of DBMS applications today, some other kinds have emerged in recent years (and are still continuing to emerge). For example, some DBMS applications now support iterative design work, where a group of engineers may collaborate on a new automobile design or a group of writers may collaborate on a book or newsletter. Such applications might have a relatively small number of concurrent users, but these users may need to work with the data (the automobile design or the newsletter) for extended periods of time. Other firms are using DBMSs to support multimedia-based applications, where the data may include video, audio, text (documents), and images. Video-on-demand applications—which would allow customers to select which movies they want shown on their TVs at what times (rather than having to accept what is broadcast by the networks)—are one example of an emerging DBMS application that relies heavily on multimedia data.

TRENDS IN THE DBMS INDUSTRY

The DBMS industry has had to continue to adapt to new customer requirements and advances in other areas of computing, such as new hardware architectures. Among the significant trends affecting the DBMS industry today are:

- Client/server (or decentralized) computing environments
- Distributed databases and mixed-vendor (heterogeneous) computing environments

- Multiprocessor environments, in which many microprocessors or reduced instruction-set computer (RISC) processors work together to form a single system
- Object-oriented concepts

Although these areas, and others, are discussed in greater detail later, it's worth taking a brief look at each now.

Client/Server Systems

In the 1970s through the mid-1980s, DBMSs were designed almost exclusively to support centralized, uniprocessor environments. These included large mainframe systems (perhaps running MVS) and midrange systems (perhaps running VMS or Unix). But the emergence of personal computers in the 1980s considerably altered the way businesses worked. No longer was all work done in a centralized environment (which, by the way, was usually managed by a separate data-processing organization in the company); instead, some work was moved to personal computers, which were relatively cheap, offered dedicated resources to individuals, and employed icons, windows, and other graphics to improve their ease of use. Gradually, departments and workgroups began linking these smaller computers directly with one another via a local-area network (or LAN). This enabled members of the workgroup to share computing resources—such as a printer—by designating one or more computers in the network as a *server*, or a system that would service requests from other systems (usually called *clients*). As the reader might expect, users in these client/server environments gradually wanted to share another type of resource—data—and this prompted the emergence of file servers and, later, DBMS servers.

Enabling a DBMS to support a client/server environment involved some work. Support for a networking interface—actually, multiple networking interfaces, since different customers preferred different ones—was mandatory. Tools and other "front-end" applications had to be moved to the client platform, which often used a different operating system and hardware architecture than the server platform. New mechanisms had to be introduced to monitor and tune overall system performance, to ensure that network traffic was minimized, to help diagnose errors, and to manage the overall environment, which had become more complex than the traditional centralized environment in many ways. These issues, and others, are discussed in greater detail in Chapter 6, "Client/Server Environments."

Open and Distributed Systems

The DBMS community has also been affected by the sheer proliferation of the number of DBMS products, operating system environments, networking platforms, and hardware platforms now at many customer sites. While it was once common to find companies using products almost exclusively from a single vendor (typically, IBM or DEC), it is now a rarity among medium- and large-sized companies. Economics, the drive toward "open systems" and standards-based computing, and the intensely competitive computer industry make it unlikely that the days of a single-supplier mentality will return. Many companies now use multiple DBMSs, including different DBMS servers for different departments, workgroups, or divisions, as well as one or more centralized DBMSs for corporate-wide functions. DBMS vendors have had to cope with this change, often by providing for *portability* of their products across multiple platforms and *interoperability* between their products and, sometimes, those of their competitors. The latter has led to the emergence of *distributed databases* and various forms of *middleware* (including *gateways*). These topics are discussed in Chapter 7, "Distributed Databases," and Chapter 9, "Middleware."

Parallel-Processing Environments

Multiprocessor environments are a hardware-driven technology that has also impacted the DBMS industry in recent years and will probably continue to do so for some time. As improvements in the capacity and power of microprocessors and RISC processors steadily improved in the 1980s and early 1990s, hardware vendors began seeing that a single computer built of multiple small processors could offer the same computing power, at significantly less cost, than systems that used a single large processor (or uniprocessor). They reasoned that such systems might be attractive to customers, not only for their cost savings, but because they offered the potential for *scalability*—that is, customers could scale the systems to meet their current requirements, increasing their power as needed by adding more processors rather than trade in one entire uniprocessor system for another larger one.

The challenge for DBMS vendors, then, was to redesign their systems to support these new environments, distributing the work across multiple processors in a manner that would exploit the available computing resources and provide near-linear performance gains. A number of research projects and commercial DBMSs now offer varying degrees of support for *parallelism*—using multiple processors to execute work in parallel. This topic is discussed in greater detail in Chapter 10, "Parallelism."

Object-Oriented Systems

Changes in programming languages and techniques are also impacting the DBMS community. In recent years, many firms have begun experimenting with or using *object-oriented* programming languages such as Smalltalk or C++. These languages differ from more traditional programming languages (such as COBOL, PL/1, and FORTRAN) in many ways; if used properly, they provide programmers with added flexibility and the potential for greater code reuse.

However, because these languages introduce new concepts and differ from their predecessors in significant ways, they often represent a considerable chalıenge for a traditional DBMS to support. For example, these languages enable programmers to create their own data types rather than settle for only the types supplied with that language compiler (such as integers, decimals, and characters). Furthermore, programmers may choose to create types of arbitrary complexity with a variety of internal structures. DBMSs have usually not supported this degree of flexibility; they traditionally supported a specific set of data types (usually those common to several popular programming languages) and a specific data structure. DBMS vendors are taking several approaches to supporting object-oriented concepts and programming languages, as is discussed in Chapter 17, "The Object Database Management System Approach," and Chapter 18, "The Extended Relational and Hybrid Approaches."

But first, a review of the data models and fundamental concepts of DBMSs is in order. These are the subjects of the following chapters.

SUMMARY

This chapter described a number of benefits associated with DBMS technology—benefits that caused this area of software to grow into a multibillion dollar industry. DBMSs offer users the ability to manage data as a shared resource, providing for such critical functions as ensuring the quality (or integrity) of the data, securing access to the data, storing the data, and ensuring that the data can be recovered in case of error. For many applications, DBMSs can help reduce development costs and coding time by providing function that would otherwise have to be coded within applications if file systems were used as a storage mechanism.

A variety of applications can take advantage of DBMSs. Batch applications, decision support applications, and online transaction-processing applications are three types that commonly use this technology. And, as hardware and other software technologies continue to advance, DBMS products are continuing to capitalize on many of these. Among the technology trends that have impacted the DBMS industry in recent years (and that are continuing to impact it) are client/server computing, distributed database environments, parallel-processing platforms, and object-oriented programming concepts. These areas are discussed more fully in subsequent chapters.

REFERENCES AND SUGGESTED READING

"Database Vendors Moving Battle to Tools Front," *Software Magazine*, January 1994, p. 61.

DATE, C. J. *An Introduction to Database Systems*, 6th ed., Addison-Wesley, 1994.

MEYER, BERTRAND. *Object-Oriented Software Construction*, Prentice-Hall, 1988.

"RDBMS Market Dynamics and Vendor Analysis," *InSide Gartner Group This Week*, Gartner Group, Dec. 8, 1993, p. 8.

CHAPTER 2
Overview of Database Models

CHAPTER OBJECTIVES

Most of today's DBMS products can be classified as using one of five general architectures: hierarchic, network (both of which are are often referred to as prerelational), relational, object-oriented, or hybrid. Many information-processing organizations use DBMSs based on two or more of these approaches, although the majority of DBMSs used commercially today are either prerelational or relational. The aim of this chapter is to provide the reader with an overview of these five database approaches, emphasizing their differences and their distinguishing features. This will provide the reader with a total picture before focusing on what is the dominant approach in the industry today.

PRERELATIONAL DBMSS

During the 1960s and early 1970s, different approaches to database management were developed. Although they may be collectively viewed as prerelational systems (because their commercial delivery predates that of relational systems), they actually were based on two different *data models* or ways of representing real-world entities in a database: the hierarchic and the network data models. These prerelational approaches are described here for several reasons. First, despite the current success of the relational database approach, large volumes of corporate data still reside in *legacy* databases managed by prerelational DBMSs. In addition, students of database technology often find that their understanding of the relational approach is enhanced by a familiarity with those database approaches that have preceded its adoption in the marketplace. Finally, it is useful for the reader to note some of the similarities between these prerelational systems and the object-oriented database approach discussed later in this book. (Of course, there are also important differences in the two approaches as well.)

Hierarchic DBMSs

The hierarchic approach, popularized by IBM's Information Management System (IMS), enables users to model their data as treelike hierarchies. These trees consist of one or more levels with just one node—the *root node*—at the top level; the lowest level is known as the *leaf* level. (Database trees are turned upside down.) A *record type* is defined by database designers for each node of the tree, including the root. A record type contains one or more fields in a specified order. There can be many records of the same type. Records are connected by branches that represent real-world connections among the entities of interest to the applications being supported. There can be multiple record types at any level except the root level.

Thus, a database designer working with a hierarchic system might create a COLLEGE tree type consisting of three levels and three record types, such as DEPARTMENT, INSTRUCTOR, and COURSE. This tree contains information about college academic departments along with data on all instructors for each department and all courses taught by each instructor within a department. The DEPARTMENT record type has the following defined fields: a department number, department name, and department location, as shown in Figure 2–1.

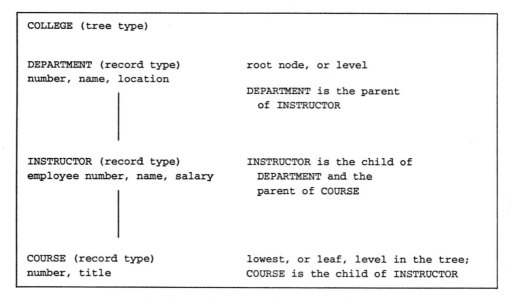

```
COLLEGE (tree type)


DEPARTMENT (record type)        root node, or level
number, name, location
                                DEPARTMENT is the parent
                                   of INSTRUCTOR
   |
   |
   |
   |
INSTRUCTOR (record type)        INSTRUCTOR is the child of
employee number, name, salary      DEPARTMENT and the
   |                               parent of COURSE
   |
   |
   |
COURSE (record type)            lowest, or leaf, level in the tree;
number, title                   COURSE is the child of INSTRUCTOR
```

Figure 2–1. Sample hierarchic database design

A single department record at the root level, such as "120 BIOLOGY 1A," represents one *instance* of the DEPARTMENT record type. Multiple instances of a given record type are used at lower levels to show that a department may employ many (or no) instructors, and that each instructor may teach many (or no) courses. Following this example, we may have data on the BIOLOGY department at the root level and as many instances of the INSTRUCTOR record type as there are instructors in the biology department. Similarly, there will be as many COURSE record instances for each INSTRUCTOR record as that instructor teaches. Thus, there is a one-to-many association among record instances, moving from the root down to the lowest level of the tree.

Since there are many departments in this college, there are many instances of the DEPARTMENT record type, each with its own INSTRUCTOR and COURSE record instances connected to it by appropriate branches of the tree. This database, then, consists of a forest of such tree instances—as many instances of the tree type as there are departments in the college at any given time. Collectively, these comprise a single hierarchic database, and multiple databases will be online at a time. (In fact, IMS supports much more complex tree structures than the one used here. Moreover, IMS trees can be interrelated and accessed as one database structure.)

Records immediately below those at a higher level are the *children* of their higher level or *parent* records. Thus, COURSE records are the children of INSTRUCTOR, their parent record type.

An important property of the hierarchic database approach is that each child can have just one parent. This can sometimes represent a significant design constraint that may require keeping *redundant data* (multiple copies of the same record). For example, if course CS909 is taught by two instructors (Professors Stonebraker and Rowe), two copies of the CS909 record are required: one connected to Professor Stonebraker's INSTRUCTOR record and one connected to Professor Rowe's record. Thus, a change to the course title of CS909 would require two database updates.

Also, the hierarchic approach can constrain the way an application can locate data. Programs are often expected to use the branches of the tree to *navigate* through record instances until position is established at the record instance that is to be retrieved. In fact, the branches of the tree are predefined access paths among record instances. Therefore, programmers must understand the tree structure of the database, including the number of levels in the tree and where the branches occur. Often, the access paths are implemented by the DBMS with embedded pointers, which specify the relative address of the next related record. Data retrieval is typically accomplished one record instance at a time.

Network DBMSs

The network data model, sometimes referred to as the CODASYL model (after its inventors, who were members of the Committee on Data Systems Languages), uses a two-level tree as its basic data structure. A designer identifies one record type as the *owner* and one or more record types as *members* of a *data-structure set* (not to be confused with the mathematical concept of a set). A data-structure set (often called an *owner-coupled* set) is similar to a two-level tree structure. Multiple data-structure sets can be defined, cascading to many levels.

The connection between an owner and its member records is identified by a link to which database designers assign a *set name;* this name is used to retrieve and manipulate data. Just as the branches of a tree in hierarchic systems represent access paths, the links between owners and their members also indicate access paths and are typically implemented with pointers.

A sample database design using a network structure is shown in Figure 2–2. Three record types—STUDENT, CRSE, and TRSCRIPT—are defined; each contains fields (or *data items*). Notice that the TRSCRIPT record type is defined as a member of two different sets, that is, as a child with multiple parents. Each of these TRSCRIPT records contains a grade for a particular student in a particular course.

Two sets identify the relationships among these types: the STU_TRS set identifies a relationship between the STUDENT record type as owner and the TRSCRIPT record type as member in the STU_TRS set. The CRSE_TRS set identifies a connection (or link) between the CRSE record type as owner and the TRSCRIPT record type as member of the CRSE_TRS set. The arrows in the diagram show that students have one or more transcripts (TRSCRIPT record instances), one for each course the student is taking. They also represent an access path from each STUDENT record to each of the student's TRSCRIPT records.

To complete the picture, note that the link between CRSE and TRSCRIPT record types indicates the availability of paths between a CRSE record for each course and its related TRSCRIPT records. (It connects a course with the grades given in that course as well as the identities of the students receiving those grades.)

Unlike the hierarchic approach, then, network-based DBMSs support multiple paths to the same record, thus avoiding the data redundancy problem associated with hierarchic systems. Generally, this approach also supports richer data structures and provides more direct support for logical data modeling of complex

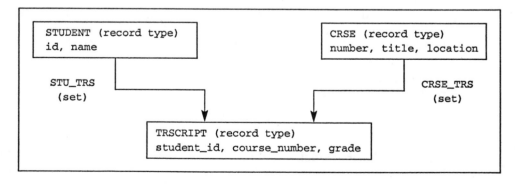

Figure 2–2. Sample database using network model

connections than does the hierarchic approach. However, this approach does place greater emphasis on data navigation, requiring the programmer to consider the available access paths to the desired record and to carefully select the most efficient path to maximize performance.

Using the database design shown in Figure 2–2, imagine that a programmer wants to retrieve information about all courses taken by one student, including the titles of these courses, that are stored in the CRSE records. In this network structure, TRSCRIPT records serve to connect STUDENT and CRSE records. (Network programmers refer to such records as *juncture records*.) There will be a chain of TRSCRIPT records for each course a student (such as R. Starr) is taking. The chain begins at the student record, as shown in Figure 2–3.

This figure is simplified. It depicts R. Starr as the only student enrolled in each course.

The program would first have to establish position at R. Starr's STUDENT record in the STU_TRS set (1). Next, it would "walk" downward through the chain in that set to locate the first TRSCRIPT record for the same student (2). This TRSCRIPT record contains grade data on the first course in which R. Starr is enrolled, and there are as many TRSCRIPT records linked to this STUDENT record as there are courses in which he is enrolled. Thus, if our student is enrolled in CS303A and CS304B and CS305A, there will be three TRSCRIPT records on the chain for our student.

Each TRSCRIPT record is also linked to its CRSE owner record in the CRSE_TRS set. Since the first transcript record for R. Starr is a member of two sets (a child of two parents), it is chained to an owner record in both of them, so that the program can now switch to the chain in the CRSE_TRS set and move upward to the owner CRSE record containing the title of R. Starr's first course (3). This sequence of moves—from owner to member in one set, to owner in a second set—is repeated (one record at a time), until the course titles for all courses taken by this student have been obtained from their respective CRSE records (4–7). The last

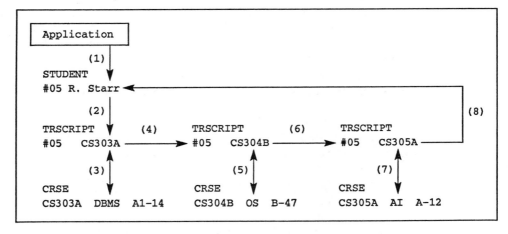

Figure 2–3. Retrieving course information about a single student

TRSCRIPT record for the student will point back to the STUDENT record (8), sig-
nifying the end of the chain.

In the 1970s and 1980s, a number of vendors offered network-based DBMSs,
including the Integrated Database Management System (IDMS) produced by
Cullinet (which has since been acquired by Computer Associates, Inc., and which
offers this DBMS today).

These prerelational approaches offered a clear advantage over conventional
access methods: they provided programmers with many paths to the data, represented as branches of a tree or links connecting members to their owners. At the
same time, however, they often presented problems when database designers
needed to change the logical structure of the database to satisfy new information
requirements. These changes would entail rearranging the previously defined
access paths to which programs had often become bound. In turn, this often
required changes to the code of production applications. When this occurred,
many users looked to the relational approach for more flexibility.

RELATIONAL DBMSs

The relational DBMS approach represented a significant and dramatic departure
from previous approaches when it was introduced in a paper by Dr. E. F. Codd,
then of IBM Research, in 1970. It simplified the user's view of the database by using
simple tables instead of the more complex tree and network structures. It also simplified the task of database programming by providing languages in which each
operation of the language could reference multiple rows—or a *set* of rows—rather
than a single record (as prerelational models did). Programmers also were not
required to navigate through structures to retrieve data. Instead, the relational
approach called for the DBMS to perform this navigation automatically and transparently, while programmers simply specified what data they wanted retrieved.

In addition, relational DBMSs helped improve programmer productivity by
providing for greater *data independence*. (enabling programs to be insulated from—
or to be independent of—changes to the underlying database representation). Prerelational DBMSs provided for less data independence because (as we have seen)
the internal database structure, including available access paths, was visible to
programmers who had to navigate through these structures to retrieve and manipulate data. This meant that when changes were made to these tightly linked tree
and network structures, modifications to production programs were also required.

Furthermore, the relational DBMS approach is based on set theory and modern logic. These subject areas give the relational DBMS approach a degree of for-
mality and precision often lacking in other approaches.

Very roughly, the relational DBMS approach relies on appropriately defined
tables as the basic objects of retrieval and update operations. The columns in these
tables are subsequently populated with data to make up rows in the table, one
row for each entity such as for an employee.

A user of a relational DBMS might create a table of employees, with columns
for their names (NAME), department numbers (DEPT), and job titles (JOB). Infor-

mation about individual employees would be represented as rows within the EMPLOYEE table, as shown in Table 2–1.

employee	name	dept	job
	richard buck	1981	potter
	sarah hunter	j522	accountant
	david mario	1981	graphic artist
	guy little	b541	manager

TABLE 2–1

It is important to remember that the rows in a table of a relational database have no inherent order. Users cannot expect a table containing data on employees to be arranged based on ascending values of an employee number or based on the spelling of employees' last names. The rows of a table can be sorted in many ways for presentation as output, but these sort operations have no effect on the table as it exists in the database.

With the relational approach, users (including application programmers) need only know the names of the tables required by their application and the names of specific columns in the tables. Furthermore, they do not specify HOW to retrieve the required data or navigate through predefined paths. Instead, they write *queries* (or inquiries) that reference the data of interest. Such a query might essentially say "Show me the names of all employees who work in department L981." The DBMS returns the answer in the form of another table or temporary relation.

This value-based (or query-based) approach at the application programmer interface (API) level represents a significant departure from prerelational systems. The most common relational DBMS query language today—and the basis for all industry standards in this area—is the Structured Query Language (or SQL), originally developed by IBM.

This provides a very simple and broad overview of the relational DBMS approach. Readers should note that today's relational DBMSs sometimes deviate from the tenets of the relational database model. A discussion of some of the popular commercial relational DBMSs appears in Part Three, "Commercial Relational Database Management Systems," while the relational model itself is discussed in greater detail in Chapter 4, "The Relational Database Approach."

OBJECT-ORIENTED DBMSS

Object-oriented DBMSs (or simply, object DBMSs) are among the more recent approaches to database management. They are closely tied to object-oriented programming languages and concepts; early developers and proponents usually had considerable experience in these areas but sometimes had less experience with traditional (relational and prerelational) DBMSs. While it is difficult to provide a precise definition of what constitutes an object DBMS because the name has been applied to a variety of products and prototypes, some of which differ considerably from one another, some generalizations can be made.

Object DBMSs differ from relational and prerelational systems in a number of respects. One of these is their emphasis on *objects*—a combination of data and code—rather than on data alone. This is due largely to their heritage from object-oriented programming languages, where programmers can define new *types* or *classes* of objects that may contain their own internal structures, characteristics, and behaviors. Thus, data is not thought of as existing by itself in these environments; instead, it is closely associated with code (*methods* or *member functions*) that defines what objects of that type can do (their *behavior* or *available services*). Because of this, designing a database for an object DBMS involves more than the organization and representation of data—it involves modeling objects, which really embody both data and code.

This approach has much to do with object DBMSs being perceived as an extension of an object-oriented programming language environment. Indeed, one of the key goals of many object DBMSs is to provide *persistence* to objects created in languages such as C++ and Smalltalk. Simply put, object DBMSs allow programmers to make their objects exist (to *persist*) after the applications that use and create them finish executing. By default, objects created in most widely used object-oriented programming languages are *transient*; like program variables, they cease to exist after the application that creates them finishes executing. By enabling programmers to make their objects persistent, object DBMSs facilitate the sharing of objects, much as other DBMS approaches facilitate the sharing of data.

The structure of an object database is highly variable. While relational and prerelational systems rely on specific ways to structure data (representing it in a tabular or hierarchic structure, for example), object DBMSs have no single inherent database structure. The structure for any given class or type of object could be anything a programmer finds useful—a linked list, a set, an array, and so forth. Furthermore, an object may contain varying degrees of complexity, making use of multiple types and multiple structures.

Finally, object DBMSs tend to emphasize programming language integration rather than programming language independence. Interfacing to the database may mean invoking C++ member functions rather than embedding a separate database access language (such as SQL, in the case of relational DBMSs). And accessing the desired objects in an object database usually means navigating to it (de-referencing or following C++ pointers, for example). Query access—the hallmark of relational DBMSs—is supported in some object DBMSs, although usually in a more limited way; it is not the predominant approach to database access in an object DBMS environment.

As the reader may have surmised, the object DBMS approach is quite different from that of the relational DBMS approach. Products that use object DBMS architectures are still relatively new and make up a small (but growing) portion of the overall DBMS community. Chapter 17, "The Object Database Management System Approach," discusses this approach in more detail, providing examples that illustrate some of its key concepts.

HYBRID OR OBJECT/RELATIONAL DBMSS

The wide use of relational DBMSs and the more recent emergence of object DBMSs have led some DBMS vendors to develop a hybrid architecture in hopes of capturing many of the strengths of each. Again, while a precise definition of an *object/relational* model is lacking, some generalizations can be made.

Like relational DBMSs, hybrid systems usually provide query-based access, employing a separate application programming interface (usually a custom or highly extended version of SQL) to provide for database access. Tabular structures represent the data, although they may deviate from traditional relational tables by supporting such features as nested tables (where the contents of a single column may actually be a reference to another table).

Like object DBMSs, hybrid systems may also support navigational data access, although this is usually not the primary means of interfacing to the DBMS. They also support the creation of new data types and enable users to associate code with these types. Hybrid DBMSs are discussed further in Chapter 18, "The Extended Relational and Hybrid Approaches."

SUMMARY

Today's database management systems are typically based on one of five different architectural approaches. Two of these, the hierarchic and network approaches, predate the relational approach. They provide users with a view of a structured database in which programs are written using a database language to search or navigate to the data of interest to the application. Prerelational databases include predefined access paths that are apparent at the application programming level. As such they often require changes to production applications when changes are made to the structure of the database to meet new information requirements.

The relational approach provides a simple tabular data structure. Users need not navigate to the data of interest. Searching the database is a function of the DBMS itself. This approach offers more powerful database languages and a higher degree of data independence than its predecessors.

The object approach to database applies the concepts and techniques of object-oriented programming languages to the database environment. It offers programmers the ability to define a rich set of data types and a wide range of data structures. Users deal with objects, defined as data and code, inextricably connected to form objects. Object DBMSs support persistent data for users of object programming languages (most notably Smalltalk and C++). Programmers make heavy use of navigational access to objects.

Hybrid or object/relational DBMSs combine features and capabilities of both the relational and the object-oriented approaches. They support query-based access (often through extended versions of SQL) as well as some forms of navigational access (which is typical of the object approach). They relax the requirement of the relational approach that the tables in which the data is stored be simple. Thus, they often support nested tables. They also support user-defined data types, a key feature of the object DBMS approach.

REFERENCES AND SUGGESTED READING

CODD, E. F. "A Relational Model of Data for Large Shared Data Banks," *Communications of the ACM* , vol. 13, no. 6, 1970, pp. 377–387.

Data Base Task Group, CODASYL Programming Language Committee, April 1971.

DATE, C. J. *An Introduction to Database Systems,* 6th ed., Addison-Wesley, 1994.

GOODMAN, NATHAN. "The Object Data Model," *InfoDB,* vol. 6, no. 1, Spring/Summer 1991, p. 2.

Object Data Management Reference Model, ANSI Accredited Standards Committee, X3, Information Processing Systems, Document Number OODB 89–01R8, Sept. 17, 1991.

"RDBMS Market Dynamics and Vendor Analysis," *InSide Gartner Group This Week,* Gartner Group, Dec. 8, 1993, p. 8.

SARACCO, CINDY M. "Object and Relational Data Base Management Systems," *Data Management Review,* vol. 3, no. 11, November 1993, p. 8.

CHAPTER 3
Major Components and Functions

CHAPTER OBJECTIVES

While Chapter 2 outlined some of the different architectures supported by today's DBMSs, it didn't discuss any of the major components and functions common to such systems. This chapter describes these components and functions. It is designed to provide readers with the necessary technical foundation for understanding more detailed, product-specific discussions later in this book.

Whenever possible, the discussion of major DBMS components and functions in this chapter is kept independent of any specific DBMS architecture. However, in some cases (such as the area of database search optimization), the focus is on their applicability to relational DBMSs.

TRANSACTIONS

It is important to understand that work involving any multiuser DBMS must be done within the scope of *transactions;* that is, all work that logically represents a single unit must be grouped together as a single transaction to ensure that all the work completes or none of it affects the database. This is necessary in order to leave the database in a consistent state. For example, a transaction might involve transferring money from a savings account to a checking account. While this would typically involve two separate database operations—first a withdrawal from the savings account and then a deposit into the checking account—it is logically considered one unit of work. It is not acceptable to do one thing and not the other; that would violate the integrity of the database. Thus, both the withdrawal and the deposit must be completed (or *committed*), or the partial transaction must be aborted (or *rolled back*), with any effects of the uncompleted work ignored.

Many database specialists often refer to the four *ACID* properties of transactions: *atomicity, consistency, isolation, and durability. Atomicity* merely means that either all the work of a transaction is applied or none of it is. *Consistency* means that the transaction's work will represent a correct (or consistent) transformation of the database's state. *Isolation* requires that a transaction not be influenced by changes made by other concurrently executing transactions. And *durability* means that the work associated with a successfully completed transaction is applied to the database and is guaranteed to survive system or media failures.

Supporting this concept of transactions as units of work plays an important role in shaping many DBMS capabilities, including concurrency control, backup and recovery, and integrity enforcement. These topics, and others, are discussed next.

CONCURRENCY CONTROL

Since DBMSs support sharing of data among multiple users, they must provide a means for managing concurrent access to the database. This ensures that the database will be kept in a consistent state and that the *integrity* of the data will be preserved. One way of achieving this is to process database requests serially, making each transaction wait until another transaction (of a higher priority or higher in a queue) has completed its work. However, this mode of processing would result in unacceptable performance for online applications.

Instead, DBMSs serve more as traffic controllers, using a software mechanism called a *lock* to provide as much throughput as possible without causing damage. What type of damage might occur without locking? One type involves lost updates, or unintentionally permitting the work of one transaction to overwrite or invalidate the work of another.

Consider the situation where John and Jane Doe own a joint savings account that has a current balance of $1000. At the same time on the same day, John and Jane separately enter two different branches of the same bank. John intends to deposit $100 into the account, and Jane intends to deposit $200. Without a concurrency control mechanism such as locking, the following situation could occur:

1. John approaches Teller No. 1, who retrieves information about the joint account from a database or file. The current balance known to the system is $1000.

2. Jane approaches Teller No. 2 at a different branch, who also retrieves information about the joint account from a database or file. The current balance known to the system is $1000.

3. Teller No. 1 increments the balance by $100, bringing her working copy of the account's balance to $1100. This is written back to the database or file.

4. Teller No. 2 increments the current balance by $200, bringing his working copy of the account's balance to $1200. This is written back to the database or file. At this point, the $100 deposit made concurrently by Teller No. 1 on John's behalf is lost because it has been "written over" by Teller No. 2's operation.

Locks prevent such problems from occurring by indicating the status of data items within the database, helping the system to determine if the desired item is available for a certain type of work (such as available for updating) or if it is currently unavailable (locked) because another process is using it.

In most modern DBMSs, locks are acquired and released transparently to the user. However, on some occasions a particular DBMS's standard approach to locking may prove to be inefficient; for these reasons, many DBMSs enable programmers to control locking mechanisms manually by issuing specific requests or instructions. But, to try to relieve most programmers of this burden, DBMSs typically use locks of different modes and lock data at different levels to satisfy the needs of various applications.

Lock Modes

Two common lock modes are *share* and *exclusive.* Share locks are associated with read operations; they signify that the transaction holding the share lock is able to read the data and that the same data remains available for other transactions to read. Exclusive locks are associated with write operations; they signify that the transaction holding the exclusive lock is eligible to update the data, but that the data is unavailable to other transactions until the prior update is complete (and the exclusive lock is released). Note that exclusive locks are incompatible with share locks (as well as with other exclusive locks on the same data); a transaction wanting to acquire an exclusive lock on some data (to update it) cannot do so until all the existing share and exclusive locks on it have been released. Figure 3–1 illustrates how share and exclusive locks might be acquired by multiple transactions over a period of time.

In many commercial DBMSs, other lock modes are also used, although share and exclusive locks are among the most common. More information about other types of locks available in commercial products is included in Part Three, "Commercial Relational Database Management Systems," as these vary considerably from product to product. (Indeed, some vendors use the same term to refer to very different types of locks. For this reason, it is important to look beyond marketing descriptions when evaluating the locking mechanisms—or other features—of a commercial DBMS.)

Granularity

In addition to providing different lock modes, DBMSs also provide different lock levels to control the scope of data that is locked. These levels dictate the lock *gran-*

TIME	USER EVENT	DBMS EVENT
T1	Transaction 1 begins. Requests to read item A.	Check lock status of A. No locks currently held. Share lock acquired for transaction 1.
T2	Transaction 1 reads item A. Transaction 2 begins. Requests to read item A.	Check status of A. A locked in share mode. Share lock acquired for transaction 2.
T3	Transaction 2 reads item A. Transaction 3 begins. Requests to update item A.	Check status of A in preparation for getting an exclusive lock. A already locked in share mode. Exclusive lock denied— transaction 3 must wait.
T4	Transaction 2 ends.	Transaction 2's share lock on A released. (Transaction 1's share lock remains.)
T5	Transaction 1 ends.	Transaction 1's share lock on A released. DBMS grants exclusive lock on A to transaction 3.
T6	Transaction 3 updates A. Transaction 3 ends.	Transaction A's exclusive lock released.

Figure 3–1. Simple locking scenario using shared and exclusive locks

ularity supported by the system, which may range from an entire database or file, to a much smaller portion of it. Different lock modes can be used at different levels of granularity.

The reason for having different levels is simple: some transactions may seek to access or update a broad scope of data in a single transaction, while others may seek to access or update a narrow scope. Providing only one level of locking could slow overall system performance. The DBMS might lock too much data at once and force other transactions to wait unnecessarily. Or the DBMS might spend much of its time trying to satisfy additional requests for locks on additional data items, thereby generating a lot of internal overhead.

Lock levels also vary from product to product, but in relational DBMSs, three common levels are row, page, and table locks. Row locks are acquired and released for a single row of a table. They represent the most granular level of locking, as shown in Figure 3–2.

Page locks are acquired and released for a single data page. Pages are usually 2K to 4K bytes (depending on the DBMS and its operating system environ-

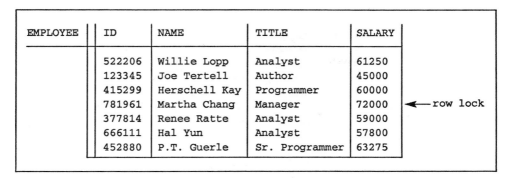

Figure 3–2. Row locks affect single rows, as this one for Martha Chang

ment), although some systems support up to 32K byte pages. Pages are not part of a data model but are a unit of storage used internally by DBMSs to manage the database. In relational DBMSs, a single page usually contains many rows and, often, a single table will be spread across multiple pages (perhaps several thousand pages or more, depending on the size of the table). In some systems, a single page may also contain rows from multiple tables.

Figure 3–3 illustrates the idea behind page-level locking. In this example, assume that a user has issued a query that affects only the rows of data that reside on page N. Although the table contains rows that reside on other pages, only the rows on page N are locked.

A third common level of locking involves the entire table. This is one of the coarser levels of locking granularity available in relational DBMSs.

As the reader might imagine, each lock level has its advantages and disadvantages. Locks of fine granularity are best suited for transactions that access a small amount of data at a time because they're less likely to tie up additional data resources unnecessarily (thereby avoiding contention). However, transactions that need to access larger amounts of data are better suited to locks of coarse granularity, as these help reduce the system overhead involved in processing many lock requests and thus can result in better performance.

Some systems also support *lock escalation*, where granular locks are expanded (or *escalated*) to a broader level. This can provide for performance improvements in situations where the default lock level (say, row-level locking) is too fine or small for a particular transaction. At some point, the cost of acquiring additional row locks (one at a time) to satisfy the needs of the transaction can simply introduce too much overhead. DBMSs that support lock escalation can sense this threshold point and determine that it is more cost-effective to acquire a single lock covering a greater amount of data (perhaps a page- or table-level lock); this is then done transparently on behalf of the transaction.

Isolation Levels

Some DBMSs also support different *lock isolation* or *lock duration* levels, which control when acquired locks are released. For locks involving read operations (such

```
┌─────────────────────────────────────────────────────────┐
│  SAMPLE    │  COLUMN 1 │ COLUMN 2 │                       │
│            │           │          │                       │
│  ─────────────────────────────                            │
│                 aaa         bbb       ◄── lock            │
│                 mmm         nnn       ◄── lock            │
│                 ccc         ddd       ◄── lock            │
│                 ggg         hhh       ◄── lock            │
│                 eee         fff       ◄── lock            │
│                 ooo         ppp                           │
│                 iii         jjj       ◄── lock            │
│                 kkk         lll       ◄── lock            │
│                 qqq         rrr                           │
│                 sss         ttt       ◄── lock            │
│                  .           .                            │
│                  .           .                            │
│                  .           .                            │
│  ── ── ── ── ── ── ── ── ── ── ── ── ── ──                │
│  PHYSICAL PAGE CONTENTS                                    │
│                                                           │
│  PAGE N                                ◄── lock            │
│                                                           │
│  . . . | aaa bbb | eee fff | ccc                          │
│  ddd | ggg hhh | mmm nnn | iii j                          │
│  jj | kkk lll | sss ttt | . . .                           │
│                                                           │
│  PAGE M                                                   │
│                                                           │
│  . . . | qqq rrr | ooo ppp | . .                          │
│  . . . . . . . . . . . . . . .                            │
│  . . . . . . . . . . . . . . .                            │
└─────────────────────────────────────────────────────────┘
```

Figure 3–3. Results of locking on
Page N

as share locks), supported isolation levels may include *repeatable read* and *cursor stability*.

Repeatable read isolation forces the DBMS to hold the (share) lock on the data until a commit point (the end of a transaction). This ensures that the locked data will not be changed during the scope of the transaction, enabling that transaction to reread it (if desired) and see the same results. Repeatable read isolation inhibits concurrency, so applications that require its use should try to complete transactions frequently (by issuing frequent commit instructions).

Cursor stability requires that the DBMS lock the data only while the transaction is actively reading it. When the *cursor* (a control structure used by applications to "point" at a row) is moved to read other data, the previously held lock is released. This provides for maximum concurrency but means that if the transaction attempts to reread data (for which a lock was acquired and then released), the data may have been changed by another transaction. For some applications, this may present a problem, and repeatable read isolation may be preferable.

Two-Phase Locking

Transactions that do not have the option of using repeatable read will not comply with the *two-phase locking* protocol. Two-phase locking is a protocol used to guarantee serializability of transactions. Serializability means that the database will be in the same state that it would have been had the transaction been processed serially (one at a time) with no concurrent execution of other transactions. With two-phase locking, transactions can be thought of as executing in two phases. In phase one, the transaction acquires lock(s) on any data it must access. This is sometimes referred to as the growing phase, because the number of locks acquired by the transaction grows at this point. In phase two, the transaction begins releasing locks; it never acquires another one during this phase. Phase two is referred to as the shrinking phase, because the number of locks held by the transaction shrinks at this point.

Deadlocks

The use of locks introduces a potential problem for DBMSs: *deadlocks.* A deadlock occurs when two or more transactions are waiting for each other to release some resource (perhaps a certain data page or a table). For example, Transaction 1 may hold an exclusive lock on page X and need to acquire an exclusive lock on page Y to proceed. But page Y may be locked in exclusive mode by Transaction 2, which cannot complete until it acquires an exclusive lock on page X. These transactions are said to be deadlocked—each is waiting for the other to release a lock.

Many DBMSs deal with this problem by providing mechanisms to detect deadlocks. If detected, the DBMS breaks the deadlock in one of several ways, such as killing or aborting one of the transactions involved in the deadlock, perhaps the one that has accomplished the least amount of work. This allows one transaction to proceed, and the other can be restarted later.

Another approach supported by some DBMSs involves deadlock avoidance. Here, all locks required by a transaction are requested and acquired at the same time. The request is granted only if all required locks are available, otherwise the request is denied. In the previous example, Transaction 1 would have requested locks on both page X and page Y. Only if locks on both pages were available at that time would they have been granted. Since Transaction 2 had already been granted a lock on page Y, the request of Transaction 1 would have been denied. This technique prevents deadlock but, of course, inhibits concurrency.

BACKUP AND RECOVERY

Preventing the loss of data is another important role of a DBMS. This is accomplished by providing mechanisms for backing up data periodically and recovering from different types of failures.

Many DBMSs enable users to make full or partial backups of their data; these are sometimes called *full* and *incremental image copies*, respectively. A full backup saves all the data in the target resource, such as an entire file or an entire database. These are useful after a large quantity of work has been completed, such as loading data into a newly created database. Partial, or incremental, backups usually record only the data that has been changed since the last full backup. These are less time-consuming than full backups and are useful for capturing periodic changes (such as the changes that occurred to a database during a given workday).

Different relational DBMSs use different backup mechanisms, which may span individual files, individual tables, groups of tables (residing in a certain area of a database or created by a certain user), an entire database, or an entire collection of databases within a DBMS. Some DBMSs also preserve more than just the data associated with these resources. For example, they may preserve the security restrictions associated with a certain resource.

In addition, some DBMSs support *online backups*, enabling a database to be backed up while it is open and in use. This is important for applications that require support for continuous operations and cannot tolerate having a database inaccessible. The reader should note, however, that some DBMS vendors use the term *online backup* to mean that the DBMS is online and available while a backup is being made, but that the particular database being backed up is inaccessible. For example, if a DBMS managed four databases and database 1 was being backed up, the other three databases could be accessible (while database 1 was not).

By using full and any available partial backups, a DBMS can restore the resource to its state as of the last backup. While this is a step in the right direction, it is often insufficient for most customers. What if the last backup was taken some time ago, and the firm cannot afford to lose all the changes that have occurred since then?

Logs

Other mechanisms exist to help resolve such problems, and these involve the use of a *log* or *journal*. A log keeps track of changes to a database and is stored on disk to guard against many kinds of failures. For added safety, the log is stored separately from the data itself—in another file or perhaps on another disk. Some DBMSs take a further precaution by providing the user with the option of maintaining *dual logs* or *mirroring* their primary log on another device. In this way, if the primary log becomes corrupted or damaged (perhaps because of disk failure), another is available.

The log currently in use is the *active log*. When this log becomes full, some systems will enable users to move the data to an *archive log*. This helps to ensure that space in the active log is available to track current transactions.

What exactly does the log contain? While this varies from system to system, in general the log contains the activities of various write transactions, each of which is given a unique, system-generated identifier. The log records the beginning of a transaction, the work of that transaction, and the end (commit point) of that transaction. The commit point indicates that the transaction has been completed and that its work can be safely applied to the DBMS. So, if Transaction 1 involved two database updates, the log might contain:

1. A record indicating the start of Transaction 1
2. A record indicating a write operation by Transaction 1, including the old value of the record or row (if any) and the new value
3. A record indicating a (second) write operation by Transaction 1, including the old value of the record or column (if any) and the new value
4. A record indicating that Transaction 1 has completed and instructed the system to commit its work

Note that these records would probably be interleaved with the records of other transactions, as multiple transactions are often performing concurrent database operations.

Typically, these log entries are kept in a buffer area (in main memory) and then "forced" or written to a log file on disk. Some DBMSs support *group commits* to improve performance. When multiple transactions commit at nearly the same time, the DBMS groups these records and performs a single write operation to the log, thereby improving performance by reducing the number of I/O operations.

Many DBMSs also use a *write-ahead logging* protocol, which requires that log records in the buffer be written to the log on disk *before* being applied to the database. This provides for recovery in case of various failures, such as a failure in the attempt to write to the database.

Undo and Redo Processing

Logging enables a DBMS to *undo* certain work if a transaction terminates unexpectedly before reaching its commit point or if a transaction instructs the system to do so for some reason (perhaps by issuing a *rollback* command). This is accomplished by working through the log and applying the *before-image* data values for log records associated with transactions that were rolled back or aborted before reaching a commit point. As mentioned previously, a write operation causes the log to record both the old and new values (the before and after images) of records or rows. In this manner, the DBMS can determine what values should be written to the database.

Furthermore, logging enables the DBMS to *redo* certain work if necessary, as might be the case should a failure occur before a transaction's committed updates can actually be written to the database on disk or should a disk fail or become damaged. Redo processing is accomplished by working forward through the log, applying all the necessary changes that were recorded in the redo log.

Checkpoints

A further log entry may be made for *checkpoints*. These indicate points at which the DBMS writes records in its log buffers to disk and writes data in its database buffers to disk files. Frequent checkpoints can shorten recovery time, although there is some overhead associated with checkpoint processing.

For many DBMSs, commit processing and database write operations occur *asynchronously*. The DBMS holds information about current (and recent) transaction activities in a log buffer. When a commit occurs, this is recorded in the active log (on disk), but the updates may not be immediately applied to the database on disk. One reason for this is that disk I/O is a relatively expensive (slow) operation. By recording the necessary information in the log and waiting until some later point to actually apply these updates to the database, a DBMS can provide better performance while still protecting against failures. However, when a checkpoint occurs, records in the log buffers and database buffers are written (forced) to disk.

If a system crash occurs after a checkpoint has been reached, all work committed prior to that checkpoint will not have to be redone (because it has already been applied to the database). Checkpoints are taken periodically by DBMSs, and many systems enable administrators to control how frequently such checkpoints occur by specifying time intervals or the number of committed transactions per checkpoint.

Sample Recovery Scenario

The relationship between checkpoints and recovery activities in the event of a system failure is often a confusing one, so an example will help here. Review Figure 3–4 and consider the recovery scenario that should occur after the system failure.

To restore the database to a consistent state after this failure, the DBMS will need to perform the following activities:

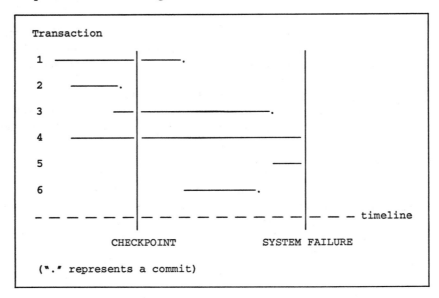

Figure 3–4. Schedule of transactions

- Redo all transactions committed after the last checkpoint but before the system failed. This affects Transactions 1, 3, and 6. These transactions were completed (committed), and their work was supposed to have been applied to the database. But, because the last checkpoint occurred before their commit points were reached, there's no guarantee that their work was actually written to the database on disk. Therefore, the DBMS must consult the log and perform redo processing for these transactions.

- Ignore transactions that were committed before the last checkpoint. This affects Transaction 2. Since it committed prior to the current checkpoint, it is safe to assume that its work was already applied to the database on disk. Therefore, it does not have to be redone.

- Undo the work for each transaction that was in progress when the system failed. This affects Transactions 4 and 5. Because these transactions had not committed their work when the failure occurred, the DBMS must ensure that their changes have not been applied to the database. Failing to do so would leave the database in an inconsistent state. Therefore, the DBMS must undo the work associated with these transactions by applying the before image copies of the appropriate log records to the database.

It is important to note that these specific recovery activities should happen automatically and transparently to the user.

Selective Logging

Some DBMSs support *selective logging*, where an administrator has the option of turning off the log (instructing the system not to log activities) for a desired period of time. This can speed performance (as the system doesn't keep log records and therefore has less work to do), but it is also dangerous as it inhibits the system's ability to recover from failure. It should be done only in isolated cases where performance needs are critical and the risks are acceptable. Such a situation might occur, for example, under test conditions (where some data loss might be acceptable) or if someone were trying to load a database with a series of images (which consume a lot of space) during off-hours when no critical transactions were being executed.

Disaster Recovery

Recovering from a natural disaster, such as an earthquake, hurricane, or tornado, that causes widespread power failure (and possibly equipment damage) requires special consideration. Many companies that use DBMSs to manage critical data cannot afford to be "down" for any extended period of time, even if a natural disaster occurs. For example, a bank that uses a DBMS to run its 24-hour automated teller machines could lose thousands or millions of dollars if these machines were made inaccessible to its customers.

Companies concerned about disaster-recovery issues typically designate a system at a remote site (in another city or state) to serve as a backup or standby system for its corporate DBMS. Keeping that backup system current (or reasonably current) is a key consideration. Another is the ability to quickly transfer processing over to the backup, should a critical failure impact the primary system. One way in which DBMS vendors can help support disaster recovery is by providing facilities for replication or mirroring of both user data and log records. Replication is discussed in further detail in Chapter 8, "Replication or Copy Management Services."

SECURITY

Securing access to data is another important function of a DBMS, particularly those used to store sensitive data. In relational DBMSs, this is achieved by granting various *privileges*—or access rights—to *authorized* users (people who can be identified as valid or legitimate users). There are many ways for a DBMS to identify legitimate users; a common means is to enable administrators to establish accounts with passwords (as is done on multiuser operating systems). Usually, it is a database administrator's or system administrator's job to specify the privileges or security constraints associated with these users.

Privileges

The types of privileges available vary from DBMS to DBMS, but they often include the ability to read certain data, write certain data, execute certain utilities or tools, and create certain parts of a database (such as a table). These privileges can be granted explicitly to one or more users or granted implicitly because of the role they perform within the DBMS environment. For example, a database administrator implicitly may possess the authority to create tables within his or her database. This administrator may also choose to explicitly authorize one or more others to do so.

Privileges are often associated with:

- All authorized individuals (or the "public"). This is a quick way of ensuring that certain data—such as a company's telephone directory—is accessible to all users of the DBMS.
- Individual users. For example, SALLY may be granted the privilege to read the contents of TABLE X.
- The creators or owners of objects. For example, the person who created TABLE X in DATABASE A can read and write to the table, as well as grant other authorized users of DATABASE A access to that table.

- A system-defined group of users, which might include one or more individuals identified as the system administrator or database administrator. For example, anyone with database administration authority has the right to determine who should be granted access to his or her database (and what restrictions, if any, should be placed on that access).
- A customer-defined group of users. Individuals may be defined to belong to a certain *"group"* (for example, all employees in the accounting department may be identified as members of the ACCOUNT group), and privileges granted to that group are available to all its members. This is a handy mechanism that can complement the organizations of many firms.

Security privileges may be cumulative across different types of users. For example, if one person is responsible for administering the entire DBMS (the system administrator), he or she is likely to have the authority to perform all the tasks of individual users and database administrators, as well as the authority to perform other tasks (such as reconfiguring certain system parameters). The system administrator can be thought of as having acquired the privileges associated with others who have lower levels of authority (such as administrators or users of individual databases within the DBMS). Furthermore, a single user who belongs to a customer-defined group (such as the ACCOUNT group) will enjoy all the privileges of that group as well as any privileges he or she was granted as an individual.

Read/write privileges can apply to an entire table or to portions of a table. For example, a firm may maintain a single table containing information about all its employees. Any employee might be authorized to read data about others in his or her department but not about those in other departments. Furthermore, the salary information for employees in any given department might be inaccessible to anyone but the department manager. Such support is often achieved in a relational DBMS through the use of *views*—a logical structure based on one or more tables that expose only the desired portions. This concept is discussed in greater detail in Chapter 4, "The Relational Database Approach."

Other Issues

In addition to these security mechanisms, some DBMSs use data *encryption* mechanisms to ensure that the information written to disk cannot be read or changed unless the user provides the encryption key that unscrambles the data. Some DBMSs also provide customers with the ability to instruct the DBMS (via *"user exits"*) to employ custom-written routines to encode the data.

In some cases, firms may wish to conduct security *audits*, particularly if they suspect the database may have been tampered with. Some DBMSs provide *audit trails*, which are traces or logs that record various kinds of database access activities (including, for example, unsuccessful access attempts). Such a facility can be particularly important to organizations dealing with highly sensitive data.

INTEGRITY ENFORCEMENT

Ensuring the quality or *integrity* of information is a key objective of a DBMS. Various types of integrity mechanisms and constraints may be supported to help ensure that the data values within a database are valid, that the operations performed on those values are valid (given what's appropriate for each type), and that the database remains in a consistent state.

Data Range Validation

A simple form of integrity enforcement involves mechanisms that support data range checking—ensuring that a column in a table or a record in a field contains a valid value. Often, a single DBMS will provide multiple mechanisms. Among those one might find in a relational DBMS are support for *domain* and *referential integrity* .

Domains define the set of valid data values for a given column in a table. Furthermore, many DBMS experts believe proper domain support also encompasses the valid operations that may be applied to those data values. For example, a column representing the SEX of a student may be defined to contain only two valid values—M (for male) and F (for female). In such a case, it would also make sense to restrict the comparison operators that can be applied to this column. Tests for equality or inequality would be acceptable ("Show me all the male students" would require testing each row to see if the data in its SEX column is equal to M). But testing for greater than or less than would not make sense.

Most relational DBMS vendors have focused on supporting domains by providing mechanisms to restrict the valid range of data values of a column. Support for specifying valid operations is much less common in commercial products. Data range checking can be implemented in a variety of ways, but a common one is through *constraints* or *rules*. In some systems, these may be specified as part of the definition of a table, with an administrator instructing the DBMS to check for certain values for a given column.

User-Defined Business Rules

One mechanism commonly used to support user-defined business rules is *triggers*, which are somewhat like miniprograms. They instruct the DBMS to enforce specific business policies, such as ensuring that no manager be given more than a 5 percent raise. Usually, such triggers are set to *"fire"* or execute when someone tries to write to a given column or table. Before allowing the write to succeed, the DBMS will automatically invoke the trigger, which can test to see if the write operation would violate the desired business policy. If so, the write attempt could be denied (perhaps by instructing the DBMS to roll back the transaction). Triggers are described in further detail later in this book, including the Chapter 5 section "Creating Stored Procedures and Triggers."

Referential Integrity

Another form of integrity is *referential integrity*. In a relational DBMS, this enables an administrator to specify that the data values of one or more columns (that represent a *key*) must be a subset of the data values of another key in the same or different tables.

This is sometimes a confusing point, so an example may help. Imagine that an insurance company maintains a list of all its policyholders in a CUSTOMER table and a list of the various claims filed in a CLAIMS table. The company wants to ensure that claims are filed only by valid customers (i.e., customers whose records appear in the master CUSTOMER table). This can be achieved by establishing a referential integrity constraint on these two tables. The DBMS would reject any attempts to write information into the CLAIMS table that would violate the constraint (such as attempts to file claims on behalf of individuals who do not own policies). Furthermore, the DBMS might take one of several actions (depending on the product and on the administrator's preference) when someone tries to remove a customer from the master list (the CUSTOMER table) when that customer is listed in the CLAIMS table as having a current claim. In this case, the administrator might choose to have the DBMS reject the attempt to remove the customer from the master list. In other cases, a different action might be appropriate. These are discussed in further detail in Chapter 4, "The Relational Database Approach."

Referential integrity is usually supported in one of two ways in relational DBMSs: through triggers and through a declarative approach. Triggers, as discussed earlier, enable users to instruct the DBMS to enforce their own business rules. Users could write triggers for each table involved in the referential integrity constraint, identifying what must be checked and what should happen if violations occur. However, this approach may require considerable coding and debugging—both of which are prone to error. If multiple triggers (of any type) are associated with any given table, it may also require that some type of ordering be established for executing these triggers. This requires that someone must be aware of all the existing triggers and understand the consequences that may occur for various interactions, which may not be an easy task.

An alternative approach—favored by many customers and adopted by the appropriate standards bodies—is the declarative approach. This requires administrators to specify (or declare) their referential integrity constraints when defining tables (or modifying the definitions of existing tables). After an administrator has done so, the DBMS will automatically enforce the integrity constraint; the administrator does not have to supply any procedural code to instruct the DBMS how to do so. This differs from the trigger-based approach, in which an administrator must specify both the constraint and the procedural logic necessary to enforce the constraint. As a result, the declarative approach requires less coding on the customer's part and therefore is less prone to error and unexpected results.

Two-Phase Commit Processing

Two-phase commit processing is often used to ensure transaction integrity when multiple resource managers (such as multiple DBMSs) are involved. This might be the case if someone was trying to wire some money electronically to another location. A debit would need to be written against one account (whose status might be maintained by DBMS 1), and a deposit would have to be reflected in another (which might require the services of DBMS 2). The two-phase commit protocol ensures that either all resource managers involved commit the changes required by the transaction or none do.

In brief, this protocol calls for one resource manager to serve as the *coordinator* for the transaction, while the other(s) serve as *participants* who respond to the coordinator's instructions. After the work requests of the transaction have been sent to each participating resource manager, the commit processing consists of two phases:

1. A PREPARE phase, in which the coordinator instructs the participating resource managers to prepare to commit the work. Each participant must answer whether or not it is prepared to do so. If no response is forthcoming (as might be the case if a DBMS failed), the coordinator interprets this to indicate that the participant cannot prepare to commit.

2. A COMMIT or ROLLBACK phase, in which the coordinator instructs the participating resource managers of the final action they must take on behalf of the transaction. The instruction will depend on the responses the coordinator received upon the completion of Phase 1. If all participants responded that they were prepared to commit, the coordinator will issue a COMMIT instruction to each. It is then each participant's responsibility to record a COMMIT in its log. If one or more participants did not successfully complete the PREPARE phase, the coordinator will instruct all participants to ROLLBACK the transaction. In this way, the integrity of the transaction is preserved.

The need for two-phase commit processing can arise in both centralized environments (in which two or more resource managers are installed on the same machine) and in decentralized or distributed environments (in which two or more resource managers that are installed on different machines must cooperate). Resource managers might include DBMSs and *transaction-processing monitors*, discussed later in this chapter under "Transaction-Processing Monitors." One resource manager serves as the coordinator during two-phase commit processing. If a transaction-processing monitor is present, it usually assumes this role.

INDEXES

Since performance is often a key area of concern for DBMSs, most support *indexes* as one potential means of speeding data access. Just as the index of a book can provide readers with one relatively quick means of locating a section of interest, indexes also provide an alternative form of data access. This can be particularly important in relational DBMSs, which do not employ a navigational-based approach to data access. Since the DBMS must determine the most efficient means to resolve a user's request, it is helpful to have a variety of alternatives made available, including appropriately defined indexes. Without them, the DBMS may be forced to conduct a full table scan (checking each row, one at a time) to search for the desired data, which can be a lengthy and inefficient process.

For relational DBMSs, although indexes are created by the system as requested, their use in retrieval and update is transparent to programmers and end-users. Indexes are automatically maintained by the DBMS. When instructing the DBMS to create an index, an administrator must specify the index *key*. An index key may be one or more columns of a table in a relational DBMS. Indexes built on two or more columns are said to be *composite*.

How do users decide which column(s) should be indexed? Columns that are frequently used as the basis for inquiry or narrowing down a search are good candidates for indexes. Thus, if bank tellers frequently seek to query account balances based on account numbers, an index on that column would be appropriate. Multiple indexes can be defined on a single table if desired.

However, careful consideration is required when creating indexes. Although indexes can be quite useful for speeding the performance of data retrieval, they do slow the performance of database writes. This is because a change to an indexed column actually requires two database writes—one to reflect a change in the table and one to reflect a change in the index. Thus, if the activities associated with a table are primarily write-intensive, it's probably advisable to define few indexes on that table. Indexes also require a certain amount of disk space, which must be considered when allocating resources to the DBMS.

Once created, indexes in relational DBMSs can be dropped (or erased) at any time. Administrators may do so if the activities of most applications aren't causing the DBMS to use the index or if the performance gains originally anticipated by use of the index are not achieved.

Indexes can be defined to be *unique* or *nonunique*. Unique indexes ensure that the values of the indexed column(s) are not duplicated. Thus, if a firm wanted to ensure that each employee was assigned a unique number for identification, establishing a unique index on the column for employee numbers would be one way to achieve this. A standard (nonunique) index will permit duplicate values for the indexed column(s).

Some DBMSs also support *clustered* indexes. When rows are inserted in a table, the DBMS will try to place the rows in the same physical order as the key values are logically ordered in the index. Clustered indexes can provide significant performance gains for certain operations, such as those that involve ordering data (like retrieving a list of all books published by a firm, beginning with those most recently released).

Although there are several different mechanisms that may be used internally to enhance access, two that are common among commercial products (relational as well as non-relational products) are *hash access* and *B+ trees*.

Hash Access

The fastest way to access data is by providing the DBMS (and its underlying file system) with the storage address of the data to be retrieved. Although this is an effective form of direct access to stored data, it is not a very practical access scheme since users rarely know the storage addresses of the data their applications need.

Hash access is a technique that enables users to provide the system with an application-meaningful search key (rather than an address) of the record to be retrieved. In the context of database systems, it is a form of direct access to data in which DBMS software transforms this key into an address that is used to retrieve the record.

One (or more) fields of the record, such as a student or employee number, is designated the *hash key*. When the record is submitted for insertion in the database, the DBMS submits the hash key value to a key transformation routine that develops the storage location at which the DBMS inserts the record. On subsequent requests to retrieve the record with the same hash key, the DBMS uses the same routine to develop the same address, which it then uses to retrieve the record. In relational systems, the primary key of a table is usually designated the hash key. There can be only one hash key for each table.

There are many algorithms for transforming key values to addresses. Those typically used in commercial DBMSs consist of relatively simple arithmetic operations. For example, one commonly used routine divides the value of the hash key by a prime number; the remainder produced by this operation is used by the system to store and locate the record. An obvious advantage of this simple scheme is that the computation that transforms the hash key value to a storage location is done at main memory speeds.

Figure 3–5 illustrates the general process a DBMS follows for performing hash access.

In relational DBMSs, the hash key is transformed to a row identifier (RID) which points to the appropriate row. One of the problems that must be addressed by DBMSs that support hash access is the occurrence of synonyms (or collisions). These are different hash key values that compute to the same addresses. Consider a personnel database for a large organization that uses employee number as the hash key. Employee numbers are six-digit integer values; they range from 000000 to 999999. A personnel database for a San Francisco office must store and process

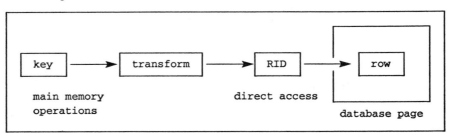

Figure 3–5. Key transformation and direct access

data for its 3000 employees assigned to that location. The key transformation routine must therefore reduce 1,000,000 *possible* employee numbers to a database with enough storage to accommodate only 3000 employees. Inevitably, there will be many sets of employee numbers that compute to the same addresses.

DBMSs handle these collisions by hashing to either the head of a chain of collision records or to an anchor that points to another page or bucket containing all of those rows that hash to the same address. There will be many such chains and anchor points. At retrieval time, the DBMS hashes to the start of the collision chain or anchor point; then it processes the chain or scans records in the bucket looking for an exact match on the hash key value to be sure that just the requested row is returned to the user. To prevent time-consuming chain chasing or bucket scans, database designers should select hash keys that will result in a fairly even distribution of rows, given the key transformation algorithm used by the DBMS.

While hash access has the clear advantage of speed of retrieval, it can be used effectively only for searches based on the hash key value. It is highly useful for applications that are retrieving single records on a random basis. This access scheme is not useful when there is a heavy requirement for retrieval based on ordered key values (such as range searches) or for applications that require sorted output.

While not all relational DBMSs support hash access for single row retrieval, several provide support for hash access as just one of several access mechanisms supported by the system. It is the job of database designers to select the best access mechanisms from those offered by vendors. For some applications, a mix of hash key access for some tables along with B+ tree indexes for other tables in a database provides desirable DBMS access support.

B+ Trees

B+ trees are multileveled structures that contain a single root page or data block with entries pointing to the next lower level of pages or blocks. The lowest level in the B+ tree holds the leaf pages or blocks, which contain every indexed data value and their corresponding row or tuple identifiers. Figure 3–6 illustrates this structure.

Because of this structure, B+ tree indexes are particularly well suited to queries that search on a range of data values for a given key ("Retrieve data on all the employees who earn between $95,000 and $125,000").

An important aspect of B+ tree indexes is that the distance between the root and each leaf node is the same and remains constant despite insertions and deletions of entries. This prevents skewing of levels and nodes on the tree. As a result, scanning the tree to access a particular leaf page or block will take about the same amount of time as accessing any other leaf page or block. Thus, the time to scan the index is uniform, regardless of the key value being searched in the index.

B+ trees also tend to grow wide faster than they grow deep. Since traversing each level of this type of a tree would cause an additional page or block access, it is desirable that B+ trees grow wide, with lots of branches per level, faster than

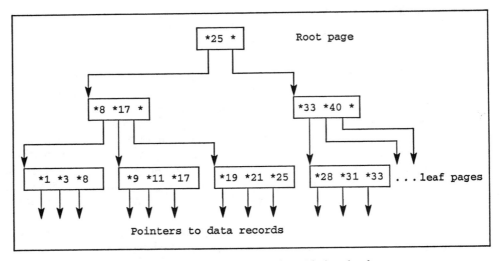

Figure 3–6. Sample B+ tree index with three levels

they grow deep. This enables the DBMS to add many index entries while still minimizing access time. The B+ tree structure is designed with this is mind.

In some cases, indexes alone can be used to satisfy a work request (or query), enabling the DBMS to save time by not retrieving the actual data pages associated with a table. This can happen if a query involves examining only indexed data. For example, if someone wanted a list of all item numbers greater than 1000 and an index was created on that column, the DBMS could retrieve this information by scanning the index, which typically requires much less time than searching the database.

Page Structure and the Use of RIDs

In the relational systems treated in this book, the hash key is transformed to what is called a *row identifier* (RID) or *tuple identifier* (TID). Similarly, the pointers in leaf pages of B+ tree indexes are RIDs. These RIDs consist of a page number and offset within a page. The offset indexes to a slot (shown at the bottom of the page in Figure 3–7, which contains the displacement within the page for the row being retrieved.

This use of page offsets containing the displacements of rows within the page facilitates the page compaction performed periodically by the DBMS. Compaction of pages eliminates the page fragmentation that results as rows are deleted from within the page. During page compaction, rows are moved into spaces made available as a result of deletions. This compaction—part of a *page reorganization* process that occurs transparently to users—produces a larger portion of contiguous free space within the page than would otherwise be available for the insertion of large rows that belong on the same page. Use of the level of indirection that is provided by the page displacements obviates the need to

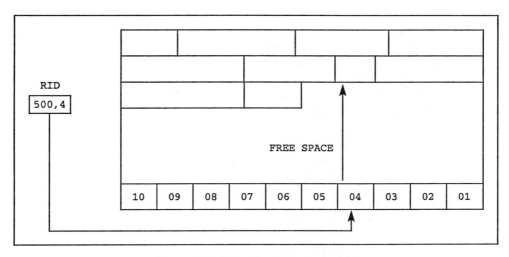

Figure 3–7. Using the RID to locate data

recompute RIDs when rows are moved within the page in this way to compact pages. The DBMS need not modify the RIDs in the leaf pages of every index that points to those rows that are moved during compaction. Instead it need only modify the displacements that are recorded in the relevant slots on the page. This can result in considerable performance gains by avoiding I/O costs to access and update the RIDs in leaf index entries.

OPTIMIZER

Optimizing access to data is a key role of relational DBMSs. Many systems that employ a navigational approach to data access rely heavily on a programmer's ability to formulate and use an efficient path to the desired data. In such environments, programmers manually perform much of the work done by an optimizer in a relational DBMS, which determines an efficient means of accessing the data (that is, an efficient *access strategy*) on behalf of the user. Relational DBMSs also develop code that implements the access strategy.

Optimizers contribute heavily to the overall performance of a relational DBMS. For this reason, many vendors have spent considerable effort improving their optimization technology and enabling administrators to see the access paths selected to further fine-tune their systems.

Rules-Based Optimization

Relational DBMS optimizers may employ a *rules-based* or *cost-based* approach when determining an appropriate access path to the data. Rules-based optimization means the DBMS examines the request (or query) and elects to follow a certain access path based upon what data was requested, what indexes (if any) are associated with the data requested, and (occasionally) *how* the data was requested (i.e., what syntax was used when making the request). A number of guidelines, or rules, are employed to help the DBMS make this decision. An example of one possible rule might be that if a user queries a table specifying a condition for a given column, and that column is indexed, the DBMS will use the index rather than conduct a full table scan.

While these rules are intended to be broadly applicable, no set of rules can be accurate or efficient for all circumstances. Furthermore, with a rules-based optimizer, good performance becomes dependent upon users' knowledge of the rules. This places an extra burden on users and violates one of the original goals of the relational approach—to eliminate the need for programmers to specify how to access the desired data. Furthermore, if the DBMS vendor changes the rules or adds new rules in a future release, some queries may need to be rewritten to achieve good performance. Again, this is undesirable.

Cost-Based Optimization

These problems are minimized, if not eliminated, with cost-based optimizers. Such optimizers consult statistics about the user's data to develop alternative search strategies. By gathering information such as the sizes of tables involved in the request, the availability and types of indexes, the minimum and maximum key values, and the overall patterns of data distribution for key values, the optimizer can estimate the amount of work (or the cost) associated with each access strategy. It can then select a low-cost option.

For a cost-based optimizer to make well-informed decisions (and, presumably, achieve good performance by selecting an appropriate strategy and access path), it must have access to current statistics about the database. Such statistics are generally recorded in a *catalog*, which is described shortly.

As the data in tables and their indexes are updated, statistical information about the new data values must be made available to the optimizer. However, updating statistics for a database every time the database is changed would involve considerable overhead and slow overall performance. Therefore, most relational DBMSs enable administrators to invoke a utility at their discretion (perhaps after regular work hours) to update these statistics. For large tables, some relational DBMSs even enable administrators to instruct the system to use a random sample of the data (maybe 10 or 20 percent) when collecting statistics; this can save considerable time and resources but still provide the optimizer with useful information.

The process of evaluating different access alternatives (or plans) and selecting one can be a relatively expensive operation itself. If the same application is executed repeatedly, this can be quite inefficient. Some systems will store the generated access plans so that they can later be reused, improving the execution time of the application and overall system efficiency.

Tuning Mechanisms

Because access path selection can be so critical to overall system performance, many DBMSs will reveal the optimizer's decision to the customer if he or she desires. This enables programmers and administrators to fine-tune the system. For example, if execution of certain queries reveals that the optimizer is not using an index, the administrator may determine that the statistics associated with it may need to be updated or that the index should be dropped entirely.

Some DBMSs provide mechanisms that enable customers to influence an optimizer's decision more directly. As mentioned previously, the decisions of rules-based optimizers often can be influenced by the way the query is written. Another technique involves writing additional statements in the application or including "hints" within the query itself to instruct the optimizer to use a certain access technique (such as a particular index).

This technique provides sophisticated users with considerable control and can offer performance gains in certain circumstances if properly used. However, such a feature should not be used indiscriminately. A poorly conceived hint can actually degrade performance. In addition, explicit access path selection can make programs dependent on the existence of certain objects (such as an index) that might later be dropped. While many DBMSs may compensate for this (perhaps by automatically selecting a new access path), doing so may require additional processing that would have been unnecessary if the user-written optimization instruction were not present. Furthermore, specific optimization instructions can prevent applications from automatically taking advantage of future optimization enhancements provided by the DBMS, unless the application is changed to remove the access path instruction.

A further optimization-tuning technique available in some DBMSs involves the ability to instruct the optimizer to base its access plan selection on the quickest way to retrieve only the first few rows that satisfy the query, rather than on an efficient means to access all the rows. This is useful for applications that are not interested in the entire answer set but only in some number of qualifying rows.

In general, today's relational DBMS optimizers are sufficiently sophisticated to make reasonable access path selections for most queries. Techniques for influencing the optimizer should be used on an exception basis only after the optimizer's decision is proven inefficient, and this decision cannot be remedied through less drastic means (such as updating the system's statistics).

CATALOG

Relational DBMSs record information necessary for operation in a *catalog*, which is actually a group of system-supplied tables. This catalog stores *meta data*, or information about the data the DBMS is managing. For example, a catalog records the names of tables stored within a DBMS, the names of users who have been granted access to these tables, and a variety of other data (which is described in subsequent sections).

The catalog is automatically created by the DBMS and consulted frequently to resolve user requests. For example, the DBMS will consult the catalog to verify that a requested table exists and that the user issuing the request has the necessary access privileges. Systems that use a cost-based optimizer will also consult statistics maintained in the catalog when evaluating different access alternatives and the relative costs of each.

Contents

Although the structure of the catalog varies from DBMS to DBMS, certain information is common to most systems. This information is usually stored in dozens of tables. These tables are automatically updated when certain database events occur, such as the creation of a new table, the removal of an index, or a change in the access privileges associated with a table.

Information about database objects is one type of data stored in the catalog. For example, the catalog will record the names of tables, indexes, views, triggers, stored procedures, and other objects that users have created within a database. Details about these objects are recorded as well. For example, the catalog typically records the column names and data types for each table, the synonyms defined for each table or view, and the integrity constraints associated with each table. Some DBMSs that support distributed database environments (discussed in Chapter 7, "Distributed Databases") also record information about remote DBMSs in their catalogs, including their locations and server names.

Information about users is also recorded in the catalog. This typically includes the names (or log-ons or authorization identifiers) of users, the privileges granted to various users for various database objects, when these privileges were granted (and by whom).

As mentioned previously, the catalog also contains statistics about user data that the optimizer may consult when formulating an access plan or that an administrator may wish to consult to fine-tune the database. Many of these statistics are only updated periodically (typically, when an administrator explicitly executes a utility) so as to minimize interference with normal database operations. Some of these statistics involve information about the number of rows in a particular table, the number of pages on which rows of the table are stored, the percentage of space occupied by active or valid rows, the number of rows that were relocated some distance away from their original position (perhaps because an update operation substantially increased the length of a record), and so forth.

The statistical factors used by various systems varies so that some optimizers are more sophisticated than others.

User Access to Catalog Data

Since relational DBMSs use tables to store catalog data, administrators can choose to make these tables accessible to their user community. Information contained within the catalog can be useful for designing and managing a relational database. It can help administrators monitor the space used within a database, audit database activities, and verify that a database design has been properly implemented (such as confirming that all the desired indexes have been created). Some programmers and users also find querying the catalog helpful, particularly if they have forgotten the definition of a table or are uncertain about their access privileges.

However, catalog data is generally intended for read-only access by users. Many DBMSs do not enable customers to change data in the catalog directly, as doing so could cause serious problems. For example, if a user removed the name of a column associated with Table_A from the catalog, the DBMS would no longer be able to retrieve user data related to that column. To the DBMS, the column would no longer exist. Many equally serious problems could occur if other changes were made to the catalog.

For this reason, most DBMSs allow only a very small portion of the catalog (if any) to be updated directly, and doing so usually requires special privileges (and perhaps resetting certain configuration parameters to override internal security mechanisms). For example, adding new information to the catalog may be acceptable if the DBMS maintains a list of names and locations of other remote DBMSs that can be accessed. As a firm adds new systems to its environment, it may be appropriate to have an administrator manually add a row to reflect this information in one or more tables in the catalog. In general, however, changes to the catalog occur automatically when a given database event occurs, such as the creation of a new table, or at periodic intervals, such as when an administrator invokes a DBMS utility that updates statistics maintained in the catalog.

APPLICATION PROGRAMMING INTERFACE (API)

All DBMSs have some sort of interface to enable applications to use DBMS services. Relational systems employ an application programming interface (API) that is independent of any programming language. They created their own data access languages, and statements from these languages are included in applications when DBMS interactions are required. Object DBMSs are a bit different; a number of these systems strive to provide close integration between the DBMS and one or more object-oriented programming languages. As such, most do not make use of a separate data access language; instead, programmers usually interact with the DBMS by writing C++ or Smalltalk applications that invoke appropriate member functions or methods. More information on this approach is provided in Chapter 17, "The Object Database Management System Approach." The remainder of this section focuses on the API for relational DBMSs.

The Structured Query Language (SQL) is the standard interface to relational DBMSs. Other languages exist (such as QUEL, which originated with the University of California at Berkeley's INGRES research DBMS project), but they are not nearly as pervasive as SQL. While a tutorial on SQL is provided in Chapter 5, "Introduction to Structured Query Language," some general points are discussed here.

Embedded and Call-Level Interfaces

The relational DBMS community offers two general approaches to supporting SQL in applications: *embedded SQL* and *call-level SQL interfaces.* Embedded SQL enables programmers working with a variety of third-generation programming languages (such as COBOL, PL/1, FORTRAN, and C) to include groups of SQL statements within their applications. These groups (which may consist of one or more SQL statements) are delineated by certain keywords and are readily identifiable. This is important, because standard language compilers cannot interpret SQL. To compile such applications, relational DBMSs provide language-specific *precompilers* or *preprocessors,* which take the source code, translate the SQL statements into DBMS calls, and produce a modified program that can be compiled, linked, and executed in the standard way. Embedded SQL was the initial approach to application programming with relational DBMSs, and it represents the most standard approach.

A number of DBMS vendors also offer call-level interfaces to their systems. These consist of programming language libraries that provide for the use of DBMS functions. SQL statements are passed as a parameter when calling a specific DBMS function. One advantage of this approach is that precompiling the application is unnecessary (since the compiler simply interprets the SQL statement as a character string to be passed as a parameter to an external library). However, these interfaces vary significantly from product to product, since they represent a newer approach to relational DBMS access and one that is not yet formally standardized.

Static and Dynamic SQL

An important performance consideration in either case is when the SQL statements are *bound* to (or provided with) a specific access plan. As noted earlier in the section "Optimizer," the process of evaluating different data access strategies and selecting an efficient one can be relatively expensive. Whenever possible, it is desirable to store and reuse the result of this process for subsequent executions of the application. Systems that support *static* or *prebound* SQL have this capability.

Static SQL is useful for applications that generate the same DBMS work at each execution. For example, if a payroll-processing application always reads the same information at the end of each week to generate paychecks for its employees, this work is static (unchanging). The DBMS workload can be reduced by optimizing and generating an access plan for this work once, then storing it and reusing it whenever the application is executed.

Some DBMSs do not support static SQL and, indeed, some applications are ill suited to it. For example, an application that prompts users to generate queries (perhaps by selecting icons and menu items on a screen) could not use static SQL—the queries that might be generated at any given time will vary. In such cases, *dynamic SQL* is required. As the name implies, these statements are optimized dynamically (at run time).

While static and dynamic SQL represent two traditional (yet somewhat extreme) alternatives, a third has emerged recently in some products. This involves the use of *stored procedures,* that include a series of SQL statements and that is somewhat similar to a miniature program. When they are brought into memory for execution (at the request of a user or an application), the optimizer generates an access plan for them. As long as they remain in memory, their plans can be reused by other applications or users who invoke the same procedure. Once the procedure is swapped out of memory, its access plan is also removed and is not stored. Further information on stored procedures is included in Chapter 5, "Introduction to Structured Query Language" and in Chapter 18, "The Extended Relational and Hybrid Approaches."

TOOLS AND UTILITIES

Most of this section has focused on components within the DBMS itself. But in addition to the DBMS (sometimes called the *engine* or *kernel*), many customers expect a suite of tools and utilities to be available to support various users, programmers, and administrators. While this book is not focused on DBMS add-on products, it's worth taking a brief look at some of the more typical facilities that are often used with DBMSs. Some of these tools and utilities emerged as a result of the growing popularity of relational DBMSs. Some exist for prerelational systems and, as of this writing, a smaller number are also available for object and hybrid DBMSs. But most DBMS tools vendors still focus on relational DBMS support.

Among the most common end-user tools are query/report writers. These enable users with limited (if any) programming background to query the DBMS for desired information and generate reports from the results. Many of these tools are menu- and icon-driven, enabling users to construct queries without actually having to learn the DBMS access language (typically, SQL). Query/report writers were one of the first types of tools developed for relational DBMSs and are often used in decision support environments (which was discussed in the Chapter 1 section "Types of DBMS Applications"). Other end-user tools include spreadsheets and graphics programs.

A variety of application development tools are also available for most commercial relational DBMSs. These include Computer-Aided Software Engineering (CASE) facilities, application generators, visual programming tools, fourth-generation programming languages, and forms generators. While precise definitions are difficult to provide for each, these tools provide professional programmers and/or other users with the ability to create some sort of DBMS application, usually at a more rapid pace than they could have otherwise created it with standard third-generation languages.

Administrators are the target audience of some tools vendors, who provide facilities designed to make DBMSs easier to manage. Such facilities might include tools for designing databases, monitoring system performance and resource consumption, estimating the system's capacity requirements, diagnosing errors, and providing additional security mechanisms.

Utilities are another common element of the overall DBMS environment. Many vendors bundle or ship their utilities with the DBMS itself, but some third-party vendors offer additional utilities as well. Utilities often provide for loading bulk quantities of data into a database, backing up and recovering a database, running internal diagnostic routines, updating statistics kept about the database for optimization purposes, reconfiguring system parameters, and starting and stopping a database. Many DBMSs also provide a means of *reorganizing* a database. This reclaims wasted space in the physical pages or blocks that contain data (which might occur after a number of records or rows have been deleted) and helps ensure that data records are physically contiguous. Doing so improves system efficiency and performance.

Since many customers have installed multiple DBMSs (often on different hardware platforms), a number of vendors also offer connectivity facilities. These include various forms of *middleware* products, ranging from specific point-to-point gateways (which enable the DBMS from one manufacturer to interface to a specific DBMS from another manufacturer) to more generic alternatives (which may try to provide a single interface to multiple DBMSs). Copy management and data replication facilities are another alternative to improving access to remote data stored on different types of systems. Different connectivity approaches are discussed in greater detail in Chapter 8, "Replication or Copy Management Services," and Chapter 9, "Middleware."

A number of vendors also offer vertical or prepackaged applications to solve certain business problems, often in specific industries. Examples include applications tailored to insurance claims processing, hospital information systems, office automation software, and legal applications. Many vendors focusing on specific industries use DBMSs as the underlying storage mechanism for supporting their applications.

TRANSACTION-PROCESSING MONITORS

In many cases, customers use transaction-processing monitors (TP monitors) as a front end to their DBMSs and file systems. These products provide specific services to applications and help manage system resources, including data resources. The earliest of these products predate relational DBMSs by approximately a decade. Their use has grown steadily over the years, with TP monitors generating more than $1 billion in worldwide revenues in 1992. TP monitors evolved in mainframe environments and provided certain services not found in the operating systems and file systems at that time; such services included a greater level of concurrency control, logging and recovery mechanisms, scheduling, and management of I/O to terminals (which was necessary to support a move from batch processing to online processing).

Today, many of these early features of TP monitors have been incorporated into operating systems or relational DBMSs. Yet TP monitors—such as IBM's

CICS and IMS/TM, NCR's Top End, and Novell's Tuxedo—are still frequently used in large online transaction-processing environments where performance is critical. These products may be used with multiple resource managers (file systems and DBMSs), including relational DBMSs. For this reason, it's worth becoming familiar with the role TP monitors can play in a DBMS environment, although a detailed discussion of TP monitors is beyond the scope of this book.

TP monitors help support applications that require access to data stored in more than one file system or DBMS. The logging and recovery facilities they provide help ensure the integrity of the transaction by guaranteeing either that work is committed by all the resource managers involved or that no resource manager commits the work. Thus, they help provide programmers with a common framework for integrating data across disparate data sources.

Relational DBMSs that support certain distributed database functions (discussed in greater detail in Chapter 7, "Distributed Databases") can offer a similar integrity guarantee without the use of a transaction manager. However, a great deal of corporate data is still not managed by relational DBMSs. Much remains in file systems, which provide very limited concurrency control and transaction management support. TP monitors can compensate for these limitations, as well as coordinate two-phase commit processing for a transaction spanning a relational DBMS and a file system (or some other managed resource). They also provide the support needed to perform transaction routing, an essential function in a distributed database environment. These functions can significantly reduce the coding that would otherwise be required for such an application.

Applications that need to support a distributed computing environment (in which work must be done on two or more separate systems) may be able to benefit from the remote procedure calls or message queuing interfaces provided by many TP monitors. TP monitors enable program-to-program communication, enabling one application on one system to call another application on a remote system. Similarly, message queuing enables an application to place a message (often, some instructions and data) in a queue associated with a given resource, which can then perform the requested service. In both cases, the TP monitor reduces the coding that would otherwise be required in such a distributed computing environment.

Performance is another reason that customers often use TP monitors. Most TP monitors—particularly those originating on mainframe platforms—have considerably more tuning mechanisms than those available with just a relational DBMS. In addition, the statistics they collect about resource utilization may be more detailed than what is available through a DBMS or native operating system facilities alone. Furthermore, TP monitors employ *multithreading* techniques, which enable more than one task to execute some system code concurrently. This can reduce overall processor overhead and improve system response time in high-end environments. Finally, facilities of most TP monitors help administrators balance the workload on a system more easily than would otherwise be possible with just operating system facilities.

A final reason for using TP monitors involves portability. For example, many mainframe applications in use today were written for CICS (which has its own application programming interface). To port these applications to other platforms, it is often easier to install CICS on those platforms than to rewrite (and, possibly, redesign) the entire application. Doing so has a further advantage of preserving an environment with which at least some of the programming staff is already familiar.

SUMMARY

Modern DBMSs are expected to feature support for concurrency control (or lock management), provide for backup and recovery (through the use of logs and other mechanisms), enforce security (through the assignment of privileges to individuals or groups of users), enforce integrity constraints, and provide various mechanisms to ensure reasonable performance (including indexes and an optimizer). Many also provide a system catalog to track relevant meta data and maintain statistics about user databases that can be helpful for optimization. The DBMS also must provide some sort of application programming interface (in a relational environment, this is usually an embedded SQL or call-level interface). As a practical matter, many customers have come to expect DBMSs to provide various types of tools and utilities to ease system maintenance, simplify application programming, and enhance end-user access. In some environments, transaction-processing monitors are used as a front end to DBMSs.

These concepts are important when evaluating the suitability of a given DBMS for certain applications. Understanding the material presented in this chapter will provide the reader with a good foundation for exploring the capabilities of the commercial offerings discussed later in this book, each of which implements these basic functions somewhat differently.

REFERENCES AND SUGGESTED READING

ASTRAHAN, M. M., et al. "System R: Relational Approach to Database Management," *ACM TODS*, vol. 1 no. 2, June 1976, pp. 97–137.

BOBROWSKI, STEVE. "Optimizer Options," *DBMS*, November 1993, p. 42.

BOBROWSKI, STEVE. "Protecting Your Data," *DBMS*, July 1993, p. 55.

BOBROWSKI, STEVE. "Safeguarding Server Data," *DBMS*, September 1993, p. 44.

BONTEMPO, CHARLES J., and CINDY M. SARACCO. "Data Integrity," *Data Base Management*, vol. 2, no 2, February 1992, p. 21.

BURRIS, PETER. *Transaction Processing: Systems, Databases, and Middleware*, International Data Corp., IDC 8026, 1993.

COMER, DOUGLAS. "The Ubiquitous B Tree," *ACM Computing Surveys*, vol. 11, no. 2, June 1979.

"Database Vendors Moving Battle to Tools Front," *Software Magazine*, January 1994, p. 61.

DATE, C. J. *An Introduction to Database Systems*, 6th ed., Addison-Wesley, 1994.

EDELSTEIN, HERB. "Using Stored Procedures and Triggers," *DBMS*, September 1992, p. 66.

ESWARAN, K. P., J. GRAY, R. LORIE, and I. TRAIGER. "The Notion of Consistency and Predicate Locks in a Database System," *Communications of the ACM,* vol. 19, no. 11, November 1976.

GOODMAN, NATHAN. "Concurrency Control in Complex Transactions," *InfoDB* , vol. 5, no. 3, Fall 1990, p. 28.

GRAY, J. N., et al. "The Recovery Manager of the System R Data Manager," *ACM Computing Survey,* vol. 13, no. 2, June 1981.

GRAY, J. N., R. A. LORIE, G. R. PUTZOLU, and I. L. TRAIGER. "Granularity of Locks and Degrees of Consistency in a Shared Data Base," *Proceedings IFIP TC-2 Working Conference on Modelling in Data Base Management Systems,* 1976.

GRAY, JIM, and ANDREAS REUTER. *Transaction Processing: Concepts and Techniques,* Morgan Kaufmann, 1993.

KNUTH, DONALD E. *The Art of Computer Programming Volume 3: Sorting and Searching,* Addison-Wesley, 1973.

MCGOVERAN, DAVID, and COLIN J. WHITE. *DataBase Associates Optimizer Evaluation Report,* Database Associates, 1991.

MOHAN, C. *Commit_LSN: A Novel and Simple Method for Reducing Locking and Latching in Transaction Processing Systems,* in *Performance of Concurrency Control Mechanisms in Centralized Database Systems,* Prentice-Hall, 1994.

MOHAN, C. *Concurrency Control and Recovery Methods for B/+/-Tree Indexes: ARIES/KVL and ARIES/IM,* IBM Research Report RJ-9715, March 1994.

MOHAN, C., and I. NARANG. *ARIES/CSA: A Method for Database Recovery in Client Server Architectures,* IBM Research Report RJ-9742, March 1994.

RODGERS, ULKA. "UNIX Facilities and Constraints for Multiuser DBMS," *Database Programming and Design,* vol. 2, no. 10, October 1989, pp. 30—37.

SCHULTE, R. "TP Monitors in an Identity Crisis," *Gartner Group Research Notes,* Gartner Group, SMS K-400–1403, 1993.

SCHULTE, R. "When a TP Monitor Helps on Unix," *Gartner Group Research Notes,* Gartner Group, SMS K-400–1402, 1993.

SELINGER, P. G., M. M. ASTRAHAN, D. D. CHAMBERLIN, R. A. LORIE, and T. G. PRICE. *Access Path Selection in a Relational Database Management System,* IBM Research Report RJ-2429, January 1979.

"Transaction Management and Client/Server," *OTM Spectrum Volume 7 Report 1,* Spectrum Reports, February 1993, p. 9.

CHAPTER 4
The Relational Database Approach

CHAPTER OBJECTIVES

Advocates of the relational database approach have always stressed the importance of understanding the *relational data model.* An understanding of the key concepts of this approach equips users to:

- Compare and evaluate relational DBMSs on an informed basis
- Appreciate the practical benefits of commercial relational DBMSs (when compared with nonrelational alternatives)
- Use the relational DBMS of their choice more effectively and efficiently in support of their applications

This chapter presents the basic concepts of the relational approach by focusing on its goals and on the key components of the relational data model. The discussion emphasizes those facets of the approach typically supported by commercial relational DBMSs, discussed in Part Three, "Commercial Relational Database Management Systems." This chapter also includes a discussion of relational algebra, with examples of how various algebraic operations are implemented in the industry's standard relational query language, SQL. (A more comprehensive discussion of SQL is included in Chapter 5, "Introduction to Structured Query Language.")

OBJECTIVES OF RDBMSs

The relational approach seeks to achieve the same basic goal of any database approach, which is to provide support for the management of data as a *shared* resource of a community of users. It tries to provide this support in a way that will increase user productivity, support responsiveness to change, preserve the integrity and security of the data, and perform adequately for a variety of applications. The relational approach seeks to realize these goals by providing:

- A *simple* data model
- A high degree of data independence
- A systematic foundation for the development and use of new DBMS capabilities

A major goal of the relational approach is to simplify the work of end users, application developers, and (perhaps most important) database designers, who often struggled with prerelational models when attempting to design a database that would satisfy the needs of many users with different application requirements. To achieve this objective, the relational database approach offers a simpler data model which, according to its originator Dr. E. F. Codd, refers to:

1. The way data is structured for users
2. The language it provides to retrieve and manipulate data
3. The rules it introduces to maintain the integrity of the database

To simplify the system for users, data always appears in the familiar format of a simple table. A database is then viewed as a collection of simple tables. It is important to note that although data is represented externally in tabular format, the relational approach does not require a similar internal representation of the data. In fact, few (if any) relational database management systems (RDBMSs) use tabular data organization at the storage level of the database. The RDBMS maps whatever data organization it uses at the storage level to tables, automatically and transparently. (The idea that relational DBMSs cannot use linked lists to represent and access data at the storage level is based on a misunderstanding of this approach, which does not rule out the use of such storage and access mechanisms. Instead, it requires that if these links are used at an internal level, they must be transparent to application developers and other users.)

From the users' standpoint, then, there are no connections (or links) that tie data together or that represent search paths through the database. And there is no significance to the relative *position* of a particular table or of rows within tables. Recall that with prerelational systems users need to be sensitive to the position of data within a tree or network structure and to the available access paths. In fact, a major task of programmers using prerelational DBMSs is to develop good strategies for navigating through such paths to the data of interest. (It is noteworthy that this can be a major task of programmers using object DBMSs. See Chapter 17, "The Object Database Management System Approach.") In exploiting these paths, applications built for prerelational DBMSs often become access path-dependent. Changes to the structure of the database that alter these paths can easily render applications inoperative or at least ineffective. Code modifications are required to repair the program. These program fixes require costly program maintenance.

Since there are no access paths apparent to the users of RDBMSs, program code is not dependent on available access paths. The result is a high degree of data independence. Program maintenance is reduced. This is a cost-avoidance benefit of the relational approach that also frees programmers' time for the development of new applications, thereby increasing programmer productivity.

But if there are no connections among the tables, how can the system respond to a request that spans two or more tables? That is, how can relationships among data elements in various tables be represented?

Consider a situation in which information about departments (including their names and department numbers) is stored in one table, while information about employees (including their employee numbers, names, and salaries) is stored in another. How is the fact that "The employee with employee number 333999 is assigned to the accounting department" reflected in the database?

In relational systems, all real-world connections (like the connections between employees and their departments) are *value-based*. That is, the fact that employee 333999 is in the accounting department is shown by representing the department number for the accounting department in the same table and row that contains other data on that employee, including the data that identifies that employee. No "extra," user-visible link between the employee and the employee's department is required. By contrast, other types of DBMSs require that a link be defined between the department record and the employee record. This concept is shown in Figure 4–1.

This simplification of the model is often expressed in the statement that the relational approach eliminates "representation clutter" from the user's view of the database and thus results in more programmer productivity. It also allows database designers more freedom to add new data and to logically rearrange data in response to changing information requirements.

As will become apparent, the relational approach is systematic since it applies some of the basic concepts of set theory and modern logic. Although users need not be concerned with the mathematical basis of this approach, they can more readily appreciate many of its features when they understand the formal foundations on which it is built. For example, conceptually the objects of retrieval and manipulation are sets, in the same sense in which mathematicians talk about sets. Also, the operations and statements of the original relational database languages have been precisely defined within the framework of that branch of mathematics known as first-order logic, and a measure of the power of relational

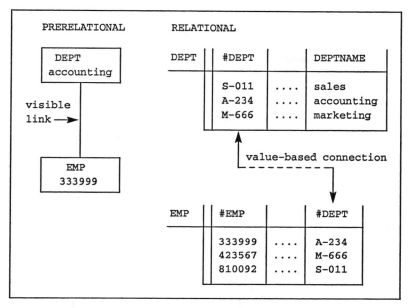

Figure 4–1.   Relationships are represented differently in pre-RDBMSs and RDBMSs.

languages has been defined, as is discussed in Chapter 5, Introduction to Structured Query Language".

Within the framework of these disciplines, the relational model introduces several basic principles of database. The resulting systematic character of the approach should not be underestimated since many of the capabilities of RDBMSs are based on these fundamental principles. Moreover, an understanding of these principles enables users to understand more easily various enhancements to RDBMSs and sometimes to anticipate these changes—which is often difficult (if not impossible) to do for DBMSs that are developed on an ad hoc basis. Users often appreciate the fact that they are not surprised and puzzled by various new features of an RDBMS.

WHAT IS A RELATION?

Users of RDBMSs deal with *relations* that are represented in the database as a collection of simple tables. A relation is a set of elements called *tuples*, a term that might be unfamiliar to the reader until it is noted that it is simply an extension of the notion of a *couple*. When we deal with a set of couples (or pairs), we work with things that are taken two at a time.

Examples of this include the relation "parent of," where p is the parent of c, and the relation "wife of," where w is the wife of h. Each element of the relation WIFE_OF is a tuple; each tuple has as its components a married female and a mar-

ried male. Table 4–1 is an abbreviated tabular representation of the relation
WIFE_OF.

wife_of	w	h
tuple →	hillary	bill
tuple →	barbara	george
tuple →	rosiland	jimmy
tuple →	betty	gerald

TABLE 4–1

A special property of a relation is that it is a set defined on other sets. Thus,
the relation WIFE_OF is defined on the set of married females and the set of married males. These sets are the *domains* of the relation. Each tuple consists of two
components (like "Hillary, Bill"), one each from the two domains. Thus, in generating the relation WIFE_OF, values are taken two at a time to make up the tuples
of the relation.

Any relation, defined as a set of tuples, can be represented in the familiar
format of a simple table. These tuples become the rows of the table. The number
of tuples or rows in the table is the *cardinality* of the relation. Application programmers do not need to be concerned with the cardinality of tables they reference.

Relations need not be restricted to elements (or tuples) whose components
are things taken two at a time. A given relation might consist of tuples whose
components are taken *n* at a time, where the value of *n* is any number that is useful for the purpose at hand. For example, we can define a relation in which we
take things three at a time, on these three sets:

    S1. the set of student identifiers
    S2. the set of student names
    S3. the set of major subjects at our university

A set of tuples can be specified by taking things three at a time, one each
from S1, S2, and S3 to form a relation called STU. The relation STU will consist of
a set of 3-tuples, since each tuple is formed by taking one value from each of the
three sets or domains. For example, STU could consist of these four *n*-tuples,
where the value of *n* is 3. (See Table 4–2.)

stu	#stu	name	major
	1074	r. starr	music
	3399	m. cuomo	government
	4274	m. jordan	marketing
	9785	r. carnap	logic

TABLE 4–2

Briefly, a relation is a set of a special kind; it is a set of tuples where each tuple has components like "4274," "M. Jordan" and "Marketing" that have significance to users.

Domains

The *domains* of the relation are the sets from which component values are taken to form tuples of the relation (or rows of the table). Domains are defined by users of the DBMS (typically, a database designer or administrator). A domain definition specifies a set of values of similar type. The type might be simple, corresponding to a conventional programming data type such as integer. In some systems, it may be richer and based on a user-defined type. A domain may then involve specification of (1) the permissible operations allowed on the data, (2) routines that will be invoked automatically to check that the data falls within a range of values, or (3) routines that transform the data when it is entered into a table.

Attributes

The *attributes* of a relation correspond to the columns of a table. When the database designer puts a domain to use, the designer assigns it to a table with an attribute name, such as #STU (student number), NSTU (student name), or MAJOR (major area of study). The *degree* of a relation refers to the number of domains on which the relation is defined. More simply, it refers to the number of columns in the table.

Domain Integrity

Only those values that conform to the definition of the corresponding domain are permitted in the column to which the attribute name has been assigned. This constraint on data values is called *domain integrity.* Enforcing this constraint is the job of the RDBMS. Domains are an important way to enrich the semantics of the data—to inform the database manager about *what the data means in the context of the applications being supported.* Assume that a domain has been defined as decimal data not to exceed 99,999.99. Used for a column called SALARY, it informs the DBMS that *in the business context being served,* SALARY connotes any decimal amount less than 100,000.00, and that an entry of 100,000.00 (or more) in the SALARY column violates the definition of "salary" and should be rejected automatically by the system.

A given domain can be used more than once in the database—and even in the same table. The domain of student numbers can be used in the STU table and can also be used in other tables like GRADE, DORM, or CURRICULUM as a way of identifying students. Moreover, multiple columns *in the same table* can reference the same domain. Thus, a table containing data on employees might contain a column #EMP and a column #MGR, both of which are defined on the domain called #PERS. See Figure 4–2.

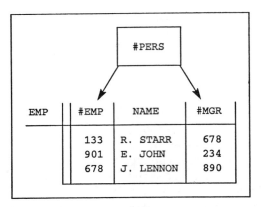

Figure 4–2. Multiple attributes on a single domain

Thus, in addition to specifying constraints on the values entered into the columns, domains eliminate the need for repetitive specification of data types for each of their uses. Consider a database in support of financial applications. A single domain of "money" might be used in tens or even hundreds of tables. Domains avoid the need for repetitive definition for each such table. Domains are important in other ways, as subsequent sections indicate. Unfortunately (as will become apparent), commercial RDBMSs don't provide full support for domains as of this writing.

Normalized Tables

Tables in relational databases are simple. Each entry in a column must be a single value from the domain on which that column is defined. Values from multiple domains cannot appear in a single row and column position, nor can multiple values from the same domain. The GRADE table in Figure 4–3 contains a set of #CRSE values for each student number in the table. This is actually a sophisticated table. It goes beyond the simplicity required by the relational data model.

The user languages associated with the relational approach generally do not decompose a single entry (row and column) that contains multiple values. This constraint on the design of tables keeps them simple and contributes toward the simplicity of relational database languages. Simple tables are often referred to as *first normal form tables*. RDBMSs "understand" and process only first normal form tables.

grade	#stu	#crse	gpa
	012	m-101, p-303, h-102	3.2
	234	p-303, a-104	4.0
	345	h-303, h-102, a-303	2.5
	.	.	.
	.	.	.

Figure 4–3. Unnormalized table

It has been noted that the relational approach borrows many of the concepts associated with mathematical sets. Thus, all relations are sets. And two important fundamental properties of mathematical sets also belong to database relations or tables: (1) there is no significant inherent order in the elements of a set, and (2) the elements of sets must be distinct. Thus, the set of positive integers from integer 1 through integer 3 might be specified as:

$$\{1, \ 2, \ 3\}$$

The *same* set might also be specified as:

$$\{2, \ 3, \ 1\}$$

As explained above, the elements of those sets that are relations are tuples; in a relational database, tuples are represented as rows in a table. Therefore, for users (including programmers) the rows in database tables have no inherent order. The DBMS can maintain an internal order on rows as requested by database designers. For example, rows might be physically clustered according to the order of index key values. Nonetheless, there is no row order in the user's view of the data. It is important to realize that indexes on tables are merely a mechanism of access that is used by the DBMS. They are transparent to users in an RDBMS and play no role in interpreting and understanding the semantics of the database. This contributes to data independence. For example, users cannot develop special search routines, such as a binary search, that exploit and depend upon row order. As a result, there is no danger of invalidating such code if the internal order of rows is modified by database administrators to achieve efficiency.

Since the elements of sets are distinct, there is no point in specifying an element more than once. This would amount to specifying the element redundantly. For example, no information is conveyed by the redundant occurrence of the integer 3 in the following set:

$$\{1, \ 2, \ 3, \ 3\}$$

Therefore, since rows represent the elements of sets that are relations, redundant rows are not allowed.

Primary Keys

One or more columns are selected as the *primary key* of a table. Values of the primary key are used to distinguish one row from another. They uniquely identify each row of a table and prevent the occurrence of redundant rows. Relational DBMSs are responsible for checking primary key values to ensure they meet this criteria. Therefore, according to the relational model, tables with redundant rows are not proper relations. (Nonetheless, the reader should be aware that for many RDBMSs, the use of primary keys is a user option so that redundant rows can be introduced by users. Many relational database proponents strongly discourage this practice.)

Missing Values

Dealing with missing information is another responsibility of a relational DBMS. Often, users may find that some information about an entity is not known when they attempt to store it in the database. For example, a college administrator entering data about a new student may find that some students have not yet declared their major subjects. In other cases, DBMS users may find that certain information about an entity is not applicable and therefore cannot be recorded in the database. For example, some colleges may not permit students to declare a major until after they have completed at least one year's worth of course work. In such a case, information about the majors of all first-year students would be missing because it is not applicable at this time.

Relational DBMSs allow users to indicate the absence or inapplicability of such data by describing it to the system as *null*. For example, to enter a row for a student with an undeclared major subject, the insertion would specify the student name, number, and any other relevant data, along with a null entry for the MAJOR column. The RDBMS enters nulls internally using a special marker on the field reserved for the missing data. Optionally, some RDBMSs allow the use of default values for missing data.

The issue of how missing values are best represented in a relational DBMS is a subject of debate among some proponents and users of relational systems. Some are opposed to the use of nulls for this purpose. Generally, opposition to the use of nulls for missing data is based on the view that:

1. Commercial RDBMSs do not handle nulls in a disciplined, and systematic way; for example, nulls appear in different places in the collating sequences of various systems.
2. The logic involved in their use is sometimes counterintuitive.
3. They sometimes produce results that are difficult to predict and therefore might be misleading.

Proponents of the use of nulls maintain that problems associated with the use of nulls occur because commercial DBMSs have not implemented their support satisfactorily.

Codd has urged RDBMS vendors to support a *multivalued logic* in predicate evaluation. In addition to evaluating predicates like "STU. MAJOR = 'MUSIC'" as either true or false, the system would also accommodate a "not known to be true and not known to be false" result in case a data value is unknown or inapplicable.

Under the proposal for a three-valued logic, the truth tables that define the usual logical connectives (NOT, AND, OR) are extended, as shown in Figure 4-4.

With this scheme for predicate evaluation, users are able to request rows for which some predicate is "maybe true-maybe false."

P	not-P		P1 AND P2	T	M	F		P1 OR P2	T	M	F
T	F		T	T	M	F		T	T	T	T
M	M		M	M	M	F		M	T	M	M
F	T		F	F	F	F		F	T	M	F

Figure 4–4. Truth table definitions for three-valued logic

Note that a null is not a *data* value. Null is a special indicator meaning "data value unknown" or "data value inapplicable." Thinking of it as a data value can lead to confusion when considering the use of nulls. For example, according to the truth table definitions above, a test for equality, "M = M" ("NULL = NULL") evaluates to "maybe." This is counterintuitive if it is viewed as a comparison of two data values. However, the test really asks whether one *unknown* (or *inapplicable)* data value is equal to another unknown (or inapplicable) data value. Thus the test asks whether one data value unknown to the system is equal to another data value also unknown to the system. When interpreted in this way, the resulting evaluation of "maybe" is no longer counterintuitive. This is why Codd refers to null as a *marker* rather than a *value*. Codd has extended his multivalued logic approach to accommodate a fourth value for the "value not applicable" cases. Truth table definitions of the connectives, as shown above, are extended accordingly to handle the four possibilities: true, false, unknown, and not applicable. Discussion of this extension to Codd's multivalued logic approach to missing data is beyond the scope of this book. (Several SQL-based systems provide a special statement to test for null.) The references listed in "References and Suggested Reading" at the end of this chapter provide comprehensive discussion of the issues involved in how to handle missing data.

Entity Integrity

Another constraint on permissible data values prohibits the use of nulls or default characters in any part of a primary key. This constraint is consistent with the requirement that each row of a table must be uniquely identifiable; each row must be distinguishable from every other row. Recording a null marker in the primary key column defined for student numbers (#STU) is tantamount to saying that the identity of the student is unknown. Of course, this allows for the possibility that the primary key value of such a student is the same as the primary key value of a student whose data is already represented in the database. This would imply that we are recording data on the same student twice. Enforcement of this rule by the RDBMS (at the user's request) assures what is called *entity integrity*.

Referential Integrity

The third integrity constraint for the relational data model enables the RDBMS to enforce certain business policies or rules automatically on behalf of users. For example, universities allow students to major only in approved subject areas. Assume that the database contains a table, OKMAJOR, whose primary key column, APMAJOR, contains all of those subjects that are approved as major subjects for undergraduate students. A relational DBMS would be expected to prohibit entries in the MAJOR column of a STU table unless it matches one value in the primary key column of the OKMAJOR table or unless it is entered as null. Figure 4–5 illustrates this concept.

Notice that the row in the STU table for Z. Manno has an entry of "poetry" in the MAJOR column; poetry is not an approved major subject. This entry violates the relational rule for *referential integrity* and should be disallowed by a relational DBMS. The DBMS can be informed of this referential constraint at data definition time, when database designers designate the MAJOR column in table STU as a *foreign key* referencing the primary key (APMAJOR) in the OKMAJOR table. Also note that the rule allows a NULL in the foreign key column when this data is unavailable or inapplicable. Since J. Christy is still undecided about her major subject, a null entry has been recorded.

Full support for this rule requires action by the DBMS if the university decides to abolish an approved major while the STU table still contains data on students with the major that is being dropped. In our example deleting the row in OKMAJOR that shows "art" as a major should result in one of the following actions by the DBMS:

okmajor	apmajor (pk)	advisor
	literature	e. wharton
	history	j. bury
	astronomy	c. sagan
	physics	a. einstein
	art	p. klee
	mathematics	k. godel
	music	i. stravinsky

stu	#stu	stuname	major (fk)
	456	a. manno	history
	567	w. herman	music
	678	z. manno	poetry
	789	d. martin	art
	890	j. christy	null
	.	.	.
	.	.	.

Figure 4–5. Two tables involved in a referential integrity constraint

1. Rejection of the delete transaction with appropriate notification to the user
2. Deletion of the row from OKMAJOR along with deletion of all rows in STU for students majoring in art
3. Deletion of the row from OKMAJOR along with a change to all values of "art" (in the STU table) to NULL

Which action the DBMS takes is a database design option.

In the previous example, the referential constraint is between data in two distinct tables. Sometimes it is useful to specify a constraint on a single table. Consider an employee table, EMP, which contains columns for each employee's serial number, name, and manager's serial number. The #EMP is defined on a domain of person number and serves as primary key of this table. #MGR is also defined on the domain of person number. In order to implement an obvious business rule that every manager must be a company employee, a referential constraint would be defined with #MGR defined as a foreign key referencing #EMP in the same table. (See Figure 4–6.)

The entries in EMP show that Sally reports to Harry and that Larry and Harry report to Sue. Since Sue is the CEO, the #MGR value for her row is NULL (not applicable). The constraint will not allow insertion of a new row with a value for the #MGR column that does not match one of the current values for the #EMP column.

Integrity Enforcement

The relational approach requires that domain, entity, and referential integrity constraints be applied automatically by the RDBMS. Centralized enforcement of these constraints by the DBMS relieves application developers of the task of developing the appropriate code. Moreover, enforcement by the DBMS avoids the possibility of redundant application code, as well as of incompatible specifications by two or more applications. And it also avoids the scenario in which an application neglects to provide this integrity check when it is needed.

EMP	#EMP	NAME	#MGR
	333	Larry	222
	444	Sally	555
	222	Sue	NULL
	555	Harry	222
	PK		FK

Figure 4–6. A table with a self-referencing referential integrity constraint

Relational DBMSs and Flat Files

The discussion thus far should serve to distinguish clearly between RDBMSs and systems that process collections of flat files. The previous sections of this chapter indicate that the tables of relational databases are highly disciplined—from the user's standpoint they contain rows with a fixed number of components; rows are not ordered; and redundant rows are not allowed. Flat files can accommodate records of multiple formats and a variable number of fields; records are normally ordered; and often there is no prohibition against duplicate records in a file.

Each row of a table in a relational database must have a primary key value. A null marker can be recorded for missing data except for any component of a primary key. In addition, the rule for referential integrity can be used to constrain the values entered in accordance with business policies and rules. It is the responsibility of the RDBMS to enforce each of these rules automatically.

RELATIONAL DBMS LANGUAGES

The second major component of the relational data model consists of the languages these systems provide for programmers, end users, and database designers. Dr. E. F. Codd designed two classes of languages for relational database processing: relational algebra-based and relational calculus-based languages. It is noteworthy that Codd's definitions of these languages satisfy the high standards for precision that one usually finds in the various branches of mathematics.

Unlike languages of prerelational systems which retrieve and manipulate one record at a time, relational languages are set-oriented. They specify operations on relations or tables and always produce relations or disciplined tables as results. Thus, relational languages enjoy the property of *closure*—another example of the systematic character of the relational approach that has highly important practical consequences. (The practical advantages due to this property are discussed in the following sections.)

In this section we examine the operations of the relational algebra, a procedural language in which users specify a sequence of one or more operations to produce the desired result. Since the relational algebra is procedural, users can exercise a measure of control with respect to how the database is searched in performing retrievals to generate the resulting table.

Languages based on the relational calculus are nonprocedural. Users specify only the result desired, that is, they define *what* users want to be materialized as a result but do not become involved in the intricacies of search logic. The standard language for RDBMSs is SQL, a language with nonprocedural properties. This section includes a brief introduction to SQL, focusing on those features of the language that are useful in subsequent descriptions of commercial RDBMSs. A more detailed discussion of SQL is provided in Chapter 5, "Introduction to SQL."

Relational Algebra

Although no major commercial RDBMS directly supports a complete version of a relational algebra language, an understanding of its operations is still necessary for users. SQL-based systems decompose SQL statements into one or more operations of the relational algebra. The optimizers of these systems, which (as discussed in the Chapter 3 section "Optimizer") develop and implement appropriate search strategies, "think" in terms of relational algebra operators. In order to understand the strategies an optimizer uses (or might use), application and database designers need to be familiar with operations of the relational algebra. Moreover, good database design presupposes a basic familiarity with the logic of these operations. Finally, many advocates of the relational approach maintain that a firm grasp of the relational algebra enables users to exploit the SQL language more effectively.

This discussion treats the following relational algebra operations:

- Restriction
- Projection
- Cross-product
- Join
- Outer join
- Union
- Intersection
- Difference

In each case the logic of the operation is described informally with (1) a brief account of what the operator does, (2) an indication of the general statement form for the operation, and (3) some examples to illustrate its use. It should be noted that the discussion centers on the *logic* of the operations. How the operations are implemented to execute internally depends on design choices of commercial RDBMS vendors. In order to introduce the reader to the SQL language, the explanation of each relational algebra operator is followed by an example of how the same operation would be expressed in SQL.

Restriction

This operator is used to extract entire rows from a table. It can be used to extract either just those rows that satisfy some condition (expressed as a predicate) or all rows in the table without qualification. The general form is:

```
RESTRICT table name <WHERE predicate(s)>
         INTO RESULT
```

The following example illustrates a restriction operation on the STU table (Table 4–3), in which the user instructs the system to retrieve all rows for students who are seniors. The primary key of STU is #STU. The entire table is presented first, followed by the results of the restriction operation shown in Table 4–4.

stu‖ #stu	nstu	yr	major
003	christy j.	4	music
101	armstrong l.	2	mathematics
115	kenton s.	4	geography
321	basie c.	3	physics

TABLE 4–3

RESTRICT STU WHERE YEAR = 4 INTO RESULT

result‖ #stu	nstu	yr	major
003	christy j.	4	music
115	kenton, s.	4	geography

TABLE 4–4

Simple queries in SQL have a simple structure, as shown here:

```
select  target data
from    table name(s) for all tables involved
        in the query
<where predicate(s)>
```

The optional WHERE clause is used to specify one or more predicates that qualify the data to be retrieved or manipulated. The SQL version of the restriction operation shown previously is:

```
select #stu, nstu, yr, major
from    stu
where  yr = 4
```

When the data to be retrieved (the target data) consists of all columns in a table, the SQL requirement to name each column can be avoided by using a "*" (pronounced "star") to indicate that data from all columns of the table should be returned. This shorthand version would be:

```
select *
from    stu
where  yr = 4
```

Projection

Just as restriction extracts rows from the named table, projection extracts columns. It can also be used to change the left-to-right order of columns within the result table. Like all operations of the relational algebra, its resulting table is always a relation. (This follows from the property of closure.) Therefore, redundant rows are removed before the result table is returned to the user. The general form of a projection is:

```
PROJECT table name ON column name(s)
      INTO RESULT
```

The following example illustrates how a user might specify that all values of the YEAR column in the STU table, Table 4–3, are to be retrieved. The results are shown in Table 4–5.

```
PROJECT STU ON YEAR INTO RESULT
```

result	yr
	4
	2
	3

TABLE 4–5

When using the SQL language for a query of this kind, to assure that the response produced is a relation, the user must explicitly call for the elimination of (possibly) redundant rows using a DISTINCT qualifier as shown below. (In this regard the SQL language departs from the relational model.)

```
select distinct yr
from    stu
```

(The subsequent examples of SQL queries omit use of DISTINCT where the query calls for the return of rows that include the primary key; this assures that redundant rows will not appear in the result.)

As mentioned previously, a projection can cause the columns in the resulting relation to be reordered. The following example extracts and reorders the #STU and YR columns in the STU table, Table 4–3. The result is shown in Table 4–6.

```
PROJECT STU ON YR, #STU INTO RESULT
```

result	yr	#stu
	4	003
	2	101
	4	115
	3	321

TABLE 4–6

In SQL, this is expressed as:

```
select yr, #stu
from   stu
```

Cross-Product

This operation is costly. It takes each row from the first (outer) named table and concatenates it with every row of the second (inner) named table. Although its use from an application standpoint is often limited, it can easily be expressed in the SQL language, so it is included here. Its general form is:

```
CROSSPRODUCT (outer) table name, (inner) table name
          INTO RESULT
```

The following example concatenates all the rows from the DORM and DEPT tables, Tables 4–7 and 4–8 respectively:

```
CROSSPRODUCT DORM, DEPT INTO RESULT
```

dorm	dormname	sloc
	fuller	c1-q3
	skinner	c1-q9

TABLE 4–7

dept	ndept	dloc
	art	c3-q1
	music	c2-q3
	literature	c1-q7

TABLE 4–8

The result of this operation appears in Table 4–9.

result	dormname	sloc	ndept	dloc
	fuller	c1-q3	art	c3-q1
	fuller	c1-q3	music	c2-q3
	fuller	c1-q3	literature	c1-q7
	skinner	c1-q9	art	c3-q1
	skinner	c1-q9	music	c2-q3
	skinner	c1-q9	literature	c1-q7

TABLE 4–9

As the example indicates, the sum of columns in the result of a cross-product operation equals the sum of columns in the outer and inner tables. The cardinality of rows in the result table is the product of the cardinalities of the outer and inner tables. In SQL, the same query is coded as:

```
select *
from    dorm, dept
```

Cross-product operations are sometimes referred to as Cartesian products in vendor literature. (They were originally called "Extended Cartesian Products.")

Join

This is probably the most useful of all the relational algebra operations. It is used to bring together rows from different tables based on the truth of some specified condition. It resembles the cross-product operation insofar as it brings together or concatenates rows from multiple named tables. But the resemblance ends there. It can only be used where the referenced tables share a common domain. (These are values in what are often called the "join columns.") It concatenates rows from the first named table (called the outer table) with rows from the second named table (called the inner table) *only* when some condition holds for the values of the join columns. Its general form is:

```
JOIN (outer) table name WITH (inner) table name
     ON domain name INTO RESULT
```

The following example concatenates rows from the STU and GRADE tables (where the join column is #STU) when a student number in the STU table matches the student number in the GRADE table. The primary key of STU is #STU. The GRADE table has a composite primary key of #STU and #CRSE. (See Tables 4–10 and 4–11.)

```
JOIN STU, GRADE on #STU INTO RESULT
```

stu	#stu	nstu	major
	003	christy j.	music
	101	armstrong l.	astronomy
	115	kenton s.	geography
	321	basie c.	physics

TABLE 4–10

grade	#stu	#crse	gr
	321	p–101	90
	101	a–099	88
	101	a–440	96
	003	m–101	89

TABLE 4–11

The result of this join operation is shown in Table 4–12.

result	#stu	nstu	major	#stu	#crse	gr
	003	christy j.	music	003	m-101	89
	101	armstrong l.	astronomy	101	a-099	88
	101	armstrong l.	astronomy	101	a-440	96
	321	basie c.	physics	321	p-101	90

TABLE 4–12

The #STU value for the first row of the outer table is compared with the #STU value for every row of the inner table. When they are equal, the row of the outer table is concatenated with the row of the inner table. This is repeated for each row of the outer table.

In SQL, the join operation is written as:

```
select stu.*, grade.*
from    stu, grade
where   stu.#stu = grade.#stu
```

The WHERE clause implies a JOIN of STU and GRADE on #STU. Column names should be preceded with a qualifying table name whenever a column name might be ambiguous.

There are several types of the join operation. The example above is an *equijoin;* it brings rows together based on the equality of values of the join columns (#STU in STU and #STU in GRADE). A join operation might be based on a similar test involving any of the standard relational comparatives (greater than, less than, greater than or equal to, less than or equal to, and not equal to).

The original definition of this operation requires a domain that is common to the tables being joined. This is another valuable use of the domain concept. This prerequisite for performing the join operation enables an RDBMS that supports domains to check for a common domain before performing the join requested. This check protects users from possible errors. For example, if a user were to ask for a join of the GRADE table and a PART table where student grade (defined as small integer) equals the weight of a part (defined as small integer), this is probably an error since a comparison of student grades and part weights doesn't usually make much sense. A domain check by the RDBMS would show that although these two columns are defined as the same data type, they are also defined on different domains. The RDBMS would issue a warning to the user and not permit the operation. However, many current commercial RDBMSs do not provide support for domains that provides this semantic check on join operations.

In the previous example of the join operation, the reader may have noticed that the RESULT table of the join contains no data on student number 115. Since that student is not currently enrolled in a course, the test for a matching student number in the GRADE table was negative. In general, the join operation does not show which rows of the outer table fail to yield a "true" result when values of the join columns are compared. And applications frequently need to know which (if any) rows in the outer table have failed to qualify. This is the motivation for the next relational algebra operator—the outer join.

Outer Join

This operation is an extension of the join described previously. It concatenates rows under the same conditions. In addition, it includes in the result any row for which the comparison yields a negative result. It takes the following general form:

```
OUTER JOIN outer table name, inner table name ON domain name
INTO RESULT
```

The following example concatenates rows from STU and GRADE when the student number in the STU table (the outer table) matches the student number in the GRADE (or inner) table. (Refer back to Tables 4–10 and 4–11.) Where there is no match, the system will concatenate the relevant row from the outer table with NULL indicators, one for each column of the inner table. (See Table 4–13.)

OUTER JOIN STU, GRADE ON #STU INTO RESULT

result	#stu	nstu	major	#stu	#crse	gr
	003	christy j.	music	003	m-101	89
	101	armstrong l.	astronomy	101	a-099	88
	101	armstrong l.	astronomy	101	a-440	96
	321	basie c.	physics	321	p-101	90
	115	kenton s.	geography	null	null	null

TABLE 4–13

The row for Kenton should be interpreted as: "There are no known courses and associated grades for Kenton S."

Although the SQL standards bodies have specified a syntax for outer joins, very few vendors support the standard syntax as of this writing. As a result, implementations of outer join operations vary from system to system (and some systems do not support the operation at all). The following is an example of how one commercial relational DBMS supports outer joins through its implementation of SQL:

```
select  stu.*, grade.*
from    stu, grade
where   stu.#stu (+) = grade.#stu
```

This is an example of how a left outer join might be expressed. A right outer join operates similarly. When the join column of any row in the inner table has no matching value in a row of the outer table, the row from the inner table appears in the result concatenated to NULL for each column of the outer table. The following example shows the results of a right outer join in Table 4–16. (For the reader's convenience, the values of the STU and GRADE tables are repeated first as Tables 4–14 and 4–15.)

stu	#stu	nstu	major
	003	christy j.	music
	101	armstrong l.	astronomy
	115	kenton s.	geography
	321	basie c.	physics

TABLE 4–14

grade	#stu	#crse	gr
	321	p-101	90
	101	a-099	88
	101	a-440	96
	003	m-101	89
	115	g-101	87
	009	b-301	70

TABLE 4–15

result	#stu	nstu	major	#stu	#crse	gr
	003	christy j.	music	003	m-101	89
	101	armstrong l.	astronomy	101	a-099	88
	101	armstrong l.	astronomy	101	a-440	96
	321	basie c.	physics	321	p-101	90
	115	kenton s.	geography	115	g-101	87
	null	null	null	009	b-301	70

TABLE 4–16

Union

This is the first of three *set operators*—so called because they are direct analogues of the basic mathematical operators on sets. The union of two sets includes in the result every row that appears in either (or both) of the two sets. The tables on which it operates must contain the same number of columns. Also, corresponding columns must be defined on the same domains. (This constraint is often relaxed in commercial RDBMSs since their implementation of the domain concept is either limited or absent. These systems require that corresponding columns be of similar

RDBMS data types.) All the set operations preserve the integrity of resulting tables as relations by eliminating redundant rows. (Some SQL systems provide an extended form of the operation that includes redundant rows in the resulting table. Strictly, such result tables are not proper relations.)

The general form of a union operation is:

```
UNION table name 1, table name 2 INTO RESULT
```

The following example retrieves rows that appear in either the INSTR1 or the INSTR2 table (Tables 4–17 and 4–18). The result of this operation appears as Table 4–19.

instr1	#instr	ninstr
	5678	star r.
	8910	john e.

TABLE 4–17

instr2	#instr	ninstr
	8910	john e.
	3456	nix s.

TABLE 4–18

```
UNION INSTR1, INSTR2 INTO RESULT
```

result	#instr	ninstr
	5678	star r.
	3456	nix s.
	8910	john e.

TABLE 4–19

In SQL, this operation is expressed as:

```
select    *
from      instr1
union
select    *
from      instr2
```

Intersection

The intersection operation includes in the result only rows that appear in *both* of the named tables. The general form is:

```
INTERSECT table name 1, table name 2 INTO RESULT
```

This example retrieves only those rows that appear in both tables (Tables 4–20 and 4–21). The result is shown as Table 4–22.

```
INTERSECT INSTR1, INSTR2 INTO RESULT
```

instr1	#instr	ninstr
	5678	star r.
	8910	john e.

instr2	#instr	ninstr
	8910	john e.
	3456	nix s.

TABLE 4–20   **TABLE 4–21**

instr1	#instr	ninstr
	8910	john e.

TABLE 4–22

In SQL, the same operation might be written as:

```
select * from instr1
intersect
select * from instr2
```

Although many RDBMSs provide explicit support for an INTERSECT operator in their versions of SQL, the same results can be obtained with an SQL EXISTS operator, as the following example shows. It also introduces the use of a nested SELECT statement whose results are input for evaluation according to the outer SELECT statement in which it occurs. The outer SELECT here evaluates each row of INSTR1 to determine whether there exists a row in INSTR2 with matching values in all columns.

```
select    *
from    instr1
where  exists
  (select    *
  from    instr2
  where   (instr1.#instr · instr2.#instr
  and instr1. ninstr = instr2. ninstr)
```

Difference

This operator subtracts from the first named table those rows that appear in the second named table. Its general form is:

```
DIFFERENCE table name 2 FROM table name 1 INTO RESULT
```

The following example retrieves all rows from INSTR1 *except* those that are in INSTR2 (Tables 4–23 and 4–24). The result appears as Table 4–25.

```
DIFFERENCE INSTR2 FROM INSTR1 INTO RESULT
```

instr1	#instr	ninstr
	5678	star r.
	8910	john e.

TABLE 4–23

instr2	#instr	ninstr
	8910	john e.

TABLE 4–24

result	#instr	ninstr
	5678	star r.

TABLE 4–25

In SQL, this operation might be written as:

```
select * from instr1
minus
select * from instr2
```

Difference can also be expressed in SQL using a subselect and the NOT EXISTS operator. This form is shown here:

```
select     *
from    instr1
where  not exists
    (select     *
    from    instr2
    where   (instr1.#instr = instr2.#instr
    and      instr1. ninstr = instr2. ninstr)
```

The outer SELECT retrieves each row of INSTR1 for which there is no matching row in INSTR2.

SUMMARY

The primary aim of the relational database approach is to simplify database processing for programmers, database administrators, and end users by providing a simple tabular data structure and more powerful languages for queries and updates to the database. Since relationships among real-world objects are represented by data values alone, relational DBMSs offer more data independence than what has been typically provided by prerelational DBMSs. Access paths are transparent to users, and users need not formulate and code access strategies. Instead these functions are performed by the RDBMS itself.

A relation is defined as a set of n-tuples. Every relation has a primary key whose values uniquely identify rows. Columns (or attributes) are defined on domains of the relation. This approach includes rules to assure domain, entity, and referential integrity of the data.

The relational algebra consists of several operators that form the basis of the standard relational language, SQL. The operations of the relational algebra provide closure so that they operate on relations and always produce relations as results. A key operation of any relational language is a join (which can take several forms). It brings together in a single table rows from multiple tables based on a comparison of values in each join column.

REFERENCES AND SUGGESTED READING

ASTRAHAN M. M., et al. "System R: Relational Approach to Database Management," *ACM TODS*, June 1976.

CODD, E. F. "Relational Database: A Practical Foundation for Productivity," *Communications of the ACM*, February 1982.

CODD, E. F. "Is Your DBMS Really Relational?" *Computerworld*, Oct. 14 and Oct. 24, 1985.

CODD, E. F. "A Relational Model of Data for Large Shared Data Banks," *Communications of the ACM*, vol. 13, no. 6, 1970, pp. 377–387.

CODD, E. F. *The Relational Model for Database Management Version 2*, Addison-Wesley, 1990.

CODD, E. F. "Relational Completeness of Data Base Sublanguages," in *Data Base Systems, Courant Computer Science Symposia Series 6*, Prentice-Hall, 1972.

DATE, C. J. *Relational Database Writings 1991–1994*, Addison-Wesley, 1995.

DATE, C. J. *An Introduction to Database Systems*, 6th ed., Addison-Wesley, 1994.

DATE, C. J. "Not IS Not 'Not,'" in *Relational Writings 1984–1989*, C. J. DATE, Addison Wesley, 1990, pp. 217–248.

DATE, C. J. "Notes Toward a Reconstituted Definition of the Relational Model Version 1 (RM/V1)," in *Relational Database Writings 1989–1991*, C. J. DATE with HUGH DARWEN, Addison Wesley, 1992. pp. 213–256.

DATE. C. J. "Null Values in Database Management," in *Relational Database: Selected Writings*, C. J. Date, Addison Wesley, 1986, pp. 313–334.

DATE, C. J. "The Nullologist in Relationland or Nothing Really Matters," in *Relational Database Writings 1989–1991*, C. J. DATE with HUGH DARWEN, Addison Wesley, 1992, pp. 181–196.

DATE, C. J. "The Outer Join," in *Relational Database: Selected Writings*, C. J. DATE, Addison Wesley, 1986, pp. 335–366.

DATE, C. J., and DAVID MCGOVERAN. "Updating Union, Intersection and Difference Views," *Database Programming and Design*, vol. 7, no. 6, June 1994, pp. 46–53.

DATE, C. J. and DAVID MCGOVERAN. "Updating Joins and Other Views," *Database Programming and Design*, vol. 7, no. 8, August 1994, pp. 43–59.

HUFF, H. W. "Why Codd's Rule No. 6 Must Be Reformulated," *ACM SIGMOD Record*, December 1988.

STONEBRAKER, M., E. WONG, P. KREPS, and G. HELD. "The Design and Implementation of INGRES," in *Readings in Database Systems*, MICHAEL STONEBRAKER, ed., Morgan Kaufmann, 1995.

STONEBRAKER, MICHAEL, ed. *The Ingres Papers: Anatomy of a Relational Database System*, Addison-Wesley, 1986.

CHAPTER 5
Introduction to
Structured Query Language

CHAPTER OBJECTIVES

While Chapter 4 included some brief examples of SQL, this chapter provides a more complete introduction to the language. The aim is to prepare the reader with sufficient knowledge of SQL to understand examples presented in Part Three, "Commercial Relational Database Management Systems."

This chapter explains the general features, uses, and components of SQL for data definition, data manipulation, and data control. It explains those SQL statements used to create databases, tables, indexes, and views; to specify data integrity constraints; and to extend and control how a database can be manipulated by its various users.

The reader is introduced to the syntax and semantics of SQL for both simple and complex queries that require multi-table joins, use of the aggregate operators, and simple arithmetic computation. Since the join operator is so important in relational database queries and applications, this chapter explains the processing logic of the various join methods used in different commercial RDBMSs and presents introductory material on when a particular method is apt to be selected by an optimizer as most efficient. (Part Three indicates which of these methods are used by the products discussed.)

Since recursive query processing is an area of increasing interest to users of RDBMSs, this chapter discusses the basic logic of such processing, with an example to prepare the reader for the material on how various vendor implementations of SQL are being extended to support such queries.

GENERAL

As the reader will recall, the Structured Query Language (SQL) is set-oriented, unlike the languages in prerelational systems. This means that the data objects referenced in SQL are always tables, and that SQL always produces results in tabular format. It is used for both batch and online applications. SQL is included in application programs through an embedded or a call-level interface. It is also used as a stand-alone query language.

SQL's main components are a data definition language (DDL), a data manipulation language (DML), and a data control language (DCL). As discussed in Chapter 4, "The Relational Database Approach," it can easily express the required operators of the relational algebra. Thus, it measures up to the standard of *relational completeness* that is required by the relational database approach. Relational completeness is a measure of the expressive power of a query language. It is defined as a language that expresses the equivalent of the basic set of relational algebra operations without resorting to iterative operations. One of SQL's most valuable features is that it gives users the ability to specify key database operations—such as table, view, and index creation—on a dynamic basis. This chapter also explains the statements used to define these database objects.

In addition to its query capability, SQL can express arithmetic operations as well as operations to aggregate data and sort data for output. Nonetheless, SQL is not a general-purpose programming language. Therefore, the development of an application requires the use of SQL with a programming language.

Not all implementations of SQL support the same general-purpose programming languages. Most systems provide support for C and COBOL. Other languages—such as Ada and Pascal—are not supported by all commercial RDBMSs. Users must determine whether a particular RDBMS supports their requirements for a specific programming language.

It is well known that although the various vendor versions of SQL comply substantially with the specifications of the American National Standards Institute (ANSI) and the International Standards Organizations (ISO), there are still differences in syntax and (in some cases) even in the semantics of the various "dialects" of the language that are offered commercially. In what follows, an effort has been made to describe a subset of the language whose semantics is common to the products described in this book. However, the reader should be aware of possible differences that might exist among the various implementations of the language.

DATA DEFINITION LANGUAGE

Once users have formulated a sound database design, they use SQL's data definition language (DDL) to describe the tables and other objects that will be managed by the DBMS. DDL statements are typically provided to enable users to create tables, indexes, views, databases, stored procedures, triggers, and other database objects. Similarly, these objects can be deleted (or dropped) using other DDL statements. And some can be changed (or altered) using DDL statements as well.

CREATE TABLE Statement

One of the more frequently used DDL statements is the CREATE TABLE statement. It defines the names of tables and columns, as well as specifies the type of data allowed in each column.

The following example defines a STU table for tracking information about students, including their identification numbers (#STU), names (NSTU), year or standing in college (YR), and subject in which they're majoring (MAJOR). Student ID numbers (#STU) form the basis for the primary key. (Line numbers are included only for easy reference in this example; they are not a part of SQL.)

```
1. create table stu
2.    (#stu        smallint     not null,
3.    nstu         char (32)    not null with default,
4.    yr           smallint,
5.    major        char (16),
6.    primary key (#stu))
```

Since #STU is the primary key, "NOT NULL" in line 2 causes the RDBMS to prohibit loading or inserting a row with a missing value for this column. Line 3 requires that missing data be represented with default characters. Finally, the primary key is explicitly identified in line 6. To avoid ambiguity, the full name of STU is X.STU, where "X" is the ID of the user who is creating the table (the table owner).

Most systems enable additional information to be specified when creating tables, such as declarations of integrity constraints that restrict the valid data values of a column.

ALTER TABLE Statement

Once created, tables can be altered to accommodate changing needs. A typical alteration might be to add one or more columns. A new column to record information about student fees might be added as follows:

```
alter table stu
    add fee      decimal (5,2)
```

The data types supported vary from DBMS to DBMS but generally include integer, floating point numbers, decimals, fixed-length character strings, and varying-length character strings. Some DBMSs also support special types for date/time data, money, double-byte character sets (necessary to support certain foreign languages), and binary large objects (BLOBs) for storing images, large documents, and other data. As discussed in Chapter 18 "The Extended Relational and Hybrid Approaches," several relational DBMSs have begun to provide support for user-defined types as well.

Synonyms or Aliases

Many DBMSs enable alternate names for tables to be defined with a CREATE SYNONYM statement. Synonyms are often used to allow reference to a table without qualifying the original table name with the user ID of the table owner. Assuming that SATCHMO is the owner of our STU table, a synonym can be defined as follows:

```
create synonym stubody for satchmo.stu
```

Column Constraints

Several DBMSs support SQL statements to check the integrity of data at the column level. Depending on the DBMS, these constraints may be written as part of the CREATE or ALTER TABLE statements or through a separate DDL statement (such as CREATE CONSTRAINT). The following example illustrates one way of ensuring that values for YR data in the STU table are 1 through 4.

```
create constraint valyr
    on stu
    check yr > 0 and < 5
```

Other RDBMSs provide a mechanism for automatic invocation of user-supplied edit and validation routines. The following is an example in which a new column is added to the STU table along with a specification of the validation routine to be used for the new column:

```
alter table stu
    add stuorgs    char(16)
    validproc      valorg1
```

Whenever an insertion of STUORGS data is made, the system will invoke the user-supplied VALORG1 routine to test for a valid student organization name.

(Each of these features that enables users to constrain data values might be viewed as partial support for the domain concept previously discussed.)

CREATE VIEW Statement

Views arc virtual tables. Although they are not directly mapped to real data in storage, they can be used for retrieval as if the data they represent is actually stored, and they can be processed as the user requests. They are one of the most useful features of relational systems, particularly since they can be created dynamically. CREATE VIEW is an executable statement. A view can be used in the same program in which it is defined.

Views are sometimes used as a security mechanism to hide sensitive information from certain users. In addition, views are often used to present a user or an application with a single logical view of information that is actually spread across multiple tables. This can be achieved by creating views based upon a join of two or more tables. The many ways to exploit the view mechanism are described in the section "More on Views" later in this chapter, along with a brief account of how an RDBMS supports this feature.

In the following example, a user needs to work with a table containing data on just those music majors who are sophomores. Only the #STU and NSTU columns are required. Instead of copying the relevant data from the STU table into a new real (or base) table, a view or virtual table is defined:

```
create view musicians
   (#stu, nstu)
   as select  stu.#stu, stu.nstu
   from       stu
   where      stu.major = 'music'
   and        stu.yr = 2
```

Column names in the view need not be the same as column names in the base table on which the view is defined. Users should determine how various RDBMSs restrict the ability to define views. Virtually all major RDBMSs support views defined on the join of two tables. However, some do not allow views defined on the union of tables.

Once the view is created, users might want to preserve its integrity by disallowing an update or insertion that would cause rows to go beyond the view definition. In our example, an update to the YR column to show that a student was now at the junior class level by changing YR from 2 to 3 could be prevented through the addition of a WITH CHECK OPTION clause to the definition given. Restrictions on view updating are necessary. These are also discussed in "More on Views."

CREATE INDEX Statement

Indexes are also defined with a CREATE statement that identifies the table being indexed and the columns that comprise the index key. Like tables, indexes can be created dynamically. The maximum number of columns in an index key varies across RDBMSs; some allow up to 64 columns. Use of a composite key has the effect of a major-to-minor ordering of key values. A composite index key of MAJOR.NSTU logically orders student names within major subjects Usually, an index on the primary key is defined as UNIQUE to prevent redundant primary key values. As mentioned previously in Chapter 3, "Major Components and Functions," creating indexes on frequently queried columns can speed performance. They are particularly useful on primary and foreign key columns since many queries require joining tables on these key columns. The performance of such queries is often enhanced through the use of these indexes.

The following example creates a unique index for the STU table. Line 1 names the index and designates it as unique. Line 2 specifies the table being indexed. Line 3 names the column being indexed and specifies the logical order of the B+ tree index to be descending. (The default order is ascending.) The cluster parameter in line 4 indicates that the RDBMS will maintain the physical row order in storage to correspond to the logical order of index key values.

```
EXAMPLE:
1. create unique index xstu
2.         on stu
3.            (#stu desc)
4.            cluster
```

Contention for index entries requires concurrency controls on indexes. Some systems offer alternative levels of granularity for index locking. Lock granularity might vary, for example, from one-sixteenth to a full index page.

It is important to note that the semantics of data stored in a DBMS does not depend on the existence of an index. Indexes are frequently created by administrators to improve performance for certain queries; programmers and end users need not be aware of the existence of any indexes and need not reference them in their SQL statements.

DROP Statement

The DROP statement can be used to drop tables and other objects. Care should be exercised in dropping tables since doing so causes all indexes, views, and synonyms defined on the same table to be dropped.

The following statement drops the STU table from the database:

```
DROP TABLE STU
```

Creating Stored Procedures and Triggers

Many relational DBMSs provide DDL statements for creating stored procedures and triggers. Stored procedures may be thought of as precoded queries or mini-programs. Most often, they consist of SQL statements and procedural logic constructs (such as if-then-else statements and loops). Users can typically pass in one or more parameters to help control the results of the procedure's execution. Stored procedures are particularly helpful in situations where the same type of work is often executed repeatedly; they help save multiple users and programmers the trouble of writing (and possibly maintaining) this code, because they can all simply use the one procedure that has been written. In client/server environments (discussed in Chapter 6), stored procedures also offer performance advantages.

In most relational DBMSs, stored procedures are created using a CREATE PROCEDURE statement. However, the full syntax of this statement is highly variable, and at least one commercial relational DBMS does not even use the CREATE PROCEDURE syntax at all. In addition, efforts to standardize the syntax for this SQL statement are still underway as of this writing. For these reasons, the authors do not present a "typical" stored procedure example here. Instead, the reader is encouraged to review different commercial implementations in Part Three, "Commercial Relational Database Management Systems."

In many DBMSs, triggers are a special form of stored procedure. Whereas a stored procedure is explicitly invoked from an application, triggers are automatically executed when a given database event occurs. This code can be used to enforce various integrity constraints. For example, if a user attempts to update the YR column in the STU table (perhaps to indicate that a student is now a sophomore instead of a freshman), a trigger could be defined to check another table to verify that the student has completed the proper number of courses required to be considered a sophomore. If so, the update would be allowed to proceed. If not, the trigger might return an error code and prevent the update from occurring.

As with stored procedures, trigger implementations vary considerably from vendor to vendor. For this reason, readers who wish to see coding examples are encouraged to review the material in Part Three.

DATA MANIPULATION LANGUAGE

Examples of simple SQL queries have been given in Chapter 4, "The Relational Database Approach." A more comprehensive version of the language as it is used for manipulating relational data is given here.

Data manipulation statements provide users with the ability to SELECT (or retrieve) data, UPDATE data, INSERT new rows into a table (or perhaps a view), and DELETE existing rows. Any of these statements may be considered a *query*, although this term is sometimes used to refer only to read-only (SELECT) statements. This book uses query in its most general sense to indicate any data manipulation statement.

The following sections illustrate SQL statements that can be issued interactively. These statements can also be included in a program, although there are additional considerations when doing so. These considerations vary according to the type of programming language interface used—embedded SQL or a call-level SQL interface. A discussion of these interfaces and programming language requirements is beyond the scope of this book.

SELECT Statement

Retrieving data from a table or view is accomplished by issuing a SELECT statement. This statement can take many forms and employ a number of optional clauses. But its most basic form (first described in Chapter 4, "The Relational Database Approach") requires specifying only the column(s) whose values are to be retrieved and the table(s) or view(s) in which the columns are defined. The structure previously given for retrieval statements is extended as follows:

```
select    <distinct> column(s)
from      table name(s)
<where    predicate(s)>
<group by column name(s)> <having condition>
<order by column name(s)>
```

Clauses enclosed in braces (< >) are optional. While the syntax for the SELECT statement may look confusing at first, it will be easier to understand if each of its clauses is explained. In order to do so, the reader will need to refer to a sample table.

The GRADE table in our COLLEGE database identifies those students who are currently enrolled, the courses in which they are enrolled, and the grades they are receiving for each course. (See Table 5–1.)

grade	#stu	#crse	gr
	321	p-101	90
	101	a-099	88
	101	a-440	96
	003	m-101	89
	003	p-101	77
	321	a-440	97

TABLE 5–1

To obtain a list of course numbers for those courses currently underway at the college, an SQL statement is formulated to query the GRADE table, since it contains all courses currently offered:

```
select   #crse (target data to be retrieved)
from     grade (table involved in processing)
```

The resulting table for this query will consist of a single column of course numbers. (See Table 5–2.) Notice that unlike the result of a projection, the result produced in this example includes redundant rows. Thus, an unqualified selection of columns in SQL is really not the equivalent of the relational algebra projection operator.

result	#crse
	p-101
	a-099
	a-440
	m-101
	p-101
	a-440

TABLE 5–2

To achieve the effect of a projection (that is, to avoid the return of redundant rows) the DISTINCT keyword is used. Here the user also requests that results be ordered by course number. (See Table 5–3.)

```
select    distinct #crse
from      grade
order by #crse
```

result	#crse
	a-099
	a-440
	m-101
	p-101

TABLE 5-3

WHERE Clause

Boolean conditions can be specified as predicates of a WHERE clause. Assuming a STU table such as Table 5–4, the user requests retrieval of the student numbers and names of senior class students majoring in astronomy. The result of this query is shown in Table 5–5.

stu	#stu	nstu	major	yr
	003	christy j.	music	4
	101	armstrong l.	astronomy	4
	115	kenton s.	geography	1
	512	buck r.	art	2
	321	basie c.	physics	3
	555	getz s.	astronomy	4
	439	vaughn s.	music	2

TABLE 5-4

```
select    #stu, nstu
from      stu
where     yr = 4
and       major = 'astronomy'
```

result	#stu	nstu
	101	armstrong l.
	555	getz s.

TABLE 5-5

To obtain the student numbers and names of students majoring in astronomy, physics, or geography, the following SQL statement expresses the appropriate disjunction of course names and produces the result shown in Table 5–6.

```
select   #stu, nstu
from     stu
where    major = 'astronomy'
or       major = 'physics'
or       major = 'geography'
```

result	#stu	nstu
	101	armstrong l.
	115	kenton s.
	321	basie c.
	555	getz s.

TABLE 5–6

Notice that in the above version of this query, the column name, MAJOR, is repeated for each value of the major subject on which the search is to be made. To avoid this repetition, the following optional form yields the same result:

```
select   #stu, nstu
from     stu
where    major in
('astronomy','physics','geography')
```

Pattern Matching

Wildcard characters can also be incorporated into the WHERE clause to perform pattern matching. For example, the following statement will query the STU table (Table 5–4) for all information on all students majoring in subjects that begin with an "a" (returning the results shown in Table 5–7).

```
select   #stu, nstu, major, yr
from     stu
where major like 'a%'
```

result	#stu	nstu	major	yr
	101	armstrong l.	astronomy	4
	512	buck r.	art	2
	555	getz s.	astronomy	4

TABLE 5–7

Note that pattern matching involves the use of the LIKE keyword (rather than an equal sign).

Arithmetic Expressions

The target list in the SELECT clause can include an arithmetic expression. Assume a table with instructor data that includes the annual salary for each instructor. A query to retrieve the name and monthly salary for each instructor sorted by *monthly* salary in ascending order (the default order) would be expressed as follows:

```
select    ninstr, sal/12
from      instrtab
order by  2
```

Since monthly salary is not a defined column for the INSTRTAB, the ORDER BY line must reference this data by numbered item in the list of target data. For some SQL implementations, only data referenced in the target list can be referenced in an ORDER BY clause. For these systems, the following is an error:

```
select    nstu, major
from      stu
order by  #stu
```

Joins

The very useful join operation is needed to retrieve the student numbers and names of those students with a grade of more than 90 in any course, as queried in the following statement. This requires processing of data in both the STU and GRADE tables (shown in Tables 5–8 and 5–9).

```
select    distinct stu.#stu, stu.nstu
from      stu, grade
where     stu.#stu = grade.#stu
and       grade.gr > 90
```

Notice that the FROM clause must reference both tables involved in the query, even though data is requested from just the STU table. The result is shown in Table 5–10.

stu	#stu	nstu	major	yr
	003	christy j.	music	4
	101	armstrong l.	astronomy	4
	115	kenton s.	geography	1
	512	buck r.	art	2
	321	basie c.	physics	3
	555	getz s.	astronomy	4
	439	vaughn s.	music	2

TABLE 5–8

grade	#stu	#crse	gr
	321	p-101	90
	101	a-099	88
	101	a-440	96
	003	m-101	89
	003	p-101	77
	321	a-440	97

TABLE 5-9

result	#stu	nstu
	101	armstrong l.
	321	basie c.

TABLE 5-10

Nested Queries

The same query can be expressed using the nested SQL format:

```
select   stu.#stu, stu.nstu
from     stu
where    #stu in
   (select   distinct #stu
    from     grade
    where    gr > 90)
```

Although the nested SQL and join statements shown here will yield the same result, in some RDBMSs their performance will *not* be the same. In these systems, queries formulated with the join syntax receive preferential treatment at the hands of the DBMS optimizer. They perform better. Other RDBMSs translate the alternative formulations into the same internal representation that is used for the join syntax *before* optimization takes place. In this way, they provide the same level of performance regardless of the user's choice of syntax.

More information about optimization of joins is included in "Join Processing" in this chapter.

Aggregate Functions

SQL provides several useful built-in functions that operate on aggregates of data:

```
  sum - computes the sum of selected values
  avg - computes the average of selected values
  max - computes the highest value of selected target
  min - computes the lowest value of selected target
count - counts the number of occurrences of values
```

To compute the average grade for all students in the GRADE table (Table 5–11), the AVG built-in function precedes the name of the column over which the function will be computed:

```
select    avg (gr)
from      grade
```

grade	#stu	#crse	gr
	321	p-101	90
	101	a-099	88
	101	a-440	96
	003	m-101	89
	003	p-101	77
	321	a-440	97

TABLE 5–11

The computed average grade is shown in Table 5–12. The result represents the average grade of all students currently enrolled in courses.

result	gr
	89

TABLE 5–12

COUNT can be used to count the number of rows in the Grade table, with the result shown in Table 5–13:

```
select    count(*)
from      grade
```

result	
	6

TABLE 5–13

To count the number of *different* values that appear in a column, COUNT DISTINCT can be used. This query counts the number of distinct values appearing in the #CRSE column of the GRADE table, with the result shown in Table 5–14.

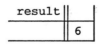

```
select    count (distinct #crse)
from      grade
```

result	
	4

TABLE 5–14

To compute the average grade *per student* (instead of the average grade for the student body), the GROUP BY clause is used with the AVG built-in function. The result is given in Table 5–15.

```
select    #stu, avg (gr)
from      grade
group by  #stu
```

result	#stu	gr
	321	93
	101	92
	003	83

TABLE 5–15

Often a user needs to compute a function, like average, for only a specified number of rows in a group. In this example, the information needed is the average grade for those students enrolled in at least three courses Their grade data appears in Table 5–16.

grade	#stu	#crse	gr
	321	p-101	90
	101	a-099	88
	101	a-440	96
	003	m-101	89
	003	p-101	77
	321	a-440	97
	321	m-101	70

TABLE 5–16

```
select         #stu, avg(gr)
from           grade
group by       #stu
having count   (*) > 2
```

The result of this query appears in Table 5–17.

result	#stu	gr
	321	85

TABLE 5–17

COUNT (*) is used to count the number of rows (including duplicates) in each group formed by the query. The HAVING keyword restricts the selection of groups (just as a WHERE clause restricts the selection of rows). In this example, only groups with more than two rows qualify for further selection.

Tuple Variables

The designers of the SQL language recognized the need to support the join operation on a completely generalized basis. This requires the ability to join a table with data from within the same table. Expressing self-joins of this sort might have resulted in considerable complication of the SQL syntax. To avoid such complexity, and to sustain the paradigm of *table look-up* in developing query logic users can introduce *tuple variables* to express the self join of a table.

It is best to think of a tuple variable (often erroneously labeled a "relation variable" in some vendor literature) as a simple place marker on one or more rows of a table. Consider a query to retrieve the names of those students majoring in the same subject as June Christy. A simple strategy is to scan the STU table (Table 5–18), looking for June Christy's major field and to mark that row. Then the DBMS could scan the STU table again from the top, marking any row whose MAJOR value matches the MAJOR value for June Christy. This strategy can be mimicked easily by introducing tuple variables or place markers, X and Y, as in the SQL formulation that follows:

```
1. select    x.nstu,
2. from      stu x, stu y
3. where     x.major = y.major
4. and       y.nstu = 'christy j.'
```

stu	#stu	nstu	major	yr	
	003	christy j.	music	4	← y-marker
	101	armstrong l.	astronomy	4	
	115	kenston s.	geography	1	
	321	basie c.	physics	3	
	555	getz s.	astronomy	4	
	439	vaughn s.	music	2	← x-marker

TABLE 5–18

Consider this query from the bottom up. Line 4 places a Y mark in June Christy's row during the first scan of the STU table. Line 3 indicates that during the second scan of STU, each row whose MAJOR value matches the MAJOR value of the row already marked Y should be marked X. Line 1 selects the student name from any row marked X. Line 2 establishes the two place markers, X and Y, on the STU table. The result appears in Table 5–19.

result	nstu
	vaughn s.
	christy j.

TABLE 5–19

Notice that a row for J. Christy appears in the result. This can be avoided by adding line 5. as follows:

```
5. and x.name <> y.name
```

Here is another way to analyze the logic of this SQL query: the FROM clause informs DBMS that the query should be processed on two copies of the STU table called X and Y. Line 4 checks copy Y, looking for a match on the NSTU column for "Christy J." Line 3 looks for a match on the MAJOR value in copy X with the MAJOR value in copy Y. Line 1 specifies projecting the name from NSTU in each row of X where the MAJOR value of that row matched the major value of copy Y.

Correlated Subqueries

Tuple variables can also be used to formulate *correlated subqueries*. Consider a query to retrieve the name of every student currently enrolled in course P-101, using the data in COSTU (Table 5–20) and COGRADE (Table 5–21) that follow.

costu	#stu	nstu
	003	christy j.
	115	kenton s.
	027	tristano l.
	101	armstrong l.
	321	basie c.

TABLE 5–20

cograde	#stu	#crse	gr
	321	p-101	90
	101	a-099	88
	101	a-440	96
	003	m-101	89
	003	p-101	77
	321	a-440	97
	321	m-101	70

TABLE 5–21

This is expressed as a correlated subquery as follows:

```
1. select    distinct #costu.nstu
2. from      costu n
3. where     'p-101' in
4.                (select #crse
5.                 from    cograde
6.                 where #stu = n.#stu)
```

In line 2, the tuple variable N is introduced. It is used in line 6 to refer to a row in COSTU. The processing logic for this query is as follows: The inner query scans the COGRADE table for a match on the #STU of row N (for example, the first row of COSTU) with a #STU in any row of COGRADE. When there is a match on student numbers, the outer query tests the course number (#CRSE) in the COGRADE row with the matching student number for a value of 'P-101.' If true, a projection is made to extract the student name from the same row in COSTU. This processing logic is performed for each tuple in COSTU. Thus the inner query processing cannot be completed in a single scan of the COGRADE table.

Compare this processing logic with the logic of the following version of the same query:

```
select    distinct #costu.nstu
from      costu
where     costu.#stu in
          (select   #stu
           from     cograde
           where    grade.#crse ='p-101')
```

Inner query processing is done first so that all student numbers for students satisfying the predicate of the inner query are retrieved from COGRADE in a *single* scan of the COGRADE table. These student numbers are used to drive a search on student numbers in the COSTU table. When any of the #STU values selected during inner query processing matches a student number in the COSTU table, the student name from the matching row is projected into a result table. Since the inner query logic is performed in a single scan of the COGRADE table, this version of the query will (in general) result in better performance.

UPDATE Statement

Database changes are made using the SQL UPDATE, DELETE, and INSERT statements. The general form of the UPDATE command is:

```
update    table name
set       column name1 = expression1
          <column name2 = expression2,...>
          <where predicate(s)>
```

For example, to change the major field for June Christy from music to philosophy:

```
update   stu
set      major = 'philosophy'
where    nstu = 'christy j.'
```

Arithmetic expressions may also be included in the UPDATE statement. The following statement adds 5 points to the grades of all students enrolled in course H-303.

```
update   grade
set      gr = gr + 5
where    #crse= 'h-303'
```

INSERT Statement

In addition to changing existing data, users must be able to add new rows to a table. This is accomplished through the INSERT statement, which takes the following form:

```
insert into   table name
              (col. name1, col. name 2,...)
values        list of values
```

The following example inserts a row containing data about a new student (Floyd, P.) into the STU table, which is repeated here for reference (Table 5–22). The effect of this INSERT is shown in Table 5–23.

stu	#stu	nstu	major	yr
	003	christy j.	music	4
	101	armstrong l.	astronomy	2
	115	kenton s.	geography	1
	321	basie c.	physics	3
	555	getz s.	astronomy	4
	439	vaughn s.	music	2

TABLE 5–22

```
insert into stu
values (177, 'floyd p.', 'music', 1)
```

```
------------After insertion------------
```

stu ‖ #stu	nstu	major	yr
003	christy j.	music	4
101	armstrong l.	astronomy	2
115	kenton s.	geography	1
321	basie c.	physics	3
555	getz s.	astronomy	4
439	vaughn s.	music	2
177	floyd p.	music	1

TABLE 5–23

Values are specified in column order. If values for all columns are inserted, column names can be omitted. Values for columns that are not included are assigned a null marker. Insertion can also be used to move data from one table to another. The following statements query the GRADE table to locate information about those students with a grade of 96 or better and inserts those rows into the BESTSTU table.

```
insert into    beststu
select         #stu, #crse, gr
from           grade
where          grade.gr > 95
```

DELETE Statement

The DELETE statement removes one or more rows from a table. It has the following general form:

```
delete
from        table name
<where      predicate(s)>
```

Thus, to delete rows for all students majoring in history:

```
delete
from        stu
where       major = 'history'
```

By eliminating the WHERE clause, the DELETE statement can be used to delete all rows from a table. However, the empty table will remain in the database until it is dropped (see the DROP TABLE discussion in "Data Definition Language," earlier in this chapter.

More on Views

Views are one of the most useful features of SQL-based systems. They can provide a high degree of data independence and data security. They can also simplify the logic and language with which queries are formulated.

As discussed previously in "CREATE VIEW Statement," views are virtual tables. Unlike base tables that contain real data, a view is a window to data in the base table(s) on which the view is defined. The RDBMS maps SQL view references to the real data in the base tables; this processing is totally transparent to users. Since views are windows on the base tables, any updates to the base tables are immediately available for retrieval and manipulation using the virtual table or view. Therefore, users need not be concerned about maintaining consistency between data in virtual tables and their corresponding base tables. A view can be defined on a subset of a base table; a view can also be defined on one or more base tables.

View definition is simple. To create a view, users (1) assign a name to the virtual table and (2) specify the makeup of the view by writing the query they would use if they were retrieving the same data from the base tables.

Here is an example that defines a view on the base table GRADE (Table 5–24). It contains the student number and average grade of each student:

grade ‖	#stu	#crse	gr
	321	p-101	90
	101	a-099	88
	101	a-440	96
	003	m-101	89
	003	p-101	77
	321	a-440	97
	321	m-101	70

TABLE 5–24

```
create view stuav
       (#stu, avgr)                    ← view column names
       as select    #stu, avg(gr)←
       from         grade              | query defining
       group by #stu                   ← the view
```

As this example shows, views can be based on computed values such as the average grades for students. Since the CREATE VIEW statement is executable, users can enter SQL queries that reference STUAV immediately following its definition:

```
select    *
from      stuav
where     #stu = 321
```

The reader will recall that "*" (star) is an abbreviation for "all columns."

Dynamic view definition is an example of one of the highly practical benefits of the systematic character of the relational approach. Recall that relational languages enjoy the property of *closure*. The operands of relational operators are relations, and they always produce relations as their results. The ability to define a view dynamically as an SQL query is due to this property of closure.

Views can be mapped to base tables by an RDBMS through a process called view merging. Consider the following example that defines a view called MUSTU. This view contains all and only those rows in the STU table for music majors.

```
create view mustu
     (#mstu, mnstu, myr)
     as select      #stu, nstu, yr
     from           stu
     where          major = 'music'
```

A user's query to retrieve only the data in MUSTU for students who are sophomores is:

```
select     *
from       mustu
where      myr = 2
```

When the RDBMS recognizes a reference to a view like MUSTU in the FROM clause of the current query, it reads the view definition from its catalog and *merges* it with the current query. The following query is the result of merging the view definition with the current query in the example above.

```
1. select    #stu, nstu, yr
2. from      stu
3. where     major = 'music'  ← predicate in view definition
4. and       yr = 2           ← predicate in current query
```

Line 2 shows that the merged version of the query references the base table STU. Lines 3 and 4 represent a merged predicate in which line 3 is taken from the view definition and line 4 is taken from the current query. It is the merged version of the query that is processed by the RDBMS optimizer.

This is a simple example of view merging. Developing the logic to perform view merging for more complex view definitions and queries is a challenging task for those who build RDBMS software. Many RDBMSs have extended the notion of view merging to support the definition of views on previously defined views. Views can be dropped at any time. When a view (or base table) is dropped, any views defined on it will also be dropped.

Views defined as the join of two tables can often be used to simplify query formulation for users. The following statement creates a view based on the join of the STU and GRADE tables. It consists of the number, name, and year of each student, along with the student's course numbers and grades.

```
create view grlist
      (#gstu, gnstu, gyr, g#crse, ggr)
      as select    stu.#stu, stu.nstu, stu.yr,
                   grade.#crse, grade.gr
           from    stu, grade
           where   stu.#stu = grade.#stu
```

As far as users of the GRLIST view are concerned, the data they require exists in a single table. This simplifies queries requiring retrieval from multiple tables that contain related data.

Although queries to retrieve data can be directed against views without restriction, problems arise in connection with view updating (that is, updates to virtual tables). Consider the following base tables, Tables 5–25 and 5–26):

stucity	#stu	#crse
	012	p-84
	023	p-84

TABLE 5–25

crsecity	#crse	city
	p-84	n.y.
	p-84	s.f.

TABLE 5–26

A view, STUCRCIT, is defined as the join of these two tables.

```
create view stucrcit
      (#cstu, #ccrse, ccity)
      as  select   #stu, stucity.#crse, city
          from     stucity, crsecity
          where    stucity.#crse = crsecity.#crse
```

Given the contents of the base tables, STUCITY and CRSECITY above, a query for all rows in the view STUCRCIT will return data as shown in Table 5–27.

stucity	#stu	#crse	ccity
	012	p-84	n.y.
	012	p-84	s.f.
	023	p-84	n.y.
	012	p-84	s.f.

TABLE 5–27

Assume now that a user enters a delete transaction to delete the row for #CSTU 023, #CCRSE P-84 and CCITY S.F. Since STUCRCIT is a window on STU-

CITY and CRSECITY, the RDBMS must delete the relevant rows in these two base tables. But what are the relevant rows in these base tables? What rows should be retained in the view? Does the user intend to delete the other rows of STUCRCIT that would be affected by the current delete transaction? Probably not. Since neither of the join columns in the base tables is a primary key, the system is unable to identify the base table rows that must be deleted to reflect the intended change in the view.

For these reasons, RDBMSs either (1) prohibit any database update using a view defined on two or more base tables or (2) allow database updates on such views only when both join columns of the base tables are primary keys. There are other problem cases of this sort involving view updating that account for similar restrictions.

Finally, the view mechanism is easily used to provide a measure of data security. If it is desirable to allow only instructors to retrieve student grades, a view might be defined on GRADE consisting of the #STU and #CRSE columns of the GRADE base table. Users other than instructors would only be allowed access to data in the GRADE base table through the view. Thus they would be able to see only student and course numbers, but they would not have access to student grades. Since any SQL query can be used to define a view, users have great flexibility in preventing unauthorized use of data in a relational database.

Join Processing

Implementing joins that execute efficiently is one of the keys to good performance. Even today, considerable research is conducted to develop new join methods that promise better performance. The researchers who produced IBM's System R (an early relational DBMS prototype) devoted considerable effort to the design and testing of various join methods. (A discussion of this is cited in "References and Suggested Reading" at the end of this chapter.) They evaluated four of the many join methods they had devised and implemented the two methods they considered best. These two methods, nested loop and sort/merge join, are used to support join processing in many commercial RDBMSs.

This section briefly summarizes some of the popular join methods in research and commercial arenas. The examples given here are stripped of any variations and enhancements that might have been made by particular relational DBMS vendors. Instead, they are described as they would work in their simplest forms in order to focus on the basic differences between them.

Nested Loop Join

To understand nested loop join processing, consider the following query that joins TABLEA and TABLEB (See Tables 5–28 and 5–29):

```
select     *
from       tablea, tableb
where      c1 = c4
```

tablea	c1	c2
	09	c
	01	b
	03	e
	04	j
	33	c
	14	b
	09	z

TABLE 5–28

tableb	c3	c4
	b	09
	e	01
	c	27
	b	33
	a	33
	d	01
	e	09

TABLE 5–29

result	c1	c2	c3	c4
	09	c	b	09
	09	c	e	09
	01	b	e	01
	01	b	d	01
	33	c	b	33
	33	c	a	33
	09	z	b	09
	09	z	e	09

TABLE 5–30

Each row of the outer table, TABLEA, is read to compare its value for C1 to the value of C4 in every row of TABLEB, the inner table. Hence, the algorithm requires a loop through TABLEB that is nested within the loop that reads TABLEA. In this example, the first row of TABLEA has a C1 value of 09, which matches the C4 value for the first row of TABLEB. These rows are concatenated and inserted into the RESULT table (Table 5–30). The system must continue to search TABLEB through its last row since any row (including the last row of TABLEB) might also have a matching value in C4. Since TABLEB must be searched to the end of table for each row of TABLEA, the cost of joining these tables is (roughly) the cost of reading each row of TABLEA *times* the cost of reading all rows in TABLEB.

This method is costly for large tables. Therefore, its use by the optimizer is unlikely when there is a large number of rows involved in the join processing. Its use is more likely when the tables involved are relatively small. The availability of an index on the inner table also makes it a more likely choice of the optimizer.

Sort/Merge Join

Another widely used join method takes advantage of the order of values in the join columns to reduce the number of rows that must be examined in the inner table. Consider how the same join query might be processed given the data shown in TABLEC and TABLED. (See Tables 5–31 and 5–32.)

```
select      *
from        tablec, tabled
where       c1 = c4
```

tablec	c1	c2
	01	b
	03	e
	04	j
	09	z
	09	c
	14	b
	33	c

TABLE 5–31

tabled	c3	c4
	e	01
	d	01
	b	09
	e	09
	c	27
	b	33
	a	33

TABLE 5–32

result	c1	c2	c3	c4
	01	b	e	01
	01	b	d	01
	09	z	b	09
	09	z	e	09
	09	c	b	09
	09	c	e	09
	33	c	b	33
	33	c	a	33

TABLE 5–33

Since there is a match on the join columns for the first rows of each table, these rows are joined. The procedure steps down to the second row of TABLED, and compares the first row of TABLEC with this row in TABLED. Again, the rows are joined. The process continues by stepping to the third row of TABLED. This time the comparison on equal is false, and the process can step to the next row of TABLEC. Applying this logic throughout, the processing avoids a full table search for every row of TABLED. The result is shown in Table 5–33. Generally, compared with nested loop this method requires far fewer comparisons to determine which rows must be joined. The cost of this method is the *sum* of the costs of reading TABLEA and TABLEB.

This method depends on the ordering of values in the join columns. If the rows are not already ordered (or there is no index that is ordered on the join columns), the optimizer will consider sorting the relevant tables as a part of its cost evaluation for this search. In addition, duplicate processing complicates the procedure and adds to its cost. Merge join is best for large tables and particularly when many rows will be joined.

Hybrid Join

Hybrid join is among those join methods implemented more recently in RDBMs. It combines some of the features of nested loop and sort/merge join. Hybrid join requires an index on the join column of the inner table. Consider a join of the following tables where column C1 equals column C2. (The RIDs, or row identifiers, are also shown in Tables 5–34 and 5–35.)

```
select      *
from      tablea, tableb
where      c1 = c2
```

tablea ‖ rid	c1
r05	09
r10	03
r11	02
r12	03
r13	06

TABLE 5–34

tableb ‖ rid	c2
r101	06
r033	01
r023	03
r034	04
r505	02

TABLE 5–35

The first step in this method is to sort the rows of TABLEA on values of the join column, C1, as is shown in Table 5–36.

tablea ‖ rid	c1
r11	02
r10	03
r12	03
r13	06
r05	09

TABLE 5–36

Next, the system scans the index on column C2 of TABLEB for values that match the values of C1 in TABLEA. For each matching value found in TABLEB, it concatenates just the RID of that TABLEB row with the matching rows in TABLEA. The concatenated rows are shown in TABLEC. (See Table 5–37).

tablec ‖ arids	c1	brids
r11	02	r505
r10	03	r023
r12	03	r023
r13	06	r101

TABLE 5–37

The BRIDs are projected from TABLEC into a result list. This result list of RIDs is sorted and used to access and join data from rows in TABLEB.

This method will avoid repeated access of rows in TABLEB for duplicate values of the join column in TABLEA. Thus, the row in TABLEB with the RID "r023" will be accessed only once. A clear advantage of this method over sort/merge join is its avoidance of duplicate processing.

Hash Join

As its name suggests, this join method exploits the speed with which addresses can be computed via hashing. Join column values of one relation are hashed for each row. The hash values reference table entries containing either the RIDs of the tuple or the entire tuples. All rows with common join key values will hash to the same bucket. Rows from the second table involved in the join are submitted to the same hash function. Rows that hash to a nonempty bucket are compared with the tuples from the first table in the same bucket. Rows with matching join column values are joined.

To increase the likelihood of processing the entire hash table in main memory, the hash table is generated for the smaller of the two tables involved in the join. Collisions on key values as well as the occurrence of duplicate values in join columns add to the cost of this method.

This method is enhanced considerably with hardware assists. Finally, this method has been extended by some vendors (such as Tandem) in order to take advantage of their system's parallel-processing capabilities. A discussion of Tandem's offering is discussed in Chapter 13, "Tandem's NonStop SQL."

Semijoins

Query processing for distributed database must consider the costs of transmitting tables from one location to another in order to perform the required relational operations, such as joins and unions. Semijoins can be used to achieve considerable reduction in the costs of interlocation data transfers. The strategy is to determine which of the rows in tables at two or more different sites will be joined by moving just the values from the join columns. Only when the rows with matching values have been filtered is all of the required data transmitted to the site at which the join is performed. Consider a request to join TABLEA (Table 5–38) at site A with TABLEB (Table 5–39) at site B as follows:

```
select      *
from      tablea, tableb
where     tablea.c1 = tableb.c10
```

tablea	c1	c2
	g	101
	k	234
	j	044
	m	213
	.	.

tableb	c10	c11	c12	...
	j	04	d	...
	j	02	e	...
	g	03	1	...
	.	.	.	....

site A
TABLE 5–38

site B
TABLE 5–39

Rather than move all the data from one site to another to perform the join, a semijoin ships the projection of one table on the join column—for example, the data values of column C10 in TABLEB (along with their RIDs)—to site A. At site A, TABLEA and an intermediate table containing the data shipped from site B are joined; this filters out the nonmatching rows in TABLEB. The RIDs of the rows that participate in the join are used to select the TABLEB rows for shipment to site A, where the join processing is completed. Often, the use of a semijoin results in a significant reduction in data transmission costs, a key factor in cost computation for distributed database.

Additional Considerations

The reader should be aware that these join methods can be supplemented and thereby enhanced with other optimization techniques. For example, additional available indexes can be used to support some of the methods described. If the query includes a restriction along with the join, the restriction predicate can be applied before the join is performed in order to reduce the number of rows that must be join processed. Furthermore, systems that support prefetching of data can take advantage of this capability during join processing.

This suggests that the number of possible query-processing strategies developed by the optimizer can be extremely large. Smart database optimizers include heuristics to quickly prune out those strategies that are ill advised and to focus on just those that appear to be more promising.

Using Multiple Indexes

All the major commercial relational DBMSs discussed in Part Three make use of indexes as part of their query-processing strategies. However, it is only recently that some systems use more than a single index per table to process a single query. The use of more than one index, called "index AND" and "index OR" processing, often results in better performance for queries with multiple predicates connected by "ANDs" and "ORs."

Consider the following query:

```
select     *
from       tablex
where      c1 = 'b'
and        c2 = 02
```

Assume that the system has two indexes on TABLEX, index1 on column C1 and index2 on column C2 (see Figure 5–1).

Each index is structured as a B+ tree; for simplicity, they are shown here in tabular form. (Actually, each row in this tabular form of the index represents an

index1	C1	RID	index2	C2	RID
	a	r099		01	r100
	b	r100		01	r266
	b	r268		02	r267
	c	r446		02	r268

Figure 5–1. Example indexes on two columns

entry in a leaf page of the index structure, as discussed in Chapter 3, "Major Components and Functions.") Each row contains a key value and its associated row identifier (RID) that represents the location of the row.

A DBMS that uses only index1 to process the query will find all and only those rows where C1 has a value of "b," but this includes a row in which the value of column C2 is 01 (rather than 02, as required by the query). Use of a single index often results in the access of rows that need not be returned to the application. The use of both indexes can ensure that each row accessed in the database satisfies both predicates, C1 = "b" and C2 = 02.

This query-processing strategy scans each index to develop two lists of RIDs (shown in Figure 5–2).

The row identifier "r268" is the only RID that appears in both lists, indicating that it is the only row that satisfies the predicates connected by AND in the WHERE clause. In fact, the intersection of these lists results in all and only those RIDs that appear in both of them. This strategy ensures that all and only those rows required by the query are accessed by the DBMS, resulting in better performance.

Now consider a query for all rows in which column C1 is value "b" or C2 is value 02. Use of just index1 in our example will locate those rows in which the first predicate is satisfied, C1 = "b." However, in order to locate those rows with column C2 = 02, all rows of TABLEX must be examined. Again, the use of both indexes results in less I/O and better performance. In this case, application of a union operation to the RID lists derived from *both* index1 and index2 will produce a RID list for rows that satisfy either or both predicates—and only for such rows. Those DBMSs that support the use of multiple indexes to perform index AND and index OR operations can provide better performance on similar queries than systems that use a single index.

ridlist	RID	ridlist2	RID
	r099		r100
	r100		r266
	r268		r267
	r446		r268

Figure 5–2. Example RID lists

Recursive Queries

In the early versions of SQL, the expressive power of the language was limited in an important way. It could not support queries that required recursive processing.

Consider the organizational structure of a company; it is easily represented as a tree structure in which data on the CEO is at the root of the tree. Data on company vice presidents who report directly to the CEO is represented in nodes at the next level, directly connected to the root node. Directors who report to vice presidents are at level three, connected to their respective superiors. The reporting structure branches downward in the tree structure to nodes at the lowest (or leaf) level, which contains data on the lowest-level employees in the organization.

These reporting relationships can also be represented in a simple table. (Table 5–40) shows the reporting relationships among the employees of a small company. It uses (somewhat unrealistically) employee names to connect an employee with his or her superior; it also indicates the title of each employee.

company	nemp.	title	supname
	carol	pres.	null
	libby	v.p.	carol
	lexa	mgr.	libby
	steve	eng.	lexa
	sean	pvgr.	lexa

TABLE 5–40

The SQL query to identify Sean's manager is straightforward:

```
select    supname
from      company
where     nemp = 'sean'
```

Next, consider a query to identify Sean's second-level manager:

```
select    supname
from      company
where     nemp =
    (select    supname
     from      company
     where     nemp ='sean')
```

A query to retrieve Sean's third-level manager is expressed by extending this SQL statement with another nested SELECT. It is clear from these examples that a query to identify the manager at any *specific* higher level (first, second, third,...) of an employee can be expressed using SQL nested selects. Similar examples can be formulated for queries that involve retrieval of data *down* the organization structure, perhaps to identify all the CEO's managers.

However, many implementations of SQL limit the number of nested selects that can be used in a single statement. A reporting structure with more levels than the maximum number of subselects allowed would present a problem.

More important, the query strategy that relies on nested selects works only when the query includes the specific level of management, (first, second, third,...) of interest, as in the examples above. Consider a query to retrieve all levels of management for an employee up to and including the CEO, where the number of levels in the organization structure is not known. This query might be expressed in English (rather than SQL) as:

```
identify all managers (for however levels of management
there are) for the employee with employee number 333999.
```

Queries that require retrieval of data from multiple levels *where the number of levels involved is unknown* require a language that can express *recursion*. General-purpose programming languages have this capability. But it was lacking in early versions of SQL and available (as of this writing) only in some commercial implementations of the language. As a result, specification of such queries necessarily requires the use of a general-purpose programming language to supplement SQL.

This has been a significant constraint on SQL because there are key applications for many customers that require recursive queries. Bill-of-materials applications, common in the manufacturing industry, have been constrained by this restriction on the expressive power of SQL. (These applications need to retrieve all components of a product at any lower levels of part assembly; conversely, they need to retrieve all components in which a particular part is used at any higher levels of component assembly.)

Recent DBMS products that include extensions to SQL in support of this capability are discussed in Part Three, "Commercial Relational Database Management Systems "

DATA CONTROL LANGUAGE

Data control language statements help confer and remove different types of privileges associated with various users. Two statements—GRANT and REVOKE—provide the means to accomplish this and are critical to implementing security constraints in a relational DBMS, as discussed in the Chapter 3 section "Security." In some systems, these statements can also be used to grant and revoke privileges beyond those involving SQL statements, such as the right to execute certain utilities.

GRANT Statement

Restricting access to base tables is achieved through the use of the SQL GRANT statement. The GRANT statement is used to grant various privileges to users. The creator of a table has full privileges on that table and can grant similar privileges to other users or groups of users on a selective basis. Privileges can be extended to all users in some systems by specifying PUBLIC in lieu of specific user IDs. Some privileges apply to rows of a table, while others apply to columns within a table. The following list indicates the broad range of privileges that a system might provide.

```
select - rows can be read
update - columns can be updated
insert - rows can be inserted
delete - rows can be deleted
alter  - columns can be added
index  - indexes can be defined
```

The general form of the GRANT statement is:

```
grant    privilege(s)
on       table/view name
to       user(s), group(s), or public
```

The following statement grants LOUISE the privilege of reading (or selecting) data from the GRADE table.

```
grant    select
on       grade
to       louise
```

If desired, LOUISE could also be granted UPDATE access to the GRADE table. This access could be rather selective, perhaps enabling her to change values in the #STU and #CRSE columns but not in the GR column. The following statement illustrates this:

```
grant    update (#stu, #crse)
on       grade
to       louise
```

A comprehensive version of the GRANT statement includes a WITH GRANT OPTION clause, an option to extend (along with a privilege) the authority to grant the same privilege to a third user. Users can also withdraw privileges on a selective basis. Any privileges extended to a third party via the WITH GRANT OPTION are automatically revoked when withdrawn by the creator of a table.

The following example grants DAVID the right to select, insert, and update data in the STU table; furthermore, DAVID can grant these same rights to others, at his discretion.

```
grant    select, insert, update
on       stu
to       david
with     grant option
```

REVOKE Statement

The REVOKE statement removes privileges that were previously conferred to one or more users. Its syntax is very similar to that of the GRANT statement:

```
revoke    privilege(s)
on        table/view name
from      user(s), group(s), or public
```

The following statement removes two of DAVID's three privileges on the STU table, leaving him with read-only access.

```
revoke    update, insert
on        stu
from      david
```

SUMMARY

SQL is the the most widely used relational API and query language today and has been officially designated the standard for relational database processing. Although each RDBMS vendor has its own dialect of the language, the commercial RDBMSs treated in this book support a large subset of the semantics and syntax of the language. SQL is relationally complete since it expresses the key operations of the relational algebra. This criterion of relational completeness was formulated by the originator of the relational approach, Dr. E. F. Codd.

SQL is a nonprocedural language: users specify what data they want retrieved and do not specify how the required search for the data should be performed by the RDBMS.

SQL views are a highly useful capability of RDBMSs. They simplify query formulation, provide data independence, and are used to control access to the data.

The various commercial RDBMSs provide various processing strategies or join methods to support those queries that require the join of multiple tables: nested loop, merge/join, hybrid join, and hash join. Not all systems support all of these methods, and each method has its own processing logic; it is the job of the RDBMS optimizer to select the best method for a given join query.

Early implementations of the SQL language did not support recursive query processing. Instead applications that required this capability (like bill-of-materials applications), had to supplement SQL statements with host language code, for example, COBOL or C, to achieve the desired results. Today vendors are extending SQL to express the recursion required in SQL without resort to the facilities of a conventional programming language.

REFERENCES AND SUGGESTED READING

BLASGEN M. W., and K. P. ESWAREN. "Storage and Access in Relational Databases," *IBM Systems Journal*, vol. 16, no. 4, 1977, pp. 363–377.

BOBROWSKI, STEVE. "Optimizer Options," *DBMS*, November 1993, p. 42.

CHENG, JOSEPHINE, DON HADERLE, RICHARD HEDGES, BALAKRISHNA R. IYER, THEODORE MESSINGER, C. MOHAN, and YUN WANG. *An Efficient Hybrid Join Algorithm: Design, Prototype, Modeling and Measurement*, IBM Research Report RJ-7884, IBM Almaden Research Center, December 1990.

CODD, E. F. *The Relational Model for Database Management Version 2*, Addison-Wesley, 1990.

CODD, E. F. *Recent Investigations in Relational Data Base Systems*, IBM Research Report RJ-1385, April 1975.

CODD, E. F. "Relational Completeness of Data Base Sublanguages," in *Database Systems*, Randall Rustin, ed., Prentice Hall, 1972.

Commands Reference Manual for SYBASE SQL Server for UNIX, Sybase, Document ID 32270-01-0491-01, 1992.

DATABASE 2 AIX/6000 and DATABASE 2 OS/2 SQL Reference, IBM Corp., SC09-1574, 1993.

DATE, C. J. "A Critique of the SQL Database Language," in *Relational Database: Selected Writings*, C. J. DATE, ed., Addison Wesley, 1986.

DATE, C. J. *An Introduction to Database Systems Volume 1*, 6th ed., Addison-Wesley, 1995.

DATE, C. J., and DAVID MCGOVERAN. "Updating Union, Intersection and Difference Views," *Database Programming and Design*, vol. 7, no. 6, June 1994, pp. 46–53.

DATE, C. J., and DAVID MCGOVERAN. "Updating Joins and Other Views," *Database Programming and Design*, vol. 7, no. 8, August 1994, pp. 43–59.

DATE, C. J., with COLIN J. WHITE. *A Guide to DB2*, 4th ed., Addison-Wesley, 1993.

DATE, C. J., with HUGH DARWEN. *A Guide to the SQL Standard*, Addison-Wesley, 1993.

FLEMING, CANDICE C., and BARBARA VON HALLE. *Handbook of Relational Database Design*, Addison-Wesley, 1989.

GASSNER, PETER, GUY M. LOHMAN, K. BERNARD SCHIEFER, and YUN WANG. *Query Optimization in the IBM Product Family*, IBM Research Report RJ-9734, March 15, 1994.

GRAEFE, GOETZ. "Query Evaluation Techniques for Large Databases," *ACM Computing Surveys*, vol. 25, no. 2, June 1993, pp. 73–170.

GRAEFE, GOETZ. " Sort-Merge-Join: An Idea Whose Time Has(h) Passed?" *Proceedings of the International Conference on Data Engineeering*, IEEE Computer Society Press, 1994, pp. 406–417.

HUGHES, JOHN. *Database Technology: A Software Engineering Approach*, Prentice-Hall, 1988.

IBM DATABASE 2 SQL Usage Guide, IBM Corp., International System Center, San Jose, GG24-1583. 1983.

IBM DATABASE 2 Version 3 SQL Reference, IBM Corp., SC26-4890, 1993.

INGRES/SQL Reference Manual, Relational Technology, Inc., 1989.

MCDERMID, JOHN, ed. *Software Engineer's Reference Book*, CRC Press, 1993.

MCGOVERAN, DAVID, "Evaluating Optimizers," *Database Programming and Design*, January 1990, pp. 38–49.

MCGOVERN, DAVID. "Relational DBMS Optimizers: An Evaluation," *InfoDB*, vol. 5, no. 3, Fall 1990, pp. 2–9.

MISHRA, PRITI, and MARGARET EICH. "Join Processing in Relational Databases," *ACM Computing Surveys*, vol. 24, no. 1, March 1992, pp. 63–113.

MOHAN C., DON HADERLE, YUN WANG, and JOSEPHINE CHENG JOSEPHINE. *Single Table Access Using Multiple Indexes: Optimization, Execution and Concurrency Control Techniques*, IBM Research Report RJ-7341, March 7, 1990.

SQL Language Reference Manual Version 7.0, Beta Draft Documentation, Oracle Corp., 778-70-0292, 1992.

TEOREY, TOBEY J. *Database Modelling and Design: The Entity-Relationship Approach*, Morgan Kaufmann, 1990.

WIORSKOWSKI, GABRIELLE. "Join Methods and Index Usage in DB2 V2 R3," *InfoDB*, vol. 6, no. 2, Fall 1991, pp. 13–17.

YAO, S. BING, *Principles of Database Design*, Prentice-Hall, 1985.

PART 2
Contemporary Database Management System Technologies

Before the mid-1980s, computing environments were largely centralized. However, as networking technology advanced and hardware improvements brought greater processing power and storage capacity to small systems, computing environments became more decentralized. This impacted the DBMS industry in a variety of ways, prompting vendors to provide support for client/server architectures, distributed database environments, data replication or copy management services, and middleware services. Although these areas differ, they were developed because of users' increased needs for connectivity and support for remote or distributed computing environments. This section describes the overall objectives of each of these approaches, outlining major capabilities associated with each as well as issues that should be considered before adopting any approach in a business environment. The reader should note that terms used to describe these areas often lack precise and formal definitions in the industry. Nonetheless, the authors have tried to exercise care in formulating precise definitions for these terms.

The final chapter in this section focuses on database parallelism, which represents another way in which distributed processing can be implemented in commercial systems. Parallel processing enables multiple processors (often installed as part of a single system) to share a workload, in some cases by breaking down a single query into multiple subtasks and executing each simultaneously on different processors. A variety of hardware and software approaches are being taken to support this, as the section "Parallelism" discusses.

CHAPTER 6
Client/Server Environments

CHAPTER OBJECTIVES

This chapter explains client/server DBMS technology and how it differs from the more traditional, monolithic approach to DBMS technology. Readers will learn what has prompted many firms to become interested in and use client/server DBMSs as well as understand under what circumstances such systems may be most appropriate. This chapter also describes three possible relational DBMS server architectures and explores various DBMS functions that can help improve performance in a client/server environment. Finally, this chapter offers guidelines for issues that should be considered before deploying this technology.

Information presented in this chapter will help the reader more fully understand some of the technical capabilities of client/server DBMS products profiled later in this book.

TECHNICAL OVERVIEW

Client/server architecture calls for a traditional DBMS environment to be split into two logical components, each of which typically executes on different systems. With relational DBMSs, this usually involves placing applications and tools on one or more *client* platforms (generally, personal computers or workstations) and connecting these systems to a DBMS *server* that resides on another system (perhaps a large workstation, midrange system, or even a mainframe system). The applications and tools act as "clients" of the DBMS, making requests for its

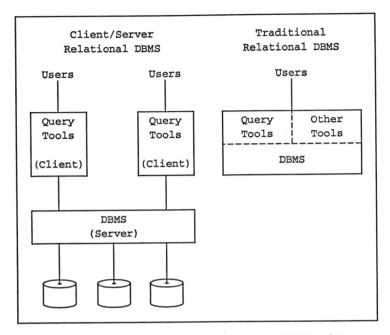

Figure 6–1.   Client/server architecture vs. traditional DBMS architecture

services. The DBMS, in turn, services these requests and returns the results to the client(s).

This approach, illustrated in Figure 6–1, is largely *server centric*, with the bulk of the DBMS work performed on the server. A server-centric approach to client/server computing can be well suited to online transaction processing and decision support applications, which tend to generate a number of relatively short transactions and require a high degree of concurrency. Further details on client/server architectures for relational DBMSs are discussed later in this chapter.

An alternate, but less common, approach to client/server support is provided by most object DBMS vendors. Such products are *client centric*, with some of the typical DBMS functions (such as query processing) executing on the client systems themselves. This alternate approach is discussed in greater detail in Chapter 17, "The Object Database Management System Approach."

MOTIVATING FACTORS AND POTENTIAL BENEFITS

As prices of smaller hardware platforms (PCs and workstations, in particular) began to decline and the processing power of these platforms began to increase, client/server computing held more appeal to users. It promised less expensive platforms to support certain applications that had previously been able to run only on larger, more expensive midrange or mainframe computers. In addition, the platforms that are so often used as clients in this architecture offered an icon- or menu-driven interface that many users found superior to the traditional command-line, dumb terminal interface typical of mainframe and midrange systems. As a result, many customers believed their user community could become more productive and make better use of existing data if they worked with client/server systems. DBMS vendors sought to support such architectures by enabling their tools and DBMS "engines" to run on different platforms, connected via one or more networking protocols.

In some firms, client/server environments were adopted because of users' frustration with a centralized Information Services (IS) organization that they perceived to be inflexible or unresponsive to their needs. In highly centralized environments, computing resources may be strictly controlled by an IS organization, which (among other things) prioritizes user requests for new applications or improvements to existing applications. Many IS organizations are unable to keep up with users' increasing (and often changing) demands, and so their requests become backlogged for weeks, months, or even years.

By deploying small, departmental client/server systems and doing much of the administrative work themselves, users often found a way to satisfy their needs more quickly. However, many later found that administering these systems was no trivial task and subsequently returned some (or all) of the responsibility back over to IS. Nonetheless, these client/server environments remained.

The desire to *downsize*, or move new or existing work to smaller systems, is another reason contributing to the increased popularity of client/server computing. The reasons that prompt a firm to consider downsizing are many, but a common motivation is cost reduction. After all, if a large mainframe costing hundreds of thousands of dollars could be replaced by a number of small systems costing only tens of thousands of dollars in total, firms could save quite a bit of money.

In the early days, client/server computing was promoted by certain vendors and analysts as a cost-savings measure. However, customers who adopted this view encountered mixed results, as the actual cost of any computing environment is more than just its hardware, software, and associated maintenance fees. Labor costs—often hard to estimate—can be high in client/server environments, particularly in initial phases. Individuals must be prepared to manage multiple systems (often from different vendors) and understand one or more networking protocols. The problem is further complicated (and, therefore, potentially more costly to resolve) if typical system management tools for problem diagnosis, performance monitoring and tuning, and security control are lacking for the DBMS, client and server operating systems, and networking environments in place.

COMPONENTS AND FUNCTIONS

Client/server environments that use relational DBMSs consist of three general components: client applications, a networking interface, and a DBMS server. The client applications—which may be tools, vendor-written applications, or user-written applications—issue SQL statements for data access, just as they do in centralized computing environments. The networking interface enables client applications to connect to the server, send SQL statements, and receive results or error return codes after the server has processed the SQL statements. The applications themselves often make use of presentation services (such as a graphic user interface) on the client.

Relational Database Server Architectures

As discussed earlier in this chapter, client/server relational DBMS applications typically place much of the processing workload on the server. It is important, then, to consider the architectural alternatives that relational DBMS vendors may use when building a DBMS server. These alternatives dictate how internal DBMS processes relate to operating system processes, which can impact the resources used on the server platform. During the past several years, at least three architectures have surfaced in commercial relational DBMSs:

- Process-per-user architecture
- Single-server architecture
- Multiserver architecture

The process-per-user architecture, illustrated in Figure 6–2, calls for each client application to be assigned its own operating system process on the server

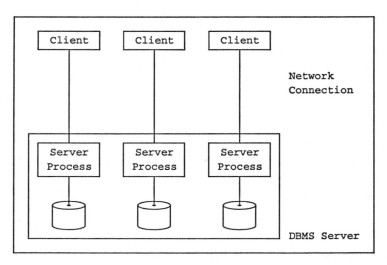

Figure 6–2. Process-per-user DBMS server architecture

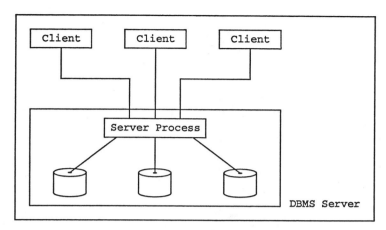

Figure 6–3. Single-server DBMS architecture

for DBMS work. Standard DBMS activities—such as logging—are handled by other, separate operating processes that are executing in the background. Dispatching and other multitasking services are performed by the operating system. This approach typically consumes more memory and makes less efficient use of system resources than the alternatives, in part because the operating system must perform the additional work involved in switching contexts for each user process.

Another architectural approach involves using a single-operating-system process for multiple client connections, as shown in Figure 6–3. This approach is sometimes called a single-server or single-process server architecture. With this approach, the DBMS server assumes the dispatching and multitasking responsibilities typically associated with an operating system; thus, the DBMS performs its own multithreading. Server resource requirements are reduced (since fewer operating system processes are required), and context switching can be kept to a minimum. However, this architecture does not lend itself well to exploiting some multiprocessor platforms.

A third approach—and one to which most vendors seem to be gravitating as of this writing—involves a multiserver architecture. As Figure 6–4 illustrates, client tasks are placed on a queue that is typically serviced by multiple server processes. (In some systems, multiple queues are established, one for each server process.) Each server process may be multithreaded or single-threaded (depending on the vendor's implementation).

Such architectures can help reduce the amount of overhead associated with each user, since one server process can service multiple clients. If the server process is multithreaded, it can service multiple client processes concurrently. If it is single-threaded, the server process works on behalf of a single client at any given point in time; when that client's work completes, the server process can service the needs of a different client.

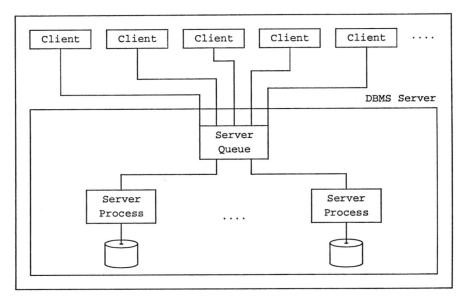

Figure 6–4. Multiserver architecture

A critical performance issue for multiserver DBMSs involves the amount of time client requests must be queued before a server process becomes available. To minimize such wait times, the dispatching work done by the DBMS must perform well. In addition, it's desirable that if a server process is "blocked" by some system activity (such as I/O or a locked resource), it can focus its efforts on other work, perhaps returning the blocked client task to the queue.

Note that the multiserver approach implies that the DBMS is taking over some of the responsibilities traditionally associated with transaction-processing monitors, discussed in the Chapter 3 section "Transaction-Processing Monitors." Some analysts have suggested that combining a transaction-processing monitor with a process-per-user DBMS server may provide performance that is similar (if not superior) to this approach. However, such a configuration may be more expensive, depending on the total pricing of a process-per-user DBMS and transaction monitor versus a multiserver DBMS.

Environmental Support

Support for multiple operating system platforms (on both the client and server sides) is a typical user requirement. As of this writing, popular client platforms include DOS, Windows, OS/2, Macintosh, Unix, and others. Popular server platforms include OS/2, Unix, VMS, MVS, and others. And, just as support for multiple operating systems is important to many customers, so is support for multiple networking protocols, such as TCP/IP, SPX/IPX, NetBios, APPC, and others.

Transparency

Enabling users and programmers to access data stored on another system raises the issue of *transparency*. People would like to be unaware that the data they need to access is stored remotely; they would like the data's location to be transparent to them or to appear as though it were local (residing on their client system). This provides for added usability as well as minimizes the amount of changes to the application that might be required if data were migrated from one server to another.

Providing for transparency helps to raise the level of abstraction for users. Irrelevant or inappropriate details (in this case, the location of the data) are not surfaced to the user, enabling him or her to concentrate on other issues.

A number of DBMSs provide for considerable location transparency, often through the use of aliases, synonyms, or some similar features. For example, an administrator may be able to define that TABLE_X really refers to TABLE_XYZ managed by DBMS_A, which resides at some specific port address. Users or programmers would not need to be aware of this information and could let the DBMS properly resolve references to TABLE_X.

Performance Issues

Performance issues also arise in client/server environments, as another component—the network—must be considered for overall system tuning. The network has a potential to become a bottleneck in client/server DBMS environments, particularly if network traffic becomes high because many requests for DBMS services are being transmitted (and many rows or error codes are being returned as a result).

A common goal of client/server DBMS vendors is to minimize network traffic, and a common technique for doing so is the use of stored procedures. Stored procedures can be thought of as miniprograms that perform functions frequently needed by one or more applications. They may contain control flow statements (such as if-then-else and loops), as well as many SQL statements. They reside on the server and may be called (or invoked) by users or applications on different client systems.

As shown in Figure 6–5, the performance benefit here is that only one call is sent across the network (the call to invoke a particular stored procedure). Without a stored procedure, each SQL statement would result in a call. Thus, a stored pro-

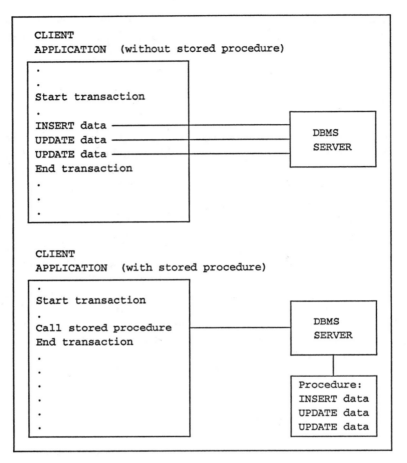

Figure 6–5. Reducing network traffic with stored procedures

cedure with three SQL statements could be invoked in one call rather than issuing three separate calls for each SQL statement. This can significantly reduce network traffic originating from the client.

Some DBMSs use other techniques to minimize network traffic, such as *record blocking* or *block fetch*. When an application issues a SELECT statement to read multiple rows from the DBMS, it declares a cursor (or control structure) and fetches data one row at a time. This can generate significant network traffic, as each FETCH request is sent from the client to the server and causes the server to return one row back to the client. To reduce this traffic, some DBMSs enable data to be returned in blocks—or groups of rows—instead of one row at a time. This is shown in Figure 6–6.

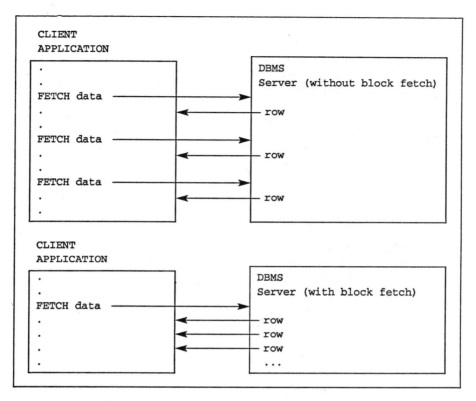

Figure 6–6. Reducing network traffic using block fetch

ISSUES TO CONSIDER BEFORE DEPLOYMENT

Client/server environments are often considered when some or all of the following conditions are true:

- Networked environments (particularly LAN-based environments) are already present, or are soon planned to be.
- Users or programmers want to use icon-driven or graphics-based tools commonly found on personal computers and workstations. Furthermore, these users or programmers require access to corporate or departmental data managed by a DBMS.
- Reducing hardware costs or floor space associated with larger systems is a priority. (Note that a reduction in hardware costs may not always translate into an overall cost savings for client/server environments, as discussed earlier.)

- The firm has made a strategic decision to downsize one or more of its applications.
- Users want to become less dependent on a centralized Information Services organization and are prepared to take on additional responsibilities (such as preparing their own reports or writing their own applications).

The operating system itself is a significant issue to consider before deploying a DBMS server. A poor choice here can affect overall performance and capabilities. Areas to consider include:

- Is preemptive scheduling supported? That is, can the operating system preempt a given task in favor of another task of higher priority? Does the operating system schedule tasks to ensure appropriate distribution of system resources?
- What degree of memory protection is supported? Can the operating system ensure that the DBMS server's memory area is not directly accessible to other applications, thereby avoiding potential corruption?
- Does the operating system use virtual memory, so that pages in memory can be temporarily swapped out to disk to make room for additional data or programs that must be brought into memory?

Other technical issues to consider include:

- What hardware, networking, and operating system platforms must be supported in this client/server environment? How does this compare with the support offered by various vendors?
- What types of applications must be supported? Decision support? OLTP? Will the applications be read-intensive or write-intensive? Many customers deploy decision support applications (which are primarily read-only) first in client/server environments, because transaction rates are usually lower and the work may be less critical to the overall business.
- What system management tools, if any, are available to make problem diagnosis, performance monitoring and tuning, security management, and other functions easier to implement? To what degree are these tools integrated with other system management tools available on the target platform(s)?
- What end-user and programming tools are available?
- What features have been incorporated into the DBMS to improve performance and minimize network traffic in a client/server environment?
- What system availability requirements apply to the client/server environment? How are these satisfied by the various software components involved?
- How much data is expected to be managed by the DBMS server? What capacity limitations, if any, apply to the DBMS, the operating system, and the hardware platform to be used for the server?

Finally, some issues are not technical in nature, but still warrant consideration. These include:

- Who will manage the environment? What kind of training will this person or group require?
- What experience already exists in the firm for installing and administering client/server environments?
- To what degree will the suppliers involved assist with diagnosing and resolving problems in a multivendor environment?

SUMMARY

Client/server DBMS architectures are those in which a DBMS-related workload is split among multiple systems. This differs from a traditional DBMS environment, in which the application and DBMS processing is done on a single system. Various events—including the introduction of more powerful PCs and workstations, organizational changes within firms, and the desire to *downsize* computing environments in hopes of cutting costs—helped fuel the demand for client/server DBMSs.

Relational DBMS architectures tend to be *server-centric* but can still vary in their internal implementations. Three possible variations are: process-per-user architectures, single-server architectures, and multiserver architectures. Important requirements for client/server DBMSs of any type include support for a variety of computing environments, location transparency, and mechanisms to ensure reasonable performance.

Client/server DBMSs are often selected by firms that want to use graphics-based tools to access departmental or corporate databases, already have networked environments in place, and are seeking to minimize hardware costs (often as a result of a strategic effort to downsize). Important considerations when selecting a client/server solution include an understanding of the type of application(s) to be used, the number of users and different types of platforms that must be supported, the skills available in-house to administer such an environment, and the system management tools available from the DBMS or third-party vendors.

REFERENCES AND SUGGESTED READING

BOBROWSKI, STEVE. "Database Security in a Client/Server World," *DBMS*, vol. 7, no. 10, Sept. 1994, p. 48.

"Confusion of DBMS Multi-Processor Support," *Database Review*, vol. 3, no. 4, August 1991, p. 1.

DAVIS, JUDITH. *Unix Relational Database Management: Vendor Strategies, DBMSs, and Application Development Tools*, Patricia Seybold Group, July 1993.

DICKMAN, ALAN. "The RPC-vs.-Messaging Debate: Under the Covers," *Open Systems Today,* August 15, 1994, p. 58.

ISO/IEC/JTC/SC21/WG7, Basic Reference Model for Open Distributed Processing—Part 2: Descriptive Model, DIS 10745–2, February 1994.

LINTHICUM, DAVID. "Client/Server Protocols: Choosing the Right Connection," *DBMS,* January 1994, p. 60.

LINTHICUM, DAVID. "Operating Systems for Database Servers," *DBMS,* February 1994, p. 62.

ORFALI, ROBERT, and DAN HARKEY. *Client/Server Survival Guide with OS/2,* Van Nostrand Reinhold, 1994.

CHAPTER 7
Distributed Databases

CHAPTER OBJECTIVES

This chapter identifies and explains the key features of distributed database management systems, emphasizing how these systems resemble and how they differ from client/server architectures. It explains the objectives and benefits of distributed database processing and discusses the key design issues that must be solved by developers of these systems, along with various approaches that have been used to deal with these technical issues.

This chapter then identifies various levels of distributed database processing; each offers different distributed database function. After reviewing this chapter, the reader will have a foundation for evaluating the capabilities of various distributed database systems that are available today (and discussed later in this book).

TECHNICAL OVERVIEW

Many people find it difficult to distinguish between client/server database environments and distributed database environments. This is understandable, as industry analysts and database consultants have debated over the precise meaning of these terms for some time. It's worthwhile, then, to review the similarities and differences between client/server and distributed database environments before focusing on many important issues specific to distributed database technology.

Distributed database systems are similar to client/server environments in a number of broad areas. Both typically involve the use of multiple computer systems, and both enable users to access data on a remote system. Both involve extensive use of interprocess communication. Both help promote access to remote data and sharing of that data. And, when the client application and the database manager reside on different machines, the client/server approach requires the use of network facilities similar in many ways to those used in support of distributed database processing.

However, there are important differences in the objectives and architectures of client/server and distributed database processing. For example, distributed database broadens the extent to which data can be shared well beyond that which can be achieved with the client/server approach. To a large extent, this is possible because in a distributed database management system, autonomous DBMSs are connected through network facilities. Note that although client/server technology can include multiple database servers supporting many clients, there are no direct network connections among database servers. Distributed database aims to support global, logical databases consisting of data that spans multiple databases and is stored and managed by DBMSs operating at different locations. The DBMSs of a distributed database system can communicate with each other using the facilities of the network. Thus, they can engage and assist each other in managing and responding to requests from users who are local to each of them. Although client/server environments clearly support distributed processing, they typically do not support a single logical database that spans multiple databases and multiple DBMSs.

Both client/server and distributed databases try to achieve greater efficiency and better performance by divide-and-conquer strategies. However, they divide the work at different places. Client/server divides the work at the boundary of the user applications and the DBMS; client applications execute in one operating environment and the DBMS executes in another. Distributed databases divide the work among multiple DBMSs, each executing in its own environment, as shown in Figure 7–1, which illustrates a distributed database configuration spanning three cities in Northern California. Note that the San Jose user community in this figure is using a client/server configuration and is also participating in a distributed database environment.

A distributed database also tries to enhance performance by taking advantage, where it can, of *locality of access.* In a distributed database environment, a portion of a database at one location can be replicated and processed at other locations in the system, thus making the replicated data easily accessible at multiple locations. Replicating data in this way allows for client access to local copies of the same data at multiple locations; local access makes for better performance and reduced communications and processing costs. Data replication is discussed in greater detail in Chapter 8, "Replication or Copy Management Services."

For some transactions and queries, a distributed database can use multiple DBMSs at different locations to work in parallel in support of a single query or single transaction. Moreover, as data volumes and transaction rates increase,

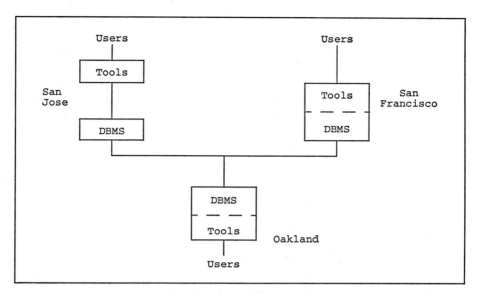

Figure 7–1.　Distributed database architecture

users can grow the system incrementally. Adding new locations to the distributed database causes less impact on ongoing operations than upgrading a centralized system to a new machine and operating environment and perhaps a new DBMS that offers more capacity and performance.

Finally, distributed database management tries to provide *local autonomy.* These systems are designed so that local administrators retain their control over local data. Local administrators determine what parts of their local database are accessible for read or write access by remote users. They retain authority with respect to who, how, and when local data is accessed by remote users. As a part of local autonomy, the distributed database is designed so that no local DBMS must depend on remote sites to perform processing on local data in support of local database applications. In this way, they are insulated from failures at remote locations and from network failure.

MOTIVATING FACTORS AND POTENTIAL BENEFITS

The ultimate design objective of a distributed database system is to enable users of their local DBMS to treat data that is physically distributed as if it were local. Ideally, users develop applications, generate transactions, and issue queries just as they would if they were referencing a single, local database even though some or all of the required data is managed by remote DBMSs. A distributed database system that achieves this objective offers its users a *single-site image.*

A single-site image provides *location transparency*. Location transparency implies that users need not be sensitive to the location of the data. It also implies that when data is moved from one location to another (perhaps to balance the workload), local applications need not be changed as a result. This is consistent with the DBMS goal of data independence. And, as noted in a previous chapter, location transparency raises the level of abstraction for users, making it unnecessary for them to learn certain details about their environment.

The Promise of Distributed Databases

In the 1970s and 1980s, database researchers realized that distributed database (as described thus far) could offer many benefits to users. Such systems promised to enable users to access remote data more quickly and easily, helping businesses compete better in a global market. They promised to give users a consistent image of data stored on multivendor hardware and software platforms in various locations. They promised to give users more flexibility when organizing corporate data centers. They promised to make more efficient use of the computing resources within a corporation by using parallel-processing techniques to split work across multiple remote systems. And they promised to hide the complexity of all this from the users.

These promises are substantial and difficult to fulfill. As of this writing, most commercial products have not lived up to all of these expectations. Furthermore, the idea of deploying distributed databases makes many customers uneasy, because such environments are inherently complex and therefore more difficult to manage than other database environments. Additional system management facilities are required, including those that will aid in data placement, monitor and audit use of the system, enforce security, and tune overall performance.

Nonetheless, several relational DBMS vendors have steadily improved their distributed database support over the years. Their distributed database support is discussed in greater detail in Part Three, "Commercial Relational Database Management Systems."

The Need for Heterogeneity

As with client/server environments, distributed DBMSs are often expected to support *heterogeneity* in a transparent manner. In other words, a distributed database system must make the data stored in different DBMSs (perhaps running on different computers, in different operating environments, and connected by different networking protocols) appear to the user as though it were stored in a single system. In practice, full support for heterogeneity is difficult to achieve. (Some of the problems involved in achieving it are noted later in this chapter.)

Vendors often take two approaches to solving this problem. Many offer *middleware* products, including *gateways* (discussed in Chapter 9). These offerings are designed to compensate for differences in system components that must operate together. Their chief design goal is *interoperability*. Other tools that deal with heterogeneity provide copy management or replication services (discussed in Chapter 8). And, as discussed in the Chapter 3 section, "Transaction-Processing Monitors," customers sometimes use TP monitors to cope with heterogeneous environments.

Regardless of which approach is taken to the problems of heterogeneity, attempting to present a single-site image to users of such distributed databases is an extremely complex task.

Providing distributed database support for *homogeneous*—or like—database managers that operate in similar environments is not as complex a task. Therefore, it is often the first step taken by a vendor to support distributed database management. And, because a homogeneous environment is easier to manage, it can be a good starting point for customers who wish to benefit from the capabilities of a distributed database environment.

COMPONENTS AND FUNCTIONS

Today's commercial relational DBMSs differ significantly in the ways they support distributed databases. Some of these differences are readily apparent to users, who are often restricted in the types of operations they may perform in such an environment. Common limitations involve the type of distributed data access that is supported. For example, some systems may enable users to join data from multiple tables that are stored at different locations, while others may not. These areas of difference are important and are discussed in greater detail in this chapter, as well as in Part Three, "Commercial Relational Database Management Systems."

However, in order to understand why some of these differences exist, it is important to first consider the design issues that must be addressed by the architects and developers of relational DBMSs. Here, the focus is on the key database and transaction management issues that have concerned the architects and system developers of commercial distributed database offerings. These are:

- Serializable transaction execution
- Global deadlock
- Coordinated commit processing
- Global optimization
- Table partitioning
- Catalog management

Each of these will be discussed in the following sections.

Serializable Transaction Execution

Drs. P. A. Bernstein and James Rothnie, two of the early researchers and architects of distributed database systems, have noted that controlling the concurrent execution of application programs to assure that they leave the database in a consistent state is probably the most difficult challenge in developing a generalized distributed database management system. A key goal of concurrency control is to achieve *serializable* execution of transactions. The reader will recall that a transaction is *atomic*. Partial effects of a transaction cannot appear in the database. As Dr. James Gray, a leading database researcher, comments: "Transactions are an all or nothing at all thing. Either you get the money and I get the ticket or the deal is off."

In order to determine under what circumstances the database is consistent, DBMS architects have adopted the criterion of serializability. "Serial execution" of transactions means that no transaction begins until its predecessor ends (or commits). "Serializable execution" implies that although transactions are executing *concurrently*, each transaction leaves the database in the same state it would be in if the transactions had executed *serially*. The two-phase locking protocol, discussed previously in the Chapter 3 section "Two-Phase Locking," ensures serializable execution of transactions. Recall that according to this protocol each transaction must (1) acquire a lock (share or exclusive) before operating on the data and (2) acquire no locks after releasing a lock. That is, all locks needed by the transaction must be acquired before any locks are released.

Consider the following sequence of operations for two transactions, TXA and TXB.

```
Time            Database Operation
-------------------------------------------------------
  t1      TXA acquires an exclusive lock on row R33
  t2      TXA updates row R33
  t3      TXA releases the exclusive lock on row R33
  t4      TXB acquires an exclusive lock on row R33
  t5      TXB updates row R33
  t6      TXB commits
  t7      TXA aborts
```

With this sequence of operations, when TXA aborts *after* releasing the lock on row R33, the committed change made by TXB to the same row is undone. TXA *appears* to be in compliance with the protocol as stated. However, the ABORT operation at time t7 directs the DBMS to reacquire a lock on behalf of TXA (to perform the required undo processing). Strictly speaking, this reacquisition of a lock violates two-phase locking. For this reason, in practice, DBMSs that support serializable execution construe the protocol as also requiring that locks be held until the transaction commits.

The reader will recall that transactions that read with cursor stability (CS) are not serializable since "locks are not held until commit" while repeatable read (RR) holds locks until commit and in doing so provides the highest level of consistency.

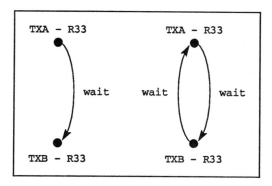

Figure 7–2. Wait-for graphs involving two transactions

Global Deadlock

A second design problem relating to concurrency control involves deadlock. Single-site DBMSs usually handle deadlock by monitoring the wait status of concurrently executing transactions. The DBMS lock manager processes lock requests, and keeps track of which transactions are waiting for other transactions to release locks. It maintains a *wait-for graph* for this purpose. When a transaction is granted a lock, the lock manager notes the transaction holding the lock on that data. When a subsequent request for the same data is made by another transaction, the requesting transaction is placed in a wait state, and the DBMS posts an entry to the graph to show the wait-for relationship between the transactions involved.

Figure 7–2 shows two transactions: TXA, which has a lock on row R33, and TXB, which is waiting for the release of the lock on R33. The nodes represent transactions; the arrows represent a wait-for state. When two transactions are waiting for each other to release a lock, the DBMS detects a cycle and interprets that as a deadlock. The right-hand side of this figure shows two transactions in deadlock; deadlocks can occur involving more than two transactions.

Handling deadlock in a distributed database system is complicated by the possibility of *global* deadlocks, that is, deadlocks that span sites or locations. Local transactions that update data at remote locations can become involved in deadlock with transactions at those remote locations. For example, assume a transaction, TRSJ, executing at a San Jose site that needs to update data at a New York location before proceeding with the remainder of its database operations on the San Jose data. The DBMS at San Jose initiates a *cohort transaction*, COTRSJ, that will execute at New York to perform the update on behalf of the original transaction, TRSJ. The cohort's request for a lock is denied by the lock manager at New York since another transaction executing at New York, TRNY, previously acquired a lock on the same data. This is illustrated in Figure 7–3.

The picture is complicated when the transaction executing at the New York location requires a lock to update data at the San Jose site. Its DBMS initiates the services of a cohort transaction, COTRNY, executing at San Jose, that requests a lock on the required data. Here the data has already been locked by TRSJ. There-

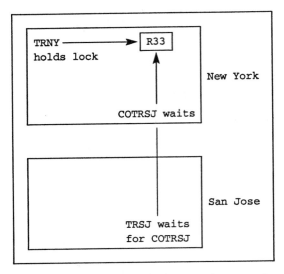

Figure 7–3. COTRSJ cannot acquire a needed lock because of TRNY

fore the cohort, COTRNY, is placed in a wait state by the San Jose DBMS. At this point, global deadlock occurs. (See Figure 7–4.)

But the wait-for graph at neither site reveals the deadlock. The graph at the New York site shows COTRSJ waiting for TRNY to release the lock on row R33. The graph at the San Jose site shows COTRNY waiting for TRSJ to release a lock on row R99. Neither graph shows all the dependencies among these transactions, including the dependency of TRNY on COTRNY and TRSJ on COTRSJ.

Of course, a centralized lock manager that handles lock requests and maintains a single wait-for graph for all locations in the distributed DBMS has enough information to detect global deadlock. However, reliance on a centralized lock manager involves a serious loss of site autonomy and could easily cause a system bottleneck.

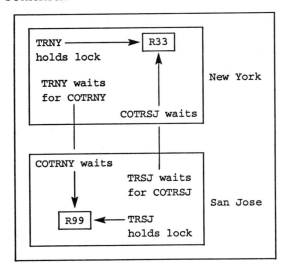

Figure 7–4.. COTRNY cannot acquire a needed lock, creating global deadlock

For this reason, researchers have suggested other approaches to handling global (or distributed) deadlocks. One noteworthy approach, described by Ron Obermarck (then of IBM Research), involves introducing a new type of node in the wait-for graph to show when a local transaction is waiting for a cohort at a remote site and when a cohort executing locally has a remote transaction waiting for it. These distinguished nodes indicate the location of the remote transactions involved. The occurrence of these nodes indicates the *potential for deadlock*. Once the potential for deadlock is recognized at a particular location, its DBMS sends the relevant part of its wait-for graph to that remote site with a transaction that might be involved in deadlock with one of its local transactions. The receiving site merges the graph sent to it with its own graph. If there is a deadlock involving transactions executing at the sending and receiving sites, it will be apparent in the merged wait-for graphs.

Although distributed deadlock detection techniques are promising, there is insufficient evidence to indicate what demands they will make on communications facilities, storage resources, and general system performance. For this reason, commercial distributed database systems typically make use of a simple "time out" mechanism as a way of handling global deadlock.

Coordinated Commit Processing

Two-phase commit processing—critical for supporting more advanced levels of distributed DBMS work—requires considerable work for a DBMS vendor to implement and can impact overall system performance. As the reader will recall from the Chapter 3 section "Integrity Enforcement," the two-phase commit protocol ensures that the integrity of a transaction is preserved when multiple resource managers (in this case, multiple DBMSs) are involved. One resource manager serves as the coordinator for the transaction and polls the other resource managers to see if they are prepared to commit the work of the transaction. If all indicate they are prepared to do so, the coordinator records the "commit" instruction in its log and instructs the other resource managers to commit the transaction. Otherwise, the coordinator records a "rollback" instruction in its log and instructs the other resource managers to roll back the transaction.

However, any distributed database environment must be able to cope with a variety of failures that may occur. A site can fail, a DBMS might be down, or intersite communications can fail. Coping with such situations has recovery and performance implications. While it is beyond the scope of this book to provide a detailed explanation of all possible problems and resolutions, it is worth reviewing a few simple examples so the reader may begin to understand the complexity of the underlying DBMS issues involved in supporting two-phase commit processing in a distributed environment.

Consider the situation where three DBMSs are involved in a distributed transaction, and one is serving as the coordinator. The two participants signaled that they are ready to commit, effectively causing the first phase (the prepare phase) of the two-phase commit process to end. The coordinator then writes a "commit" record in its log and attempts to send a "commit" message to the two participants. However, the second of the two participants has since become unreachable, perhaps because of a temporary network failure.

What happens? The transaction has been committed at the coordinator's site and at the first participant's site. It *must* be committed at the second participant's site; otherwise the integrity of the transaction would be violated. In such a case, the coordinator will repeatedly try to send the "commit" instruction to the second participant until it receives some sort of acknowledgment. This may take many attempts and span a considerable period of time (if the network failure is severe), but it is necessary if the integrity of the transaction is to be preserved. Meanwhile, the relevant data at the troubled site remains locked and unavailable.

Consider a very similar situation in which two participants complete the first phase (the prepare phase) and are awaiting instructions from the coordinator. The coordinator logs the "commit" record but *its* network connection fails, making it unable to transmit the "commit" message to the other sites.

What happens? As part of the prepare phase, these other sites have acquired locks on the necessary tables and written log records about the work in progress. They are now waiting to be informed whether they need to post a "commit" record for this transaction in their logs. These sites will continue to wait until a message is received from the coordinator; otherwise the integrity of the transaction could be violated. During this time the data resources locked at these sites on behalf of the transaction will continue to remain locked, possibly causing other transactions to wait and thereby degrading performance.

These are just two situations that can arise from communication failures. But networks aren't the only components of a distributed database environment that are subject to failure. DBMSs can fail or be taken off-line by a system administrator; similarly, computer systems can fail (perhaps because of a power outage) or be taken off-line by an administrator.

Consider what might happen if the prepare phase is completed by all sites, the coordinator transmits a "commit" instruction to each participant, and one participant fails before the commit record is written to its log. Perhaps the computer system suffered a power outage or the DBMS simply crashed. When the DBMS is subsequently brought online, it will begin a recovery process, reading its log and attempting to undo any uncommitted transactions at the time of failure. However, the undo processing of this DBMS must take the distributed database environment into consideration. The DBMS must determine if any of the uncommitted transactions were involved in a distributed transaction before simply undoing (or rolling back) their work. If this is the case, the DBMS must check with the coordinator to determine if the transaction should be committed or rolled back. This can mean that the recovery of this DBMS will become more time-consuming, as it must perform additional processing and possibly wait for a message from the coordinator. However, this compromise must be made if the integrity of the transaction is to be preserved. Otherwise, the recovering DBMS could roll back a transaction that the coordinator and other participating sites have already committed, leaving the databases involved in an inconsistent state.

The two-phase commit protocols should be implemented to:

- Guarantee transaction atomicity
- Minimize overhead involved in logging and messaging

Enhancements to the protocol, called presumed commit and presumed abort, focus on reducing the amount of I/O associated with logging as well as the number of messages the protocol otherwise requires.

Global Optimization

Another issue that vendors of distributed relational DBMSs must consider involves optimization. As discussed in the Chapter 3 section "Optimizer," relational DBMSs rely on an optimizer to determine an efficient access path to the requested data. Determining an efficient access path to remote data is a more complex issue, yet one that must be addressed in order to ensure reasonable performance in a distributed environment.

Perhaps an example will help illustrate some of the complexity involved in optimizing data access in a distributed environment. Consider an environment with three DBMSs at different sites. The table containing data on departments with 500 rows is stored at location A, and a table containing data on employees with 50,000 rows is at location B. A query from location C requires the join of these two tables. A distributed database system might use one of three processing strategies:

1. Move both tables to location C and perform the join at that location.
2. Move the employee table to location A and perform the join there, returning the result to location C.
3. Move the department table to location B and perform the join there, returning the result to location C.

This example is one of many that point out the crucial importance of a smart global optimizer in achieving acceptable performance with a distributed database system. Option 3 offers the best performance, as it minimizes the amount of data that must be moved over the network.

Bernstein and Rothnie cited examples of alternate processing strategies for the same query that yielded widely varying processing times. In one of their examples, a smart global optimizer made the difference between a processing time of less than two seconds and one of 22.5 hours! The cardinality of tables (that is, the number of rows in each table) and communications costs are two important factors that must be considered. However, an ideal global optimizer will consider a number of other factors as well. Dr. Michael Stonebraker, a DBMS researcher, explained that these factors include:

- Current workloads of participating sites
- Differences in machine speeds

- Differences in network characteristics
- Administrative constraints
- Cost constraints
- Space constraints

The optimizer should take into account current workloads when distributing the workload among its participants. For heterogeneous systems, differences in machine speeds (as well as operating systems) can make an important difference in performance of the transaction. Distributed databases with participating sites connected to different networks require that the optimizer must understand differences in the capacities and speeds of the networks that might be involved in processing the transactions. Some participants might constrain remote access to their data so as not to conflict with their peak production schedules, in which case alternate sites must be selected by the optimizer. Some users may want the optimizer to select the least expensive processing strategy for those transactions where performance is not critical. In some cases, performing a join at one location might be the least expensive when evaluated in terms of transmission costs, but the same location may not have the resources to accommodate the tables involved. Finally, Stonebraker notes that the complexity of the factors to be considered increases the search space way beyond what is required for local database optimizers. Search space refers to the number of *possible* search/processing strategies that can be taken into account. And the factors discussed here become much more complex when dealing with heterogeneous distributed databases.

To effectively optimize access to distributed data, a global optimizer will need access to statistics about remote databases. This raises questions about the role of catalogs in a distributed database environment, discussed in the section "Catalog Management," later in this chapter.

Table Partitioning

The use of multiple DBMSs in a distributed database environment raises a number of design considerations for administrators. How should the data be distributed? In some cases, administrators may wish to partition a single table across multiple sites—either horizontally (by rows) or vertically (by columns). This design technique is referred to as *horizontal or vertical partitioning,* although some vendors refer to it as *fragmentation.* (IBM has referred to such partitions as *distributed tables.*) Such a design may yield performance benefits, as administrators can place portions of a single table at those locations requiring most frequent access to it.

Figure 7–5 illustrates a situation in which a single table is partitioned horizontally (by row) across two sites. In this case, an insurance firm with two branch offices may wish to maintain a single table listing its clients and their policies. All clients with policy numbers greater than 1000 are serviced by Branch_A; all others are serviced by Branch_B. However, agents at either branch might occasionally need to access data at the other's location. In addition, managers may wish to

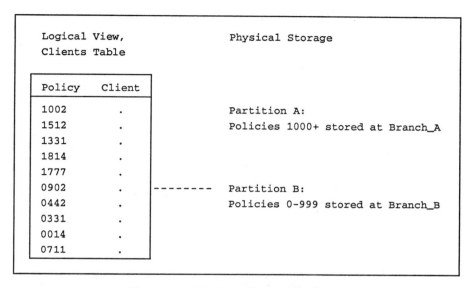

Figure 7–5. A horizontally partitioned table

periodically generate reports about all clients of the firm. A partitioned table may be appropriate for this situation.

In addition to splitting a single table across multiple locations, administrators may wish to maintain multiple copies of a table in different locations. At least two designs for these copies are possible—*snapshots,* which involve a read/write table at one location and multiple read-only copies at other locations, and *replicates,* which involve multiple copies of a table that can be updated at any site, with the DBMS propagating updates to the remote replicates. These alternatives, and others, will be discussed in greater detail in Chapter 8, "Replication or Copy Management Services."

Catalog Management

A global optimizer requires access to the catalog entries of each participating site for the data that is subject to remote access. This raises questions relating to the design and location of the distributed catalog and to the names assigned to those tables that participate in the distributed database system.

An obvious answer to the first question, and one adopted by some commercial systems, is to maintain and process a universal catalog that contains entries for all the tables in the distributed database. These entries include statistics used by the optimizer. Thus the universal catalog is used by the distributed DBMS to perform search optimization for requests originating from any site in the distributed database environment. Since this approach is vulnerable to bottlenecks as well as to site failure, some systems provide facilities for replicating the universal catalog and maintaining it at multiple locations.

A second approach to catalog management is to maintain entries on a distributed basis. Each system contains entries for just the data managed locally. All remote queries and transactions requiring these entries make use of a multipart name to reference the table, and a part of this name indicates the location of the relevant catalog entry for the data. Aliases are converted to multipart names by local DBMSs so that users need not remember and deal with the complex name structure.

Another approach tries to maximize location transparency by including as a part of the *systemwide* name the "birth site" of every object in the distributed database system. The birth site is the location at which the table was created. There is always a catalog entry for the object at the table's birth site. If an object is moved, this entry is updated by the local DBMS to point to the new location of the object. This entry update is performed at the birth site again if the object is migrated to a third site. In this way, every catalog entry in the system can be obtained from any remote site with no more than two remote accesses regardless of the number of times it has moved. Location transparency is enhanced. However, when a location is inoperative or inaccessible by remote sites, catalog entries for all data "born" at that site are unavailable. Global optimization for queries referencing those tables is forestalled.

The reader is reminded that a benefit of location transparency is that data can be moved without impacting current applications.

Levels of User Access

Given all the issues vendors must consider when building a distributed relational DBMS, it's not surprising that commercial products vary considerably in their implementations. One broad area of difference involves the different levels of user access to distributed data that are supported.

The most advanced level enables users to read data from multiple sites within a single query statement (such as a join of tables from two different locations) and to update data at multiple sites in a single transaction, with the system automatically providing two-phase commit integrity. However, not all applications require such functions. The lists below cite some possible access levels that distributed database management systems may support. The most advanced levels of function appear at the end of each list.

```
READ ACCESS
   - Read data from one site per transaction or unit of work
   - Read data from multiple sites per transaction or unit of work
   - Read data from multiple sites per query statement

WRITE ACCESS
   - Write data to one site per transaction or unit of work
   - Write data to multiple sites per transaction or unit of work
   - Two-phase commit processing manually coordinated by user/programmer
   - Two-phase commit processing automatically enforced by system
```

While this can help serve as a useful guide for customers who are trying to define their distributed database requirements, the reader should also be aware of other classifications frequently cited in the industry. These classifications were first published by IBM and are often used by IBM and other vendors to describe the level of distributed database support they have implemented in their products.

- Remote requests: Users can read and update data in a remote system. Only one SQL statement is permitted per unit of work or transaction. (The reader will recall that a single SELECT, INSERT, UPDATE, or DELETE is an "SQL statement.")

- Remote unit of work: Users can read and update data at one remote DBMS within a single unit of work or transaction. Multiple SQL statements are permitted per transaction, although all must reference the same DBMS instance.

- Distributed unit of work: Users can read and update data in multiple DBMSs per unit of work or transaction, provided that each SQL statement references only one DBMS. Updating data at different locations presupposes support for the two-phase commit protocol.

- Distributed requests: Users can read and update data on multiple DBMSs per unit of work or transaction; a single SQL statement can reference multiple DBMSs. Systems that support this level of distribution should also make use of a global optimizer (see the earlier section "Global Optimization") in order to achieve good performance when multisite joins and multisite unions are requested.

Figure 7–6 illustrates the functions provided by these different levels of support.

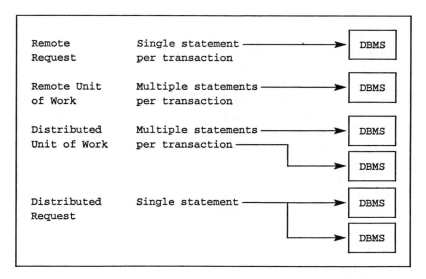

Figure 7–6. Levels of distributed database support; based on IBM classification.

In general, commercial products that employ distributed database technology have focused more on data access issues (supporting multiple environments, two-phase commit processing, and gateways to other DBMSs) rather than on system management and distributed data placement issues.

ISSUES TO CONSIDER BEFORE DEPLOYMENT

While distributed database issues were a frequent topic for discussion in the late 1980s and early 1990s, relatively few customers have deployed production applications that use distributed databases as of this writing. One reason for this may be that some vendors have been slow to provide robust support. Another reason may be because managing such an environment is inherently complex. Nonetheless, many database specialists view distributed database as a key technology area in the near-term future.

Distributed database environments are best considered a solution when:

- Critical business data is distributed across multiple systems in multiple DBMSs and is likely to remain so.
- Users require access to *current* or "live" data distributed across these systems. Accessing data that may be slightly out of date is not acceptable.
- Users' data access needs are highly unpredictable. Queries are frequently ad hoc and may require access to a variety of different data sources in different DBMSs.

SUMMARY

Distributed database management systems provide users with a single-site image of data that is physically distributed over multiple (possibly remote) locations. This means that users can develop their applications *as if* all the required data resides on their local systems when, in fact, some or all of the data is distributed. These systems provide users with location transparency so that interlocation movement of data does not impact production applications.

Although client/server database architectures support an important form of distributed processing, they differ from true distributed database management systems since they typically do not support user views of a single logical database whose components are physically distributed over diverse locations.

Distributed database can provide users with improved performance through locality of reference and by sometimes processing requests on a parallel basis. They also allow for incremental growth to accommodate increased workloads and data volumes.

With distributed database management systems, the problems associated with data sharing are more complex. Thus, these systems must solve complex problems relating to concurrency control (including global deadlock handling), coordinated commit processing, global optimization, and catalog/directory management.

Various levels of distributed database capability are available in current distributed database product offerings ranging from *remote request* to *distributed request,* which is regarded as the most advanced form of distributed database processing.

REFERENCES AND SUGGESTED READING

BELL, DAVID, and JANE GRIMSON. *Distributed Database Systems,* Addison-Wesley, 1992.

BERNSTEIN P. A., and NATHAN GOODMAN. "Concurrency Control in Distributed Database Systems," *ACM Computing Surveys,* vol. 13, no. 2, June 1981, pp. 185–222.

BERNSTEIN, P. A., VASSOS HADZILACOS, and NATHAN GOODMAN. *Concurrency Control and Recovery in Database Systems,* Addison-Wesley, 1987.

BERNSTEIN, PHILIP A., and NATHAN GOODMAN, "Concurrency Control in Distributed Database Systems," in *Readings in Database Systems,* MICHAEL STONEBRAKER, ed., Morgan Kauffman, 1988.

DATE, C. J. *An Introduction to Database Systems Volume 1,* 6th ed., Addison-Wesley, 1995.

DATE, C. J. "Twelve Rules for a Distributed Data Base," *Computerworld,* June 8, 1987, p. 75.

Distributed Relational Database Architecture Reference, IBM Corp., SC26-4651, 1990.

EPSTEIN, R., M. STONEBRAKER, and E. WONG. "Query Processing in a Distributed Data Base System," *Proceedings of the 1978 ACM-SIGMOD Conference on the Management of Data,* May 1978.

GRAY, JAMES, "Notes On Database Operating Systems," IBM Research Report RJ2188, February, 1978.

GRAY, JAMES, and REUTER, ANDREAS. "Transaction Processing: Concepts and Techniques," Morgan Kaufman, 1993.

ISO/IEC/JTC1/SC21/WG7, Basic Reference Model for Open Distributed Processing—Part 2: Descriptive Model, DIS 10745-2, February 1994.

LINDSAY, BRUCE. "Object Naming and Catalog Management for a Distributed Database Manager," IBM Research Report RJ-2914, August 1980.

McGOVERAN, DAVID. "Distributed Not Yet Delivered," *Computerworld,* June 6, 1994, p. 112.

MOHAN, C., INDERPAL NARANG, and JOHN PALMER. "A Case Study in Migrating to Distributed Data Base Recovery Using Multiple Logs in the Shared Disk Environments," IBM Research Report RJ-7343, May 1990.

NonStop SQL, A Distributed, High-Performance, High-Availability Implementation of SQL, Tandem Computers, Technical Report 87.4, part number 83061, April 1994.

OBERMARCK, RON. "Distributed Deadlock Detection Algorithm," *ACM Transactions on Database Systems,* June 1982, pp. 187–208.

ROTHNIE, J. B., and N. GOODMAN. "A Survey of Research and Development in Distributed Database Management," in *Tutorial: Distributed Database Management,* IEEE Computer Society, 1978.

STONEBRAKER, MICHAEL, ed. *Readings in Database Systems,* Morgan Kauffman, 1988, p. 189.

YOST, ROBERT A., and LAURA M. HAAS. "R*: A Distributed Data Sharing System," IBM Research Report RJ-4676, April 1985.

CHAPTER 8
Replication or Copy Management Services

CHAPTER OBJECTIVES

This chapter explains the capabilities of various types of copy management services, many of which are referred to as replication services in popular trade literature. Readers will learn why many firms are turning to copy management offerings as a means of coping with remote data, and they will be able to explain how these replication services differ (in many cases) from the distributed database environments discussed earlier.

The reader is introduced to the capabilities of three types of copy management services, as well as to administrative issues and architectural alternatives. Finally, this chapter presents a number of issues that should be considered before deploying replication or copy management solutions and guidelines for determining when such solutions may be appropriate.

This chapter also provides the reader with the foundation necessary for understanding the commercial implementations of replication products, which are profiled later in this book.

TECHNICAL OVERVIEW

Replication or copy management services enable firms to maintain copies of the same data in different DBMSs. The reasons for doing so are varied but often include a desire to:

- Improve response time for end users (who might otherwise be constrained by network traffic when accessing remote data)
- Improve data availability (by minimizing reliance on a network and remote systems)
- Create a standby database that can be used if the primary remote system crashes or must be shut down
- Simplify system management issues

Copy management facilities are known by various names, but they are typically referred to as extractors, replication servers, snapshot facilities, and propagators.

In most cases, the data contained in these various copies is not synchronized—for example, a "master" copy of a table may contain current data, but secondary copies of this table may be slightly (or significantly) out of date. While this may sound somewhat strange, many applications do not require access to absolutely current data.

For example, a software development firm may maintain a central database containing abstracts and other information about new scientific reports in the computing industry. If this firm has engineers at many locations worldwide who need access to this data, it can send copies periodically (perhaps every day) to each location, thereby reducing network traffic, improving response time for users, and promoting better overall data access. The fact that local copies of this database may be slightly out of date with the central database is not a significant problem for this type of application.

MOTIVATING FACTORS AND POTENTIAL BENEFITS

The idea of maintaining multiple copies of data is hardly a new one to the computer industry. For decades, many firms have extracted or dumped the contents of databases and files to some device (often a tape), shipped or electronically sent these extracts to a remote location, and manually loaded the data into a DBMS or file at that location.

But more recently, DBMS vendors have provided ways to automate this process and, in some cases, to update copies in a near synchronous fashion. As a result, replication or copy management services have attracted the attention of many firms, particularly those that have found commercial distributed database support lacking or too difficult to manage.

Indeed, copy management products are sometimes touted as a more practical alternative to two-phase commit processing in a distributed database environment. However, the two are not synonymous. Two-phase commit processing in a distributed database environment ensures that either all DBMSs involved in a transaction commit the work or none do. This is critical for certain applications, such as funds transfers. If two-phase commit processing were applied to remote copies of a table, all copies would remain in sync with one another. Thus, if TABLE_A existed at three sites, two-phase commit processing would ensure that an update to TABLE_A would be committed at all sites (including the site at which the update transaction originated) or at none.

Most commercial replication facilities do not support two-phase commit processing across multiple sites and therefore do not guarantee that copies of tables will be in sync with one another at any given time. Instead, changes are queued or otherwise tracked, and later they are propagated to remote sites (perhaps immediately, or perhaps at some user-specified interval).

Copy management facilities emerged because of several problems inherent with distributed databases. Providing users direct access to production data on a remote system can impact the performance of the remote system, slow response time for the user, and force the user to contend with limited availability (because of network failures or problems at the remote site). Furthermore, support for two-phase commit processing in a distributed database environment was slow to emerge in commercial DBMSs and often carried significant limitations (particularly if DBMSs from multiple vendors needed to be supported). Finally, designing an efficient distributed database environment and managing it is no easy task, often involving considerable coordination among people at various sites. For these reasons, copying data to various sites holds appeal to many customers.

CAPABILITIES AND FUNCTION

Copy management facilities can involve support for extracts, snapshots, and replicates. Although similar in some respects, each provides different capabilities for managing redundant data (or copies of data).

Extracts

Extracts were among the earlier forms of copy management services. Extract products typically enable administrators to identify portions of a file or of a relational or prerelational database to be copied, extract this data, and load it into another data source (usually a relational database). If the initial and target data sources use different structures (if, for example, someone wanted to copy data from a hierarchic system to a relational system), administrators must specify how the facility should map one structure to another. This can be a labor-intensive process.

Furthermore, most extract facilities do not contain built-in scheduling facilities (which could force new copies to be generated every hour or every day). In addition, most do not support incremental copies (where only the changed data is

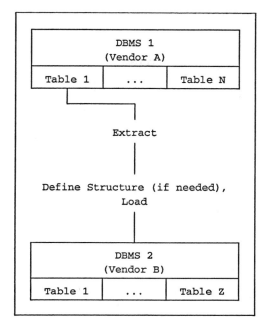

Figure 8–1. Using a data extract facility

sent, rather than all the data). Figure 8–1 illustrates how an extract facility might be used to copy data from one relational DBMS to another.

Snapshots

Snapshots provide a more automated approach to copy management. However, current commercial implementations often support only relational-to-relational DBMS copies. Snapshot facilities enable administrators to copy one table (or part of a table) to one or more remote DBMSs. One site is defined to contain the master or primary copy, to which any necessary updates are applied. The other sites store read-only copies of this table, which are periodically updated (or "refreshed") to reflect any changes made to the master table. This refresh process is usually automatic after some initial administrative work has been completed.

Snapshots are beneficial in situations where remote sites require only read access to data, and some lack of synchronization between the snapshots and the master table is tolerable. For example, consider a small company that operates three stores and maintains a separate headquarters facility. To keep prices consistent across all stores, the headquarters facility is responsible for setting these prices and redistributing any changes to the stores every Sunday, in preparation for the chain's weekly sales on Monday. Snapshots can be well suited for this situation. Headquarters can spend the bulk of each week changing prices in anticipation of the following week and have these changes automatically sent to each store once a week. Figure 8–2 illustrates this use of snapshots.

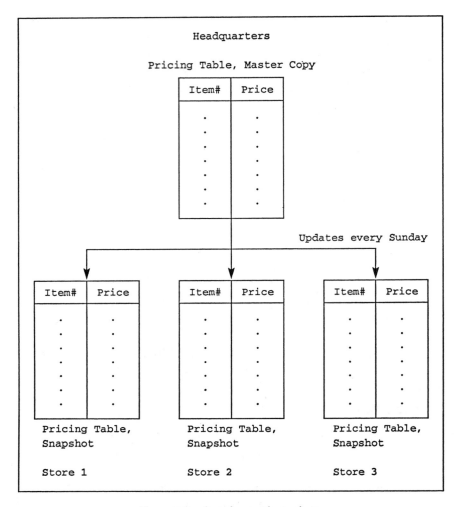

Figure 8–2. Sample use of snapshots

Replicates

Replicates differ from snapshots in one critical way: each location containing a copy of the data has read/write access to it. This implies that there is some two-phase commit capability provided to keep all replicates in sync—a technique that preserves integrity but mandates that all sites involved be accessible and able to complete the update in order for it to be allowed.

More recently, some vendors have been using the term *data replication* to apply to cases where each site has read/write access to copied data but may not use two-phase commit processing. How is this achieved?

In at least one case, updates to data at secondary sites are not applied to the secondary site directly. First, they are rerouted to the master site, which updates its data, thereby causing secondary sites to be notified that they must apply the necessary changes as well. Thus, direct write access is *simulated* at secondary sites, although the user may not be aware of this.

Other vendors support write access at all sites by providing a conflict resolution mechanism in case two or more transactions at different sites update the same data at or near the same time. In such cases, the system will resolve the conflict by following instructions previously specified by the customer. For example, priority might be given to one update over another, based upon the most recent update.

Both snapshots and replicates typically support only relational DBMSs today. To understand when replicates might be useful, consider a public library system with three branches, each of which has its own local computer system. If a patron enters any library and cannot find the desired book, each library would like to be able to determine if one of the others has the book in stock. This might be accomplished by creating a single table to contain all the books owned by all the libraries. With replicates of this table stored at each library, any librarian could query the table (to see if a book is in stock) and insert or update data in that table (to add a new book or put a hold on an existing book). Figure 8–3 illustrates how replicates might be used in this situation.

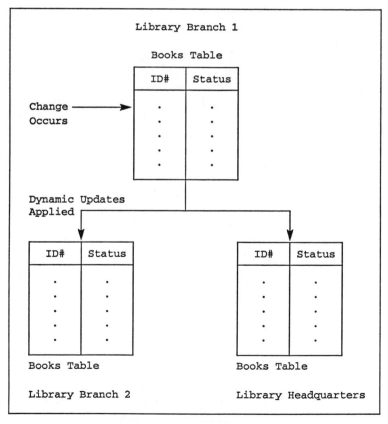

Figure 8–3. Sample use of data replication

Administrative Issues for Snapshots and Replicates

For both snapshots and replicates, it's most desirable if the system sends only the changes (rather than a complete copy of the table) to the remote sites. This minimizes resource consumption and helps prevent potential performance problems. In addition, it's also desirable for systems that support snapshots to enable administrators to specify when refreshes are to be made. For example, an administrator may wish to specify that refreshes should occur during off-hours (such as every night at 11 P.M.) or after a certain number of changes have been made. Again, this can help prevent performance problems and ensure that resources are being used as desired.

Another desirable feature is the ability to specify that only portions of a table—a certain set of rows and columns—should be copied. For example, if the headquarters of a company maintained a single table containing information about all of its employees, it might want to give each site copies of only those rows containing information about employees that work at that site. Many commercial products support this.

At least one commercial product also supports the creation of copies based on aggregate functions. These copies really appear more as derived tables than as mirror images of master tables. For example, the marketing division of a bank could create a derived table to contain the average opening balance of different types of new accounts. Information about new accounts might be inserted into a master ACCOUNTS table at headquarters. A copy management facility would track this information, periodically compute the average opening balance for each account type, and make this information available to the marketing division.

In addition, at least one commercial product enables administrators to maintain a record of the changes made to a master table over an extended period of time. This can be helpful for performing temporal or time-based analysis, such as "Show me the sales figures for store X on this same date last month."

Furthermore, some vendors are providing support beyond copying data. At least one enables users to copy stored procedures from one site to others.

Alternatives for Capturing Data Changes

As of this writing, vendors are taking at least two broad approaches to capturing data changes for propagation to other sites. One involves the use of triggers, and the other involves the use of log records.

The trigger-based approach requires that a trigger be established on all source or master tables that are to be copied. This trigger is typically designed to "fire" or execute whenever someone inserts, deletes, or updates information in the source table. In this way, database changes can be captured so that they can be propagated to other sites as desired.

Certain issues should be considered when evaluating products that use this approach. For example, many products provide an administrative facility (perhaps even one that is graphics-based) to enable customers to easily identify the data they wish to copy and the site(s) that should receive such copies. After such information is specified, it is desirable that the product automatically generate a trigger to capture the changes to the source table. This can minimize coding requirements.

Using a trigger to capture data changes has the potential to slow update, insert, and delete operations at the source site. If the trigger executes before the data change is applied (or committed), local work will have to wait until the trigger's execution is completed. For this reason, it's often desirable to specify that the trigger be executed only after the local data change has been applied.

In addition, some DBMSs restrict the number of triggers that may be created for a given table. In such cases, a trigger-based copy management facility should be capable of tolerating triggers that execute user-defined business rules *as well as* the necessary data capture logic. Failure to provide this support can force users to trade off enforcement of certain integrity constraints in favor of replication.

An alternate approach to capturing data changes relies on the use of log records. As the reader will recall, DBMSs commonly record *before-image* and *after-image* data in logs for recovery purposes. Some copy management or replication products use this log information to obtain the after-image data, which reflects the change to the database. In some cases, this log information is read directly from buffers (in memory) to avoid additional disk I/O and capture the changes as early as possible.

Reading log data can represent an efficient and reliable means of "trapping" data changes. However, different DBMSs use different logging techniques and different formats for their log records. Occasionally, the log record formats may even change slightly from release to release (perhaps due to various product enhancements). Therefore, relying on log records for capturing data changes means that vendors may have a more difficult time capturing data from many DBMSs, as this can represent a considerable coding effort.

Alternatives for Applying Data Changes

Once the changes to the data have been captured in some way, they must also be applied to the target sites. This application process can occur in one of two ways: changed data can be "pushed" out to other sites, or other sites can "pull" changed data from the source site.

Pushing data out to target sites implies that the source site (containing the data to be copied) knows where and when the data must be sent. The changed data is typically read once and sent out to all target sites immediately or at some predetermined interval. If a network connection is down, the source site is responsible for reestablishing a connection and retrying the operation.

By contrast, pulling data in from a source site places greater responsibility at each target site involved. It allows each site to request data as desired (perhaps at different time intervals), but doing so implies that the changed data will be read multiple times (once for each request from each target site).

Some individuals have argued that a push-based approach to propagation is best suited to OLTP environments, as it provides the greatest chance for near-synchronous replication. Once the data is captured, the source site can immediately begin propagating this data (that is, pushing this data) to other sites. By contrast, a pull-based approach is sometimes considered best suited for decision support environments because different sites may require different levels of data currency and may possibly wish to perform other processing on the data before making it available to local users.

Environmental Support

A frequent requirement of copy management facilities is the ability to support multivendor environments. This involves not only multiple hardware, operating system, and networking platforms, but also multiple data sources. As of this writing, most snapshot and replication facilities focus on supporting relational-to-relational DBMS copies. Furthermore, many facilities support only homogeneous database environments (in which copies are managed by products supplied by a single vendor), although recent developments suggest that this will change.

ISSUES TO CONSIDER BEFORE DEPLOYMENT

Replication or copy management solutions are best considered when most or all of the following conditions are true:

- Access to data managed by one or more remote systems is required.
- Access needs are fairly predictable. To a large degree, administrators know in advance what data is going to be accessed by which users.
- Absolute currency of data is not required. Users are able to work with data that may be slightly out of date.
- Networked-based environments are already in use, or are planned to be.
- DBMS response time to users' requests is critical. In such cases, it may be better to copy data and have it available to users locally than to have each user repeatedly issue remote requests.
- Overhead in a production DBMS environment must be kept to a minimum. In such cases, it may be best to prevent many users from directly accessing production data and instead copy the data to a less heavily loaded system where users can then access it.

With many kinds of copy management facilities available, interested customers have a number of issues to consider when evaluating alternatives. These include:

- What needs to be copied? Data, or some combination of data and other objects (such as stored procedures)? Entire tables, subsets of tables (certain columns and rows), or derivations of tables based on aggregate functions?

- What are the source(s) and target(s) for these copies? Do they involve products of different architectures (such as file systems, relational DBMSs, and nonrelational DBMSs)? What hardware and operating system platforms are these products running on?
- What type of access to copied data is required at each site? Read-only or read/write?
- How should copies be sent to other sites? Synchronously (which would require two-phase commit processing)? Near synchronously? Or at some other interval?
- Are copies automatically propagated to the appropriate sites, or is this a manual process?
- What scheduling facilities, if any, exist for the copy management solution? Are they based on time periods (such as every hour or every Friday at midnight)? On the number of changes that have occurred (such as every 1000 changes)? Or on some other basis?
- What work must an administrator do to set up the copy management environment? After setup, what additional maintenance work (if any) is required?
- What performance features are provided to minimize network traffic and the impact of copy management services on the sites involved (particularly any production DBMSs that contain the master tables)?
- Is support for temporal data analysis required? Can the copy management facility support this, or is some other mechanism provided with the DBMS?

SUMMARY

Replication or copy management services provide an automated means of managing multiple remote copies of data. There are at least three basic types of copy management facilities: simple extracts, read-only snapshots, and read/write replicates. The latter two are the most common area of focus in today's DBMS environment. Among the important technical issues affecting replication offerings are techniques for minimizing resource consumption and improving performance, alternatives for capturing changes to data that must be propagated to other sites, and alternatives for applying these data changes. Replication offerings are best suited to situations where data access needs to remote sources are fairly predictable and absolute currency of the data is not required. If access needs are unpredictable and/or data currency is paramount, a distributed database or middleware solution may be more appropriate. These are discussed in other chapters of this book.

REFERENCES AND SUGGESTED READING

ASK INGRES/Replicator Technical Background and Competitive Overview, The ASK Group, 1993.

Data Replication: The IBM Solution, IBM Corp., May 1994.

EDELSTEIN, HERB. "Replicating Data," *DBMS*, June 1993, p. 59.

GOLDRING, ROB. "A Discussion of Relational Database Replication Technology," *InfoDB*, Spring 1994.

GUERRERO, JORGE. "RDF: An Overview," *Tandem Systems Review,* October 1991, p. 34.

LEINFUSS, EMILY. "Replication Synchronizes Distributed Databases Over Time," *Software Magazine, Client/Server Computing Special Edition*, July 1993, p. 31.

LYON, JIM. "Tandem's Remote Data Facility," *Digest of Papers, COMP Spring 90*, Thirty-Fifth IEEE Computer Society International Conference, IEEE Computer Society Press, Feb. 26–March 2, 1990.

Oracle7 Symmetric Replication Asynchronous Distributed Technology, Part A13824, Oracle Corp., September 1993.

Replication Server: A Component of SYBASE System 10, Sybase, 1993.

ROTI, STEVE. "Replication in Ingres and Informix," *DBMS*, September 1993, p. 83.

STACEY, DOUG. "Replication: DB2, Oracle, or Sybase?" *Database Programming and Design*, vol. 7, no. 12, December 1994, p. 42.

ITEM CHARGED

Patron: Srinivas Yada
Patron Barcode: 60179600188
Patron Group: Graduate Stud

Due Date: 8/8/98 23:59

Title: Database man
Author: Bontempo, Ch.
Item Barcode: 39346006896

CHAPTER 9
Middleware

CHAPTER OBJECTIVES

This chapter explores the role of data access middleware, a type of software that simplifies data manipulation across various data sources. The reader will learn about the major components and functions of such middleware offerings and be able to explain the potential benefits of this technology. This chapter also explains when a middleware solution may be most appropriate and outlines a number of issues that should be considered before it is deployed.

Information in this chapter will help the reader understand the discussions of commercial middleware and DBMS gateway offerings presented later in this book.

TECHNICAL OVERVIEW

In the early 1990s, a number of vendors began promoting various *middleware* offerings designed to help customers deal with disparate, heterogeneous environments more effectively. Since then, the term "middleware" has come to mean different things to different people, especially those who specialize in different software disciplines. At its broadest, middleware may be thought of as software that provides an application with a consistent interface to some underlying (and often remote) services, shielding the application from the different native interfaces and complexities required to execute the services. Middleware might be responsible for routing a local request to one or more remote servers, translating the request as needed (from one SQL dialect to another, in the case of data access middleware), supporting various networking protocols, converting data from one format to another, coordinating work among various resource managers, and performing other functions.

Such a definition of middleware is admittedly very broad and encompasses several software disciplines. The remainder of this section discusses *data access middleware*—a form of middleware that is particularly relevant to the DBMS industry. Such software provides customers with a consistent interface to multiple data sources (relational DBMSs, nonrelational DBMSs, and file systems). *Gateways* can be thought of as one form of data access middleware.

MOTIVATING FACTORS AND POTENTIAL BENEFITS

A primary goal of middleware is to simplify software development and maintenance by eliminating the need for programmers to code many environment-specific requests or calls in any application that needs access to current data rather than copies of such data. In this way, programmers can be isolated (at least to some degree) from the particular interfaces of the networking environments, data sources, and other system-dependent services that they must otherwise learn when working with the heterogeneous (and often distributed) platforms common in most firms. This enables programmers to concentrate primarily on writing software to solve the problem at hand and can serve to protect the investment made in the development of that software. Presumably, a major rewrite would not be necessary if data were moved from one DBMS to another, because direct requests or calls to these DBMSs would not be included in the application itself (they would be handled by the middleware). Therefore, data access middleware can be thought of as a way of raising the level of abstraction for programmers by enabling them to avoid dealing with various environment-specific and data source-specific interfaces.

In addition to helping simplify a complex environment for programmers and for end users by providing transparent access to diverse data sources, middleware is also seen as a means of protecting investments. Traditionally, business applications have included direct calls to native system services. For example, a payroll application written for IBM's IMS might have included a number of DL/1 calls. Similarly, an accounts payable application written for Oracle's relational DBMS might have included a number of embedded SQL statements written to Oracle's SQL dialect. This worked fine but meant that migrating data to a new DBMS (perhaps because of changes in a firm's requirements) would have a significant impact on existing applications; most would have to be rewritten (if not redesigned), and programmers would have to learn the new interface of the current data source.

Many customers have since recognized that their computing environments are unlikely to remain the same over several years. To prepare to cope with whatever changes they may face, many customers have already begun using a layered approach when implementing new applications. Business applications may no longer call many native system services directly, but must instead invoke specific subroutines or functions written strictly for that purpose. In effect, such subroutines become in-house middleware, isolating the business application from system-specific interfaces. This helps protect the longevity of such applications, as the "volatile" portions are carefully isolated in specific routines.

Commercial middleware attempts to complement such in-house efforts by providing a consistent interface to multiple back-end services. Instead of coding much of the routing, translation, and other functions into specific subroutines, these programs could call commercial middleware products that would handle many of these functions themselves.

Data access middleware is also intended to appeal to third-party software vendors. In the mid- to late-1980s, for example, firms offering query/report writers, 4GLs, decision support facilities, and other DBMS tools had to rewrite portions of their software to get them to support a variety of DBMSs. Although this was often critical to the success of their product, it took time away from additional product enhancements. Middleware offers the potential to shield tools vendors from the differences among the native interfaces of many DBMSs, freeing those vendors to concentrate on other improvements to their software.

CAPABILITIES AND FUNCTIONS

In the DBMS arena, middleware products provide a consistent interface to different local and remote data sources. Often these data sources are relational DBMSs, but middleware offerings may support file systems, prerelational DBMSs, other data sources, and sometimes even other data access middleware. Typically, data sources are supported through one or more specific *drivers* that (among other things) pass requests to a given data source and enable the results to be returned to the application. In most (if not all) middleware offerings, these drivers are tailored to a specific data source and are responsible for the translation of SQL and data types.

The application, however, doesn't deal with these drivers directly; instead, it writes to the interface of a middleware engine that manages these drivers and may perform other functions (such as access optimization). Often, the middleware engine uses a call-level SQL interface, although some support non-SQL commands as well. Figure 9–1 illustrates a sample middleware architecture.

From a customer's viewpoint, typical elements of data access middleware offerings include an application programming interface, a middleware "engine" for routing requests to various drivers and performing other functions, and drivers for various back-end data sources. Many middleware products have a client/server architecture and access data residing on multiple remote systems. Therefore, networking interfaces may be provided between the client and the middleware, as well as between the middleware and the data sources. Specific

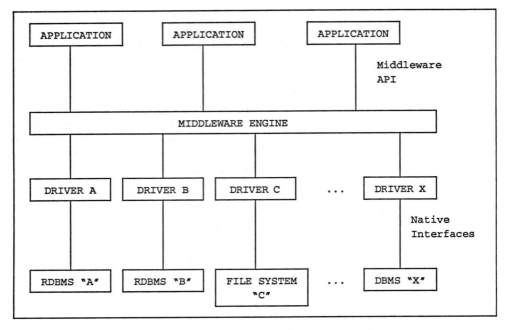

Figure 9–1.   Sample architecture of data access middleware

configurations vary from product to product. Some middleware offerings are largely client centric, with the middleware engine and some (or all) of the drivers residing on a client workstation or PC. Others are largely server centric, with a small layer of software on the client provided to connect it into the remainder of the middleware solution, which resides primarily on a LAN server or host system.

"Data access middleware" is a relatively new term that is being applied to technology that has previously existed (at least in part). Products designed to provide enhanced connectivity (such as DBMS gateways) have been available for some time. But recent trends point to a greater focus on improving transparency, conforming to standards, and adding more function beyond the mere ability to route a request and a corresponding reply. Thus, middleware is often used to refer to products that provide certain functions beyond the early gateways of the 1980s.

Application Programming Interface (API)

The application programming interface (API) of data access middleware usually consists of a series of available function calls (often for a programming language such as C), as well as a series of data access statements. Typically, these data access statements are dynamic SQL, although certain middleware offerings support other interfaces as well, such as navigational and query-by-example interfaces. Call-level interfaces (rather than embedded SQL interfaces) are most common.

The API employed is important; many dialects of SQL exist, each providing different capabilities. Call-level interfaces also vary, including those based on formal or informal standards, as well as those proprietary to certain vendors. This means that two middleware products could support the same call-level interface but still differ in the SQL statements (and perhaps data types) they consider to be valid.

Finally, the idea of having a single API for multiple back-end data sources raises questions about function, transparency, performance, and vendor independence. For example, does the API support all the functions of the various back-end data sources or just a subset? Does the API promote location (and DBMS) transparency, or must the programmer be sensitive to these issues? What is the performance impact of translating between the middleware API and the native APIs of the various back-end data sources? And to what degree does the middleware API conform to industry standards (which could help provide for vendor independence)?

Several approaches may be taken when designing an API, each of which has trade-offs. One approach is to support only a subset of SQL (typically, the lowest common denominator among the more popular SQL-based systems). This provides for a high degree of standards conformance and enables the middleware vendor to support a wide range of data sources relatively quickly. However, it can prevent the user from taking direct advantage of any advanced functions the native (or back-end) data source may support.

Another approach—one that some DBMS vendors are taking—is to provide an API based on a given SQL dialect (usually the dialect supported by the vendor's DBMS). This helps to make foreign systems look like a single vendor's system. For customers who already are familiar with this vendor's API and seek to standardize on it, this approach is probably reasonable. It enables them to leverage their existing skills and expand their reach to other data sources with minimal (if any) retraining. But it can also lead customers to question the openness and vendor independence provided by a system whose API is based largely (if not entirely) on one vendor's SQL dialect.

More commonly, one of these two approaches is complemented by a *pass-through* mechanism. Such a mechanism instructs the middleware not to evaluate the SQL statement or command stream itself but instead to simply pass it along to the target data source for processing. When doing so, the user must give up transparency and learn the native interface of the target data source; in return, he or she can exploit the underlying (and unique) features of the data source and may be able to achieve some performance gains.

Middleware Engine

A middleware engine handles data access requests that have been issued. How it handles a request differs considerably from product to product, but some of the general approaches are described in this section.

Some middleware engines merely examine the request and route it to the appropriate driver for handling. Engines that lack a global catalog or directory of some sort will not support location transparency. This means that users will have to tell the middleware engine which data source is the intended recipient (and, therefore, which driver should be given the request). In this case, the engine acts much like a traffic controller or an information pipeline. An advantage of this approach is that the engine can be "lightweight," consuming relatively few resources and possibly requiring little administration. A disadvantage of this approach is that the engine may be able to do little to optimize performance or add value beyond access to multiple data sources.

An alternate approach involves providing additional capabilities in the middleware engine beyond routing requests. This might include support for a global catalog or directory to aid location transparency. It might include an optimizer to help determine an efficient means of resolving requests that involve multiple data sources. It might include supporting certain SQL operations—such as joins and unions—across different data sources. And it might include supporting (or simulating) certain functions not present in a given back-end source, such as support for a particular data type or SQL statement.

This approach calls for the middleware engine to look like a DBMS with remote (instead of local) storage mechanisms that are really other DBMSs or file systems. The advantage of this design includes greater potential for added value, particularly in the areas of location transparency, performance, and enhanced function. However, such an approach is more ambitious and therefore more difficult to build; it is also likely to require processing resources more typically found in a workstation or LAN server than in a small PC.

Drivers

Since SQL dialects and other types of APIs vary significantly from system to system, most middleware offerings use a number of drivers to translate requests issued through the middleware API to a format intelligible to the target data source. Translation services may include SQL translation, data type translation, and error messages and return code translation.

Driver support can be a critical issue for middleware customers, who may require that drivers be available for a number of target data sources. If the driver for an important remote DBMS is poorly designed or implemented, performance may become unacceptable or errors may arise.

While in most cases a driver supports a single back-end data source, a few vendors have discussed or are offering drivers to other middleware products, which in turn may support multiple back-end data sources. This can be a quick and relatively simple means of expanding the breadth of any middleware offering, but it does introduce another level of indirection and translation, potentially opening the door for performance and other problems.

Environmental Support

Finally, environmental support is another aspect of middleware that deserves consideration. Given the goals of most middleware offerings, support for a variety of client and server hardware and operating system platforms is essential, as is support for popular LAN- and WAN-based networks.

Middleware and Gateways

Gateways may be considered an early attempt at middleware. These products usually provide specific point-to-point connections between one DBMS and others. In some sense, they are similar to the drivers in Figure 9–1.

The distinction between gateways and middleware is often a bit fuzzy and certainly varies from product to product. However, gateways traditionally have not focused on providing broad-based connectivity but rather on providing specific point-to-point connectivity. In addition, some gateways offer limited translation facilities, often requiring the programmer to understand the SQL dialects, data types, and error codes of multiple systems; this can hardly be thought of as providing a consistent API. Finally, some gateways may lack some of the additional functions found in broader middleware products, such as support for transparency, joins, optimization, and simulation of nonnative functions.

As of this writing, a number of early gateway vendors have begun enhancing their products to provide broader support for middleware by including some of the features previously discussed.

ISSUES TO CONSIDER BEFORE DEPLOYMENT

Data access middleware is best considered when many or all of the following statements are true:

- Access to a variety of data sources is required.
- Access needs vary from day to day or perhaps week to week. That is, different tables at different locations may need to be accessed on an ad hoc basis. (This is often typical of decision support applications, in which queries are rather random.)
- Access is expected to involve read-only activity or read activities with limited updates.
- Transparency is somewhat or highly desirable. This can include both location transparency (where remote systems appear to be local) and API transparency (where different back-end sources appear to have the same interface).
- Standardizing on one or two data sources, operating systems, and hardware platforms is not likely. The environment is, and is expected to remain, heterogeneous.
- Network-based environments are already heavily in use, or are planned to be.
- Some performance degradation is tolerable for single-source queries. Middleware introduces a layer of software between the application and the target data source, which will cause additional instructions to be executed; this can create overhead that may affect performance. In addition, if the middle-

ware must interface to a production DBMS, the performance of that DBMS may be impacted as well.

Once the reader has determined that data access middleware is a potential solution to a current problem, other issues need to be considered. These include:

- Environment support issues, such as
  - What operating systems, hardware platforms, and networking systems need to be supported? Does the middleware solution support each of these environments?
  - What data sources need to be supported?
  - Are any production data sources involved? If so, what performance impact (if any) will be tolerable?
  - How many people are expected to make use of the middleware software? At how many locations? What additional hardware or software, if any, will be needed for these people (such as additional memory, LAN cards, and software upgrades)?
  - Which existing decision support, application development, and systems management tools, if any, will need to interface to the middleware software?
- Application programming interface issues, such as
  - What programming languages need to be supported?
  - What type of interface is preferred? One that is SQL-based?
  - How important is vendor independence and support for standards-based computing to the customer?
  - Is the customer willing to compromise transparency and portability for function and performance on occasion? If so, a middleware offering with a pass-through feature (enabling programmers to bypass the middleware API and write directly to the native API) may be desirable.
- Functional issues, such as
  - What type of data access must be supported? Read-only or read/write? If read/write access is needed, what restrictions (if any) will be acceptable (such as the ability to write to only one underlying data source per unit of work)?
  - What SQL statements and functions must be supported? For example, will users expect to be able to join data stored in two or more different DBMSs? SQL data manipulation statements are the most common area of focus for today's middleware vendors. Support for data definition and data control statements is considerably more difficult to find (imagine, for example, trying to support a user's request to create a table in DBMS A that requires a referential integrity constraint to be established on a remote table in DBMS B).

- What data types must be supported? For example, will users expect to be able to work with very long fields even if the underlying data source does not support this function directly?
- To what degree is performance (both response time and throughput) expected to be a concern? If performance is expected to be a high concern, customers should seek out products that provide mechanisms to reduce network traffic, support global optimization, prefetch data, and employ drivers that make intelligent use of native data interfaces (among other things).
- What mechanisms are provided to aid problem diagnosis?
- What availability requirements apply to the middleware solution? That is, how much down time (if any) is acceptable?
  - General issues, such as
    - What training and consulting services are available? If the middleware solution actually consists of products from multiple vendors (say, an engine and some drivers from Vendor A, as well as additional drivers from Vendors B and C), will these vendor support services apply to the entire solution or just to one vendor's pieces of it?
    - How will problem resolution be supported, particularly if the middleware solution involves products from multiple vendors?
    - What type of administrative support is required for the system? How much setup work is involved?

Finally, in some situations, middleware may not represent the total solution to the problem. Data access middleware may be helpful for a variety of applications within a firm, but it may be inappropriate for others. Providing dozens, hundreds, or thousands of applications and users with access to a heavily loaded production DBMS may simply be unacceptable. In such a case, copy management facilities (discussed in Chapter 8, "Replication or Copy Management Services") can complement the middleware solution by enabling customers to propagate important data (and changes to that data) from the production DBMS into less critical resources, such as one or more departmental DBMSs running on LAN servers, which would then be accessible through the middleware. This can represent an effective compromise: impact to the production DBMS is kept to a minimum, and access to its data is improved.

SUMMARY

Data access middleware provides users with a consistent interface to multiple DBMSs and file systems in a transparent (or near-transparent) manner. Key goals of such offerings include the abilities to simplify heterogeneous environments for programmers and provide users with an easier means of accessing live data in multiple sources. Although middleware architectures can vary from product to product, they often consist of an application programming interface, a middleware engine, one or more drivers, and one or more underlying data sources (DBMSs or file systems).

Middleware is often considered when data access needs vary from day to day or week to week, yet location transparency and a consistent means of accessing remote data are desired. Important issues to evaluate before deployment include the number and types of data sources required, the type of data access required (read or read/write), the mechanisms available to ensure good performance, and overall system management and support issues.

REFERENCES AND SUGGESTED READING

BERNSTEIN, PHILIP A. *Middleware: An Architecture for Distributed System Services*, Digital Equipment Corporation, Cambridge Research Lab, March 1993.

FINKELSTEIN, RICHARD. "Benchmarking Middleware," *DBMS*, November 1993, p. 82.

ISO/IEC/JTC1/SC21/WG7, Basic Reference Model for Open Distributed Processing—Part 2: Descriptive Model, DIS 10745-2, February 1994.

ROFER, C. ALLAN. "Midware: A New Approach to Distributed Data Delivery," *Database Programming and Design*, September 1992, p. 29.

SARACCO, C. M. *An Introduction to Data Access Middleware*, IBM Corp., Santa Teresa Laboratory Technical Report 03.529, October 1993.

WHITE, COLIN. "Getting Past the Buzzwords," *Database Programming and Design*, May 1993, p. 29.

CHAPTER 10
Parallelism

CHAPTER OBJECTIVES

This chapter describes ways in which DBMS products are designed to support parallel database processing in multiprocessing environments and outlines the potential benefits of database parallelism, as well as technology and business trends that are leading more firms to use parallel DBMS products. It describes major multiprocessor hardware architectures, the potential strengths and weaknesses of each, and how the choice of hardware architectures impacts internal DBMS design considerations.

The reader will also learn about the different types of parallel-processing support that may be provided by a DBMS and be able to discuss significant issues that apply to parallel DBMS installations, such as data partitioning. Finally, this chapter describes when a parallel DBMS may be an appropriate solution and outlines several issues that should be considered before selecting and installing such a product.

Information presented in this chapter provides the reader with sufficient background to understand the commercial implementations of parallel DBMS support profiled later in this book.

TECHNICAL OVERVIEW

Support for *parallelism* has become an area of increased focus for relational DBMS vendors in recent years. In part, this is due to the increased availability of multiprocessor systems. These systems enable multiple activities or operations to be executed simultaneously (that is, *in parallel*) by different processors, which offers potential for substantial performance improvements. Note that parallel execution is different from concurrent execution. With parallel execution, two or more transactions or queries can be serviced simultaneously by the system. With concurrent execution, these transactions might appear to users as though they are executing simultaneously, but in reality the CPU work for each of them is being interleaved.

Parallelism offers customers two potential advantages over a more traditional approach to data processing: *scale-up* and *speed-up*. Scale-up enables customers to increase the sizes of their databases while maintaining roughly the same response time. Speed-up enables customers to improve the response time of their queries, assuming the sizes of their databases remain roughly the same. To achieve either objective, new hardware (processors and disks) is added to the system, and the databases involved are redistributed (or partitioned) appropriately.

DBMSs stand to benefit a great deal from the parallel approach to computing. Moreover, DBMSs based on the relational database approach are well suited to take advantage of parallel systems architectures. The tabular data structure facilitates the assignment of subsets of databases and tables to different processors in a parallel system. In addition, the use of a set-oriented language facilitates parallel processing of queries since (1) each of the high-level statements of the language can be easily assigned to multiple processors for parallel processing, or (2) each such statement can be decomposed into various lower-level operations that are parceled out for processing by multiple processors.

MOTIVATING FACTORS AND
POTENTIAL BENEFITS

DBMS support for parallelism was motivated by several events. As relational technology gained acceptance in the 1980s, people gradually began storing more and more data in relational DBMSs. While early relational DBMSs may have managed only a few megabytes to hundreds of megabytes of data, it is not uncommon for customers to want to store considerably more data (ranging from several gigabytes to several terabytes or more) in their systems. Searching through these large amounts of data (to satisfy some condition specified in a query), as well as retrieving a large amount of data, poses a considerable performance challenge. Parallelism offers one means of helping to improve performance in such situations.

In addition to storing more traditional types of data (such as character strings, decimals, and integers) in relational DBMSs, many customers have sought to store "unusual" data types in their databases to support multimedia-based applications. These data types, which might include audio, image, and video, add to the complexity of a traditional database environment and introduce more demanding performance requirements, some of which are satisfied more readily through the use of parallelism.

However, coping with increased amounts of data wasn't the only factor motivating relational DBMS vendors to explore parallelism. Increasingly complex queries—either coded manually by programmers who have gradually become more comfortable with SQL or generated automatically by various query tools—were another reason. Such queries, particularly those that involve multitable joins or many levels of nested subqueries, are resource-intensive to process. Again, parallelism can help DBMSs support such queries in a more responsive manner.

In addition, as customers sought to make their businesses more competitive by more effectively using their corporate data, many wrote DBMS applications that involved more complex operations. For example, historical data on customers' buying patterns is important to many retail stores and mail order firms who seek to customize their promotional mailings to the needs of specific market segments. Some firms may wish to electronically mail such promotional literature (as well as sales catalogs and order forms) directly to their customers' home computers to minimize mailing and labor expenses. Yet analyzing this wealth of data can become a resource-intensive and time-consuming task; servicing hundreds or thousands of incoming electronic requests can also become quite burdensome. In such cases, database parallelism can be used to achieve more acceptable performance levels and support such environments more effectively and more economically.

Finally, as relational DBMSs were used to support more and more applications, transaction volumes increased. At some point, the increased workload slowed the overall response time of the system, often forcing customers to upgrade their hardware (which could be costly) or to try to off-load some work (and possibly data) to another system (which sometimes created administrative problems and hindered overall user access to corporate data). Multiprocessing systems offer an alternative approach to coping with increased system workloads: upgrades to the system can be incremental and relatively small, possibly involving the addition of a few new processors and disks. Presumably, the DBMS can be made aware of these new resources and use them to further divide the workload.

Providing reasonable performance for complex or resource-intensive workloads is perhaps the primary objective for many DBMS vendors who have sought to support multiprocessing environments. Price and performance issues—or the relative cost of executing a given transaction (including queries) in one environment versus another—are also relevant. A number of DBMS vendors have sought to position their offerings as a more cost-effective solution than those running in large (uniprocessor) mainframe environments. Traditionally, these latter environments have offered the greatest processing power (measured in MIPS, or millions of instructions executed per second) but have also been the most expensive. Multiprocessing environments, particularly those that make use of low-cost microprocessors, can often offer considerable processing power at a lower cost per MIP. Thus, DBMS vendors who support such multiprocessing platforms can potentially support complex, resource-intensive workloads (previously possible only for mainframe-based DBMSs) at a lower hardware and software cost per transaction.

Parallel DBMS technology can be applied to a variety of application areas, including those that involve OLTP and decision support activities. However, at least two vendors have begun focusing on using parallelism to support video-on-demand applications, where a large multiprocessor system might be used to store video data (such as popular films) on behalf of cable TV and telecommunications firms. Individuals could then request that a desired video be shown on their home television at a given time. This is another example of how parallelism might be used to support a data-intensive and (potentially) transaction-intensive workload.

OVERVIEW OF HARDWARE ARCHITECTURES

To understand how relational DBMSs might support parallelism, it is useful first to become familiar with the different multiprocessor hardware architectures available. Since any computer system typically contains memory, disk(s), and one or more processors, the different hardware architectural alternatives of a multi-processor environment can be categorized by what resources (memory and disk) are shared by the different processors. Three general options are available:

- Shared nothing. Neither disks nor memory are shared among processors.
- Shared disk. Each processor has its own memory, but data stored on disk(s) is accessible to all processors.
- Shared memory. Memory is shared among processors, and each processor has access to disk(s).

These different architectural alternatives are illustrated in Figure 10–1. The reader should note that some commercial systems are a combination of two or more of these approaches. For example, one vendor provides a two-tier multiprocessor system that uses shared memory at the top tier and shared nothing at the bottom tier. However, it is beyond the scope of this book to provide a comprehensive discussion of different commercial, multiprocessing hardware configurations.

Shared-Nothing Environments

Shared-nothing environments, as their name implies, involve no sharing of memory or disk resources. Each processor has its own copy of the operating system, its own copy of the DBMS, and its own copy of a portion of data managed by the DBMS. By not sharing these resources, shared nothing architectures minimize contention among processors and therefore offer a high degree of *scalability*. Thus, adding more processors and more disks enables the system to grow (or scale) in a manner that is proportionate to the power and capacity of the newly added components. This provides for scalability that is nearly linear, enabling customers to get a large return on their investment in new hardware (theoretically, close to a 100 percent return on their investment). Near-linear scalability also makes it easier to project performance gains that might be realized by adding more hardware. Furthermore, with no contention over disk or memory resources, traffic over the interconnection mechanism is minimized.

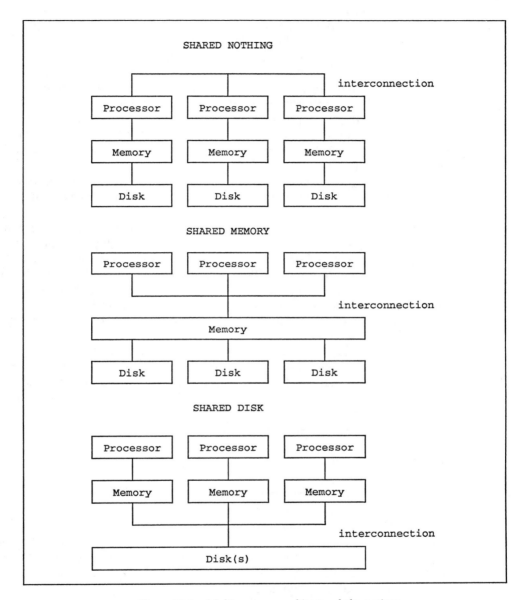

Figure 10–1. Multiprocessor architectural alternatives

Shared nothing environments are well suited to exploiting relatively cheap microprocessor technology. Since scalability is high, customers can start with a relatively small (and low-cost) system, adding more relatively low-cost processors to meet increased capacity needs. The shared-nothing approach often forms the basis for *massive parallel processing* systems, some of which support thousands of processors as of this writing.

While shared-nothing environments have a number of potential strengths, they also carry some drawbacks. Among these is that they are difficult to *load-balance*. In any multiprocessor environment, it's necessary to split the system workload in some way so that all system resources are being used efficiently. Splitting—or balancing—this load properly across a shared-nothing system requires an administrator to properly partition or divide the data across the various disks such that each processor is kept roughly as busy as the others. In practice this is difficult to achieve. If most transactions tend to access the same data, placing it on one disk will mean that one node can become overworked while others remain nearly idle.

Adding new processors and disks to a shared-nothing environment also means that the data may need to be redistributed in order to take advantage of the new hardware.

Another potential disadvantage of shared-nothing environments is that they introduce a single point of failure to the system. Since each processor manages its own disk(s), data stored on one or more of these disks becomes inaccessible if its "owning" processor goes down. Some commercial systems attempt to circumvent this problem by providing backup mechanisms or built in redundancy. In addition, shared-nothing environments require an operating system that is capable of accommodating the heavy amount of messaging required to support interprocessor communications.

Readers should note that a distributed DBMS environment (discussed in Chapter 7, "Distributed Databases") could be viewed as a shared-nothing, parallel environment. Each DBMS instance in the network could be tapped to perform work in parallel with other instances. As of this writing, support for parallelism through a widely distributed DBMS environment (involving different hardware and operating system platforms) is not common.

Shared-Disk Environments

Shared-disk environments involve multiple processors, each of which has its own memory but all of which have access to the same disk or, more commonly, to a shared array of disks. To accomplish this, a common interconnection mechanism is provided between the memories of each processor and the disk(s). Scalability is then largely determined by the capacity and throughput of this interconnection mechanism. Since memory is not shared among processors, each node has its own copy of the operating system and the DBMS.

With the same data accessible to all nodes, it's possible that two or more nodes may want to read or write the same data at the same time. Some sort of global locking scheme must be in place to ensure that data integrity is preserved. This often involves the use of a *distributed lock manager,* which is responsible for setting and releasing locks for data blocks or pages, depending on the status of work of the various processors.

A distributed lock manager is also used to help manage the *coherency* of the buffers or cache associated with each processor. This also has integrity implications. With each processor having access to the same data, it's possible that two or more processors might have the same data block or page in their own local caches at the same time. If one of these processors changes the data and writes the changes back to disk, the old copy of the data could still be in another processor's cache. Allowing subsequent transactions to view this outdated data would violate the integrity of the system. Therefore, the system must ensure that this processor is forced to reread this data from disk. Locking mechanisms controlled by a distributed lock manager help ensure this will occur.

Shared-disk environments tend to be easier to load-balance than shared-nothing environments, because data does not have to be "permanently" divided among available processors. Although all processors have access to the same data, only one processor can be updating a certain piece of data at any one time. Therefore, it's still important for administrators to try to ensure that transactions executing on different processors do not frequently try to update the same data at the same time; if they do, performance will degrade, as one or more transactions will need to wait for the data while another transaction has it locked for the update.

Shared-Memory Environments

Shared-memory environments use global memory that is shared by all processors. This means that a single copy of a multithreaded operating system and multithreaded DBMS can support multiple processors. Thus, an eight-processor, shared-memory system can execute eight of the highest priority tasks in parallel. This removes some of the bottlenecks of the system, as each processor can execute all tasks.

However, contention over shared memory and the bandwidth of the interconnect mechanism can make scalability difficult. Each time a new processor is added, it has the potential to interfere with the work of existing processors, as the new processor must request use of the same shared memory. For this reason, most commercial shared-memory systems can effectively accommodate a relatively small number of processors before scalability becomes hampered. One way to cope with this situation is to use more powerful individual processors, but this drives up overall system costs and can make shared memory architectures economically unattractive. Furthermore, sharing memory introduces a single point of failure into the system.

Other Hardware Issues

While focusing on what system components are shared is perhaps the simplest way of understanding different multiprocessor architectures, the reader may occasionally be confronted with other terms, such as *tightly coupled, loosely coupled,* and *symmetric multiprocessing* systems. Tightly coupled systems refer to those in which memory is shared among processors. Loosely coupled systems traditionally referred to those in which nothing was shared. However, in recent years, some vendors have begun using the term to refer to any system in which memory is not shared (but, perhaps, in which disks *are* shared). Symmetric multiprocessing (SMP) systems are tightly coupled (shared memory) environments in which any processor is capable of processing a given request or activity. In asymmetric multiprocessing environments, one or more processors are dedicated to specific tasks rather than being available to perform any type of work.

DBMS IMPLEMENTATIONS

Most relational DBMS vendors have announced—or shipped—enhancements to their products to support one or more types of multiprocessor hardware architectures. It's worth exploring just how relational DBMSs have been (and can be) enhanced to support parallelism. Details on specific product implementations are provided in Part Three, "Commercial Relational Database Management Systems."

Two common approaches to DBMS parallelism are parallel transaction processing (in which multiple transactions are executed in parallel, one by each processor) and parallel query processing (in which parts of a single query are processed simultaneously by different processors). As of this writing, most relational DBMS vendors have focused on these approaches, although some offer support for other kinds of parallelism, such as parallel utility execution and parallel index processing. It's worth noting that these different kinds of database parallelism can be implemented on different multiprocessor architectures, although the hardware architecture certainly influences internal changes DBMS vendors must make to their products.

Parallel Transaction Processing

Parallel transaction processing, sometimes called *interquery parallelism*, is often used in support of OLTP applications. With this approach, individual transactions are executed in parallel on different processors. Thus, a four-processor system supporting parallel transaction processing could execute four different transactions in parallel, as shown in Figure 10–2.

To support this kind of processing effectively, the DBMS should use some means of task or transaction dispatching. This helps ensure that incoming requests are routed to the least busy processor, enabling the overall workload to be kept balanced. However, it may be difficult to fully automate this process, depending on the underlying hardware architecture. For example, a shared-nothing environment dictates that data stored on certain disks be accessible only

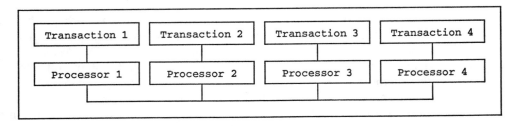

Figure 10–2. Parallel transaction processing

to certain processors. Therefore, requests that involve this data cannot be dispatched to just any processor. But DBMSs running in shared-disk environments could provide task dispatching to help ensure that all available processors are being used effectively.

Efficient lock management is another issue that arises for DBMS vendors seeking to support parallel transaction processing, particularly in shared-disk environments. Here, the DBMS must understand the locks held by different transactions executing on different processors in order to preserve overall data integrity. If memory is shared among processors, lock information can be kept in buffers in global memory and updated with little overhead (much as is done in uniprocessor environments). However, if only disks are shared (and not memory), this lock information must be kept on the only shared resource—the disk. In a number of environments, DBMS vendors will rely on the services of an operating system component—a distributed lock manager—to coordinate at least some of the locks on its behalf. However, this still involves disk I/O, which is an expensive operation. For these reasons, parallel transaction processing on shared-disk systems performs best when transactions that execute in parallel do not access the same data. In other environments, DBMS vendors will make use of special hardware to assist with locking. This can reduce the amount of processing overhead required.

Parallel Query Processing

Parallel query processing, sometimes called *intraquery parallelism*, involves using multiple processors to simultaneously work on behalf of a single query, as shown in Figure 10–3. This type of parallelism can be beneficial for decision support applications that issue complex, read-only queries (including those involving multitable joins).

At least two different approaches to parallel query processing may be supported: each processor can execute the same request against some portion of the data, or the request may be divided into different subtasks, with each processor executing a different subtask. Both approaches generally presume the data is partitioned across disks in an appropriate manner.

The first approach (in which multiple processors execute the same query in parallel over a different portion of the data) is perhaps the most common approach to parallel query processing in commercial products as of this writing. To understand how this approach might work, consider how a single query—

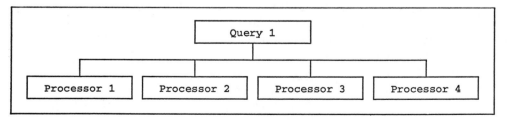

Figure 10–3. Parallel query processing

such as "SELECT * FROM EMPLOYEE"—might be processed by a four-processor, shared-nothing system. The EMPLOYEE table would be partitioned in some manner across each of the system's four disks. In parallel, each processor would retrieve all the data from the partition of the table on its disk. Next, the result would be merged into a temporary table and returned to the user.

The principle is the same, but the processing more complex, for a join operation. Imagine this same system is storing an EMPLOYEE table and a LOCATION table. The EMPLOYEE table contains employee identification numbers, employee names, salaries, and the building numbers at which each employee works. The LOCATION table contains all the building numbers within the company, as well as their site names and mailing addresses. Each of these tables is partitioned across the system's four disks in some manner. Consider a query that joins these two tables, EMPLOYEE and LOCATION, on BLDGNO:

```
select *
from employee, location
where employee.bldgno = location.bldgno
```

This query might be processed as follows.

1. The DBMS determines an efficient means of processing the join. Assuming the LOCATION table contains substantially fewer rows than the EMPLOYEE table (as would be the case for most firms), the DBMS might choose to temporarily replicate the entire LOCATION table on each disk. In doing so, the LOCATION table would be sorted in some order (such as ascending order).
2. Each processor then sorts its portion of the EMPLOYEE table in the same order that the building numbers in the LOCATION table are sorted. This work is done in parallel.
3. Each processor joins its portion of the EMPLOYEE table with the LOCATION table in parallel. The results of each processor's work are then merged and returned to the user.

An alternative approach to parallel query processing involves having different processors execute different subtasks associated with a single query. To understand how this might be supported, consider a join of two tables that involves conditions associated with both tables. For example, imagine that someone wanted to query the EMPLOYEE and LOCATION tables (described previously) to get a list of all the names, salaries, and mailing addresses of all employees who work at "Headquarters" and earn more than $75,000 per year. In SQL, this might be written as

```
select employee.name, salary, address
from employee, location
where employee.bldgno = location.bldgno
and location.name = 'Headquarters'
and salary > 75000
```

To simplify the situation, imagine that this query is to be executed on a two-processor, shared-nothing system in which the EMPLOYEE table is stored on one disk and the LOCATION table is stored on another. This query could be broken down into different subtasks, including:

- A restriction operation on the LOCATION table, where the DBMS would search for the row(s) that have "Headquarters" for the site name
- A restriction operation on the EMPLOYEE table, where the DBMS would search for the row(s) for employees who earn more than $75,000
- A join operation of the two temporary tables that resulted from the previous restriction operations

By breaking the query down in this manner, the system could perform the first two subtasks (the two restriction operations) in parallel, and then join the results afterward. This is one simple example of how parallel query processing can be supported by dividing a single query into multiple subtasks and having multiple processors service these subtasks in parallel.

As the reader may have suspected, efficient support for parallel query processing can place great demands on the optimizer of the DBMS. It is this component's responsibility to evaluate different ways of accessing the data specified in a query and to choose a reasonably efficient access path. Thus, optimization in a multiprocessor environment can require knowledge of how the data is partitioned across the available disks, what ways in which a query may be decomposed into different subtasks, the overhead involved when processors must send messages or data to one another, and how the work of various processors can be coordinated to provide a single, accurate response back to the user. This work is in addition to the typical responsibilities of an optimizer working in a uniprocessor environment, such as understanding what types of indexes (if any) are available for the tables involved in the query.

Shared-nothing environments, which commonly play a role in parallel query support, make this problem even more challenging. As noted previously, shared-nothing platforms place many of the same burdens on a DBMS that a distributed DBMS must deal with (because the DBMS consists of multiple systems at remote locations, none of which share memory or disks). In such a scenario, how can any one processor (or node) generate an efficient access path for data managed by other processors (or nodes)? One solution is to provide a global optimizer (or to enable any processor servicing a query to perform the global optimization for that query). In such cases, the global optimizer needs to have access to catalog entries containing statistics on tables that are processed by other processors/nodes to develop an overall access plan. However, replicating the catalogs across multiple processors/nodes (or maintaining a "global catalog") can be costly. An alternative is to distribute the optimization work among all the processors/nodes involved, but this introduces considerable complexity into the process of writing an optimizer.

Other Forms of Database Parallelism

While processing multiple transactions in parallel and processing a single query in parallel are two of the common areas of focus for DBMS vendors, some systems support other forms of parallelism. These include parallel index processing and parallel utility processing. Although these activities are more internal to the system and may be done without the user's awareness, they can nonetheless, provide significant performance gains in many situations.

Parallel index processing can be used to speed updates to tables containing indexed columns. When new rows are inserted or deleted, the DBMS must update the indexes associated with those tables to reflect the database changes. Some DBMSs enable this index maintenance activity to be done in parallel in some situations. For example, if a table had two indexes defined on it and these two indexes resided on different disks, a DBMS that supported parallel index processing could update both indexes in parallel. This could save time processing the update. A similar situation can occur with index processing for reads. For example, if an index is partitioned over multiple disks, read activities for the index can be processed in parallel.

Running utility tasks in parallel can also improve performance. Such utilities might include making backup or image copies of data, loading data into a table, reorganizing a database, recovering data, and updating catalog statistics. As an example, consider how recovery might be achieved in a shared-nothing environment. Since each DBMS running on each processor has its own logs, recovery from a systemwide failure (such as a power outage) could be done in parallel, with each DBMS reading its log records and taking the appropriate actions.

Data Partitioning

As the reader may have surmised, data partitioning can be critical in ensuring good performance in both parallel transaction-processing and parallel query-processing environments. Four general approaches can be taken to partitioning data, although most relational DBMS vendors support only a subset of these options. These approaches are:

- Hash partitioning, in which a hash function is applied to the value of a key. The output of this function causes the data for that row to be targeted for placement on a particular disk.
- Range partitioning, in which an administrator specifies that key values within a certain range are to be placed on a certain disk. For example, rows for employee numbers 1–1000 might be placed on disk 1, rows for employee numbers 1001–2000 might be placed on disk 2, rows for employee numbers 2001–3000 might be placed on disk 3, and so forth.
- Round-robin partitioning, in which disks "take turns" receiving new rows of data. For example, a system with four disks would place row A on disk 1,

row B on disk 2, row C on disk 3, row D on disk 4, row E on disk 1, row F on disk 2, and so forth.

• Schema partitioning, in which different tables within a database are placed on different disks.

Figure 10–4 illustrates these different approaches to data partitioning.

Hash partitioning has the advantage of providing for even distribution of data across the available disks, helping to prevent skewing (which can slow performance caused by one or more processors and disks getting more work than others). Hash partitioning is particularly suited to queries involving exact

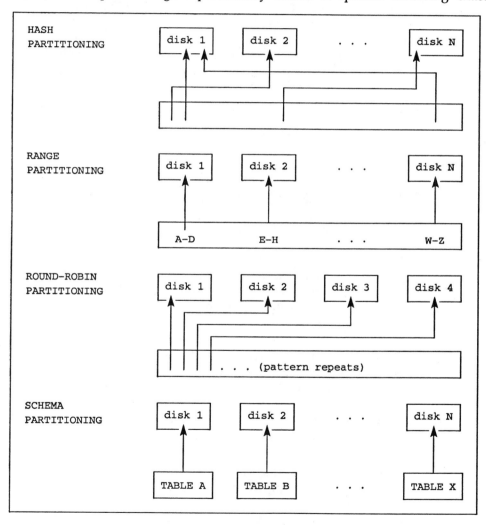

Figure 10–4. Data partitioning alternatives

matches on key values (such as "SELECT * FROM EMPLOYEE WHERE EMP_NO = 11242"), because the search can be confined to one disk. However, hash partitioning obviously will not perform as well for queries involving range searches (such as "SELECT * from EMPLOYEE WHERE SALARY > 75000 and SALARY < 150000"). In such a case, the search would have to involve most (or all) disks over which the table has been partitioned.

Range partitioning involves placing rows containing key values that fall within a certain range on a particular disk. This offers good performance for range-based queries and also provides reasonable performance for exact-match queries involving the partitioning key. However, range partitioning can cause skewing in some cases. Consider an EMPLOYEE table that is partitioned across disks according to employee identification numbers. If rows containing numbers 1–1000 are placed on disk 1 and rows containing numbers 1001–2000 are placed on disk 2, data will be evenly distributed if the company employs 2000 employees. However, if the company employs only 1300 employees currently, and most are assigned numbers 1–1000, the bulk of the rows for this table will be skewed toward disk 1.

Round-robin and schema partitioning are simpler alternatives. Schema partitioning can be more prone to data skewing. Most vendors support schema partitioning as well as one or more other approaches.

ISSUES TO CONSIDER BEFORE DEPLOYMENT

Although initial support for database parallelism first surfaced in relational products in the 1980s, it was only in the early 1990s that most vendors began shipping support for parallelism in earnest. Implementations vary from system to system. Furthermore, effective use of database parallelism requires skills that are new to users of more conventional systems. Nonetheless, a parallel database environment should be considered when most or all of the following conditions are true:

- Members of the computing staff already have significant experience with relational DBMSs.
- Overall DBMS workload has increased substantially, with the DBMS managing large amounts of data (perhaps hundreds of gigabytes, several terabytes, or more), and/or servicing complex queries.
- Price/performance is a key concern.
- One or more administrators are available to learn performance tuning, load balancing, problem diagnosis, and other system management techniques that become increasingly important in multiprocessor environments.

Once a parallel database environment is selected, a number of issues should be considered when evaluating various alternatives. Among these are:

- What type(s) of applications will the DBMS need to service? Is parallel query processing or parallel transaction processing required (or some combination of both)?
- What type of hardware architecture must be supported? What features does the DBMS contain to support this architecture?
- What performance features has the DBMS incorporated to take advantage of parallel processing? For example, how is load balancing achieved? What are the available data partitioning schemes? What extensions have been made to the optimizer?
- How well does the DBMS's performance scale in parallel environments? To what degree can the DBMS take advantage of newly added resources? At what point does scale-up become hampered by internal constraints?
- What additional work must the administrator perform when new resources are added to the system? What facilities, if any, are provided to automate this process?
- What additional requirements, if any, are placed on application programmers who must work with a parallel DBMS?

SUMMARY

DBMSs that exploit multiprocessor environments can enable customers to scale up their workloads or speed up system response time to existing workloads. A number of events are contributing to the demand for database parallelism, including increased data volumes, increased numbers of users, increasingly complex queries, and new types of applications.

The underlying hardware architecture heavily influences the internal design of DBMSs. Three hardware architectures that can be used to support parallelism include shared nothing, shared disk, and shared memory; each presents technical challenges to DBMS vendors.

DBMSs can be (and, in some cases, have been) enhanced to support two different types of database parallelism: parallel transaction processing or inter-query parallelism, and parallel query processing or intraquery parallelism. Other types of database parallelism also include parallel index processing and parallel utility processing. Data partitioning schemes can also play a key role in balancing overall system workload. Four major partitioning approaches include round-robin, key range, hash, and schema partitioning.

Parallelism is best considered when price/performance is a key concern, users are already familiar with relational DBMSs, capacity or performance requirements cannot be met by a more traditional uniprocessor environment, and someone is available to learn the administrative and performance tuning skills unique to multiprocessing platforms. Issues to consider before deployment include the type of hardware architecture desired, the degree to which the DBMS selected can exploit this architecture, and the types of operations that can be performed in parallel by the DBMS (such as parallel query processing or parallel transaction processing).

REFERENCES AND SUGGESTED READING

DeWitt, David J., and Jim Gray. "Parallel Database Systems: The Future of Database Processing or a Passing Fad?" *SIGMOD RECORD*, vol. 19, no. 4, December 1990, p. 104.

Ferguson, Mike. "Parallel Query and Transaction Processing," *InfoDB*, vol. 7, no. 3, Summer 1993, p. 18.

Englert, Susanne, and Jim Gray. "Performance Benefits of Parallel Query Execution and Mixed Workload Support in NonStop SQL Release 2," *Tandem Systems Review*, October 1990, p. 24.

Hsiao, Hui-I. *Parallel Database System Technology*, IBM Research Report 18866, IBM T. J. Watson Research Center, April 1993.

Mohan, C., H. Pirahesh, W. G. Tang, and Y. Wang. "Parallelism in Relational Database Management Systems," *IBM Systems Journal*, vol. 33, no. 2, 1994, p. 349.

Moore, Mark, and Amardeep Sodhi. "Parallelism in NonStop SQL Release 2," *Tandem Systems Review*, October 1990, p. 36.

Pirahesh, Hamid, C. Mohan, Josephine Cheng, T. S. Liu, and Pat Selinger. *Parallelism in Relational Data Base Systems: Architectural Issues and Design Approaches*, IBM Research Report RJ-7724, IBM Almaden Research Center, October 1990.

Walter, Stephen. "Put Multiprocessing Systems to Work," *Unix Review*, vol. 12, no. 13, December 1994, p. 43.

PART 3
Commercial Relational Database Management Systems

Until now, this book has focused on database concepts and technology trends. The first part provided a solid foundation for understanding key concepts and principles of database management, while the second part described several contemporary technologies that are impacting the DBMS industry.

This section bridges the gap between theory and practice, concentrating on how these concepts and technologies have been addressed in various commercial products. To provide the reader with exposure to a variety of implementations in a manner that is not overwhelming, this section profiles five relational database management systems: DB2 from IBM, NonStop SQL/MP from Tandem, Oracle from Oracle, CA-OpenIngres from Computer Associates, and SQL Server from Sybase. These products were selected because of their wide installation base and/or their technical innovations in certain areas discussed earlier in this book. Nonetheless, these products are only a subset of the relational DBMSs available today. Many other products, some of which provide highly desirable and highly competitive functions, are also offered from other vendors.

All information is based upon publicly available materials. In those cases where the vendor has publicly disclosed future plans or directions of its DBMS, this information is also included. However, readers should be aware that the profile of each product is not intended to be exhaustive. Further details on each product may be obtained directly from the vendor.

Because information presented on these products is often quite detailed in some areas, the reader may wish to review material presented in Chapter 3, "Major Components and Functions," for tutorial information about key DBMS functions (such as concurrency control and recovery).

CHAPTER 11
Introduction and Sample Database

CHAPTER OBJECTIVES

This chapter outlines the sample database that will be used in examples in subsequent sections of this book, which detail five relational DBMS products. DBMS topics discussed for each product include data management, administration, query capabilities, distributed database support (including middleware and replication), performance considerations, and database parallelism. A number of these discussions refer to the sample tables outlined in this chapter.

SAMPLE DATABASE

Most examples in the following sections use a common set of tables. These tables support applications that provide online access to a series of critiques about restaurants in various cities. Collectively, these tables reside in the DINING database shown in Figure 11–1.

RESTAURANT Table

The RESTAURANT table contains detailed information about every restaurant for which a critique is available. The ID column is a number that uniquely identifies each row and serves as the table's primary key. A unique index (REST_INX) is also defined on this column. In addition to the restaurant's name, address, geographic region, and phone number, this table also identifies the type of cuisine served (such as Japanese or French) and the price range of its menu (such as inex-

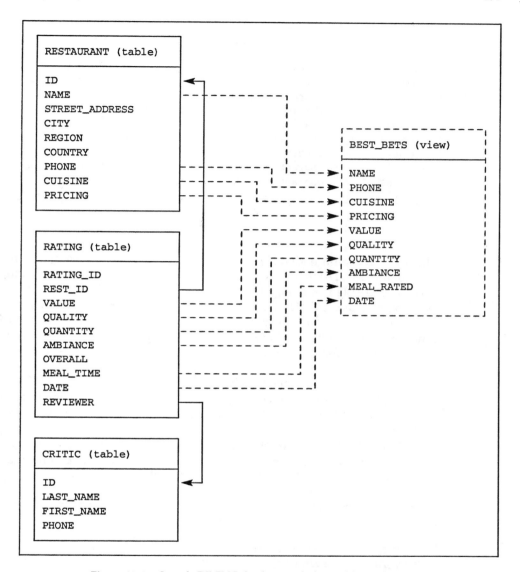

Figure 11–1. Sample DINING database with three tables and one view

pensive, moderate, or expensive). A secondary index (CUISINE_INX) is defined on the CUISINE column. Figure 11–2 illustrates this table in more detail. Data types cited here are generic; actual specifications would vary, depending on the commercial system being used to support this table.

RATING Table

The RATING table contains the critiques of various restaurants. The RATING_ID column uniquely identifies each critique and serves as the table's primary key.

```
                            RESTAURANT TABLE

   ID                unique numeric identifier and primary key. not null.
   NAME              character string for restaurant name. not null.
   STREET_ADDRESS    character string for street address. not null.
   CITY              character string for city. not null.
   REGION            character string for state/province/etc.
   COUNTRY           character string for country. not null.
   PHONE             number. not null.
   CUISINE           character string. (example: continental)
   PRICING           character string. (example: expensive)
```

Figure 11–2. Detail of RESTAURANT table.

The REST_ID column identifies the restaurant that was reviewed; it is the foreign key to the RESTAURANT.ID column. Reviewers rate each restaurant on its VALUE, QUALITY of food, QUANTITY of food, and AMBIANCE. An OVERALL assessment is also provided. Each reviewer also notes the MEAL_TIME at which he or she was served (such as breakfast or dinner) and the DATE when he or she dined at the restaurant. The REVIEWER column identifies who conducted the review; it is the foreign key to the CRITIC.ID column, which is discussed in the next section.

At a minimum, one index is defined on this table for the OVERALL column. Some systems require that the uniqueness of a primary key must be enforced through the creation of a unique index. In such cases, one would be created for RATING_ID as well.

Figure 11–3 illustrates this table in more detail. Data types cited here are generic; actual specifications would vary, depending on the commercial system being used to support this table.

```
                            RATING TABLE

   RATING_ID    unique numeric identifier and primary key. not null.
   REST_ID      foreign key to RESTAURANT.ID. not null.
   VALUE        number 1 - 5 for value of meal (5=best). not null.
   QUALITY      number 1 - 5 for quality of meal (5=best). not null.
   QUANTITY     number 1 - 5 for portion size (5=best). not null.
   AMBIANCE     number 1 - 5 for ambiance (5=best). not null.
   OVERALL      number 1 - 5 for overall rating (5=best). not null.
   MEAL_TIME    character string for meal served (such as dinner)
   DATE         date of dining at restaurant.
   REVIEWER     employee number of the reviewer. foreign key to CRITIC.ID.
```

Figure 11–3. Detail of RATING table

```
                         CRITIC TABLE

   ID            unique numeric identifier and primary key. not null.
   LAST_NAME     character string for reviewer's last name. not null.
   FIRST_NAME    character string for reviewer's first name.
   PHONE         number. not null.
```

Figure 11–4. Detail of RATING table

CRITIC Table

The CRITIC table describes each of the reviewers who have provided critiques about one or more of the restaurants in the database. It contains the employee numbers for each reviewer, which are unique and serve as the primary key. It also cites the reviewer's name and phone number. This table is expected to have relatively low usage and to contain a small number of rows. Thus, no indexes are defined on it, unless a unique index is required to enforce the uniqueness of the primary key.

Figure 11–4 illustrates this table in more detail. Data types cited here are generic; actual specifications would vary, depending on the commercial system being used to support this table.

BEST_BETS View

Finally, one view has been defined to serve the needs of most of the database's users. The BEST_BETS view joins the RESTAURANT and RATING tables (on the RESTAURANT.ID and RATING.REST_ID columns) to extract data about the top-ranking restaurants (those that have earned a "5" rating in the OVERALL category in the RATING table). Figure 11–5 illustrates this view. Note that the join column and the OVERALL rating column are not included in this view.

```
                         BEST_BETS VIEW

   NAME          name of restaurant. RESTAURANT.NAME
   PHONE         phone number of restaurant. RESTAURANT.PHONE
   CUISINE       type of cuisine served. RESTAURANT.CUISINE
   PRICING       price range of meals. RESTAURANT.PRICING
   VALUE         value of meal. RATING.VALUE
   QUALITY       quality of meal. RATING.QUALITY
   QUANTITY      portions served. RATING.QUANTITY
   AMBIANCE      ambiance. RATING.AMBIANCE
   MEAL_RATED    meal rated. RATING.MEAL_TIME
   DATE          date of review. RATING.DATE
```

Figure 11–5. Detail of RATING table

SUMMARY

This chapter described the sample database and tables that are used in examples in subsequent sections of this book; these sections describe the capabilities of five commercial relational DBMS products: IBM's DB2, Tandem's NonStop SQL/MP, Oracle's Oracle, Computer Associates' CA-OpenIngres, and Sybase's SQL Server.

CHAPTER 12
IBM's DB2

CHAPTER OBJECTIVES

This chapter describes IBM's DATABASE2 (DB2) and a number of related offerings. The focus is on DB2 for MVS/ESA, a widely installed relational DBMS for mainframe platforms. The chapter discusses major areas of product function, including those that provide for lock management, resource management, backup and recovery, data integrity, security, query support, and performance tuning. Additionally, there is discussion of IBM technology that supports replication, middleware, distributed databases, and parallelism.

This chapter provides the reader with insight into how a commercial DBMS product has actually implemented the technologies discussed earlier in this book.

OVERVIEW OF DBMS AND RELATED PRODUCTS

Announced in 1983, IBM's DB2 for MVS/ESA is IBM's flagship relational database management system. The product is the most commonly selected relational DBMS on MVS platforms. In recent years, IBM has attempted to broaden its focus to include midrange and workstation platforms. Other members of the DB2 product family now include DB2 for OS/2 (sometimes called DB2/2), DB2 for AIX (sometimes called DB2/6000), DB2 for VM and VSE (formerly known as SQL/DS), DB2 for OS/400 (sometimes called DB2/400), DB2 for HP/UX, and DB2 for Sun Solaris.

Since the MVS-based product is arguably IBM's most successful relational DBMS to date, this chapter focuses on that product. For simplicity, the remainder of this chapter refers to DB2 for MVS/ESA simply as DB2. Other family members are discussed briefly in the section "Other DB2 Products."

IBM's relational DBMS products were based on work on relational theory performed by Dr. E. F. Codd, then an IBM research scientist. His theoretical work formed the basis for System R, IBM's relational database prototype. System R, in turn, formed the basis for DB2.

Although IBM has placed considerable marketing and development focus on its DBMS engines, it also offers a number of tools to support its products. Figure 12–1 illustrates some of the decision support, application development, and system administration tools that are part of IBM's relational-product family.

In addition, a large number of third-party vendors supply tools and applications that support DB2. These include connectivity tools, decision support facilities, computer-aided software engineering (CASE) tools, system administration tools, and various applications.

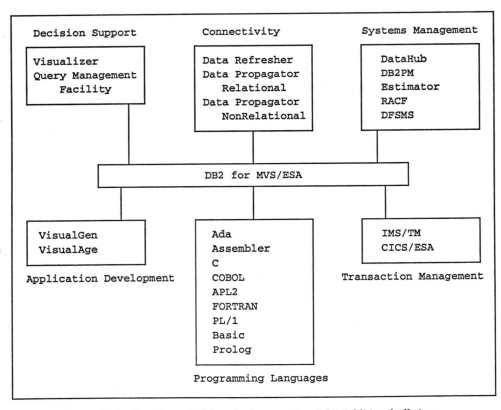

Figure 12–1. Sampling of IBM products supporting DB2. Additional offerings are available but not shown.

The remainder of this chapter focuses on Version 3 of DB2. A summary of major enhancements featured in Version 4, announced but not generally available as of this writing, is also included.

DATA MANAGEMENT

DB2 supports the basic relational objects—databases, tables, views, indexes—and stores its data in VSAM (virtual storage access method) data sets, a storage method common in the MVS environment. Databases contain one or more *tablespaces*, each of which may contain one or more base tables, as defined by users. (The reader will recall that base tables, unlike virtual tables or views, contain real data.) Since the tablespace concept may be new to the reader, DB2's support of it is discussed next.

Tablespaces

Tablespaces are a collection of pages that are mapped to one or more VSAM data sets. A tablespace may hold multiple tables, each of which may range up to 64 GB. Each tablespace is divided into equal-sized pages (or blocks) of either 4K or 32K. Administrators may determine the page size by selecting one of four buffer pools for the tablespace. To provide administrators with flexibility in the assignment of tables to tablespaces, three types of tablespaces are supported:

- Simple
- Segmented
- Partitioned

The data administrator's choice of a tablespace will depend upon the anticipated processing requirements of the application. The aim is to select the option that efficiently uses storage devices and provides acceptable performance.

Simple Tablespaces

Simple tablespaces may contain multiple tables and can result in a mix of rows from different tables on the same page, as shown in Figure 12–2. This can be beneficial if all tables in the simple tablespace are closely related and are often retrieved together, perhaps as part of a join operation. Recall from Chapter 11 that the DINING database contains one table (RATING) that tracks information noted in reviews of various restaurants, such as the quality and value of the food served. A second table (RESTAURANT) contains generic information about these restaurants, including their names, phone numbers, and addresses. If most queries retrieve data from both tables, placing these tables in the same simple tablespace is likely to yield performance benefits because DB2 can search within the same tablespace (and possibly the same pages) to retrieve rows from both tables.

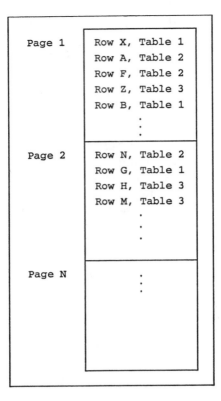

Figure 12–2. Logical structure of a simple tablespace

However, storing multiple tables in a simple tablespace may not always be the best solution. Consider a query referencing data in just one of the tables in the tablespace, perhaps data in the RATING table. Use of the simple tablespace (containing data for both RATING and RESTAURANT) can force DB2 to read data from *both* tables, even though the data in one of these tables is not relevant to the current query. This will result in additional I/O activity. In some circumstances, DB2 may even lock the entire tablespace, including data that is not needed for the current transaction. In such situations, other transactions would be prohibited from accessing this data, even though the initial transaction had no real need to lock it. This can be circumvented through the use of segmented tablespaces.

Segmented Tablespaces

Segmented tablespaces may contain multiple tables, and a single table can occupy more than one segment in the tablespace. However, no single segment contains rows from more than one base table. Each segment contains the same number of pages (always a multiple of 4, ranging from 4 to 64).

Segmented tablespaces can help improve performance involving table scans by eliminating the need to scan the entire tablespace. Segmented tablespaces can also help eliminate needless I/O processing because queries involving a single table will help prevent DB2 from reading pages that contain data from multiple tables.

Table 1	Table 1	Segment 1
Table 1	Table 1	
. . .		
Table X	Table X	Segment N
Table X	Table X	

Figure 12–3. Logical structure of a segmented tablespace. In this case, each segment contains four pages.

Segmented tablespaces also help improve concurrency by eliminating the need to lock data from multiple tables unnecessarily. Users can elect to lock a single table within a segmented tablespace, thus avoiding a lock on the entire tablespace. Figure 12–3 illustrates the structure of a segmented tablespace.

Partitioned Tablespaces

Partitioned tablespaces contain only a single table and are not segmented. They are particularly useful for large tables, because the partitions (or portions) of the table reside in different data sets. Indexes on partitioned tables are partitioned themselves; they are also clustered, causing the data to be clustered by the index key values. This also helps improve performance, particularly for large tables in which queries require grouping or ordering of many records.

A single partitioned tablespace may contain between 1 and 64 partitions. The number of partitions specified determines the maximum partition size (1 to 16 partitions yields a maximum of 4 GB each; 17 to 32 yields 2 GB each; 33 to 64 yields 1 GB each). Each partition is stored in one data set. Frequently accessed data can be placed on faster devices to yield performance gains. A clustered index is required for a partitioned tablespace. Figure 12–4 illustrates a partitioned tablespace.

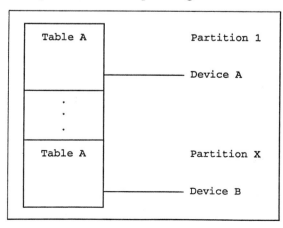

Figure 12–4. Logical structure of a partitioned tablespace

Tables

Given this background on DB2 tablespaces, let's turn to DB2's treatment of tables. Administrators may create one or more tables within a simple or segmented tablespace. Only one table is permitted per partitioned tablespace.

DB2 tables may contain up to 750 columns, and each row may contain up to 32K of data. When a table is created, users may specify certain integrity constraints (discussed in the section "Integrity") and identify user exit routines that will be invoked when certain operations occur. Similarly, when a tablespace is created, administrators may specify a number of options, including the buffer pool to be used, the smallest lock size that may be used, and the amount of free space to be provided when a table is loaded or reorganized. Buffer pool selection affects the size of pages for the tablespace. The size of locks, discussed later in the section "Concurrency Control," can affect concurrency and performance. Free space enables customers to instruct DB2 to plan for additional columns or rows that may be added to the table later. This foresight can help improve performance by minimizing index page splits and the number of necessary reorganizations of the data

Index Spaces

Just as DB2 supports tablespaces, it also supports index spaces. However, these are automatically created on behalf of the user when the user creates an index. Each index occupies its own index space. DB2 supports unique indexes to enforce uniqueness of primary keys and clustering indexes, as well as indexes built on a single column or multiple columns. Up to 64 columns may form the composite key of the index, and these columns need not be contiguous. Indexes are B+ trees.

Version 4 of DB2 introduces a new kind of index, which IBM sometimes refers to as a Type 2 index. Certain other functions new to Version 4 are dependent on this new type of index; these involve improvements in the areas of locking and parallelism. Type 2 indexes have no subpages and are multileveled. Row IDs of nonunique indexes are ordered, allowing for improved performance when a large number of duplicates are present. In addition, locks are not acquired on index pages of Type 2 indexes; only data pages are locked.

Data Types

In addition to supporting various data objects, DB2 also supports a number of data types. These include:

- CHAR(n), a fixed-length character string of 1 to 254 bytes.
- VARCHAR(n), a varying-length character string with n bytes ranging from 1 to slightly less than the page size (which may be up to 32K). If the length is greater than 254 bytes, it is considered a LONG VARCHAR.
- LONG VARCHAR, a varying-length character string of at least 254 bytes

- GRAPHIC(n), a fixed-length graphic string with 1 to 127 double-byte characters.
- VARGRAPHIC(n), a varying-length graphic string with n bytes ranging from 1 to slightly less than the page size (which may be up to 32K). If the length is greater than 127 bytes, then it is a LONG VARGRAPHIC.
- LONG VARGRAPHIC, a varying-length graphic string greater than 127 bytes.
- SMALLINT, a 16-bit binary integer (–32,768 to 32,767).
- INTEGER, a 32-bit binary integer (–2,147,483,648 to 2,147,483,647).
- FLOAT(n), a single-precision or double-precision floating-point number, depending on the number specified for n.
- DECIMAL(p,s), a packed decimal number with a precision of p (ranging from 1 to 31) and a scale of s (ranging from 1 to less than the precision value).
- DATE, a three-part value for year, month, and day.
- TIME, a three-part value for hours, minutes, and seconds.
- TIMESTAMP, a seven-part value for year, month, day, hour, minute, second, and microsecond.

Character and graphic strings may consist of double-byte characters. This enables DB2 to support Kanji and other characters used in certain national languages.

Integrity

DB2 was the first commercial relational DBMSs to support declarative referential integrity constraints. Users may specify referential integrity constraints when creating or altering tables; this is accomplished by identifying primary and foreign keys. DB2 will then enforce referential integrity constraints between these tables automatically.

The following example illustrates how a referential integrity constraint may be defined when two tables are created. In this case, the RESTAURANT table contains a list of all restaurants that have been reviewed. The ID column is unique to each restaurant and serves as the primary key. An index is created on this column to enforce uniqueness. In addition, a RATING table provides detailed reviews of these restaurants. The RATING.REST_ID column is defined as a foreign key (referencing the RESTAURANT.ID column) to ensure that every restaurant review refers to one of the restaurants in the master list.

```
create table restaurant
    (id              smallint    not null,
     name            char(30)    not null,
     street_address  varchar(70) not null,
     ...
     primary key     (id))
```

```
create unique index rest_inx on restaurant(id)

create table rating
     (rating_id        smallint      not null,
      rest_id          smallint      not null,
      value            smallint      not null,
      ...
      primary key      (rating_id),
      foreign key      (rest_id) references restaurant
           on delete restrict))
```

Note that this example instructs DB2 on how to proceed should a transaction attempt to delete a restaurant from the RESTAURANT table when reviews for it still exist in the RATING table. In this case, DB2 is restricted from doing so. Other alternatives are to permit the row to be deleted from the primary table and remove any corresponding rows in the dependent table (a *cascade* action), or to permit the row to be deleted from the primary table and set the corresponding rows in the dependent table to null (a *set null* action). The latter option would not be possible with this example, as the foreign key (RATING.REST_ID) was defined as not permitting nulls.

Updates to primary and foreign keys also face certain restrictions. Primary keys that have a dependent row cannot be changed. (In the example above, the ID for a given restaurant could not be changed in the RESTAURANT table if that restaurant were referenced in the RATING table. Doing so would violate the referential constraint, because the RATING table would then list the identifier of a restaurant that no longer belonged in the master RESTAURANT list.) Similarly, users cannot change foreign key data unless the change would match one of the primary key values. (In the example above, data in the RATING.REST_ID column could not be changed unless it matched a corresponding value in the RESTAURANT.ID column. This ensures that all restaurant reviews in the RATING table correspond to a restaurant in the master RESTAURANT table.)

In addition to referential integrity support, DB2 also provides other mechanisms to help preserve data integrity. For example, DB2 enables users to write data validation routines and specify these when tables are created. Whenever someone attempts to load, insert, update, or delete data from such tables, the validation routine will be executed to determine if the operation should be allowed to proceed for the given row(s). Similar user exit facilities are provided for other functions, such as data encoding.

Views also serve as a mechanism to provide some level of domain support. Views may be created with a CHECK OPTION, which effectively enforces the restrictions on data values that are specified in the WHERE clause when the view is created. For example, imagine that the PRICING column of the RESTAURANT table should be defined to contain only one of three values: expensive, moderate, or inexpensive. The following view can be created:

```
create view rest_view
     (id, name, street_address, city, region, phone, cuisine, pricing)
```

```
  as select id, name, street_address, city, region, phone,
     cuisine, pricing
     from restaurant
     where pricing = 'expensive' or pricing = 'moderate'
           or pricing = 'inexpensive'
with check option
```

If users are restricted to updating or inserting information into the underlying table only through this view, then DB2 can ensure that the PRICING column will only contain one of the three "valid" data values. Whenever someone tries to insert or update data through this view, DB2 will reject any attempts that would violate the constraint specified in the WHERE clause of the view.

Version 4 of DB2 will support data value constraint checking through extensions to the CREATE TABLE and ALTER TABLE statements. The following statement illustrates how the RESTAURANT table might be created with a CHECK constraint that will ensure that values for the PRICING column are "expensive," "moderate," or "inexpensive." This represents an alternate way of enforcing data range checking and eliminates the need for administrators to create a view with the CHECK option.

```
create table restaurant
  (id   smallint not null,
  ...
  pricing char(11)
          check (pricing in ('inexpensive', 'moderate', 'expensive')),
  ...)
```

Constraints may apply to a single column of a table (as shown previously) or to multiple columns of a table. Check constraints are enforced for SQL INSERT, UPDATE, and DELETE operations, as well as when executing the LOAD, CHECK DATA, and RECOVER utilities.

When altering a table or running the LOAD utility, administrators have the option of specifying that constraint checking be deferred. However, this places the tablespace containing the table in a "check pending" state, preventing users from issuing DML statements against tables in that tablespace and from performing certain other functions. (If the tablespace is partitioned, only the affected partition(s) are placed in a the check pending state.) An administrator can clear the tablespace of this state by running the CHECK DATA utility (which will remove invalid rows from the table(s) and copy them into "exception tables").

ADMINISTRATION

Like other DBMSs, DB2 provides a number of mechanisms to address various administrative concerns. Administration or system management issues have been an area of focus for DB2 even in its early releases, as mainframe customers often had high expectations in this area.

Security

DB2 supports the standard SQL GRANT/REVOKE statements for assigning privileges. Its privilege list is quite granular, enabling administrators to tightly control the types of operations performed on the system. Privileges are associated with different types of resources (including databases, tables, views, the system catalog, utilities, and other resources). Privileges may be assigned in a variety of ways to restrict the actions of individuals. For example, a user may be permitted to create tables and tablespaces but not to perform certain utility operations against them.

In addition to its privilege set, DB2 provides six predefined user classes (for system administrators, system operators, database administrators, database maintenance operators, database control operators, and the public). Users who belong to these groups automatically inherit a certain set of privileges. DB2 also provides a "secondary authorization ID" mechanism that can be used to support additional user-defined groups. DB2 works with IBM's RACF (Resource Access Control Facility) to verify user IDs, authorization for connection to DB2, protection of DB2 data sets, and other functions.

Information about DB2 objects stored in various databases is tracked in a single system catalog. This catalog actually consists of a number of tables, which DB2 consults and updates as appropriate. Data in these tables is not automatically available to all DB2 users (for security reasons); however, administrators may grant access to all users if they wish.

To track access or attempted access to various DB2 objects, an audit trace facility is provided. Users can determine which events to trace by specifying one or more classes. The following example shows how to instruct DB2 to audit all explicit use of GRANT/REVOKE statements (part of class 2) affecting all tables that are eligible to be audited. Audit trace records are being directed to GTF, a common MVS facility.

```
-start trace (audit) class (2) aest (gtf)
   comment ('Trace grant/revoke statements')
```

A similar command could have been issued to instruct DB2 to record the actual SQL statements that were issued for data manipulation operations (select, insert, update, or delete). This is an additional security feature, and DB2 is one of the few products to support it.

DB2's trace facility also collects accounting information. Information about locks, buffers, SQL activity, and remote access are among the items that may be tracked through accounting traces. The syntax for initiating such a trace is similar to that shown in the previous example (on the audit trace).

Concurrency Control

To preserve data integrity when multiple transactions are executing concurrently, DB2—like other DBMSs—provides various locking mechanisms. These include standard *transaction locks*, which are acquired to process various SQL statements, and *drain locks*, which are acquired only to process DB2 commands and utilities. The product also uses *latches* to control certain internal events. Transaction locks are typically a greater area of focus for administrators and programmers, so it is these locks that are discussed in this section.

Lock Levels and Lock Modes

The administrator can specify lock granularity (or the size of locks) when creating a tablespace. However, many administrators choose a lock granularity of ANY, which directs DB2 to escalate the lock size automatically to a broader lock granularity when it deems it prudent.

Three broad levels of lock granularity are provided: page-level locks (which lock a single page), table-level locks (which lock an entire table and apply only to segmented tablespaces), and tablespace-level locks (which lock an entire tablespace). Version 4 of DB2 supports row-level locking. This function relies on the use of a Type 2 index. The majority of this section discusses locking in DB2 Version 3, as details of Version 4 capabilities were not publicly available as of this writing. However, major changes included in Version 4 are also discussed.

Although the reader might think these lock levels are mutually exclusive, DB2 may actually use a combination of these levels to service any given request. This is because DB2 features some special modes of table and tablespace locks—generically called *intent* locks—that work in synergy with page locks to enable the DBMS to balance the (sometimes conflicting) requirements for high concurrency, high performance, and deadlock avoidance.

The modes (or types) of page locks supported by DB2 are the easiest to understand, so they are discussed first. Next, the modes of table and tablespace locks are discussed, with an emphasis on the types of intent locks supported at this level. Finally, the synergy between the page lock modes and the table and tablespace lock modes is discussed briefly to illustrate how this can enhance concurrency and improve performance.

Three modes of page-level locking are supported: *share, update,* and *exclusive.* Share locks offer the most concurrency (enabling multiple processes to read the same page), and exclusive locks are the most restrictive (the lock owner can read or change the data, but no one else can access the page). Update locks enable the owner to read, but not change, the page. To change the page, the update lock must be upgraded to an exclusive lock. Update locks allow for greater concurrent access than do share and exclusive locks. They permit other transactions to acquire share locks on the page (to read the data), but do not allow other transactions to acquire update or exclusive locks. They can also help prevent deadlocks when the lock owner is merely reading data to determine whether or not it should be changed. In this way, update locks are used to balance the desire for concurrency with the need to minimize (or avoid) deadlocks.

Table and tablespace locks may also be granted in share, update, and exclusive modes. These modes are the same as those described for page-level locks. The only difference is that these modes are now being applied to a greater amount of data (to all the pages of a single table, in the case of segmented tablespaces, or to all the pages of a single tablespace).

However, DB2 also supports intent locks for tables and tablespaces. Assuming that page-level locking is available to DB2 for a given tablespace, DB2 will often choose to acquire an intent lock before acquiring any page locks. With an appropriate intent lock acquired, DB2 can then try to acquire the necessary page lock(s).

Three types of intent locks are supported: *intent share, intent exclusive,* and *share with intent exclusive.* These are summarized briefly below:

- Intent share is used for read operations. It enables the owner to subsequently try to lock one or more pages to read data. These attempts will succeed provided these pages are not already exclusively locked by other processes. Intent-share locks permit other transactions to read pages within the table or tablespace as well.
- Intent exclusive is used for write operations. It enables the transaction to subsequently try to lock one or more pages to write data. These attempts will succeed provided other transactions do not already have update or exclusive locks on these pages. Transactions that hold intent-exclusive locks may also try to acquire share locks for reading pages. Intent-exclusive locks permit other transactions to acquire share locks on pages (provided these pages are not already exclusively locked), update locks on pages (provided these pages are not already subject to an exclusive or update lock), and exclusive locks on pages (provided no other locks are held on the page).
- Share with intent exclusive is used for write operations. It is similar to the intent-exclusive lock (described previously), except that it does not permit other transactions to acquire locks for writing data to any page within the table or tablespace. This is true even if the other transactions want to write to a page that is not currently locked in update or exclusive mode. As the name implies, this type of lock can be thought of as involving a share lock on the entire tablespace (preventing other transactions from locking any given page in exclusive mode) *as well as* an intent-exclusive lock.

At this point, the reader may be wondering why these different intent locks are part of DB2. What benefits do they provide? By using these table- and tablespace-level intent locks, and combining them with page-level locks, DB2 is able to minimize some locking overhead that typically occurs in a high production environment in which many transactions are executing concurrently. This lock overhead can occur when the DBMS must determine if a new transaction can be granted the desired locks for reading or writing data. Without intent locks, DB2 might have to examine many individual page locks to see if any incompatibilities exist between these existing locks and the lock it wishes to grant. With intent locks, DB2 can make that determination more quickly by reviewing the anticipated intent of other transactions that are operating on data within that table or tablespace.

Users may influence both the lock size and the initial lock modes that DB2 will use. The LOCKSIZE parameter of the CREATE TABLESPACE statement helps control the lowest level of granularity permitted for a tablespace. Note that specifying a LOCKSIZE of PAGE will *not* prohibit DB2 from acquiring table or tablespace locks. However, specifying a LOCKSIZE of TABLESPACE *will* prohibit DB2 from acquiring locks at a lower level.

Programmers may use the LOCK TABLE statement to influence the initial lock modes used by DB2. This statement enables programmers to immediately request either a share or an exclusive lock for the entire simple or partitioned tablespace. For segmented tablespaces, the LOCK TABLE statement is still valid but results in acquisitions of share or exclusive locks for the table and intent-share or intent-exclusive locks for the entire tablespace.

DB2 also locks index data as necessary. Through the SUBPAGES clause of the CREATE INDEX statement, administrators can control the granularity of index locks. SUBPAGES specifies the number of subpages for each physical index page, and DB2 will lock index data at this subpage level. Valid values are 1, 2, 4, 8, or 16. A "1" value would cause DB2 to lock index data at the coarsest level (one page at a time), while a "16" would cause DB2 to lock index data at the finest level (one-sixteenth of a page at a time). Indexes defined on write-intensive tables (such as tables for which INSERTs are frequently made) should have their SUBPAGES value set to 1 to minimize lock overhead.

Version 4 of DB2 introduces a new type of index that does not make use of subpages. Furthermore, DB2 does not lock index pages with this new type of index. To maintain consistency, it uses page-level latches, which are internal concurrency control mechanisms that are typically held for shorter durations than locks. These latches are used with other internal functions to ensure that the integrity of the index is not compromised.

Lock Duration, Isolation Levels, and Deadlock

Programmers may influence the duration for which locks are held by specifying certain options when binding or rebinding their programs. Binding is a process that causes DB2 to validate SQL statements, perform certain authorization checks, select the appropriate access paths, and build a control structure (or *plan*) to enable DB2 to access the data when the program is executed.

The ACQUIRE and RELEASE options help determine when table and tablespace locks are acquired and released; their main purpose is to help DB2 avoid deadlocks, which is discussed shortly. The ISOLATION option helps determine when page locks are released.

DB2 supports two isolation levels: cursor stability and repeatable read. Cursor stability ensures that page locks for read operations, that is, share locks, are held only while the cursor is positioned on that page. Repeatable read ensures that all page locks acquired within a transaction remain locked until the transaction completes. Cursor stability promotes the most concurrency, but it does not ensure that all rows retrieved within a transaction will remain unchanged for the duration of the transaction. For this, repeatable read is required, but this provides less concurrency.

Version 4 of DB2 offers an additional isolation level: uncommitted read. This provides greater concurrency than cursor stability, but it means that transactions may read uncommitted data. This isolation level is sometimes referred to as supporting *read-through* locks.

As mentioned previously, the ACQUIRE and RELEASE options can help DB2 avoid deadlock. They enable programmers to instruct DB2 to try to acquire all needed locks when a plan is allocated. If DB2 is able to do so, the application can be executed immediately and will not be involved in a deadlock. If DB2 is unable to acquire all the needed locks, the application must wait. In this way, the transactions in the application never lock a resource while waiting to acquire a lock on another needed resource, which could cause a deadlock.

Working under this locking scheme is at the user's discretion. If all applications do not use this approach, deadlock can still occur. DB2 maintains wait-for graphs to detect deadlocks and will resolve these deadlocks automatically. For example, if two transactions are deadlocked, DB2 will select one to become the "victim" and roll back its work, freeing the necessary resource(s) for the other transaction to use.

Backup and Recovery

Backing up data in DB2 is performed through the COPY utility. This enables users to make full or incremental image copies of their data. Copies may be made of an entire tablespace, a single partition within a partitioned tablespace, or a single VSAM (virtual storage access method) data set. Backups on multiple partitions or multiple data sets of a single tablespace may be made in parallel to improve performance.

Incremental image copies enable DB2 to back up only the data that has been changed since the last backup occurred, reducing the time and resources required to make a safe backup of the user's data. However, if a single tablespace has one full image copy and multiple incremental image copies associated with it, this can lengthen recovery time, as DB2 must dynamically merge these copies before recovering. For this reason, IBM provides a MERGECOPY utility to merge the image copies associated with a single tablespace.

The RECOVER TABLESPACE utility uses image copies, as well as log records, to recover data to a point of consistency (sometimes called a *commit point* or *sync point*). Most often, this is used to recover the tablespace to a consistent state immediately prior to the failure.

The RECOVER TABLESPACE utility consults information in a catalog table to determine the most recent full image copy of the tablespace to be recovered, as well as any subsequent incremental image copies. Once these changes have been applied, the RECOVER TABLESPACE utility applies any committed work registered in the log subsequent to the last incremental image copy. Again, a catalog table notes the appropriate starting point in the log, based upon information about when the last image copy was taken. Different partitions of a tablespace may be recovered in parallel to improve performance. DB2 also enables users to restore a single page or a range of pages, an index, or the system catalog.

Log records are important to the recovery process of DB2. DB2 logs both before- and after-image copies of data. The product also supports both active logs and archive logs, and administrators are encouraged to maintain dual copies of the active log for added safety.

When database events occur, DB2 creates log records, assigns them to output log buffers (in memory), and eventually writes them to one of the data sets on disk containing the active log. Group commit processing is supported to minimize I/O and improve performance. Later, administrators can instruct DB2 to move old log records to an archive log (stored in other data sets, perhaps on tape). The RECOVER TABLESPACE utility, and certain other utilities, retrieve log records by specifying the relative byte address (RBA) or starting point within the log. DB2 attempts to locate the desired record by first searching the buffers, then the active logs, and then the archive logs. Performance is best when the desired record is in memory or at least in the active log.

Although administrators typically recover their data to its most recent point of consistency, they can choose to recover to a specific point in time. This is accomplished by specifying an option when invoking the RECOVER TABLESPACE utility that instructs DB2 to apply log records only up to a certain point (only up to a given log RBA).

The bootstrap data set (BSDS) is also an important mechanism for recovery and logging. This VSAM data set includes information about the active and archive log data sets, the log records included in these data sets, and checkpoints. Administrators may occasionally find it useful to review information contained in the BSDS; a batch utility (print log map utility) enables them to do so.

Although the RECOVER TABLESPACE and RECOVER INDEX utilities are sufficient for most recovery requirements, DB2 also provides an online mechanism for repairing data that has somehow become damaged. The REPAIR utility enables users to replace invalid data with valid data. It is intended primarily for emergency situations when there may not be enough time to recover using the normal processes available. It should be used with caution, as improper use can result in further damage or possibly even system failure.

A REPORT utility provides administrators with information useful when planning for recovery. Such information includes historical recovery data, log ranges, locations of archive logs and image copies, and data about all the partitions or data sets of a tablespace.

Continuous operations and high availability are considerations somewhat related to recovery. DB2 enables users to read and write data while performing copy operations. This is accomplished by invoking the COPY utility with a share level set to CHANGE. In some cases, such image copies may contain uncommitted data. When working with such image copies for recovery, administrators typically use the default parameters of the RECOVER TABLESPACE utility to ensure that subsequent log records are applied (and uncommitted data is not made visible to users). In addition, DB2 enables users to read data while an index is being created on a table, further supporting continuous operations.

In the area of high availability, DB2 supports specialized IBM hardware to help protect users against unplanned outages and to support disaster recovery. This includes the 3990 Model 6 storage control units, which supports extended remote copy (XRC) for asynchronous shadowing of DASD (direct access storage device) volumes and peer-to-peer remote copy (PPRC) for synchronous shadowing of DASD volumes. In addition, the IBM RAMAC Array DASD provides for fault tolerance and higher data availability through the use of RAID technology (redundant array of independent disks).

Version 4 also includes support for data sharing on IBM Parallel Sysplex hardware. Multiple DB2 subsystems can be running on this hardware platform. If one DB2 subsystem fails, a transaction can switch new requests to another DB2 subsystem that shares access to the same data. This can improve overall availability. More information on Parallel Sysplex, and DB2's support of this hardware, is provided later in this chapter in the section "Parallelism." Finally, certain Version 4 features help improve availability when DB2 is installed on certain IBM multiprocessor hardware. This is also discussed in "Parallelism."

Other Issues

Controlling system resources is often an area of concern for administrators. One aspect of this sometimes involves limiting runaway or wild queries that can potentially consume a significant amount of resources. DB2 provides a facility for limiting processor time consumed by any dynamic data manipulation statement (INSERT, UPDATE, DELETE, SELECT). Users create a resource limit specification table and specify the number of processor service units permitted for queries issued by a given user (or all users) and a given plan (or all plans). Optionally, users may specify limits for requests originating at one or more remote sites. This facility, often called the governor, will terminate queries that exceed their resource consumption limit.

DB2 also supports data compression, wherein byte strings that repeatedly occur in tables (such as city names or numbers with many zeros) are replaced by shorter strings. A *compression dictionary*, built by running the LOAD or REORG TABLESPACE utilities, enables DB2 to map bit strings to their shorter representations. If compressing a record doesn't result in a shorter length (as might be the case if there were few or no repeating byte strings), DB2 does not store the record in a compressed format. An option of the CREATE TABLESPACE statement, compression can help administrators reduce overall storage requirements for their databases, offering them a potential cost savings on storage devices.

Finally, diagnosing and resolving potential problems is often a concern to administrators. In addition to a variety of error messages and return codes, DB2 also provides several trace facilities (including a diagnosis trace facility) and formatted dumps. Log records, certain utilities (such as CHECK), and certain DB2 commands (including -DISPLAY commands) provide further diagnostic information.

QUERY CAPABILITIES

SQL was developed by IBM Research as part of its System R project, and DB2 has supported SQL as its native language since the product was first delivered. Its SQL implementation helped to serve as the basis for the first ANSI/ISO specifications for a relational DBMS language. DB2 continues to support the basic elements of SQL (including data manipulation, data control, and data definition statements) and was the first commercial relational DBMS to extend the language to support declarative referential integrity. The product also supports basic arithmetic, Boolean, and character operations.

Supported SQL functions include AVG (average), MIN (minimum), MAX (maximum), COUNT, and SUM. A variety of scalar SQL functions (which return a single data value) are supported as well. These support such functions as computing the length of a character string (and certain other data values), extracting the date, hour, or other portions of a timestamp value, and returning a decimal representation of another numeric value.

DB2 supports both dynamic and static SQL, which may be embedded in a variety of programming languages. These include COBOL, C, FORTRAN, PL/1, assembler, Ada, APL2, Prolog, and IBM Basic.

Version 4 of DB2 supports left outer joins, right outer joins, and full outer joins. The following example illustrates how users might be expected to write a query that performs a full join of TABLE1 and TABLE2, both of which are presumed to possess a NAME column. The results will include paired rows for both tables. For those rows in TABLE1 that do not contain a corresponding match with TABLE2, null values will be concatenated. Similarly, for those rows in TABLE2 that do not contain a corresponding match with TABLE1, null values will be concatenated.

```
select *
    from table1 full join table2
    on table1.name = table2.name
```

Other SQL enhancements in Version 4 of DB2 are support for table expressions, stored procedures, and user-defined default values for columns. Table expressions enable a table expression (such as a SELECT statement) to be included in the FROM clause of a query. In previous releases, only table or view names could be included in the FROM clause of a query.

Stored procedures offer performance benefits by helping to reduce network traffic. DB2 stored procedures are written in a programming language such as COBOL, PL/1, C, assembler, or VisualGen. Applications can call these stored procedures through an SQL CALL statement.

Finally, Version 4 of DB2 enables users to specify their own default values for columns of a table. Previous releases supported default values, but these relied on DB2-supplied defaults.

Certain other members of the DB2 family provide additional SQL statements to support triggers, user-defined types, and other features. These are described briefly later in this chapter in "Other DB2 Products."

DISTRIBUTED DATABASE

DB2 enables users to read and write data in multiple DB2 systems within a single transaction or logical unit of work, provided no SQL statement spans more than one system. This means that DB2 supports distributed unit-of-work processing, using two-phase commit processing to ensure the integrity of transactions that span multiple sites. This two-phase commit processing is automatically managed on the user's behalf, so customers need not manually coordinate the processing.

Distributed Relational Database Architecture (DRDA)

DB2's distributed database support is based largely on IBM's Distributed Relational Database Architecture (DRDA), which specifies protocols and data formats to enable DBMSs to communicate with one another. These formats and protocols encompass such issues as network support, data encoding, and process flows. DRDA is based on other architectures, including SNA LU 6.2, Distributed Data Management Architecture, SNA Management Services Architecture, Formatted Data Object Content Architecture, and Character Data Representation Architecture. (DB2 also uses private protocols for supporting distributed unit-of-work processing in DB2-to-DB2 only environments.)

In brief, DRDA outlines responsibilities for *application requestors* (applications or DBMSs that request data from another source) and *application servers* (DBMSs that respond to data requests). Any SQL dialect is supported, and programmers working with DRDA-enabled systems may embed static (pre-bound) or dynamic SQL statements into their applications. Support for static SQL offers potential performance benefits, as does support for blocking and prefetching data (which is also part of DRDA). DRDA's data-encoding protocols also help improve performance by ensuring that data transformations occur no more than once (and, on some occasions, may not need to occur at all).

DB2 Version 3 features both application-requestor and application-server support for performing DRDA-compliant distributed unit-of-work processing. DB2 can service requests from any other DRDA-compliant application or DBMS, and it can make requests of other DBMSs (and participate in two-phase commit processing) with other systems that have implemented the appropriate DRDA application server logic. As of this writing, IBM has announced or shipped both requestor and server support for DRDA remote unit-of-work processing for its DB2 products that run on AIX, OS/2, OS/400, and VM platforms. This means that users of these systems can manually connect to a single IBM DBMS—perhaps DB2 on MVS—and issue data definition, data manipulation, and data control statements. However, remote unit-of-work processing requires that users read or write data to only one site per transaction.

A number of other vendors have announced or shipped products that support DRDA, including Oracle and Informix (another relational DBMS vendor). As of this writing, these DRDA-enabled products typically feature application-requestor support (enabling them to request data, but not service requests) at a remote unit-of-work level.

Administrative Issues

To enable their systems to participate in a distributed database environment, DB2 administrators create a communications database (CDB) as part of the installation process or by issuing SQL statements. The CDB, created at each DB2 site that wants to participate in a distributed environment, consists of catalog tables that map VTAM LUNAMES to DB2 location names and perform other functions. Administrators must populate the CDB with appropriate information. The example below shows how an administrator might update the SYSLOCATIONS table of the CDB to specify that the DB2 location of NEWYORK maps to the VTAM LUNAME of LUNY:

```
insert into sysibm.syslocations (location, linkname)
       values ('newyork', 'luny');
```

Once the CDB is populated, administrators must activate the distributed data facility (DDF) to enable a DB2 system to participate in a distributed environment. This is accomplished with the -START DDF command. At this point, users who have been granted appropriate privileges (by personnel at the remote sites) can access remote objects directly by specifying the full, three-part table name (*location.owner.object*).

The example below shows how a DB2 user at one location might issue an interactive query to retrieve information about various Italian restaurants. This data is stored in another DB2 system (in New York). Private DB2 protocols will be used to process the request.

```
select name, phone, pricing
   from newyork.spy.restaurant
   where cuisine = 'italian'
```

Optionally, users may create aliases to make the location of the data more transparent. The example below defines a local alias of REST for the RESTAURANT table in New York and subsequently queries that table.

```
create alias rest for
   newyork.spy.restaurant

select name, phone, pricing
   from rest
   where cuisine = 'italian'
```

Had the RESTAURANT table resided in a DB2/VM system (or another DBMS that was enabled as a DRDA server), the application would have first established a connection to that server (issuing a CONNECT statement) and then queried the table. Establishing and releasing connections are required when using DRDA protocols.

Performance and Programming Considerations

Remote static SQL execution is supported through the use of *packages*, part of the DRDA protocol that is supported by DB2. Packages are individually bound database request modules that enable users to bind an application into smaller, more easily maintained increments than DB2 had previously allowed. To use packages in a distributed environment, users at the requesting (or client) site must (1) bind the individual packages required, (2) bind these packages into a plan, and (3) connect to the desired server at BIND PLAN time or within an application. If multiple servers must be accessed within a single application, the application must manually switch between servers after a commit point.

The example below provides a brief overview of how this might be achieved. Packages stored at two different locations (one in SF, one in NY) are bound at the requesting location (in this case, Chicago) and are subsequently bound into a plan, with the initial server location set to SF. The user's program later switches to the server in NY for queries after issuing a commit.

```
User at Chicago issues these commands:

    bind package (sf.eat) member (food)
    bind package (ny.eat) member (food)
    bind plan (test) pklist (sf.eat.food, ny.eat.food)
        currentserver (sf)

show1 program issues these commands:
    select name, phone from restaurant /* executed at SF */
        .
        .
        .
    commit
        .
        .
    Set host_variable to NY
    connect to host_variable
        .
        .
    select name, phone from restaurant /* executed at NY */
        .
        .
```

To simplify debugging for programmers, IBM has implemented a common set of return codes to further aid transparency between its DB2 systems on various platforms.

GATEWAYS AND MIDDLEWARE

IBM's efforts to provide access to non-IBM DBMSs were originally focused on specifying an appropriate architecture (DRDA) and encouraging other vendors to implement products based on this architecture. As such, it did not develop point-to-point gateway solutions in the 1980s, as certain other vendors did. Although support for DRDA has increased since its debut, IBM has explored additional ways of providing access to non-IBM data sources. One of these involves a partnership with Information Builders, Inc., makers of the EDA/SQL product line, which provides read/write access to various relational and nonrelational DBMS sources on IBM and non-IBM platforms. The EDA/SQL product line can be considered one type of middleware offering.

More recently, IBM announced DataJoiner, a data access middleware product it developed internally. DataJoiner is based on DB2 for AIX (using it as the middleware engine, described in Chapter 9, "Middleware") and enables customers to join data from multiple IBM and non-IBM data sources through standard SQL statements. Users can also define multi-location views. The product uses various drivers to support DRDA-enabled servers (such as DB2 on MVS). It also supports Oracle, Sybase SQL Server, and other sources.

A consistent interface to these data sources is provided through the use of the SQL dialect native to DB2 for AIX, as well as support for Microsoft's Open Database Connectivity (ODBC) call-level interface. For situations demanding high performance, a pass-through mechanism is supported as well (which enables customers to code statements native to a particular data source in their applications). The product also features a global optimizer to help improve performance. A global catalog contains statistics to help the optimizer determine reasonable access paths.

REPLICATION

IBM provides a suite of products to enable customers to maintain multiple copies of their data at different locations. Data Refresher (formerly known as DXT) is an extraction facility that enables customers to export data from IMS, VSAM files, and other data sources for loading into DB2. Data Propagator NonRelational is designed to support customers who use both DB2 and IMS databases. This product enables customers to propagate IMS data to DB2 tables.

Data Propagator Relational is IBM's newest offering in the copy management area. Both incremental changes and entire tables can be propagated asynchronously from a source database to a target database. Currently, the product supports copying of incremental changes from DB2 for MVS, DB2 for OS/400, and IMS (when used with Data Propagator NonRelational) to DB2 for OS/2, DB2 for AIX, and other DRDA-enabled DBMSs. Copying entire tables (rather than just propagating changes) from DB2 for OS/2 and DB2 for AIX to other DB2 for OS/2 and DB2 for AIX systems is also supported. An interface is provided to enable customers to write code to support additional sources and targets, and IBM is expected to support additional DBMSs as well.

Data Propagator Relational captures data changes by reading log records (often when still in buffers) and recording relevant information in "staging tables" at the source site. These tables include a CHANGE DATA table to track changes to the source table and a UNIT OF WORK table to record transaction boundaries (including commit points). Because Data Propagator Relational reads data from the log as changes occur, it can capture uncommitted work. The product enables customers to either propagate uncommitted work (by reading information in the CHANGE DATA table only) or propagate only committed work (by joining data from the CHANGE DATA table with the UNIT OF WORK table).

Figure 12–5 illustrates a simple scenario in which Data Propagator Relational is used to maintain a copy of a DB2 table at another location, perhaps running DB2/2 on a small workstation. In this case, only committed changes made to the source table are propagated to the target table. Other copy management scenarios are possible with the product but are not illustrated here.

Secondary sites maintain copies of source data, "pulling" or requesting updates as desired. Such copies are generally read-only, as updates to target copies are not propagated to other locations (including the source location). A sched-

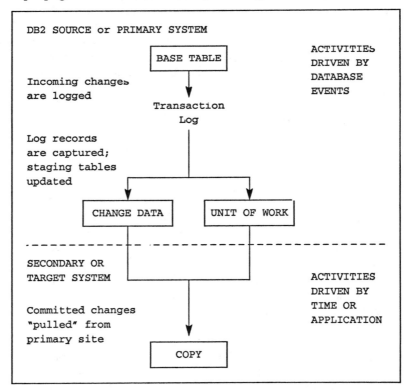

Figure 12–5. Sample scenario using Data Propagator Relational

uling mechanism enables each secondary site to request updates at appropriate (and potentially different) time intervals, such as every 12 hours.

Use of staging tables at the source site enables customers to apply a variety of SQL functions, including aggregate functions, on the data before propagating it. Thus, if one site is interested in seeing only the average opening balance for new checking accounts, it can obtain only this information by writing an appropriate query. It does not need to propagate individual rows about all new accounts and then calculate the average opening balance at the target site. Eliminating this requirement can offer performance benefits. Use of staging tables also enables customers to maintain a history of changes that occurred to various tables, and this information can be used for temporal analysis. Customers also have the option of basing copies on joins of multiple source tables, or subsets of source tables.

PERFORMANCE

DB2 offers a number of mechanisms to help users achieve their desired performance levels. The product was one of the first to support static SQL, which can provide significant performance advantages by eliminating the need to regenerate an access plan each time the same query (embedded in an application) is executed. DB2 also exploits native MVS facilities, such as the IMS/TM and CICS transaction monitors, to help maximize performance.

The DB2 optimizer traces its heritage back to the first optimizer developed for the System R research prototype. Many significant enhancements have been made since then, and IBM considers its optimizer technology as one of its strongest assets in the area of database management. Among the table statistics used by the optimizer in developing an efficient search strategy include:

- Number of rows in the table
- Number of pages the table occupies
- Number of pages in a tablespace
- Available indexes
- Number of index levels for indexed columns
- Number of leaf pages in the index
- Number of distinct (different) values in an indexed column
- Second highest index key value
- Second lowest index key value

Often the optimizer uses only the available index(es) to produce the query result; several examples of this follow. A request for the highest value of a SALARY column can be satisfied by consulting an index on SALARY and avoiding any search of the database, which usually involves more I/O processing. Using data on the number of distinct values for an indexed column, the optimizer computes an expected number of rows that will be included in the query result. To avoid the effects of possible data skewing when computing an expected number of qualifying rows, the optimizer uses second highest (or lowest) values rather than the highest (or lowest) value of the relevant column. The optimizer can also take into account the actual distribution of values, a statistical factor that is kept for the 10 most frequently occurring values of an indexed column.

DB2 can perform query transformation to provide additional possible access strategies for consideration by the optimizer. Consider the following query requesting a three-table join:

```
select     *
from     tablea, tableb, tablec
where    tablea.c3 = tableb.c4
and      tableb.c4 = tablec.c5
```

DB2 can append the following join predicate to this query:

```
and      tablea.c3 = tablec.c5
```

This transformation, referred to as "computing the transitive closure" for join operations, is done automatically by the system on behalf of users. It introduces additional possible access strategies for the optimizer's consideration. In addition, DB2 is able to "flatten" certain subqueries (nested SELECTS) into their equivalent join operations, which can help speed performance. The optimizer is capable of using index ANDing and ORing. DB2 supports sort/merge, nested loop, and hybrid join processing, a join method recently developed by DB2 researchers and developers. When the optimizer recognizes its usefulness, it will adopt a prefetch strategy that can result in the transfer of up to 32 pages in a single I/O operation.

DB2 includes utilities to enable users to reorganize their data (REORG) and update the catalog statistics used by the optimizer as needed (RUNSTATS). A resource limit facility (or governor) helps administrators guard against runaway queries that could consume too much processor time and slow performance. Version 4 of DB2 supports stored procedures to help minimize network traffic.

As mentioned previously, DB2 provides a number of trace mechanisms that can be useful for monitoring and tuning performance. Among these are accounting traces, performance traces, and statistics traces. Often, users invoke a reporting facility (such as DB2PM) to format these statistics and display them in a tabular or graphic report.

In addition, DB2 provides an EXPLAIN facility to help users determine the access path selected by the optimizer for a given query. Users create a PLAN_TABLE and invoke the EXPLAIN facility, which causes the optimizer to select an access plan for the given query but does not force the query to be executed (potentially saving considerable resource consumption and I/O). Data about this access path is then stored in the table, and its contents may be queried.

The following example shows how EXPLAIN might be used to determine the access path for a given query on the RESTAURANT table. Once the EXPLAIN command is executed, a subsequent query on the PLAN_TABLE is made, revealing that DB2 used the RESTINX index to satisfy the query (detected by interpreting the ACCESSTYPE and ACCESSNAME columns) and that DB2 acquired an INTENT

SHARE lock on the tablespace (indicated by the "IS" value in the TSLOCKMODE column). Data pages were read in advance through a page list prefetch (indicated by the "L" value in the PREFETCH column). Prefetching data helps reduce the amount of I/O processing, as multiple pages can be read in a single I/O operation. Note that this PLAN_TABLE was defined to contain 28 columns; DB2 enables administrators to define PLAN_TABLEs that contain fewer or more columns, provided the table conforms to a valid format specified in the product manuals.

```
explain plan set queryno = 1 for
    select * from restaurant
    where id = 1234

select *
    from plan_table
    where queryno = 1
```

QUERYNO	1
QBLOCKNO	1
APPLNAME	
PROGNAME	DSQIESQL
PLANNO	1
METHOD	0
CREATOR	SARACCO
TNAME	RESTAURANT
TABNO	1
ACCESSTYPE	I
MATCHCOLS	1
ACCESSCREATOR	SARACCO
ACCESSNAME	RESTINX
INDEXONLY	N
SORTN_UNIQ	N
SORTN_JOIN	N
SORTN_ORDERBY	N
SORTN_GROUPBY	N
SORTC_UNIQ	N
SORTC_JOIN	N
SORTC_ORDERBY	N
SORTC_GROUPBY	N
TSLOCKMODE	IS
TIMESTAMP	199302018464208
REMARKS	
PREFETCH	L
COLUMN_FN_EVAL	
MIXOPSEQ	

Version 3 of DB2 also enables users to influence optimization through the OPTIMIZE FOR n ROWS clause of the SELECT statement. Through this clause, users can instruct the optimizer to select an access path based on the assumption that the number of rows retrieved will not exceed a specified number (n). In certain cases, this can improve performance. However, if the application attempts to fetch more than n rows, performance may degrade (although the retrieval will still be permitted).

DB2 also maintains information about nonuniform distribution of data values in tables. The RUNSTATS utility, which updates catalog statistics, records the most frequent values for the first key column of an index key for a table. For tables stored in nonpartitioned tablespaces, RUNSTATS records the 10 most frequent values. For tables stored in partitioned tablespaces, RUNSTATS stores a maximum of 12 values per partition.

DB2 also provides certain features to help improve its performance in a distributed environment. The traces, for example, can describe the amount of activity on a local system caused by remote requests. In addition, DB2 uses a block fetch mechanism to help reduce the number of remote requests that must be made from a given application to satisfy remote queries. Remote static SQL execution, through the use of packages (discussed earlier), can also provide performance benefits.

PARALLELISM

As previously noted, Version 3 of DB2 supports parallel processing for certain utility operations, including COPY (for making backup copies of data) and RECOVER TABLESPACE (for recovering data). It also supports transaction parallelism, using multiple processors to service the needs of multiple transactions. And Version 4 contains additional enhancements to support hardware platforms that allow for data to be shared among multiple DB2 subsystems.

This section first focuses on support for parallel query processing present in Version 3 of DB2. Next, it describes expected enhancements in Version 4 to further exploit multiprocessor environments.

Parallel Query Processing

In addition to its support for parallel utility operations and parallel transaction processing, DB2 Version 3 provides some form of parallel query processing. Specifically, I/O processing for a query involving partitioned tablespaces can be executed in parallel. This can significantly improve performance for queries over large tables (stored in partitioned tablespaces) requiring full table scans.

Before Version 3, DB2 read partitions sequentially. This sometimes lengthened response time, as the system had to wait for these I/O operations to complete. The query was said to be *I/O bound*. Version 3 of DB2 improves performance of such queries by initiating multiple I/O requests for a partitioned tablespace and performing I/O processing in parallel.

Tables that were not created in partitioned tablespaces may still benefit from parallel I/O processing because DB2 may partition such tables into multiple work files if doing so would prove beneficial. In the case of sort/merge joins, DB2 might partition the sorted data into multiple files and join these in parallel.

DB2's support for parallel I/O processing was designed for read-only queries involving one or more tables. When optimizing such a query, DB2 will evaluate its estimated I/O processing time and its estimated CPU processing time. If the query appears to be I/O bound, DB2 will activate parallel sequential prefetches on multiple partitions to improve performance. Key range partitioning is often most effective in such cases. DB2 also supports schema partitioning (where multiple tables and indexes may be placed on different disks).

Version 4 Enhancements

Version 4 of DB2 further exploits multiprocessor environments. Improvements are expected in the area of parallel query processing to enable DB2 to use multiple processors in parallel on behalf of a single query. IBM sometimes refers to this as *query CPU parallelism*. When combined with DB2's existing support for parallel I/O processing of a single query, this can provide additional performance benefits, particularly for queries involving tablespace scans and certain types of join operations.

Version 4 also is expected to include additional support for data sharing on IBM's Parallel Sysplex hardware. The hardware, illustrated in Figure 12–6, consists of a group of central processor complexes (CPCs), each of which may be thought of as a node in the system. Memory is shared among multiple processors within each CPC. In addition, a *coupling facility* provides for some shared memory across participating CPCs (or nodes). Finally, all CPCs (or nodes) can be configured to share access to the same data. A timer synchronizes timestamps for participating DB2 subsystems.

With this architecture in mind, it's worth briefly exploring how DB2 supports this multiprocessor hardware. A simple configuration might involve using

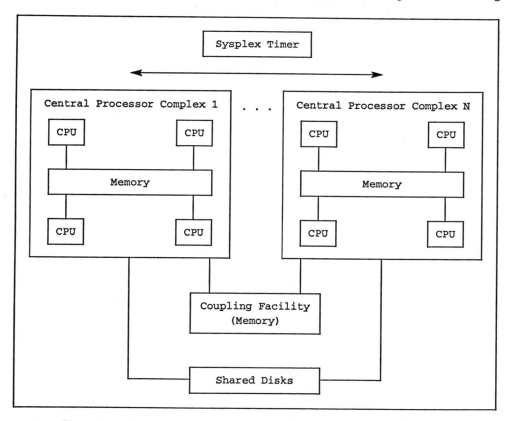

Figure 12–6. Overview of IBM Parallel Sysplex (sample configuration)

one DB2 subsystem per CPC or node. All CPCs may be configured to share access to the same user data; in other words, these CPCs are said to be participating in the same *data sharing group*.

Because of this, certain data and structures are shared among participating DB2 subsystems. These include group locks, group buffer pools, the DB2 system catalog, and user-created databases. However, certain data and structures are also private to individual DB2 subsystems. These include local locks, local buffer pools, work databases, and log data. Figure 12–7 illustrates this approach.

The group buffers and group locks (managed through the coupling facility) help control access to data of interest to multiple DB2 subsystems. Each group buffer pool corresponds to local buffer pools private to individual DB2 subsystems. For example, if two DB2 subsystems each had local Buffer Pools 0 and 1, there would be corresponding Group Buffer Pools 0 and 1 in the coupling facility. The group buffer pools cache data that is of interest to two or more DB2 subsystems sharing common data. When necessary, this data can be read from the group buffer pools into local buffer pools to satisfy transaction requests.

Group locks (also called *data sharing locks*) help ensure data integrity, as multiple DB2 subsystems might wish to update the same data pages concurrently. It's important to note that these group locks, because they are cached in memory of the coupling facility, do not incur the same I/O overhead associated with distrib-

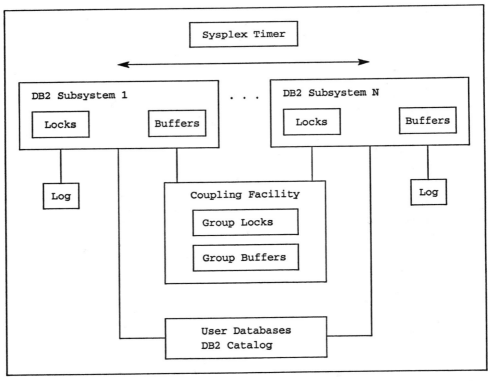

Figure 12–7. DB2 Version 4 data sharing configuration on IBM Parallel Sysplex

uted locks on other hardware platforms, which are typically written to disk. Reducing potential I/O in this manner offers performance benefits.

It might be helpful to explore how DB2 supports update processing in a data-sharing environment. Imagine that Transaction 1 on DB2 Subsystem 1 wishes to update data residing in page X. DB2 will check to see if the page resides in its local buffer pool or in the corresponding group buffer pool. If not, it reads the data from disk into its local buffer pool and updates the data. To do so, appropriate local and group locks are acquired to prevent potential conflicts.

Shortly thereafter, Transaction 2 on DB2 Subsystem 2 tries to update the same page. An existing group lock indicates that the page is in use by another transaction. When that transaction completes, DB2 Subsystem 1 writes the changed page to the group buffer pool. DB2 Subsystem 2 can then acquire a group lock on it and change it as needed. After DB2 Subsystem 2 commits its changes, the page is copied back into the group buffer pool and the (outdated) copy in the local buffer pool of DB2 Subsystem 1 is invalidated. Thus, if DB2 Subsystem 1 subsequently needs to access this data page again, it will know that it must ignore the copy in its local buffer pool and read the current copy from the group buffer pool.

What happens when data must be removed from the group buffer pool and written back to disk? Because there is no direct connection between the coupling facility and the disks, the data must first pass through a private buffer in a DB2 subsystem. However, this is a different buffer than the local buffer pool used to cache data for active transactions.

Other Forms of Parallelism

IBM also supports parallel processing in a shared-nothing environment through its DB2 Parallel Edition product. Since this product is based on DB2 for AIX technology, it is discussed in the next section, "Other DB2 Products."

OTHER DB2 PRODUCTS

As mentioned earlier in this chapter, IBM offers a number of other products that bear the DB2 name. These include DB2 for AIX, DB2 for OS/2, DB2 for OS/400, and DB2 for VM and VSE (formerly known as SQL/DS). In addition, IBM has ported DB2 for AIX to non-IBM environments, including Sun Solaris and HP/UX. While a thorough discussion of these products is beyond the scope of this chapter, this section highlights a number of important features of some of these offerings.

DB2 for AIX and DB2 for OS/2 support stored procedures and block prefetch, which can provide performance benefits in client/server environments as they help reduce network traffic. IBM's implementation of stored procedures differs from that of other vendors profiled in this book. IBM's stored procedures—sometimes called server procedures—are written in a third-generation language (such as C) with embedded SQL. By contrast, most other vendors support stored procedures through an extended version of SQL (a particular SQL dialect that has been enhanced to support procedural logic constructs, such as if-then-else statements and loops).

A potential advantage of IBM's approach is that users can take advantage of all the power of the third-generation programming language; their capabilities are not restricted by the SQL extensions the vendor has chosen to implement. A potential disadvantage is that the coding, testing, and debugging process of such stored procedures may require more advanced programming skills; sophisticated end users may be able to write their own stored procedures in extended SQL, but they are less likely to be able to write stored procedures in languages such as C.

In addition, Version 2 of DB2 for AIX and DB2 for OS/2 supports columns of up to 2 GB through the addition of three large object data types: binary large objects (BLOBs) for handling compressed video, audio, and image data; character large objects (for handling text documents); and double-byte character large objects (for handling text documents written in certain national languages). The products also support triggers to enforce user-defined business rules, event alerters, constraints (through a CHECK clause in the CREATE TABLE statement), user-defined scalar functions, and user-defined distinct types (based on existing system-supplied types). These products also support recursive queries and two object-oriented programming languages: C++ (via embedded SQL) and Smalltalk (via a separately purchased product, VisualAge). IBM has said it expects to incorporate a number of these, and similar, extensions into other members of its DB2 product family over time.

DB2 for AIX Version 1 serves as the basis for another IBM DBMS offering—DB2 Parallel Edition for POWERparallel Systems. These systems are RS/6000-based multiprocessors that feature a shared-nothing architecture. One copy of the DBMS (as well as the AIX operating system) can be installed on each node to support parallel query processing. The product can support parallel processing of SELECT, INSERT, UPDATE, and DELETE statements, as well as execute various utilities in parallel. Hash partitioning and schema partitioning are supported.

SUMMARY

This chapter described IBM's DB2 for MVS, a popular relational DBMS for mainframe environments that enjoys a wide installation base. It explained how the product supports key DBMS functions, including lock management, recovery, integrity, and other areas. It also described IBM's support for emerging technologies profiled earlier in this book, including distributed database support, replication, parallelism, and middleware. Finally, it summarized significant capabilities of other members of the DB2 family, including those that run on OS/2 and AIX.

REFERENCES AND SUGGESTED READING

BONTEMPO, CHARLES J. *DataJoiner—A Multidatabase Server*, IBM White Paper, IBM Corp., October 1994.

CHENG, J. M., C. R. LOOSLEY, A. SHIBAMIYA, and P. S. WORTHINGTON. "IBM DATABASE 2 Performance: Design, Implementation, and Tuning," *IBM Systems Journal*, vol. 23, no. 2, 1984.

CRUS, R. A. "Data Recovery in IBM Database 2," *IBM Systems Journal*, vol. 23, no. 2, 1984, pp. 178–188.

Distributed Relational Database Cross Platform Connectivity and Application, IBM International Technical Support Organization, Boeblingen Center, GG24-4311, May 1994.

FECTEAU, GILLES. *DATABASE 2 AIX/6000 Parallel Technology*, IBM Software Solutions Laboratory, North York, Ontario, Canada, March 17, 1994.

GASSNER, PETER, GUY M. LOHMAN, K. BERNHARD SCHIEFER, and YUN WANG. "Query Optimization in the IBM DB2 Family," *Bulletin of the Technical Committee on Data Engineering 16,4*, December 1993, DAVID LOMET, ed., IEEE Computer Society, pp. 4–18. (Also available as IBM Research Report RJ-9734, March 15, 1994.)

GOLDRING, ROB. "A Discussion of Relational Database Replication Technology," *InfoDB*, vol. 8, no. 1, Spring 1994, p. 2.

HADERLE, D. J., and R. D. JACKSON. "IBM Database 2 Overview," *IBM Systems Journal*, vol. 23, no. 2, 1984, pp. 112–125.

HAUSER, D., and A. SHIBAMIYA. "Evolution of DB2 Performance," *InfoDB*, Summer 1992.

HOOVER, CHUCK, JANET RIZNER, and RICHARD YEVICH. "DB2 Version 4: Our Dreams Come True?" *IDUG Solutions Journal*, October 1994, p. 12.

IBM DATABASE 2 Version 3 Administration Guide Volume I, IBM Corp., SC26-4888, December 1993.

IBM DATABASE 2 Version 3 Administration Guide Volume II, IBM Corp., SC26-4888, December 1993.

IBM DATABASE 2 Version 3 Administration Guide Volume III, IBM Corp., SC26-4888, December 1993.

IBM DATABASE 2 Version 3 Application Programming and SQL Guide, IBM Corp., SC26-4889, December 1993.

IBM DATABASE 2 Version 3 Command and Utility Reference, IBM Corp., SC26-4891, December 1993.

IBM DATABASE 2 Data Sharing: Planning and Administration, Preliminary Planning Version, IBM Santa Teresa Laboratory, Software Solutions Division, April 5, 1994.

IBM DATABASE 2 Version 3 SQL Reference, IBM Corp., SC26-4890, December 1993.

KRILL, PAUL. "IBM to Offer Middleware for Uniform Data Access," *Open Systems Today*, June 6, 1994, p. 1.

MOHAN, C. *Commit_LSN: A Novel and Simple Method for Reducing Locking and Latching in Transaction Processing Systems*, in *Performance of Concurrency Control Mechanisms in Centralized Database Systems*, V. KUMAR, ed., Prentice Hall, 1994.

Object Support and the DB2 Family, IBM White Paper, IBM Corp., May 1994. (This paper is a reprint of IBM technical report 03.551, Santa Teresa Laboratory, by C. M. Saracco and Charles J. Bontempo.)

SARACCO, C. M., and CHARLES J. BONTEMPO. "Applying Object Concepts to the DB2 Family," *IDUG Journal*, vol. 2, no. 1, January 1995, p. 28.

SELINGER, P. G., M. M. ASTRAHAN, D. D. CHAMBERLIN, R. A. LORIE, and T. G. PRICE. *Access Path in a Relational Database Management System*, IBM Research Report RJ-2429, January 1979.

STODDARD, D. "DB2, 10 Years Later," *Database Programming and Design*, October 1993.

CHAPTER 13
Tandem's NonStop SQL

CHAPTER OBJECTIVES

This chapter describes Tandem's relational DBMS and a number of related offerings. It discusses major areas of product function, including those that provide for lock management, resource management, backup and recovery, data integrity, security, query support, and performance tuning. Additionally, there is discussion of Tandem technology that supports replication, middleware, distributed databases, and parallelism.

This chapter provides the reader with insight into how a commercial DBMS product has actually implemented the technologies described earlier in this book.

OVERVIEW OF DBMS AND RELATED PRODUCTS

Tandem first released its relational DBMS, NonStop SQL, in 1987. The product complemented other aspects of Tandem's hardware and software line, with a special emphasis on functions that support fault tolerance, high availability, and online transaction processing (OLTP). Because NonStop SQL is tightly integrated with facilities available through Tandem's operating system (the NonStop Kernel, formerly known as Guardian 90), it was one of the first commercial relational DBMS to deliver certain features to the market, particularly in the area of distributed databases.

The product is in its third major release as of this writing and is properly known as NonStop SQL/MP. For simplicity, this book refers to the product merely as NonStop SQL.

The current release of NonStop SQL includes a number of features that help broaden its appeal beyond its initial OLTP base. In addition, Tandem has been pursuing alliances and partnerships with various hardware and software vendors in the industry. In the DBMS arena, Tandem has announced joint development or marketing agreements with Oracle, Informix, Sybase, and others. Some of these agreements involve support of Tandem's Unix-based hardware line, which does not run the NonStop Kernel operating system or NonStop SQL. Tandem has also formed agreements with a number of software vendors, as well as with various value-added resellers.

Aside from NonStop SQL, Tandem produces fault-tolerant hardware systems, including the Himalaya line and the Integrity line. The Himalaya line runs the NonStop Kernel, which supports NonStop SQL. The Integrity line runs UNIX, and certain non-Tandem DBMSs are available for this hardware platform.

Included with NonStop SQL is a conversational interface to SQL (SQLCI), as well as support for C, Pascal, and COBOL. Other Tandem software products include system management tools and network facilities. Tandem also has a number of agreements with other vendors to provide customers with a variety of DBMS tools that interface to NonStop SQL.

Although the emphasis of this portion of the book is on functions related to relational DBMSs, the reader must have some knowledge of Tandem's hardware architecture and operating system components to fully understand the implementation and features of NonStop SQL. For this reason, a brief hardware and operating system overview is provided. However, only those components of particular relevance to NonStop SQL are discussed.

HARDWARE INTRODUCTION

Tandem provides a number of hardware offerings, from massively parallel processing systems to smaller platforms with as little as two processors. As noted previously, some of these hardware platforms support the NonStop Kernel, and some support UNIX. Since NonStop SQL requires the use of the NonStop Kernel, this section discusses the hardware architecture of its Himalaya line.

Since the company's formation in 1974, Tandem has developed systems that offer redundant hardware components and special software to provide fault tolerance. Generally, a single system will consist of multiple processors and disks. Each processor contains its own memory and executes its own copy of the NonStop Kernel. Disks may be attached to each processor, and disk mirroring is often used to provide for hardware-level fault tolerance in case of a disk failure.

System-level processes are typically executed as *process pairs* to provide for software-level fault tolerance. Process pairs are discussed in more detail shortly.

But briefly, this involves running a primary copy of a process on one processor and a backup copy of this same process on another processer. If the primary process fails for some reason, its backup can take over.

As of this writing, up to 16 processors can be interconnected to form a *node* (sometimes referred to as a *named system*). Up to 256 such nodes can be interconnected using a wide-area network or local-area network. NonStop SQL and the native Tandem operating system contain certain features to support location transparency across these various nodes, as this chapter discusses in the section "Distributed Databases."

Figure 13–1 illustrates the hardware architecture of a single Tandem node; note that the architecture enables customers to add more processors and disks to accommodate future workload increases or improve system response time for an existing workload. Limits on expansion vary with each hardware platform. The architecture is based on a shared-nothing approach.

As noted previously, each processor has its own private memory and may be configured to access a subset of the available devices (such as disks and tape drives). System processes and user processes (such as applications) run on each processor. System-level processes (such as disk processes, I/O processes for communications and tape, and various monitor processes) are run as process pairs to provide for fault tolerance. User processes (such as applications) typically are not.

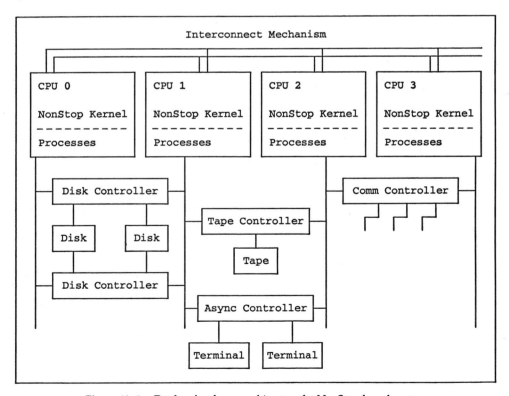

Figure 13–1.   Tandem hardware architecture for NonStop-based systems

In such cases, programmers can use PATHWAY (an application development facility, discussed in the section "PATHWAY"), to compensate for the resultant loss in fault tolerance.

It's important to note that process pairs can execute in any pair of processors. In the previous illustration, CPU 0 might execute the primary process for process pair $X, and CPU 1 might execute the backup process for this same process pair. Similarly, CPU 3 might execute the primary process for process pair $Y, while CPU 0 might execute the backup for this same process pair.

The primary process of a process pair periodically checkpoints critical operations to its backup process. If the primary process (or its associated processor) fails, the backup process can take over from the state as of the last checkpoint. Communication between processes is achieved through messages. Thus, Tandem's architecture is representative of a loosely coupled system, and as such, its operating system is especially oriented toward message processing.

OPERATING SYSTEM OVERVIEW

A number of operating system components are of particular interest to NonStop SQL administrators, as they provide a means of monitoring overall system performance, recovering data, and managing remotely replicated data. The operating system facilities discussed here are the Measure performance monitor, the Transaction-Monitoring Facility, and the Remote Duplicate Database Facility. In addition, the PATHWAY environment offers application development support for database applications. A brief overview of these Tandem facilities is provided here. When appropriate, details about these and certain operating system commands is discussed in subsequent portions of this chapter that address administrative, data management, and distributed database functions of NonStop SQL.

Measure

Measure helps administrators monitor the performance of their systems over short and long periods of times. Measure collects data on a variety of system activities involving processors, disks, files, communication lines, and SQL statements. After specifying activities to be monitored, start/stop times, and intervals for data gathering, users may request performance reports. Additional products may also be purchased to work with Measure; these include Surveyor (for organizing, maintaining, and querying historical measurement data), and the Offender line (for real-time performance monitoring with graphical displays).

While it is beyond the scope of this book to detail the capabilities of these performance-monitoring facilities, a brief example of output that can be generated through Measure may prove useful. The following example presumes an administrator has activated Measure and configured it to track a wide range of system activities, including all SQL statements, processes, and other activities. A query is then run using the SQL conversational interface, and the results are returned.

```
>> add define =customers, file $mos23e.tpcdsf1.custs
>> select c_nation, avg(c_acctbal) from =customers group by c_nation;
```

```
                          C_NATION              (EXPR)
                          --------------------  -------
                          ALGERIA               4436.76
                          ARGENTINA             4400.45
                          BRAZIL                4368.69
                          CANADA                4566.53
                          CHINA                 4654.39
                          EGYPT                 4574.05
                          . . .
                          RUSSIA                4580.81
                          SAUDI ARABIA          4572.79
                          UNITED KINGDOM        4276.80
                          UNITED STATES         4464.62
                          VIETNAM               4383.91
                          --- 25 row(s) selected.
```

As is apparent, the query shown in this example involves a table containing customer financial data. The user has requested the average account balance of customers grouped by their countries of residence. The first line in the example makes use of a DEFINE statement, explained in detail in the section "Distributed Databases." However, it is used here to introduce "customers" as a synonym for the table referenced in the four-part name that also appears in the same statement. The second line in the example contains the actual query; the equality symbol in the FROM clause is appropriate syntax for NonStop SQL queries that reference previously DEFINE synonyms.

At this point, the measurement may be stopped and information about the executed SQL statement requested. Among other things, the subsequent report will note the number of records accessed, the number of disk reads required, and the elapsed time required for the sort operation.

```
SQL Statement
Procedure SQLX-EXECUTE                              Index #1
Process    0,62              Pri 149   Program  $SYSTEM.SYSTEM.SQLCI2
Userid    1,217   Creatorid 1,217      Ancestor 0,63
Local System \PSYCHO  From   9 Sep 1994, 12:51:23   For 27 Seconds


Calls                       32 #
Elapsed-Busy-Time        25.03 sec
Records-Used            15,000 #
Records-Accessed        15,000 #
Disc-Reads                 210 #
Messages                   486 #
Message-Bytes        1,967,590 #
Sorts                        1 #
Elapsed-Sort-Time        19.64 sec
Recompiles
Elapsed-Recompile-Time
Lock-Waits
Timeouts
Escalations
```

Similarly, the administrator may request other information. For example, assume the administrator requests to see measurement data on the processes that executed, ordered by the amount of CPU time consumed by each. In this case, three processes are relevant: the SQL conversational interface process, which is reported first and which consumed 9.19 seconds of CPU time; the sort process, which is reported second and which consumed 3.99 seconds of CPU time; and the disk process on which accessed the customer table. The measurements associated with this process are reported last and illustrate that 3.61 seconds of CPU time were consumed. The following three examples illustrate measurement data that might be reported for each of these three processes.

```
Process   0,62              Pri 149    Program $SYSTEM.SYSTEM.SQLCI2
Userid    1,217   Creatorid 1,217      Ancestor 0,63
Local System \PSYCHO  From 9 Sep 1994, 12:51:21    For 29.8 Seconds

Cpu-Busy-Time            9.19  sec   Ready-Time             13.32  sec
Mem-Qtime                            Dispatches               802  #
Page-Faults                          Vsems
Pres-Pages-Qtime         1,785 sec   Pres-Pages-Max            60  #
Ext-Segs-Qtime          89.30  sec   Ext-Segs-Max               4  #
Recv-Qtime              77.39  ms    Recv-Qlen-Max              2  #
Messages-Sent            637   #     Messages-Received         33  #
Sent-Bytes             568,044 #     Received-Bytes           990  #
Returned-Bytes       2,485,932 #     Reply-Bytes              990  #
LCB-Allocations          670   #     LCB-Alloc-Failures
LCBs-Inuse-Qtime        57.65  sec   Max-LCBs-Inuse             3  #
Checkpoints


Process   0,145             Pri 149    Program $SYSTEM.SYS21.SORTPROG
Userid    1,217   Creatorid 1,217      Ancestor 0,62
Local System \PSYCHO  From 9 Sep 1994, 12:51:25       For 25 Seconds

Cpu-Busy-Time            3.99  sec   Ready-Time              6.62  sec
Mem-Qtime              271.04  ms    Dispatches               541  #
Page-Faults              201   #     Vsems
Pres-Pages-Qtime         4,495 sec   Pres-Pages-Max           229  #
Ext-Segs-Qtime          71.18  sec   Ext-Segs-Max               3  #
Recv-Qtime               2.64  sec   Recv-Qlen-Max              1  #
Messages-Sent            88    #     Messages-Received        137  #
Sent-Bytes             606,642 #     Received-Bytes        542,606  #
Returned-Bytes         606,772 #     Reply-Bytes           540,728  #
LCB-Allocations          225   #     LCB-Alloc-Failures
LCBs-Inuse-Qtime        16.13  sec   Max-LCBs-Inuse             2  #
Checkpoints


Process   2,9      ($MOS23E) Pri 220    Program $SYSTEM. SYS21.OSIMAGE
Userid   255,255 Creatorid 255,255      Ancestor Unknown
Local System \PSYCHO From 9 Sep 1994, 12:51:20       For  30.5 Seconds

Cpu-Busy-Time            3.61  sec   Ready-Time              3.75  sec
Mem-Qtime                            Dispatches             1,234  #
Page-Faults                          Vsems
Pres-Pages-Qtime         6,528 sec   Pres-Pages-Max           245  #
```

```
Ext-Segs-Qtime        91.52 sec    Ext-Segs-Max                  3 #
Recv-Qtime            52.37 ms     Recv-Qlen-Max                 2 #
Messages-Sent             4 #      Messages-Received           484 #
Sent-Bytes            1,288 #      Received-Bytes           24,174 #
Returned-Bytes                     Reply-Bytes           1,919,712 #
LCB-Allocations         494 #      LCB-Alloc-Failures
LCBs-Inuse-Qtime       7.74 sec    Max-LCBs-Inuse                4 #
Checkpoints               3 #
```

If desired, further performance measurements can be explored, such as the amount of time spent waiting for logical and physical I/O on the table. For brevity, examples of these, and other measurements, are not included here.

Transaction Monitoring Facility (TMF)

The Transaction Monitoring Facility (TMF) provides recovery facilities for NonStop SQL and other data sources. Its primary purpose is to ensure the integrity of transactions, particularly if a media or other failure should occur. It provides for transaction management support (based on the X/Open model) and database recovery facilities.

Although a prerequisite for NonStop SQL, TMF protection is optional. When creating NonStop SQL tables, users can decide whether or not TMF protection is to apply to that table. The role of TMF for NonStop SQL is discussed more fully in the section "Backup and Recovery" later in this chapter.

As of this writing, Tandem recently announced a new product for transaction management and recovery. NonStop Transaction Manager/Massively Parallel (NonStop TM/MP), to be offered with newer releases of the NonStop Kernel operating system, provides function similar to TMF but includes some additional enhancements. Tandem is expected to provide a migration path for its customers. Since existing TMF applications are expected to be compatible with NonStop TM/MP, this chapter notes the TMF functions relevant to database management. Where appropriate, it also notes expected transaction management improvements in the new NonStop TM/MP product.

Remote Duplicate Database Facility (RDF)

The Remote Duplicate Database Facility (RDF) is an extension of TMF. It enables customers to maintain redundant copies of their databases in a highly automated fashion. It was primarily conceived as a means to support disaster recovery, wherein a remote location could stand ready to take over processing from another location should some serious problem occur. The function of this product is described in more detail in the section "Replication" later in this chapter.

PATHWAY

PATHWAY is an optional facility that enables programmers to develop requester/server applications for database access. Such applications typically separate the user interface (or terminal handling) procedures into a requester module, while the data access operations are coded into a server module. These modules may reside on different processors and use messages to communicate with one another. PATHWAY provides a means of centralized control over these requester/ server-based applications and also assists in load balancing. For example, if a particular PATHWAY server reaches peak activity, the PATHWAY environment can cause additional copies of the server to be created dynamically to handle the additional work. Similarly, users can create additional copies of the requesters, should additional terminals or transactions need to be accommodated.

With these hardware and operating system design points in mind, readers are now ready to delve further into the function offered by NonStop SQL. The remainder of this chapter discusses the third major release of this product.

DATA MANAGEMENT

NonStop SQL supports databases, tables, views, and indexes. It also supports partitions, which are of particular interest in distributed database and parallel processing environments. Such environments, and their use of partitions, are discussed later in sections on "Distributed Database" and "Parallelism."

Each NonStop SQL database may contain data that resides on multiple disks. A catalog exists for each database, and this may be placed on any desired disk. Each table corresponds to an operating system file within a given subdirectory and is tracked by at least one catalog.

NonStop SQL's naming convention for objects is derived from the NonStop Kernel operating system. With this operating system, files may be referred to by *node.disk_volume.subvolume.file*. The *node* is the name by which an individual system is known. (The reader will recall that each named Tandem system may consist of up to 16 processors. Many such nodes or systems may be interconnected to form a larger overall computing environment.) The *disk_volume* identifies a specific disk on that node. The *subvolume* refers to a specific area (or directory) on the disk where the desired *file* resides. Because NonStop SQL is highly integrated with the NonStop Kernel, its table naming convention is the same.

Databases

Although NonStop SQL actually lacks a CREATE DATABASE statement, administrators can apply many of the logical concepts of a database in a NonStop SQL environment. For example, administrators may create multiple catalogs, each of which will maintain data about a specific collection of tables or table partitions. Multiple catalogs may be created on a single disk, and tables associated with a given catalog may reside on any of a number of available disks.

The following example uses the CREATE CATALOG statement to create a new catalog called DINING, which will reside on the $VOL1 disk volume of the node currently executing this statement.

```
create catalog $vol1.dining
```

With this catalog created, users may create objects (such as tables) that will be tracked by this catalog. This is accomplished through the CATALOG clause of the CREATE TABLE statement. The following example creates a RATING table containing restaurant reviews; it will reside on disk volume $VOL2 in the FOOD subvolume. The final clause specifies that this table will be registered in the DINING catalog, which was previously created and resides on a separate disk.

```
create table $vol2.food.rating
        (rating_id    smallint    no default,
         rest_id      smallint    no default,
         value        smallint    no default,
         quality      smallint    no default,
         quantity     smallint    no default,
         ambiance     smallint    no default,
         overall      smallint    no default,
         meal_time    char(9)     default "dinner",
         date         date        no default,
         reviewer     smallint    no default)
catalog dining
```

This example also illustrates the use of a user-defined default value for the MEAL_TIME column. Optionally, this table could have been partitioned across multiple disks or multiple sites.

Each node also contains a master catalog, which notes information about the catalogs created on that node. This master catalog is considered to be a write-only file from NonStop SQL's point of view. However, administrators may read from it to locate all catalogs on this particular node.

Indexes

Tandem supports B-tree indexes for key-sequenced data. Indexes may be defined on a single column or multiple columns of a table (these columns need not be adjacent). Indexes may be unique or nonunique; they may also be clustered.

In addition, NonStop SQL enables users to define a primary key for key-sequenced tables. If none is defined, the system will automatically create a SYS-KEY column for the table to serve as its primary key. This SYSKEY value may also be used in a search predicate (if desired) in subsequent queries. Primary keys must be unique and cannot contain NULLs or be updated.

Users may also define clustering keys for key-sequenced tables to force related rows of a table to be stored physically close together. Clustering keys can be primary keys or a key based on any other column (or columns), even non-unique columns. If a clustering key is not defined on the primary key, NonStop SQL will attach a unique, system-generated value to the clustering key.

Tandem's support of alternate or secondary B-tree indexes is somewhat unusual and deserves a brief discussion. Alternate indexes will contain entries for data associated with primary keys. Assume a GRADE table has been defined for columns for student number (STU_NO), course number (CRSE_NO), and grade

(GR); see Table 13–1. Also assume that a STU table has been defined with the names (NAME) and numbers (STU_NO) of all students; see Table 13–2.

grade	stu_no	crse_no	gr
	003	p-207	81
	003	e-101	67
	143	h-105	95
	.	.	.
	.	.	.
	.	.	.

TABLE 13–1

stu	stu_no	name
	003	janice jacobs
	143	chris webb
	.	.
	.	.
	.	.

TABLE 13–2

The primary key of the STU table is STU_NO, and a B-tree index exists for this. The primary key of the GRADE table is a composite of the STU_NO and CRSE_NO columns, and a B-tree index exists for this. In addition, a secondary B-tree index is defined for the GR column. This B-tree index will contain data values from *both* the secondary key and the primary key, as shown below:

```
GR    STU_NO    CRSE_NO
81    003       P-207
67    003       E-101
95    143       H-105
(Sample Index Contents for Tables 13-1 and 13-2)
```

A query to locate the student numbers of all students with a grade of 90 or better in any course will use just the alternate index of the GRADE table. However, a query to find the student numbers and names of all students who have a grade of 90 or better will cause NonStop SQL to scan the alternate GRADE index for grades greater than 90. Next, it will use the STU_NO data for a given student (number 143, in the previous example) to scan the STU table's B-tree index on STU_NO to access the student's name.

Data Types

Data type support in NonStop SQL includes:

- CHAR, up to 4061 fixed-length characters.
- PIC X DISPLAY, same as CHAR.

- VARCHAR, varying-length character strings of up to 4059 characters.
- NUMERIC(1,s) to NUMERIC(18,s), binary numbers with an optional scale of s. May range from 1 to 18 digits (2 to 8 bytes).
- PIC S9V9 COMP to PIC S9(18) COMP, the same as NUMERIC.
- DECIMAL(1,s) to DECIMAL(18,s), decimal numbers with an optional scale of s that are stored as ASCII characters. May range from 1 to 18 digits (byte length equals the number of digits).
- PIC S9V9 DISPLAY to PIC S9(18) DISPLAY, the same as DECIMAL.
- SMALLINT, binary integers from -32,768 to 32,767.
- INTEGER, binary integers from -2,147,483,648 to 2,147,483,647.
- LARGEINT, binary integers from $-2**63$ to $2**63-1$.
- FLOAT(p), single-precision floating-point numbers with an optional precision of p. May be stored in 4 or 8 bytes.
- REAL, a 22-bit floating-point number providing approximately 7 decimal digits of precision.
- DOUBLE PRECISION, a 54-bit floating-point number providing approximately 16.5 decimal digits of precision.
- DATETIME, a specific point in time, including any subset of the following contiguous fields: YEAR, MONTH, DAY, HOUR, MINUTE, SECOND, and FRACTION of a second (up to 6 digits).
- TIMESTAMP, a specific point in time using all contiguous fields described for DATETIME.
- DATE, a specific point in time including the YEAR, MONTH, and DATE fields.
- TIME, time of day using a 24-hour clock. Uses the DATETIME HOUR, MINUTE, and SECOND fields.
- INTERVAL, a duration of time. The value is in the YEAR/MONTH range of the DAY/HOUR/MINUTE/SECOND/FRACTION range.

Integrity

A common integrity requirement involves the ability to specify the valid data values for a column. In NonStop SQL, this is accomplished through the CREATE CONSTRAINT statement. The example below shows how to ensure that the ID column of the CRITIC table will always contain a value between 0 and 9999. (The full table name is shown here; \SYS1 defines the node containing the data, $VOL1 defines the volume, DINING defines the subvolume or directory, and CRITIC defines the table or file. Specifying the full name is optional.)

```
create constraint valid_critic_id
on \sys1.$vol.dining.critic
check id > 0 and id < 9999
```

Expressions and calculations may also be included in the constraint specification.

Storage Structures

When creating tables, users may choose from three file structures: key-sequenced, entry-sequenced, or relative files. Rows in key-sequenced tables are ordered by primary key values, and B-tree access is supported. Rows in entry-sequenced tables are inserted only at the end of the file, and records cannot grow once inserted. Rows in relative tables are directly addressable records. Key-sequenced files are the default storage mechanism for NonStop SQL. When necessary, Non-Stop SQL generates unique keys for each table (regardless of which storage method is used).

Tables may also be divided into a number of partitions, enabling users to place different portions of the table on different devices. The length of the primary key determines the maximum number of partitions for a given table. Partitioning a table is particularly helpful for leveraging parallel processing, which is discussed later in the section "Parallelism." Each partition may contain up to 2 GB, and the maximum size of each table is 2 GB multiplied by the maximum number of allowable partitions. Tables are limited to 255 columns with a maximum row size of 4062 bytes.

ADMINISTRATION

As mentioned previously, NonStop SQL is highly integrated with Tandem's Non-Stop Kernel operating system. Effective administration of the DBMS involves use of these native facilities for security, recovery, and other purposes, as this section discusses.

Security

Security is one issue of concern to administrators and one in which NonStop SQL relies upon operating system facilities. Because of this reliance, NonStop SQL does not conform to ANSI/ISO SQL standards in the security arena. There are no GRANT/REVOKE statements for privileges in NonStop SQL. The security scheme is built around standard NonStop Kernel file protection mechanisms; in addition, those sites that purchase Tandem's SAFEGUARD security software may also use its facilities against NonStop SQL data.

The Tandem security scheme bears some similarity to that of certain midrange operating systems. Data access privileges involve reads, writes, execution, and purges. NonStop Kernel users can issue commands to reveal the privileges associated with any file. Figure 13–2 attempts to map Tandem security mechanisms to SQL equivalents common in other commercial relational DBMSs.

```
TANDEM PRIVILEGE                    POSSIBLE SQL EQUIVALENT
_____                _____

READ (R)                            GRANT/REVOKE SELECT
WRITE (W)                           GRANT/REVOKE INSERT, UPDATE, DELETE
EXECUTE (E)                         GRANT/REVOKE EXECUTE
PURGE (P)                           GRANT/REVOKE CREATE ..., DROP ...


TANDEM LOCAL USERS                  POSSIBLE OEM EQUIVALENT
_____                _____

SUPER.SUPER (-)                     System Administrator
OWNER (O)                           Object Owner
GROUP (G)                           Group, secondary authorization ID
ANY USER (A)                        PUBLIC


TANDEM DISTRIB SYSTEM USERS         POSSIBLE OEM EQUIVALENT
_____        _____

USER (U)                            Object Owner
COMMUNITY (C)                       Group, secondary authorization IDs
NETWORK (N)                         PUBLIC
```

Figure 13–2. Comparing Tandem security terminology to possible OEM terminology

Note that Tandem has two separate user classifications: one for local systems only and one for systems participating in a distributed environment.

Interpreting Tandem's security may seem a bit strange to a someone with strictly an SQL background. But it may be very easy to those familiar with certain workstation and midrange operating systems, particularly VMS from DEC. Using a NonStop Kernel command (FILEINFO), a user might obtain this output describing the security levels of the RATING table:

```
> fileinfo $vol2.dining.rating

Code    EOF     Last Modif    Owner     RWEP    . . . . .
101     5324    9-May-94      24,206    NGOO
```

This output shows that user 206 in group 24 owns the table. (Another command could be issued to retrieve the name of this user.) Any user (local or remote) can read the table, all members of group 206 (a local group) can write to the table, and only the owner can purge or drop the table.

Because Tandem's security scheme is based on operating system components, it applies only to physical objects (tables). Privileges cannot be granted against views directly, but only to the tables (files) underlying them. In addition, write access is used to address three different SQL operations: insert, update, and delete.

Auditing is another topic related to security. (The term is used here to discuss the ability to track events that occurred in the DBMS; it should *not* be confused with how Tandem uses the term to refer to logging or journaling facilities.)

Some support for auditing NonStop SQL objects is provided through SAFE-GUARD. This audits user log-on attempts (to NonStop Kernel) and disk file activities, such as attempts to access a file or to change security attributes for a file. It does not provide SQL statement granularity. For example, an administrator could use SAFEGUARD to determine that a given user wrote to TABLE5, but this administrator could not determine if that write involved an INSERT, UPDATE, or DELETE statement.

Concurrency Control

Tandem uses disk processes to manage locks. Although these disk processes may use more than 20 different modes of locks, only two are visible to NonStop SQL programmers: share locks (for reading data) and exclusive locks (for writing data).

Row locks, generic locks, and partition locks are used to provide different levels of granularity. Row-level locks affect a single row, while partition locks affect a single partition. Locking the entire table is achieved by acquiring locks on all its partitions.

Generic locks, available for key-sequenced tables, offer a different level of granularity: they affect a series of rows that have the same primary key. The *lock length* parameter of generic locking enables a programmer to specify the granularity of the key. (For example, a 10-character key value with a lock length of three would cause the system to lock all rows whose first three bytes matched the user-defined search argument.) To some degree, generic locking can be compared to page-level locking in that it usually locks more than a single data row and less than an entire table. However, generic locking provides users with more control over how much data is locked than can be achieved with page-level locking. Generic locking is requested in a NonStop SQL data definition language (DDL) statement.

Figure 13–3 illustrates the data that might be locked by a SELECT statement when row locks, generic locks, and partition locks are used. (Here, the BOOKS table is presumed to consist of a single partition.)

This figure presumes that the system is using the default lock isolation level of providing *stable* access (or cursor stability). *Repeatable access* (or repeatable read) is also supported. In addition, NonStop SQL offers a *browse access* level of isolation. Transactions operating under this mode acquire no locks at all; in this way, they can read data that other transactions have changed but not committed (and may never commit at all). Users may be subjected to viewing "dirty" data and, as a result, this is *not* the default isolation level. However, it is an appealing option to users who demand high concurrency and aren't planning to make critical decisions with the data they are browsing.

The NonStop SQL optimizer, discussed later in the section "Performance," normally selects the appropriate lock mode and lock level for each SQL statement. However, the disk processes that manage locking can alter this selection if needed. This might be the case if too many row-level locks are acquired; the disk process can automatically escalate these locks to a coarser level of granularity.

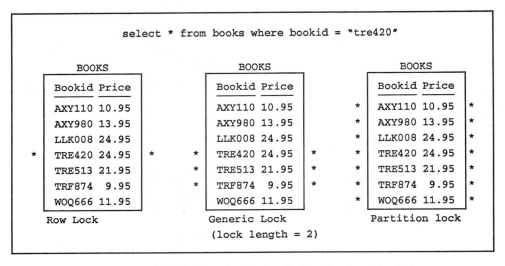

```
                    select * from books where bookid = "tre420"
```

Figure 13–3. Data locked as a result of various lock modes. Asterisks show rows that are locked.

Another means of providing for high concurrency is to control the length of time spent waiting for locked resources. A CONTROL TABLE statement enables programmers to avoid ever waiting for a locked resource. (Doing so is sometimes referred to as using a *bounce lock*.) When a needed resource is locked, NonStop SQL will not wait for it to become available. Instead, it will return immediately to the application, raising an exception (or error). The application can then take appropriate action. Proper use of the CONTROL TABLE statement can be particularly useful for sophisticated customers who want to fine-tune their systems, as it operates on an SQL statement basis (rather than on a table, transaction, or application basis).

Like many other DBMSs, NonStop SQL also gives programmers control over when to acquire and release locks. Deadlocks are resolved through time-outs.

Backup and Recovery

TMF is the primary means for recovery of NonStop SQL data. By default, NonStop SQL tables are subject to TMF logging (or *auditing,* as Tandem calls it). All updates affecting logged tables are part of a TMF transaction, and log records are automatically generated. TMF is a prerequisite for NonStop SQL because all catalog tables are subject to TMF auditing.

Administrators may opt not to activate logging for specific tables, although Tandem does not recommend doing so. Nonaudited tables can be updated outside the scope of a transaction. Even if changes are made to nonaudited tables within a transaction, the normal transaction properties do not apply. For example, if the transaction is rolled back, the changes to the nonaudited table will still be applied. In addition, nonaudited tables cannot make use of the online dump facility of TMF (for backups) or its automatic recovery mechanisms, both of which are described shortly. Thus, turning off logging for a specific table can prevent the system from being able to recover that table from certain kinds of failures.

Before discussing NonStop SQL's recovery abilities further, it's important to note that the overall architecture of Tandem systems provides for automatic recovery from any single hardware failure and from many software failures. This is because of its use of redundant components as well as its notion of process pairs; these features were discussed briefly in the section "Hardware Introduction."

TMF maintains a log (which Tandem refers to as an *audit trail*) that records before- and after-image copies of new or changed data, as well as information about when checkpoints (or *control points*) were taken. To improve performance, group commit processing is supported. For added safety, the log is kept on a disk that is separate from the databases. When certain types of failures occur, TMF will automatically recover the database to a consistent state (once a system operator has started TMF).

To recover from media loss or corruption, users can rely on the *roll-forward recovery* capabilities of TMF. Here, backup copies of audited database files are applied, as well as appropriate log records. This returns the database to its most current status before the failure. Recovery to a specific point in time is also supported.

Database files can be backed up to tape using the *online dump* (OLD) facility of TMF. These files may include individual tables, specific partitions of a given table, or indexes. Dumps are taken when the database is online and in use. These are sometimes called *fuzzy* dumps.

The BACKUP and RESTORE utilities can be helpful for protecting nonaudited tables against media failure. When users are not updating such a table, the BACKUP utility may be run to create a copy of it on tape. Later, it can be restored if necessary. However, any updates that occurred to the table since its last backup will be lost.

High availability—or the ability to recover quickly from unplanned outages (such as natural disasters)—has been another area of focus for Tandem. RDF provides for "hot site" backups to minimize down time should a severe problem occur at one location. RDF enables a primary site to replicate data at a remote location so that the remote site can stand ready to take over operations should some significant failure befall the primary site. An extension of TMF, RDF's replication facilities are discussed in more detail in the section "Replication."

NonStop TM/MP supports *overflow audit volumes* that can be used if all active log files (or audit files) become full. This helps promote availability, as activities involving logged files would otherwise have to stop if no space were available in the active log. When NonStop TM/MP reaches a user-defined overflow threshold, it copies the oldest log file from its active volume to an overflow volume. In this way, DBMS applications are less likely to be stopped because of lack of space for log records.

Other Issues

A related function is support for continuous operations, which enables users to access and update data while regular maintenance operations are being conducted. A key component of supporting continuous operations is support for online utilities. NonStop SQL provides online support for creating indexes, copying data, reorganizing the database, recovering data and indexes, modifying partitions, and renaming objects.

In addition, NonStop SQL features a PURGEDATA PARTONLY command that enables users to quickly purge the data in a single partition of a logged table. In some other systems, this is accomplished by issuing a DELETE statement, but that can generate substantial log activity. The PURGEDATA command minimizes log activity, accomplishing the delete operation more quickly.

QUERY CAPABILITIES

The current version of NonStop SQL includes support for nulls, unions, date/time data, and outer joins—all elements of various levels of the ANSI/ISO SQL standard.

Outer joins are supported through the use of the LEFT JOIN clause in the SELECT statement. The following query performs an outer join on the RESTAURANT table (which lists the names, addresses, phone numbers, and other information about various restaurants) and the RATING table (which contains critiques of various restaurants). Here, the name and address of each restaurant will be returned, along with its overall rating. If no rating exists, a null value will be returned for that column (usually represented as a question mark in the printed version of the report).

```
select name, street_address, overall
from restaurant, rating
left join rating
on restaurant.id = rating.rest_id
```

An additional query capability enables users to rename objects without forcing them to drop, recreate, and secure the object. This rename facility was created to handle ENSCRIBE data (a Tandem nonrelational DBMS) and has been incorporated into NonStop SQL.

A previous section of this chapter ("Data Management") illustrated how NonStop SQL supports default values. When creating tables, users may define defaults for various columns in lieu of using nulls. If a row is inserted that does not contain values for these columns, NonStop SQL will automatically store the default for each.

In addition to interactive queries, Tandem supports embedded SQL access through COBOL, C, and Pascal. The NonStop ODBC Server, a separately purchased product, provides a call-level interface to NonStop SQL data. Both the Sybase DB-Library (Open Client) and Microsoft ODBC call-level interfaces are supported through this product. As mentioned earlier, Tandem users may also purchase PATHWAY for generating screen-based applications.

DISTRIBUTED DATABASE

Distributed database support was one of the original design goals of NonStop SQL, and it has included a significant number of distributed database capabilities since its first release in 1987. Most of these apply to homogeneous (NonStop SQL-to-NonStop SQL) systems and are discussed in this section. Gateway support is described in a later section on "Gateways and Middleware."

NonStop SQL supports multisite reads (or internode reads) within a single query statement as well as multisite updates (or internode updates) within a single transaction. Two-phase commit processing, as well as presumed-abort protocols, is automatically supported in a manner that is transparent to programmers. This is distributed request processing, as defined in Chapter 7, "Distributed Databases."

The ability to support distributed requests means that Tandem users can join data from multiple nodes. This example shows how a NonStop SQL user might retrieve data from two tables at different nodes (installed in different cities) using a single SELECT statement:

```
select name, phone, meal_time, overall, date
from \node1.$disk4.dining.restaurant,
     \node2.$disk3.reviews.rating
where restaurant.id = rating.rest_id
and city = "PARIS"
and country = "FRANCE"
```

Because NonStop SQL supports distributed requests, users can create views based on joins of tables located at any nodes in the system—local or remote. This example shows how to create a BEST_BETS view based on two tables (RESTAURANT and RATING) that reside on two different nodes:

```
create view \node1.$vol1.dining.best_bets
    (name, phone, cuisine, pricing, value, quality, quantity,
    ambiance, meal_rated, date)
as select a.name, a.phone, a.cuisine, a.pricing,
       b.value, b.quality, b.quantity, b.ambiance,
       b.meal_rated, b.date
from \node1.$vol1.dining.restaurant a,
     \node7.$vol4.dining.rating b
where a.id = b.rest_id
catalog \node1.$vol1.dining
```

Transparency

For users who don't want to use full object names in queries, NonStop SQL provides a DEFINE mechanism to make the location of the data transparent. This mechanism is similar in function to aliases supported by other vendors, except that DEFINE is not recorded in the system catalog and therefore are coded into each application that wishes to use them.

A NonStop SQL programmer seeking to create a more flexible application might first create a series of DEFINEs to specify the full names of the objects to which he or she will refer in the application. For example, if the program must query the RESTAURANT table, managed by the SF node, a programmer might write this statement:

```
define =rest, file \sf.$disk1.dining.restaurant
```

The body of the program would refer to the RESTAURANT table simply as "=rest", forcing the system to translate this variable into its full name (at compile or run time). For example, a SELECT statement against the RESTAURANT table might now be written as:

```
select name, phone from =rest where cuisine="italian"
```

Partitioned or Distributed Tables

Another distributed database feature offered to NonStop SQL users is the ability to create tables and indexes that are partitioned across multiple nodes. Partitioning is often used on a single node to place data in a single table on different disks, perhaps to reduce contention and improve performance. The same concept applies in a distributed database environment. In this case, NonStop SQL enables administrators to partition (or split) data in a single table horizontally across multiple nodes, which may be located in different cities. Thus, rows of a table can be placed closest to those most likely to access it.

Consider an insurance company with branch offices; although the company may wish to maintain a single CLIENTS table, it might like each of its branches to have top response time when accessing data related to its local customers. Partitioning the table across multiple systems can help solve this problem. The example below illustrates how to create a CLIENTS table, partitioning the data across two sites. Since policy numbers (POLICY) greater than 1000 are handled by personnel at Site 2, these rows are placed at that location.

```
create table \site1.$vol3.corp.clients
   (policy     integer,
    type       char(15),
    clientid   integer,
    salesrep   char(20),
    key (policy))
catalog \site1.$vol3.corp
partition
    (\site2.$disk5.branch.clients
     catalog \site2.$disk5.branch
     first key 1000)
```

Support for multi-site partitioning often leads people to wonder if local autonomy has been violated. For example, if Table A is divided between Site 1 and Site 2, and Site 1 retained the sole definition of this object, users at Site 2 would not be able to access the local rows of Table A if Site 1 were to become disconnected from the network. Making Site 2 dependent on Site 1 violates one of the common design goals of a distributed database.

To resolve this, NonStop SQL replicates catalog data about the partitioned object at every node involved. Thus, local users always have access to local data, even for objects partitioned across multiple nodes. However, this design has an impact on data definition statements, since creating or dropping a partitioned object requires changes to catalogs at multiple nodes. Here, NonStop SQL has chosen to violate local autonomy by refusing to execute DDL statements unless all affected sites are available. The alternative—to allow local DDL execution anyway—would preserve local autonomy at the expense of system integrity.

GATEWAYS AND MIDDLEWARE

Much of Tandem's focus to date on distributed database support had related primarily to homogeneous environments (where multiple NonStop SQL DBMSs can communicate with one another to satisfy various user requests). However, NonStop SQL is not confined to working strictly in a homogeneous environment. In the early 1990s, Tandem announced gateways between its NonStop SQL DBMS and those offered by Oracle and Sybase. In addition, some third-party vendors provide gateways or middleware offerings that provide connectivity to Tandem's DBMS.

More recently, Tandem announced a NonStop ODBC Server. Although not strictly a middleware offering (as the term has been used in this book), the product does enhance client application access to Tandem data. Applications running on Windows can access NonStop SQL data.

REPLICATION

As this chapter has already noted, Tandem supports data replication through RDF. Unlike many of the other snapshot and replication offerings profiled in this book, RDF focuses primarily on supporting disaster recovery. Nonetheless, the product can be used for other purposes as well, such as maintaining a local copy of a remote database for decision support use. However, doing so requires some consideration, as is discussed later in this section.

Administrators identify one or more sites as the primary location, and another site as a backup or secondary location. Disk volumes at the primary sites are identified for replication. Since RDF is an extension of TMF, only the audited tables stored on these disk volumes (or tables for which changes are logged) are actually replicated. (A future release of RDF is expected to support Tandem's NonStop TM/MP as well as TMF.)

Figure 13–4 illustrates the architecture and replication process used by RDF. RDF relies on an *extractor* process to read the TMF log (or audit trail) from disk to capture changes made to databases at a primary site (1). RDF then copies these

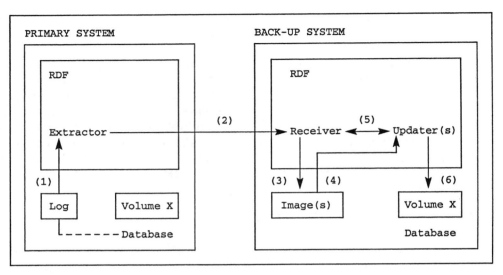

Figure 13–4.   Overview of RDF

records immediately to the backup site (2). When a transaction commits, TMF writes the appropriate record in its log and then waits for RDF to copy this commit record to an image file at the backup site. If desired, users can reset a configuration option to avoid this wait period.

A *receiver* process at the backup site receives the data, storing it in RDF image files (3). One or more *updater* processes also run at the backup site. (At least one updater process exists for each primary disk volume that is replicated.) The updater processes read the RDF image files, looking for data changes affecting the primary disk with which they're associated (4). When a record is found, the updater consults with the receiver process to determine the status of the transaction that caused the data change (5). The receiver keeps this status information in memory to speed processing. Once the updater learns whether the transaction has been committed or aborted, it can take appropriate action. If the transaction committed, the updater modifies the backup database accordingly (6). If the transaction aborted, the updater ignores its work and does not apply it to the backup database.

As mentioned earlier, RDF was originally designed with disaster recovery in mind. Although it can be used for decision support work, users who do so should be aware of certain considerations. For example, the backup database may be slightly "stale," as the primary site will not wait until the updates have been applied to the backup database (only until the updates have been applied to the RDF image files). In many cases, this may not be a problem. A further consideration is that RDF does not cause locks to be held at the backup site while updater processes are updating the database. Among other things, this means that a query against the backup database may see only partial effects of a transaction.

A future release of RDF is expected to support multiple backup databases (or secondary sites).

Independent of RDF, NonStop SQL also provides for automatic, synchronous replication of catalog data in which tables are partitioned across multiple sites. This is necessary to support distributed database processing, as discussed earlier.

PERFORMANCE

NonStop SQL includes a number of features designed to help users obtain good performance. Among these are support for static SQL, rebinding options, an EXPLAIN command, and a facility for feeding the optimizer hints. Parallel processing, also an important means of improving performance, is discussed later in the section "Parallelism."

Like certain other DBMSs, NonStop SQL enables users to code static (or compiled) SQL. Programmers then compile and *bind* these applications, forcing the optimizer to determine an access path and store this for possible reuse later.

NonStop SQL also includes a number of compilation options designed to improve performance and availability. For example, programmers using static SQL can instruct NonStop SQL to resolve object names at execution time instead of at compile time. In this way, programs can be executed against different tables (perhaps in different databases) than the tables for which they were initially compiled, provided both sets of tables have identical schemas. This can be helpful for migrating applications from a test environment to a production environment without incurring the expense of additional recompilation. Another feature of NonStop SQL involves the ability to tolerate certain data definition language (DDL) statements—which might include the addition of a partition or an index—without invalidating the program's execution plan and automatically recompiling the program. Additional compilation options are also supported; see "References and Suggested Reading" for more information.

Like other DBMSs, NonStop SQL provides a facility to determine the access path selected by the optimizer, which can help users evaluate the effectiveness of their database design. This is accomplished through the EXPLAIN command, which will note the type of operation performed (such as a table scan or nested loop), the percentage of rows in the table expected to be selected, the type of lock mode in use, whether or not the query predicate was evaluated by a disk process, and other data.

To help the optimizer select an efficient access path, accurate catalog statistics are necessary. Users may invoke the UPDATE STATISTICS utility to periodically update these statistics. Administrators have two options for regulating how statistics are collected: EXACT and SAMPLE <n> BLOCKS. EXACT gathers statistics based on all actual data values. SAMPLE <n> BLOCKS gathers statistics for the specified number of blocks. If neither option is specified, NonStop SQL will read all rows for partitions of 1000 blocks or less. If the size of a partition exceeds 1000 blocks, an average of 500 blocks is read per partition. If the table is not partitioned, all rows in up to 1000 blocks are read. (Blocks are 4K in size, by default).

NonStop SQL's optimizer is capable of performing nested loop, hash, and sort/merge processing of joins. Some variations on these—such as a hybrid hash join—are supported as well. However, a discussion of these features is beyond the scope of this book. Readers are encouraged to consult the sources cited in "References and Suggested Reading." For joins spanning local and remote tables (or partitions), NonStop SQL's optimizer makes certain assumptions about the cost of accessing the remote data and factors these assumptions into its evaluation of access alternatives.

As noted earlier, NonStop SQL includes a CONTROL TABLE statement for tuning purposes. This statement may be used to influence the optimizer's access path (perhaps by instructing the optimizer to select the best path for retrieving the first few rows quickly rather than selecting one that minimizes total execution time). If desired, users can invoke the CONTROL TABLE statement to force NonStop SQL to choose a specific access path (such as using a given index or performing a certain type of join operation).

The following example illustrates how the CONTROL TABLE statement might be used to instruct NonStop SQL to use the REST_INX when accessing data in the RESTAURANT table.

```
control table restaurant access path index rest_inx
```

CONTROL TABLE also permits NonStop SQL programmers to control lock wait durations, lock modes, and lock isolation levels. This example shows how an application might override default wait times on a query:

```
control table rating wait if locked timeout 1.5 seconds
```

In addition, information about locked resources can be obtained from various operating system components and additional products. For example, the File Utility Program (FUP) contains a LISTLOCKS command that shows locks currently held, as well as processes that are waiting for locks. This information can apply to all tables on a given disk volume, or to a single table. Measure can report on the number of requests per disk volume that were blocked (because a resource was locked) and the number of lock escalations that occurred (if any) for a given SQL statement. Furthermore, SQL performance statistics are available to the application independent of the Measure facility. These statistics include the elapsed and CPU time for a query, the names of tables accessed, the number of rows examined and used, the disk reads for each table, and so forth.

To further improve performance, NonStop SQL supports *sequential block buffering*. This mechanism enables blocks of data (rather than individual rows) to be returned from disk to a system process. Both *physical* buffering (which returns a physical data page) and *virtual* buffering (which returns selections and projections of data) are supported. The system can filter data at the disk process level, reducing the amount of data that must be transmitted to higher levels of the DBMS for additional processing. For example, in certain circumstances the system performs projections and aggregations (GROUP BY) at the disk process level. For batch applications, the system can take advantage of the bulk I/O capability of the NonStop Kernel operating system, which transfers either 28K or 56K of data with one I/O. Bulk I/O is used by the NonStop SQL optimizer to perform sequential prefetch.

PARALLELISM

Tandem has supported parallel database processing since its first release of Non-Stop SQL. The product supports both parallel transaction processing (sometimes called *interquery parallelism*) as well as parallel query processing (sometimes called *intraquery parallelism*). As the reader will recall, parallel transaction processing enables a system to process multiple transactions simultaneously. Parallel query processing enables a system to use multiple processors to work on a single query simultaneously. This can involve dividing a single query into subtasks, each of which is performed by different processors in parallel, or it can involve replicating the query across processors, with each performing the work against its portion of the data in parallel. If appropriate, all processors within a node can be used to support parallel transaction and parallel query processing.

Figure 13–5 illustrates a situation in which NonStop SQL is processing multiple transactions in parallel. Here, the Tandem system has been configured with four processors. In this case, NonStop SQL is processing two different transactions in parallel, each of which is working with different tables. (Parallel transaction processing can also be used if multiple transactions are working with different partitions of the same table, provided each is on a different disk managed by a different processor.)

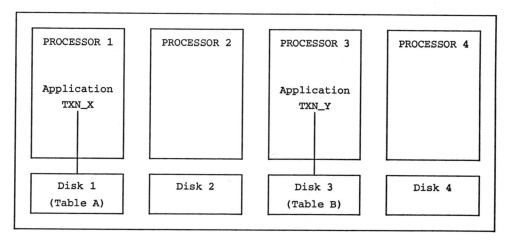

Figure 13–5. Processing two transactions in parallel

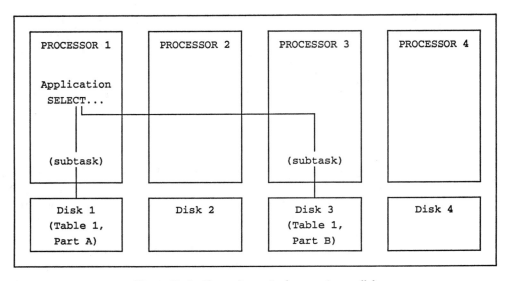

Figure 13–6.   Processing a single query in parallel

NonStop SQL can also use multiple processors to work in parallel on behalf of a single query, as shown in Figure 13–6. Again, the system shown here uses four processors. In this case, one table is partitioned across disks associated with two processors. The query might require NonStop SQL to read data from both partitions (perhaps to perform a full table scan); this can be done simultaneously to improve performance. (Parallel query processing can also be applied when a single query needs to access data from two or more tables, each of which resides on different disks managed by different processors.)

NonStop SQL's support for parallel query processing is not limited to read-only operations (or SELECT statements). Write operations (INSERT, UPDATE, and DELETE statements) can also be processed in parallel.

To enable parallel query processing, programmers must issue a specific instruction (CONTROL EXECUTOR PARALLEL EXECUTION ON) before compiling the query. Although this may seem a bit unusual, it provides customers with an additional tuning mechanism. In some situations, customers may determine that maximizing transaction throughput (or being able to service a larger number of transactions) is of greater importance than minimizing response time to a particular query. The CONTROL EXECUTOR mechanism allows them to do so (by determining whether or not parallel query processing is enabled). It should be noted that enabling parallelism does not always mean that the optimizer will choose parallel access. The actual access strategy selected depends on a number of factors, but parallel processing is considered as an alternative.

NonStop SQL's parallel query processing features support for parallel joins. A number of join processing strategies are supported, and their use depends, in part, on how the data is partitioned. A discussion of NonStop SQL's approach to parallel join processing is beyond the scope of this book; however, readers are encouraged to consult material cited in "References and Suggested Reading."

In addition to support for parallel transaction processing and parallel query processing, NonStop SQL also provides parallel index maintenance. If a write operation occurs involving a table on which multiple indexes have been defined and these indexes reside on disks managed by different processors, NonStop SQL can update the different indexes in parallel. The system will also perform parallel processing in support of sort operations when the FASTSORT PARALLEL option is used.

Figure 13–7 illustrates a configuration in which there are four processors, each with its own disk. On one disk is Table A, and on each of the other three disks is one of the indexes for Table A. When an INSERT operation occurs on Table 1, the process of modifying the table and its associated indexes is done in parallel. This occurs automatically, regardless of whether or not parallel query processing has been turned on.

As the reader has probably surmised, the way in which data (in both tables and indexes) is partitioned across the system plays a significant role in determining how effectively NonStop SQL may use parallel-processing techniques for either speeding up existing workloads or scaling to meet the needs of increased workloads. Administrators may use range partitioning for their NonStop SQL databases. Partitioned tables need not be located on nodes at the same site; partitions located at different sites can also be processed in parallel. In addition, administrators can partition the schema of their databases, perhaps storing a table on one disk and its indexes on other disks.

If administrators do not partition their data, or if they partition their data in such a way that is ineffective for a given query, NonStop SQL's optimizer may instruct other system components to *dynamically* repartition the data at run time. The optimizer does so only when it expects that the cost of repartitioning the data and processing the query over the resulting temporary set of partitions is less than the cost of processing the query given the current distribution of the data. In such

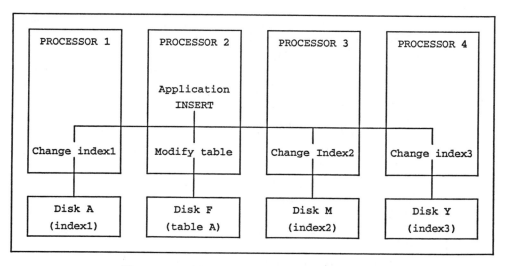

Figure 13–7. Maintaining multiple indexes in parallel

cases, the data is temporarily repartitioned (using a hash technique) over disks associated with all processors in the node.

SUMMARY

This chapter described Tandem's NonStop SQL/MP, a relational DBMS that runs on the NonStop operating system (formerly known as the Guardian 90 operating system). Because many of the product's key functions are derived from its exploitation of Tandem hardware and native operating system services, an introduction to both of these areas was provided. Key DBMS functions were explained in some detail, including lock management, recovery, integrity, and other areas. Emphasis was also placed on understanding Tandem's support for distributed databases and parallel processing, as the vendor was an earlier commercial implementer of these technologies. Related products in such areas as transaction management, replication, and performance tuning were also discussed.

REFERENCES AND SUGGESTED READING

BORR, ANDREA. "Technical Paper: High-Performance SQL Through Low-Level System Integration," *Tandem Systems Review*, July 1988, p. 52.

CHANDRA, MALA, and DAVE EICHER. "Enhancing Availability, Manageability, and Performance for NonStop TM/MP," *Tandem Systems Review*, July 1994, p. 58.

COHEN, HOWARD. "Overview of NonStop SQL," *Tandem Systems Review*, July 1988, p. 2.

Concepts and Facilities Student Text, Tandem Computers, Part No. 21620, 1989.

ENGLERT, SUSANNE, and JIM GRAY. "Performance Benefits of Parallel Query Execution and Mixed Workload Support in NonStop SQL Release 2," *Tandem Systems Review*, October 1990, p. 12.

ENGLERT, SUSANNE, JIM GRAY, TERRYE KOCHER, and PRAFUL SHAH. "The NonStop SQL Release 2 Benchmark," *Tandem Systems Review*, October 1990, p. 24.

FENNER, CLAUDE. "NonStop SQL Reliability," *Tandem Systems Review*, July 1988, p. 39.

GRAY, JIM. "A Census of Tandem System Availability Between 1985 and 1990," *IEEE Transactions on Reliability*, vol. 39, no. 4, October 1990.

GUERRERO, JORGE. "RDF: An Overview," *Tandem Systems Review*, October 1991, p. 34.

HO, FRED, ROHIT JAIN, and JIM TROISI. "An Overview of NonStop SQL/MP," *Tandem Systems Review*, July 1994, p. 6.

HOLBROOK, ROB, and DON-MIN TSOU. "NonStop SQL Data Dictionary," *Tandem Systems Review*, July 1988, p. 52.

LYON, JIM. "Tandem's Remote Data Facility," *Digest of Papers, COMP Spring 90*, Thirty-Fifth IEEE Computer Society International Conference, IEEE Computer Society Press, Feb. 26–March 2, 1990.

MAHBOD, HALEH, and DONALD SLUTZ. "NonStop ODBC Server," *Tandem Systems Review*, July 1994, p. 40.

MOORE, MARK, and AMARDEEP SODHI. "Parallelism in NonStop SQL Release 2," *Tandem Systems Review*, October 1990, p. 36.

MOSHER, MALCOLM JR. "RDF Enhancements for High Availability and Performance," *Tandem Systems Review,* July 1994, p. 68.

NonStop SQL, A Distributed, High-Performance, High-Availability Implementation of SQL, Tandem Computers, Technical Report 87.4, Part Number 83061, April, 1994.

PONG, MIKE. "An Overview of NonStop SQL Release 2," *Tandem Systems Review,* October 1990, p. 4.

PONG, MIKE. "NonStop SQL Optimizer: Basic Concepts," *Tandem Systems Review,* July 1988, p. 14.

PONG, MIKE. "NonStop SQL Optimizer: Query Optimization and User Influence," *Tandem Systems Review,* July 1988, p. 22.

SENF, WOUTER. "Concurrency Control Aspects of Transaction Design," *Tandem Systems Review,* March 1990, p. 46.

SHARMA, SUNIL. "Late Binding and High Availability Compilation in NonStop SQL/MP," *Tandem System Review,* vol. 10, no. 4, October 1994.

SLUTZ, DON. "Gateways to NonStop SQL," *Tandem Systems Review,* October 1990, p. 76.

SMITH, GARY S. "Online Reorganization of Key-Sequenced Tables and Files," *Tandem Systems Review,* October 1990, p. 52.

TRIOSI, JIM. "NonStop Availability and Database Configuration Operations," *Tandem Systems Review,* July 1994, p. 18.

VAISHNAV, JAY. "The Outer Join in NonStop SQL," *Tandem Systems Review,* October 1990, p. 60.

CHAPTER 14
Oracle's Oracle

CHAPTER OBJECTIVES

This chapter describes Oracle's relational DBMS and a number of related offerings. It discusses major areas of product function, including those that provide for lock management, resource management, backup and recovery, data integrity, security, query support, and performance tuning. Additionally, there is discussion of Oracle technology that supports replication, middleware, distributed databases, and parallelism.

This chapter provides the reader with insight into how a commercial DBMS product has actually implemented the technologies discussed earlier in this book.

OVERVIEW OF DBMS AND RELATED PRODUCTS

Since its foundation in 1977, Oracle has grown from a small start-up company in Northern California to one of the largest independent software vendors in the world. The company enjoys a sizable installation base spanning more than 80 different computing platforms.

In 1979, Oracle became the first company to offer a commercially available, SQL-driven relational DBMS, basing its product on technical papers by Dr. E. F. Codd, who invented the relational database model while at IBM Research. After establishing a foothold among VAX/VMS users, Oracle began porting its DBMS to numerous hardware and software platforms—a practice it continues today, as its products span from massively parallel processing systems to small desktop systems. In addition to its DBMS, Oracle offers various end-user tools, application development tools, application packages, and networking interfaces. Most can be tied together to support client/server computing and distributed database technologies.

In addition to marketing its own products, Oracle has signed numerous joint marketing agreements with hardware vendors, including DEC, Sun, and Sequent. It has also prompted a number of third-party vendors and value-added resellers to support its products.

Its product line is broad, featuring a set of tools common to most Oracle-supported platforms, a set of turnkey application packages, a set of computer-aided software engineering (CASE) tools, a series of precompilers for third-generation programming languages, a set of gateway and connectivity products, and some specialized tools for PCs, the Macintosh, and portable computers. A number of these products are part of Oracle's Cooperative Development Environment (CDE), which attempts to provide an integrated set of offerings that span the application development life cycle.

Oracle's tools and applications support the Oracle DBMS or server. (In some cases, Oracle products also support non-Oracle DBMSs.) The Oracle7 DBMS (or Oracle Version 7) may be purchased with the Distributed Option (which supports distributed database access and replication), the Parallel Server Option (which supports parallel transaction processing), and/or the Parallel Query Option (which supports parallel execution of queries, data loading, and index creation). In addition, a high-security version of the Oracle DBMS is available as Trusted Oracle.

Figure 14–1 illustrates some of the tools, applications, and other offerings available from Oracle for Oracle7.

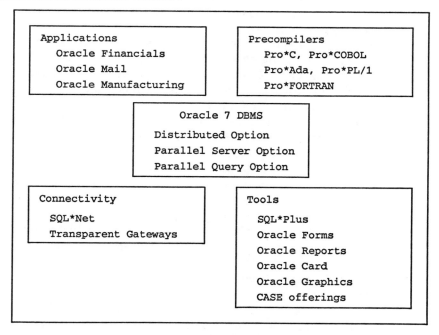

Figure 14–1. Overview of Oracle product line. Not all products offered by Oracle are shown.

The remainder of this chapter focuses on Oracle7, including release 7.1. When applicable, information about expected enhancements in future Oracle releases is also discussed.

DATA MANAGEMENT

Like most relational DBMSs, Oracle supports multiple databases, tables, views, and indexes per system. Each database contains a set of system catalog tables, a log, certain Oracle software files, a control file, and user data.

User data—such as indexes and tables—is associated with *tablespaces*, which are logical storage structures that make use of one or more physical files (stored on one or more disks). At a minimum, each database contains at least one tablespace—the SYSTEM tablespace, which is automatically created for new databases. The SYSTEM tablespace contains the catalog tables (sometimes referred to as the Oracle *data dictionary*) for that database.

Tablespaces contain *segments*, each of which is allocated for a particular data structure. For example, each table in the database is stored in its own data segment, and each index is stored in its own index segment. Each database also contains one or more rollback segments (for recovery, described later in the section "Backup and Recovery"), a bootstrap segment (which contains catalog definitions), and possibly one or more temporary segments (created by Oracle to process certain operations, such as sorting). Segments cannot span tablespaces but they may span multiple physical files within a single tablespace.

Each segment consists of one or more *extents*, which are contiguous data blocks or pages (usually 2K or 4K each, although the size is configurable by the user, subject to operating system constraints). As the user's table grows, additional extents may be allocated to accommodate its storage requirements. Extents are available only for use by the table for which they were allocated; they are reclaimed for use by other objects when the table is dropped.

Figure 14–2 illustrates the logical architecture of an Oracle database. Note that the database contains a SYSTEM tablespace, which also contains the catalog as well as user data (in this case).

As the figure indicates, users may define one or more B*-tree indexes for their tables. Indexes can be unique or nonunique, as well as based on a single column or multiple columns (up to 16, which need not be adjacent). If tables are stored in *clusters* to be discussed shortly), a cluster index must be created.

Clusters enable users to store one or more related tables so that their rows are physically grouped together. A cluster key indicating the related columns must be used to form the basis for the cluster index. Clusters can improve performance if the tables contained are frequently queried together (as would be the case with join operations).

An alternative data structure involves *hashed clusters*. This provides hashed access to data in tables and can be particularly useful if queries frequently involve exact matches on the hash key (such as "select name, phone from restaurants where id = 19820").

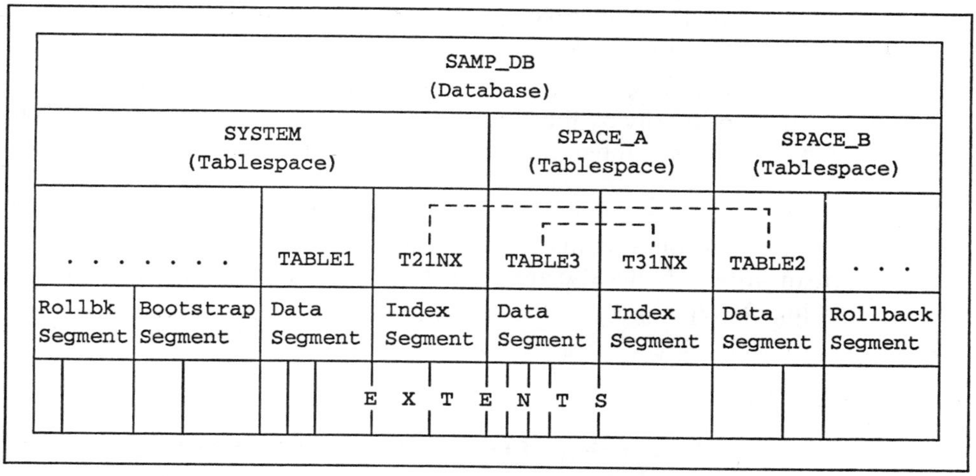

Figure 14–2. Logical architecture of an Oracle database

In addition to tables, views, indexes, and clusters, Oracle databases may also contain other objects, such as stored procedures, triggers, and database links. Examples of these are included later in the sections "Stored Procedures,' "Triggers," and "Distributed Database."

Release 7.1 also enables administrators to alter their tablespaces to make them read-only. This is designed to enable administrators to modify existing tablespaces (to prevent write activities) and then copy their contents (associated files) to read-only media, such as CD-ROMs or WORM drives. Read-only tablespaces are not subject to the same backup and recovery concerns as read-write tablespaces. Read-only tablespaces may be particularly useful for data archival and certain multimedia applications.

Data Types

Like other relational DBMSs, Oracle supports a variety of data types. These include:

- CHAR(n), fixed-length character data of n bytes, up to a maximum of 255 bytes.
- VARCHAR2(n), variable-length character data of n bytes, up to a maximum of 2000 bytes.
- LONG, variable-length character data of up to 2 GB.
- NUMBER(p,s), fixed- or floating-point numbers ranging from $1 \times 10^{**}\text{-}130$ to $9.99 \times 10^{**}125$; p specifies the number's precision and may range from 1 to 38; s specifies the number's scale and may range from -84 to 127.
- DATE, which records date/time information. Each DATE value includes information relating to the century, year, month, day, hour, minute, and second. Dates may range from January 1, 4712 B.C. to December 31, A.D. 4712.

- RAW(n), fixed-length binary data of n bytes, up to a maximum of 255 bytes.
- LONG RAW, variable-length binary data of up to 2 GB.
- ROWID, a hexadecimal string representing the unique address of a row. It is used primarily by the "ROWID" pseudocolumn present in all Oracle tables. The values of the pseudocolumn can be queried, if desired.

Null values are also supported, but they will not be stored unless they occur between two columns that contain data; in such a case, they will consume one byte of storage. Nulls also aren't stored if they occur in trailing columns, thus conserving disk space.

Integrity

Oracle provides a variety of facilities to enforce different types of integrity constraints. These facilities enable customers to specify the valid range of data values for one or more columns, identify referential integrity constraints, and write triggers for enforcing local business policies.

Data Range Checking

Data range checking—which provides some support for domains—is accomplished by specifying CHECK constraints when creating or altering tables. The example below illustrates the syntax for creating a CHECK constraint on the RESTAURANT table to ensure that pricing information is classified as "EXPENSIVE," "MODERATE," or "INEXPENSIVE." The constraint for the PRICING column is given a name ("pricing_schema"). If none had been supplied, Oracle would have generated one automatically.

```
create table restaurant
    (id          number      primary key,
     .
     .
     .
     pricing char(11)
             constraint pricing_schema
             check (pricing in ('EXPENSIVE','MODERATE','INEXPENSIVE')) )
```

This example also specifies that the ID column should serve as the primary key for the table. The relevance of this is discussed shortly, in the section "Referential Integrity."

CHECK constraints may also involve Boolean comparisons as well as AND/OR logic. The following example involves a typical business constraint designed to verify that only employees in the sales division of a company are allowed to receive commissions.

```
create table emp
   (empno      number,
    comm       number,
    dept       char(5),...
 constraint comm_chk
    check ((comm > 0 and dept = 'SALES') or comm is null))
```

Referential Integrity

Oracle also supports declarative referential integrity. When users create tables, they can specify which columns serve as primary and foreign keys. Oracle will then automatically enforce referential integrity constraints between the primary key and foreign key(s).

The following example illustrates how a user might define a referential integrity constraint involving the RESTAURANT table and the RATING table. (As the reader will recall, RESTAURANT lists the name, address, phone numbers, and other information about all restaurants tracked in the database. RATING includes critiques of those restaurants.) In this case, the constraint requires that all restaurants that have been rated or reviewed must belong to the master list of restaurants stored in the database.

```
create table restaurant
   (id            number        constraint pk_rest primary key,
    ...)

create table rating
   (rating_id     number        constraint pk_rating primary key,
    rest_id       number        constraint fk_restid
                                references restaurant(id),
    ...)
```

First, the RESTAURANT table is created, with its ID column identified as the primary key. (The designer has chosen to name this constraint "pk_rest.") Nulls will not be allowed for the ID column, and Oracle will automatically create an index on it. Next, the RATING table is created. The RATING_ID column serves as the primary key. A constraint on the REST_ID column indicates it is a foreign key, referencing the ID column in the RESTAURANT table (which is the primary key for this referential integrity constraint). Creating these two tables in this manner ensures that all values in the REST_ID column will reference a valid restaurant listed in the RESTAURANT table.

Deleting information from the RESTAURANT table may violate referential integrity, as some rows in the dependent table may reference the values about to be deleted. Oracle's implementation of declarative referential integrity enables customers to specify that one of two actions should be taken in such cases where someone attempts to delete data from the parent table that is referenced by one or more dependent tables. The default option (and the one that will be taken for the example shown previously) will prohibit such deletions from occurring. A second option involves cascading the delete operations, automatically removing any dependent rows. Users who wish Oracle to take some other course of action—such as setting dependent data to null or to a default value—can write triggers to enforce referential integrity rather than use the declarative approach illustrated here.

Triggers

Triggers also enable users to enforce site-specific business policies. Written largely in PL/SQL (Oracle's version of SQL that incorporates procedural logic constructs), they are a special form of stored procedures (which are discussed later in "Stored Procedures"). Each trigger is associated with a table and automatically executes when a given database event occurs (such as an INSERT, UPDATE, or DELETE operation).

The following example illustrates a simple trigger designed to prohibit anyone from inserting or updating information in the CRITIC table on the weekends.

```
create trigger critic_modify before insert or update on critic
declare
        weekend exception;
begin
        if (to_char(sysdate,'DY') in ('SAT','SUN')
                then raise weekend;
        end if;
exception
        when weekend then raise_application_error(-20100,
                'Adding or changing information is not permitted on weekends');
end;
```

This example creates a trigger called "critic_modify" that will execute before an INSERT or UPDATE statement is processed for the CRITIC table. An exception condition is declared and given the name of "weekend." Depending on the results of a subsequent test, this exception may be raised, causing Oracle to take additional action. The test itself involves using two Oracle-supplied functions (SYSDATE and TO_CHAR) to retrieve the day portion of the current date and time and convert this to a character string. This string is then tested to see if it is either "SAT" or "SUN," which would indicate that someone is trying to change the CRITIC table on a Saturday or Sunday. If so, the "weekend" exception is raised. This causes Oracle to return an error code to the calling application, along with a message of explanation. The INSERT or UPDATE statement is not permitted to execute.

Oracle enables users to define triggers that execute either BEFORE or AFTER an event. The previous example was of a BEFORE trigger, which will execute before an INSERT or UPDATE statement occurs. Triggers can also be defined to execute once for each triggering statement or once FOR EACH ROW for each triggering event. Thus, there are four general types of triggers available: BEFORE statement triggers, BEFORE row triggers, AFTER statement triggers, and AFTER row triggers.

Multiple triggers of each type may be defined for UPDATE, INSERT, and DELETE operations on a single table. Therefore, a single Oracle table may have an unlimited number of triggers defined on it. If multiple triggers of the same type are defined on the same table, Oracle will choose an arbitrary order in which to execute the triggers. If desired, users can specify that UPDATE triggers apply only to specific columns.

In addition, a WHEN clause can be included in the definition of row triggers to restrict execution of the trigger body. If the Boolean SQL expression specified in the WHEN clause evaluates to FALSE or unknown (as might be the case for null values), the trigger body will not be fired for that row. The following example illustrates a simple use of this clause. Here, the trigger will fire only when INSERTs into the RESTAURANT table include a value for the ID column that is greater than 0.

```
create trigger sample before insert on restaurant
for each row
when (new.id > 0)
    /* declarations and trigger body follow */
    .
    .
    .
end;
```

Oracle also enables administrators to enable or disable triggers as desired. Temporarily disabling a trigger can be helpful when a user is loading large amounts of data and wishes to avoid executing the trigger repeatedly for performance reasons. A trigger might also be disabled if it references additional objects that are not currently available for some reason. Finally, Oracle enables triggers to be nested to an unlimited depth, subject to available memory.

Save Points

A final issue sometimes associated with integrity involves *save points*. These are markers within a program that are used with long transactions to divide up the work. They serve to identify points to which the transaction can be rolled back if certain conditions detected by the application indicate it is appropriate to do so.

ADMINISTRATION

Oracle provides a number of features to enable customers to administer their systems. Among the features discussed here are those involving support for security, recovery, and concurrency control. Performance issues are discussed in a section with the same name later in this chapter.

Security

Oracle's security mechanisms are provided by GRANT/REVOKE statements. These statements control the privileges associated with each user. Oracle also supports security based on roles, which is discussed shortly.

Privileges

For each database defined in the system, users may be granted one or more *system privileges, object privileges,* or a *role.* System privileges are usually granted to administrators, as they confer the authority to create and drop database objects (such as tables, views, and triggers), add or delete new user accounts for a database, manage tablespaces, and perform other functions necessary to manage a database. Oracle identifies additional types of system privileges that may be granted (or revoked) to users.

Object privileges apply to specific database objects, such as tables, views, and stored procedures. Users may be granted the right to select, insert, update, or delete data in tables or views; execute a stored procedure; reference a table when defining a referential integrity constraint; and perform certain other functions.

Roles are named groups of privileges. Administrators may create roles, grant these roles certain privileges, and then grant users the privilege of using certain role(s). The following example creates a DINER role (with a password of "hungry"), grants that role the ability to select information from the RESTAURANT and RATING tables, and then grants five users (DAVID, LOUISE, FRANK, DENNIS, and CHERYL) the privilege to assume the DINER role (and thereby query the RESTAURANT and RATING tables).

```
create role diner
    identified by hungry

grant select on restaurant to diner
grant select on rating to diner

grant diner to david, louise, frank, dennis, cheryl
```

Oracle also enables roles to be granted to other roles, which can be useful for defining hierarchical security schemes. In addition, roles may be selectively enabled from among authorized roles. Roles may have passwords associated with them; applications can enable a role on behalf of a user who is authorized for the role but who does not know its password.

In addition to user-created roles, Oracle automatically creates five roles when each database is created: CONNECT, RESOURCE, DBA, EXP_FULL_DATABASE, and IMP_FULL_DATABASE. Different privileges are automatically associated with each of these roles, the specific details of which are beyond the scope of this book. However, they encompass privileges such as creating tables, views, triggers, procedures, sequences, clusters, database links (for distributed database environments); altering the characteristics of the current user session (perhaps to enable a trace); and obtaining other system privileges.

Auditing

A related security issue involves the ability to maintain an audit trail of various events that occur within a database. A number of options are available to administrators to help them determine which events should be audited. Among these is the ability to audit the types of SQL statements executed or the activities that involve a given database object. For example, administrators may specify that all executions of an SQL statement (such as all INSERT statements) should be audited, or that certain SQL statements should be audited only if they are issued by certain users, or that only successful or unsuccessful access attempts should be audited. With this approach, auditing is not specific to a given database object (such as a specific table or view).

An alternate approach to auditing involves specifying a particular object (such as a table or view) to be audited. With this approach, all DML operations against the table or view will be audited, as well as certain other options (such as altering the table's definition).

Audit facilities are manually activated and stopped by object owners or administrators (through the AUDIT and NOAUDIT commands). Once activated, the audit facility collects data, storing it in system catalog tables. Users may review the audit records using standard Oracle query facilities. Information that is recorded in the audit trail varies according to the audit options selected, but all options will record information about the user who executed the statement, a numeric action code that indicates the type of statement executed, the object(s) referenced in the statement, and the date and time the statement was executed. Users who wish to create audit records that store the old and new data values can write triggers to do so.

Concurrency Control

Like other multiuser DBMSs, Oracle provides various locking mechanisms to manage concurrent access to its data. Oracle provides several kinds of locks, some of which are used only to protect internal database structures or are required only in parallel-processing environments. It also makes use of *latches*, which are internal concurrency control mechanisms. *Data locks* (or *DML locks*) are those that are typically of most concern to Oracle customers, so it is these locks that will be discussed here.

This discussion of Oracle's approach to concurrency control assumes that users have retained default settings for the ROW_LOCKING and SERIALIZABLE initialization parameters. By default, ROW_LOCKING is set to ALWAYS, enabling multiple update transactions to change a single table concurrently by each acquiring locks on different rows of the table. Alternatively, this parameter may be reset to INTENT, which enables multiple transactions to query the same table concurrently but forces transactions to update the table serially. By default, the SERIALIZABLE parameter is set to FALSE. If reset to TRUE, locks are held at the table level and Oracle schedules concurrent transactions so that the result of their execution would be the same as if each were executed serially. However, holding locks at the table level can inhibit concurrency; for this reason (and others), the default settings specify row-level locking and do not enforce serializability.

Lock Levels and Lock Modes

Oracle can lock data at the row or table level, although row-level locking is the default. Different lock modes correspond to these different levels. When row-level locks are acquired, Oracle also acquires certain types of table-level locks to prevent conflicting data definition operations from occurring and to protect the transaction from other conflicting DML statements. The synergy between row and table locks is discussed after the modes available for each are explored.

Oracle acquires *row locks* (sometimes called *exclusive row locks*) on rows when a transaction attempts to change data. Row locks prevent other transactions from updating the same row at the same time.

However, Oracle is somewhat unique in that read activities are not blocked by write transactions, and Oracle does not acquire share locks on rows for read operations. Instead, it gives readers access to a version or snapshot of the data that was consistent when the query or transaction began. Thus, an exclusive row lock will *not* prevent others from seeing what may be an earlier version of that row's contents. This is due to Oracle's *multiversion consistency model*, which is discussed shortly.

While only one mode of row-level lock is used, a number of different modes are used for table-level locks. These are:

- Row share table locks. These imply that a transaction has (exclusive) locks on rows of a table and intends to update the locked rows. This lock is acquired for DML statements involving SELECT...FROM..FOR UPDATE OF. Other transactions can change or lock other rows in the table (provided these rows are not already locked). However, other transactions cannot explicitly lock the table in exclusive mode.
- Row exclusive table locks. Locks of this type are acquired when a transaction has modified a table (through an INSERT, UPDATE, or DELETE statement). Other transactions can change or lock other rows in the table for which exclusive locks are not currently held. Other transactions cannot explicitly lock the table in share or exclusive modes.
- Share table locks. These locks are acquired only when users explicitly issue the LOCK TABLE...IN SHARE MODE command. It prohibits other transactions from updating any data in the table, although other transactions may read data in the table. If no other concurrent transactions hold share table locks, the owner of this lock can acquire row locks to write data.

- Share row exclusive table locks. These locks are acquired only when users explicitly issue the LOCK TABLE... IN SHARE ROW EXCLUSIVE MODE. Only one transaction may acquire such a lock on a table at any given time. Other transactions may query data in the table, but none may write to it. In addition, no other transactions may acquire share, share row exclusive, or exclusive locks on the table.

- Exclusive table locks. This lock is acquired when a user explicitly issues the LOCK TABLE... IN EXCLUSIVE MODE. The owner may write data, but no other transactions may do so. However, other transactions may query the table. Only one transaction may hold an exclusive table lock on a particular table at any given time.

Multiversion Consistency Model

As mentioned previously, Oracle is somewhat unusual among the DBMS products profiled in this book as it does not normally acquire share locks for read operations. Its multiversion consistency model enables users to control the level of read consistency enforced by the system, which may be either *statement-level read consistency* or *transaction-level read consistency*.

By default, Oracle enforces *statement-level consistency*, wherein the results of a single query are guaranteed to be consistent for the point in time at which the query began. To do so, Oracle notes the system change number (or SCN) that is current as of the time the query enters its execution phase. (A system change number is recorded in the redo log whenever a transaction commits.) Oracle compares this SCN with the SCNs written for data blocks it must use to satisfy the query. Data blocks with the observed SCN (or an earlier SCN) can be used directly, as they contain data that was committed at the time the query entered its execution phase.

However, data blocks that contain a more recent SCN are not used directly, as these could surface data that has changed since the query entered its execution phase. In such cases, Oracle uses log records (stored in its rollback segments) to reconstruct a snapshot or version of the data that is consistent as of the time the query began. Statement-level consistency, as described here, provides for the highest level of concurrency in an Oracle environment.

The multi-version consistency model is sometimes referred to as a *non-blocking query technique*. This is because readers don't block writers, and writers don't block readers. Queries still see consistent data (more so than those executing on other DBMSs running in a cursor stability isolation level), although the data may not be as current (a long-running query will not see data that has been committed by another transaction before the query execution completes).

Optionally, users may instruct Oracle to enforce *transaction-level read consistency*, which is comparable to repeatable reads. It guarantees that all queries within a single transaction will see a consistent version of the data. To provide this level of consistency for transactions that perform write (or read/write) operations, users must acquire exclusive locks on tables or rows. (Read-only queries within such transactions can issue SELECT...FOR UPDATE statements to acquire exclusive row-level locks.) This use of exclusive locks decreases concurrency, as other transactions cannot perform write operations on tables or rows that have been locked exclusively.

If the transaction requiring repeatable reads is identified as a read-only transaction (by the SET TRANSACTION READ ONLY statement), exclusive table locks are not required. Instead, Oracle guarantees transaction-level consistency for read-only transactions through the use of system change numbers and log records. It notes the current system change number when the transaction begins and presents a version of the data that is consistent for that point in time.

Other Lock Issues

As noted previously, Oracle enables users to manually acquire table locks. This is accomplished through the LOCK TABLE...IN...MODE command. Any of the modes of table-level locks previously described may be acquired in this manner.

If desired, users may also override the default locking scheme for row-level locks (which are automatically acquired for INSERT, UPDATE, DELETE, and SELECT...FOR UPDATE statements). For example, users who want to acquire an exclusive row lock for read operations can write their SELECT statements as SELECT...FOR UPDATE statements and then not actually update the row. When acquiring row locks with a SELECT...FOR UPDATE statement, users may also specify whether or not they want to wait to acquire the locks. If the NOWAIT option is specified, Oracle will return an error if the desired row lock cannot be granted immediately. If the NOWAIT option is omitted, the transaction will wait until the requested lock can be acquired.

This raises the issue of deadlocks. Oracle uses wait-for graphs to detect local deadlocks. It resolves these by selecting a victim and rolling back one of the statements causing the deadlock. A message is sent back to the transaction responsible for this statement, which can either roll back the entire transaction or retry the rolled back statement. In distributed database environments, global deadlocks are handled by time-outs.

Backup and Recovery

Providing for backup and recovery of databases is another issue of concern for administrators. This section describes how such functions are supported in an Oracle environment.

Backup Options

Oracle administrators may use operating system commands to back up all files that comprise a database (including all data files, online redo log files, and the control file) or back up only some of the files associated with a database (such as individual data files). Issuing various queries and commands can help administrators determine the names of files that should be backed up, depending on the objective. For example, certain queries and commands can help administrators determine the names of all files that comprise a given database or only the names of data files associated with a given tablespace.

Many administrators choose to make full or partial backups of their databases while they are online (open and in use). This helps support continuous operations, as users can still access a database while it is being backed up. Online backups are sometimes referred to as *fuzzy* backups because they are not guaranteed to be consistent for a specific point in time. This is because user activity may cause database changes during the backup period. For this reason, log records are typically applied to online (or fuzzy) backups to bring them to a consistent state.

Optionally, administrators may create offline backups of their databases, when these databases are shut down and inaccessible to users. Offline backups are guaranteed to be consistent for a specific point in time.

Logging

Although backups are necessary for recovery, log records are also important. Oracle records log information for *undo* processing in one or more *rollback segments*. It also maintains a *redo log* for *redo* (or roll-forward) processing. Both active (online) and archive redo logs are supported. Archive logging must be enabled for Oracle to fully recover from media errors and to support online backups of tablespaces. The online redo log may be mirrored so that dual copies are maintained on separate disks; this avoids a single point of failure.

The online redo log actually consists of two or more files that are used in a cyclical fashion. When the first file becomes full, the log records are written to the next file; when the last available file is full, log records are once again written to the first file. The action of changing the current log file being written to is called a *log switch*.

By default, checkpoints occur only at log switches. Users specify other intervals at which checkpoints should occur through the LOG_CHECK-POINT_INTERVAL and LOG_CHECKPOINT_TIMEOUT initialization parameters. Frequent checkpoints can speed recovery but do incur some processing overhead.

To improve performance, Oracle supports group commits. Work that is committed at or near the same time is transferred from log buffers to disk in a single I/O operation, reducing the number of I/O operations that would otherwise have to occur.

Recovery Options

A common concern of administrators involves recovery from media errors (such as failure or corruption of a hard disk). The process involves first restoring backup copies of the damaged files associated with a database. Next, the RECOVER command is invoked through SQL*DBA to roll forward any committed changes since the last backup and roll back any uncommitted work at the time of failure. Administrators may perform media recovery on the entire database, individual tablespaces, or individual data files used by a tablespace. Recovery of one tablespace can proceed while other tablespaces are in use

Oracle also enables users to conduct incomplete media recovery, in which the database is recovered only up to a specific point in time (specified by a given date and time, accurate to the second), up to a specific system change number, or up until the user cancels the operation manually. Incomplete recovery applies to the entire database.

Import and Export Utilities

In addition to the backup and recovery facilities described so far, Oracle also offers Import and Export utilities. Although these are designed to help customers move Oracle data (perhaps from one Oracle system to another), they also provide a means for creating backups of data and reloading these backups.

Export enables users to back up all objects within a database, all objects owned by a given user within a database, or one or more specific tables owned by a user within a database. Such exports may be full copies or incremental copies. If many incremental copies were taken since the last full copy, administrators may make a cumulative copy, which condenses the changes recorded in all the incremental exports. The Import utility provides a way to reload data into a database after export copies have been made.

Other Administrative Issues

In large, multiuser environments, it's often important for administrators to be able to limit the amount of resources a single user can consume. Oracle permits administrators to do so by defining *profiles* for users. These profiles can be used to limit the amount of CPU time consumed (in one-hundredths of a second), the number of logical data block reads permitted (from both memory and disk), and other resources. After creating a profile specifying such limits, an administrator can associate this profile with one or more user accounts. If desired, these accounts (and their associated profiles) can be altered later as needed.

Diagnosing and resolving problems is a final area of administrative concern. Like other products, Oracle provides a variety of error messages to help users pinpoint problems. It maintains a chronological log of various errors in an ALERT file for administrators to consult.

QUERY CAPABILITIES

Oracle was the first vendor to support SQL in a commercial product, although the language itself was originally developed as part of a research project at IBM. Oracle supports dynamic embedded SQL, as well as a call-level interface (OCI, or Oracle Call Interface). A variety of programming languages are supported, including C, COBOL, FORTRAN, Ada, PL/1, and Pascal. Future releases of Oracle are expected to include certain object-oriented features.

As the reader has seen, Oracle supports triggers through the use of PL/SQL, a feature that offers procedural logic constructs within SQL (such as if-then-else statements, GOTO statements, and loops). These triggers are really a special form of stored procedures, which are discussed next.

Stored Procedures

Stored procedures help promote code reuse and can provide performance benefits in a client/server environment. They consist of blocks of PL/SQL code. The following example illustrates a simple Oracle stored procedure for updating PRIC-ING information in the RESTAURANT table:

```
create procedure price_change (rest_no in number, cost in char(11)) as

begin
   update restaurant
      set pricing = cost
      where id = rest_no;
  if sql%notfound then
      raise_application_error (-20014,'Invalid restaurant number.');
   end if;
end price_change;
```

The first line creates a procedure called "price_change" that expects two input parameters: a number representing the restaurant's ID ("rest_no") and an 11-character string representing the new pricing information ("cost"). The "rest_no" parameter corresponds to the ID column of the table, while the "cost" parameter corresponds to the PRICING column of the table. Restaurant pricing is presumed to be classified as "EXPENSIVE," "MODERATE," or "INEXPENSIVE." The procedure begins by updating the RESTAURANT table, resetting the PRIC-ING information for the specified restaurant. A test is made to determine if the update actually occurred. If not (because the restaurant ID value passed in via the "rest_no" parameter was not found in the table), an error is raised before the procedure completes.

If desired, administrators may create *packages* to group together a related set of stored procedures. PL/SQL, which forms the basis for stored procedures and certain other functions offered by Oracle, is used extensively by many Oracle customers. Although a few of its capabilities have been illustrated in this chapter, further discussion is beyond the scope of this book. Readers are encouraged to consult sources cited in "References and Suggested Reading" for more information.

Recursion

As the reader will recall from the Chapter 5, "Introduction to SQL," support for recursive queries can be useful for several types of applications. Oracle supports recursive queries through two extensions to SQL. The CONNECT BY and PRIOR statements enable users to write recursive queries that can be used to give a hierarchical representation of tabular data. For example, imagine an EMPLOYEE table with a list of employees and their managers. Each employee has a number

(EMPNO), a name (NAME), a title (TITLE), and an entry indicating the employee number of his or her manager (MGR). The following query would print an organization chart, starting at the top (with the president):

```
select * from employee
connect by prior empno = mgr
start with title = 'PRESIDENT'
```

The CONNECT BY clause specifies a relationship between "parent" and "child" rows in a hierarchical query. In this case, the child rows of a parent row are those that have the employee number of the parent row as their manager number. The final line identifies the starting point in the hierarchy (or the "root" row) to be that of the president of the company.

Similarly, a user could take a "bottom-up" approach to this problem, perhaps by creating a report listing all of Ms. Ward's managers:

```
select * from employee
connect by empno = prior mgr
start with name = 'WARD'
```

Operators and SQL Functions

In the area of arithmetic operations, Oracle supports the basic functions of addition, subtraction, multiplication, and division. In addition, it supports more specialized functions, such as modulo division, square root, and exponentiation.

Release 2.1 of PL/SQL includes support for user-defined functions that can be referenced in any SQL expression (including SELECT statements, the WHERE clause, GROUP BY clause, and ORDER BY clause). These functions are defined through the CREATE FUNCTION statement and stored as database objects. The functions themselves are written in PL/SQL.

Like most relational DBMSs, Oracle provides various mechanisms to support wildcard searches. In addition, Oracle provides a phonetic search capability through the SOUNDEX function. This enables users to search on words that are spelled differently but sound alike in English. For example, users can enter this query to search for all restaurant critics whose last names are spelled in such a way that they sound like "SMITH":

```
select last_name, first_name, phone from critic
    where soundex(last_name) = soundex('SMITH')
```

Outer Join

Oracle also supports the use of outer joins through the use of the "(+)" symbol in the join clause. The following example shows how Oracle users might obtain a list of all restaurants and their overall ratings, even if a restaurant hasn't been reviewed yet (in which case, null values would fill out rows that did not match on join column values).

```
select name, overall
from restaurant, rating
where restaurant.id (+)= rating.rest_id
```

Column Defaults

Like certain other DBMSs, Oracle enables users to specify default values for columns. If users do not explicitly provide values for these columns when they update or insert information into the table, Oracle will automatically include the default value specified when the table was created. The following statement specifies that the default value for the DATE column of the RATING table should be set to the current date when the update or insert operation occurred. (This is achieved through the SYSDATE function supplied by Oracle.)

```
create table rating
    (...
    meal_time      char(9),
    review_date    date default (sysdate),
    ...)
```

DISTRIBUTED DATABASE

Oracle supports distributed database processing at a distributed request level, described in Chapter 7, "Distributed Databases." In other words, insert, update, and delete operations within a single transaction can be directed to local and remote Oracle databases, and two-phase commit processing will automatically be supported in a manner that is transparent to the user. In addition, Oracle enables users to write a single SQL statement (perhaps involving a join operation) that involves data managed by multiple Oracle DBMSs.

Products that contribute to Oracle's distributed database capabilities include:

- SQL*Net. This interfaces to various networking products. It is used for both client/server and distributed database configurations.
- Oracle7 DBMS with the distributed option. This provides the distributed database functions described previously, as well as support for remote procedure calls in a distributed database environment.
- Transparent Gateway products (formerly SQL*Connect products). These are optional gateways that provide for heterogeneous distributed database support, enabling Oracle applications to access non-Oracle DBMSs. For details, see the section "Gateways and Middleware."

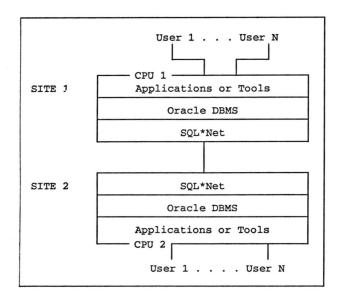

Figure 14–3. Distributed database environment with two Oracle DBMSs

Figure 14–3 illustrates a simple distributed database configuration, in which applications at different sites can each access their local Oracle databases and/or remote Oracle databases.

Users working in distributed database environments often prefer that the location of the data be transparent to them. To support this, Oracle enables users to create *database links* and *synonyms*. The example below shows how a user might create a database link named "sf." The USING clause specifies "sf_path" as the *connect descriptor;* such descriptors are stored in the TNSNAMES.ORA file and identify the specific Oracle DBMS instance to be accessed. After the database link is created, a user could query remote tables to which he or she had previously been granted access (by the table owner or database administrator at that site).

```
create database link sf
using 'sf_path'

select name, cuisine, pricing, phone
from dining.restaurant@sf
```

However, to make the user's access to the RESTAURANT table more transparent, the user could create a synonym and reference this in his or her query. The example below shows how this is accomplished.

```
create synonym rest
for dining.restaurant@sf

select name, cuisine, pricing, phone
from rest
```

Oracle also provides facilities for copying remote tables into a local table and for joining remote data with local data. This example inserts data into the local

TEMP table, copying the contents from the REST table. As the reader has seen in the previous example, REST is actually a synonym for the remote RESTAURANT table (identified by the SF database link).

```
insert into temp
   select * from rest
```

Similarly, the local RATING table can be joined with the remote REST table, as shown below.

```
select overall, date, name, pricing
   from rating, rest
   where rating.rest_id = rest.id
```

For queries such as this, Oracle can perform global optimization to help ensure reasonable performance. To do so, the local Oracle DBMS dynamically reads statistics contained in remote catalogs (in this case, statistics related to the RESTAURANT table in San Francisco, referenced by the REST synonym). This enables the local Oracle optimizer to determine an efficient access strategy for satisfying this query. More information about Oracle's optimization techniques is included in the section "Optimizer."

A separately purchased product, Oracle Names, can be used with Oracle7 release 7.1 and SQL*Net release 2.1 to make network addresses and database link information available to all sites participating in a distributed database environment. This helps ease overall system administration, enabling local users to use database links without specifying connect strings. Instead, all database link definitions can reside at a central location.

GATEWAYS AND MIDDLEWARE

Up until now, only homogeneous distributed database support from Oracle has been discussed. Oracle provides a number of gateway products to enable its customers to access data stored in non-Oracle environments, including DB2 for MVS, DB2 for VM, DB2 for OS/400, Ingres, SQL Server, and RMS files (from DEC). At a minimum, these gateways support remote unit-of-work processing, enabling applications to read or write to a single non-Oracle data source within a given transaction. A subset of SQL statements is supported for use with these gateways.

In the case of the Oracle Transparent Gateway for DB2/MVS (formerly SQL*Connect to DB2), Oracle enables users to update data in multiple Oracle7 DBMSs and one DB2 DBMS within a single transaction. Oracle7's two-phase commit processing coordinates this distributed update work. Access to DB2 is via its Call Attach Facility. Figure 14–4 illustrates a sample distributed database environment involving Oracle and DB2. In this case, Oracle is installed on one system, and both Oracle and DB2 are installed on another MVS system. With this configuration, users can create Oracle database links and synonyms for DB2 tables. This helps hide the fact that Oracle users will be accessing remote data in a non-Oracle DBMS.

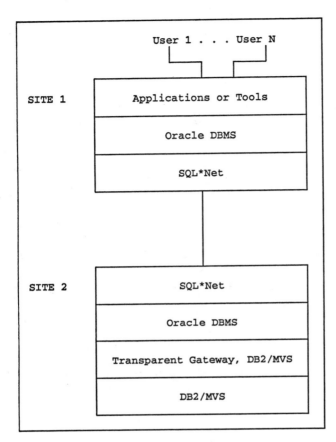

Figure 14–4. Sample distributed database environment with a gateway

In addition, Oracle offers a number of other gateway products, including one for IBM DRDA. This product serves as a DRDA application requestor, providing remote unit-of-work support based on DRDA protocols. Users can access any data source that has implemented DRDA application server logic (including various members of the DB2 family). Using Oracle7 protocols, this gateway enables users to update data managed by multiple Oracle DBMSs and any single DRDA-enabled data source.

For those who wish to build customized gateways to data sources not supported by other Oracle products, the firm also offers Open Gateway Toolkits.

Another middleware offering from Oracle is Oracle Glue. It provides a consistent application programming interface to multiple data sources, relying on gateway products to bridge to non-Oracle environments. As of this writing, the product supports Windows clients and can be used with Microsoft's Visual Basic.

REPLICATION

Oracle provides a number of options for users who wish to maintain copies of their data at multiple sites. With the distributed option of Oracle7, users can maintain read-only snapshots of source tables (or subsets of source tables) at multiple locations. Enhancements for release 7.1 enable users to maintain read/write copies of their data at multiple locations. This section first discusses read-only snapshots and then discusses some of the newer features associated with release 7.1.

Read-Only Snapshots

Beginning with release 7.0 of Oracle7, Oracle offered customers the ability to maintain read-only snapshots of their data at multiple locations. This release supports two kinds of read-only snapshots: *simple snapshots,* in which the query defining the snapshot has no subqueries, joins, set operations, GROUP BY, or CONNECT BY clauses; and *complex snapshots,* in which the query defining the snapshot has at least one of these clauses or operations. Complex snapshots require regenerating the entire table when the data must be updated at the target site(s). Simple snapshots may be defined to have *snapshot logs* associated with them; in such cases, only incremental changes are sent to the target site(s) rather than the entire table. With both simple and complex snapshots, data changes are propagated asynchronously.

Snapshots are defined at the target site. Included in their definition is a query that references the appropriate table(s) at one or more source sites. The following example creates a simple snapshot (with no snapshot log) based upon the remote CRITIC table.

```
create snapshot snap_critic
    refresh complete
    start with '01-DEC-94'
    next sysdate + 7
    as select * from critic@sf;
```

This creates a snapshot called SNAP_CRITIC at the the local site. Complete refreshes—or entire copies of the table—will be transmitted whenever propagation occurs since no snapshot log was defined at the SF site. In this case, the user has specified that the first propagation should occur on December 1, 1994. Subsequent propagations will occur at one-week intervals (seven days from the most recent refresh). The snapshot itself is based on a very simple query that selects all rows from the CRITIC table, which resides at the location referenced by the SF database link.

To enable automatic refreshes to occur, at least one snapshot refresh process must be running on the local server. (Initialization parameters control whether or not any background refresh processes are running.) Such processes "wake up" periodically (every second to every 60 minutes, depending on information specified by the SNAPSHOT_REFRESH_INTERVAL initialization parameter) to check if any snapshots need to be refreshed. If so, the local Oracle DBMS can then issue the appropriate query, causing the necessary data to be retrieved from the source site. Optionally, users may manually refresh snapshots if desired.

Simple snapshots may also be defined to process snapshot logs, which allow for incremental changes to be propagated from the source site to the target site. These logs reside in the same database as the source table. Creating a snapshot log implicitly causes Oracle to generate an AFTER ROW trigger on the master table. This trigger inserts information about changes to the source table into the snapshot log, which can then be consulted to determine what information should be propagated when the next refresh cycle occurs.

The following example shows the commands issued at two different locations (the source and target locations) to define a snapshot log and create a snapshot, respectively. First, the site in Boston (the source site) defines the snapshot log for its local CRITIC table. Next, the site in New York creates a local snapshot of this table, specifying that FAST refreshes (or incremental changes) are to be propagated every three days. Here, "bstn" is presumed to be a previously defined database link that identifies the appropriate Oracle DBMS in Boston.

```
BOSTON:     create snapshot log on restaurant

NEW YORK:   create snapshot snap_rest
                refresh fast
                start with '01-DEC-94
                next sysdate + 3
                as select * from restaurant@bstn;
```

A distinctive feature of Oracle's snapshot support is its notion of a *snapshot refresh group*. Tables involved in referential integrity constraints may be identified as belonging to the same refresh group (through the use of the system-supplied MAKE procedure that is part of the DBMS_REFRESH package). This ensures that related snapshots will be updated consistently to a single point in time. Any snapshot can belong to only one refresh group at any time. Oracle automatically creates a snapshot refresh group for an individual snapshot created with a refresh interval (assuming an administrator did not define this snapshot as already participating in another group). In this case, the "group" contains precisely one member—the individual snapshot.

Instructing Oracle to automatically refresh snapshots at some given interval may lead the reader to wonder what happens if Oracle is unable to complete the refresh as scheduled, perhaps because of a network or other failure. It will retry the refresh after one minute; if unsuccessful, it will repeat the attempt, doubling the retry interval each time until it successfully completes or until the retry interval exceeds the normal refresh interval. In the latter case, Oracle continues to retry at the normal refresh interval. In extreme cases, if Oracle continues to encounter problems with the refresh attempt after 16 retries, it considers the snapshot refresh group to be "broken." Administrators can determine this status by examining system-supplied views. They can then resolve the situation by manually refreshing the group; successfully doing so will cause Oracle to reset this status and subsequently continue with automatic refreshes.

Updatable Snapshots and N-Way Replication

As mentioned previously, release 7.1 of Oracle7 includes additional replication capabilities. Among these are support for *updatable snapshots* and *n-way replication*, both of which enable customers to maintain multiple read/write copies of their data at various sites.

Updatable snapshots are similar in many respects to the read-only snapshots previously described. Updatable snapshots may be based on an entire table or on a subset of a given table. For best performance, a snapshot log is created at the source (or master) site so that only changed data is propagated during refresh periods. And the refresh cycle is determined by the receiving or target site, which pulls the data from the source site on demand. However, read-only snapshots may be *complex,* based on join or aggregate queries. Updatable snapshots cannot be complex.

N-way replication provides customers with read/write access to copies of their data. However, n-way replication differs from updatable snapshots in a number of key respects. Here, each participating site is considered to have a master copy of the table. Each replicate must consist of a full table (not table subsets). Changes to any of the replicates are still captured by system-generated triggers. However, these changes are pushed out to other replicate sites by system-generated stored procedures. N-way replication, therefore, relies on *store-and-forward* technology to queue these changes and propagate them, based on events at the originating site. Administrators may control when these refreshes are automatically pushed out by specifying a time interval to control the frequency of propagation. Manual refreshes are also supported.

It should be noted that updatable snapshots and n-way replication can be combined to form a hybrid configuration. For example, n-way replication can be used at multiple hub sites to maintain full copies of one or more tables. Other sites attached to a given hub may contain updatable snapshots of these master tables (or portions of these master tables)

Figure 14–5 illustrates the new configurations possible with release 7.1 of Oracle 7.

With both updatable snapshots and n-way replication, asynchronous remote procedure calls (RPCs) are used to propagate and apply changes to master copies. This might lead the reader to wonder what will happen if users at different locations attempt to update their copies at or near the same time. Conflicts are likely to occur, but how will these be resolved?

Conflict resolution routines instruct Oracle on how to deal with such cases. Customers may write their own routines (in PL/SQL) or use one of the routines supplied by Oracle. Among the simpler of these Oracle-supplied routines are those that give priority to updates at a particular site, to the most recent update, or to the update that involves some minimum or maximum value. Additional routines are also supplied.

A future release of Oracle is expected to support heterogeneous replication. Oracle's replication mechanisms are expected to work with Oracle gateways to replicate data from Oracle DBMSs to non-Oracle targets in the form of read-only snapshots. Non-Oracle sources are also expected to be able to provide master copies of data that will be propagated to Oracle DBMSs in the form of read-only snapshots.

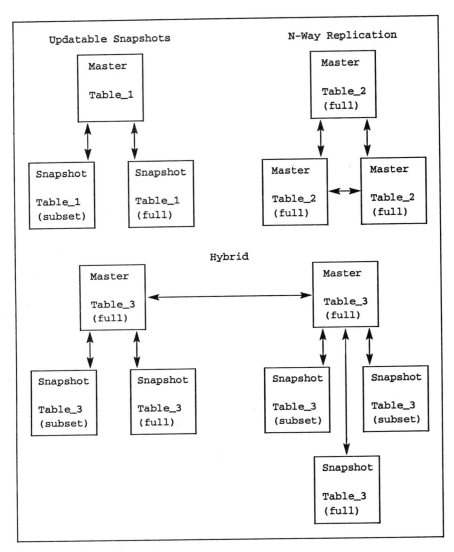

Figure 14–5. Sample Oracle replication scenarios

PERFORMANCE

Most relational DBMS vendors, including Oracle, view performance as a key factor in gaining customer acceptance. Among the performance-related features provided by Oracle are an optimizer, an EXPLAIN PLAN facility, and an SQL Trace facility. Previous sections of this chapter have already mentioned other Oracle functions that enable customers to improve their system performance, such as the use of stored procedures.

Optimizer

Oracle's approach to optimization differs from that of several other vendors in that it can use either cost-based or rules-based optimization. Cost-based optimization relies on statistics to determine an efficient access path to the data. With rules-based optimization, access path selection can be significantly influenced by the syntax of the query. Rules-based optimization is automatically used if no statistics are collected and no optimizer "hints" are provided in the query. However, Oracle has indicated that future releases of its DBMS will not continue to support rules-based optimization.

Statistics are collected by issuing the ANALYZE command. These statistics may be based on an exact computation involving all rows in the table, or they may be based on a random sampling of data.

Oracle also enables users to include hints to the optimizer about the access path it should select for a DELETE, UPDATE, or SELECT statement. A hint may instruct Oracle to use a COST based approach to optimization or a NOCOST approach (a rules-based approach) to optimization. Moreover, hints can instruct the optimizer which access path to use to resolve a statement. This path will be chosen provided it is valid. (For example, if a user includes a hint to use a nonexistent index, Oracle will ignore it.)

The following query includes a hint instructing Oracle to use the DATE_INX on the RATING table to retrieve the necessary information. This hint is enclosed in comments ("/* */") and specifies the name of the table and the desired index.

```
select /*+ index(rating date_inx) */
    rest_id, rating_id, overall
    from rating
    where review_date = '01-DEC-94'
```

Hints may be very specific. For example, users may instruct Oracle on how to perform a join operation, using sort/merge or nested loop processing. In addition, users can specify (via hints, or at the database or session level) an optimization goal: response time for retrieving the first set of rows, or response time for retrieving all rows that satisfy the query.

In the area of join processing, Oracle is capable of "flattening" certain subqueries into their equivalent join statements to select a more efficient access path. With some exceptions, joins involving more than two tables are generally processed two tables at a time. (In other words, the optimizer typically chooses which of the two tables to join first, then joins this result with the next table, and so on.)

EXPLAIN PLAN and SQL Trace

To further understand the workings of the optimizer and tune their queries, users may invoke the EXPLAIN PLAN command to record information about access plan selection in a *plan table* (created by the user). The command records such information as the timestamp, type of operation performed, the name of the object involved, and other data.

The SQL trace facility provides another mechanism for users who wish to understand more about the activities involved to satisfy their queries. For each desired SQL statement, this facility can collect statistics on the CPU and elapsed times required for processing, the number of rows processed, the number of physical and logical reads required, and other data. Oracle initialization parameters and the ALTER SESSION command enable users to control when the SQL trace facility is active. Oracle then writes the appropriate trace data to one or more files, and this data must be translated by the TKPROF command for review. If desired, the SQL trace and EXPLAIN PLAN data can both be combined in a report generated by TKPROF.

Other Facilities

As mentioned previously, Oracle offers a variety of performance-tuning mechanisms through its INIT.ORA file, which enables administrators to control buffer sizes, cache usage, the maximum number of allowable processes per system, and other factors. In addition, the SQL*DBA MONITOR helps administrators understand lock usage (perhaps to pinpoint contention problems that are impacting performance), I/O activity, and ways in which the system is being used.

PARALLELISM

Oracle Parallel Server, based on Oracle7, supports parallel transaction processing in shared-disk environments. This means that multiple Oracle servers (or *instances*) can be started on different nodes of a multiprocessor environment, and the Oracle Parallel Server can process multiple different transactions in parallel. Among the hardware platforms supported by the Oracle Parallel Server are DEC VAXclusters, IBM HACMP/6000 clusters and SP1 system, the NCR 3600 series, and nCUBE's massively parallel processing system.

Oracle also recently announced support for parallel query processing, in which a single Oracle instance can use multiple CPUs to process multiple subtasks associated with a single query in parallel. This support is part of the Parallel Query Option for Oracle 7.1. This option is often used on tightly coupled (shared-memory) systems. However, it may be combined with the Parallel Server on certain types of hardware platforms to provide for both parallel transaction and parallel query processing. This section first discusses the Parallel Server (which supports parallel transaction processing) and then discusses the Parallel Query Option (which supports parallel query processing, as well as parallel data loading and index creation).

Parallel Server

The overall architecture of Oracle instances that comprise the Oracle Parallel Server is very similar to the architecture of Oracle7 in uniprocessor environments. Each instance contains several components and processes, as illustrated in Figure 14–6.

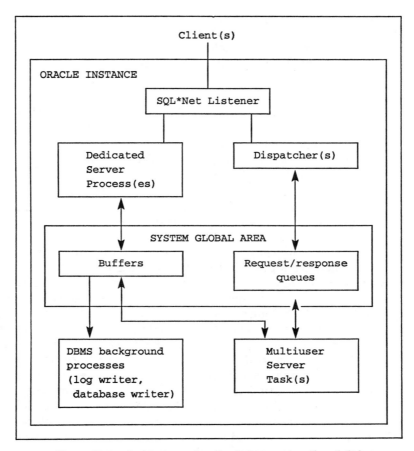

Figure 14–6. Architecture of an Oracle instance in a shared-disk environment

Components and processes associated with the Oracle Parallel Server include:

- A System Global Area (SGA) containing memory structures private to that Oracle instance. The SGA contains caches for database blocks and catalog information, a buffer for the redo log, and other structures. An additional structure was added to the SGA to accommodate distributed lock information (which is discussed later in this section).
- Several background processes for writing logs, making checkpoints, writing modified database blocks to disk, monitoring system processes, and so forth. Dispatcher tasks are among these background processes; they place SQL requests on queues and pick up results.
- Dedicated server tasks, each bound to a specific user or process fo⸱ the duration of the task's lifetime.

- Multi-user server tasks, each bound to a specific user or process only until the necessary work for that user or process has been completed. Thus, multi-user tasks are tasks that are available to many users, but each task can service only one user at a time (one task cannot service multiple users concurrently).
- An SQL*Net listener task, which "listens" for incoming SQL requests. Depending on how the SQL*Net connection was specified, the request will be routed to either a dedicated server task or to a dispatcher, which will place it on a queue for an available multiuser server task to pick up. (In most environments, it is routed to the dispatcher by default. However, users can often specify "SRVR = DEDICATED" as part of their SQL*Net connection string to force the work to be routed to a dedicated task.) If appropriate, SQL*Net listener tasks can route requests to other instances, depending on information specified at connection time.

With multiple instances having access to the same database (in a shared-disk environment), it's possible that two or more instances may both seek read (or read/write) access to the same data at the same time. Oracle uses two distinct locking mechanisms to manage this situation: distributed locks (which rely on the services of an operating system's Distributed Lock Manager component) and standard transaction or data locks (discussed previously in "Concurrency Control").

Distributed locks ensure consistency (or "coherency") among the local caches of each instance. Without such locks, each instance may read the same database block into its local cache at different times to satisfy different requests. Since this block would remain encached as long as memory was available, an instance might attempt to reaccess that block to satisfy subsequent requests. However, if another instance had committed changes to that block in the interim, the system would be expected to reread the block into memory so that the most current, committed data was used to satisfy the new request. To achieve this, a mechanism must be in place to manage the use of in-memory data blocks across instances; distributed locks—specifically, parallel cache manager (or PCM) locks—are this mechanism. Such locks are also a useful way of coordinating updates to the same block by different instances.

Distributed locks may be acquired in shared mode (for read access) or exclusive mode (for write access). A single lock may cover a single database block or many blocks, depending on parameters set at system configuration. It's important to note that an instance never releases a distributed lock unless another instance requests access to the block; this is true even if the original instance has already committed its transaction that involved the block.

But distributed locks are only one piece of the puzzle. A second, separate locking mechanism is also required for maintaining transaction integrity. Here, Oracle uses its standard row-level locking mechanism to ensure that transactions don't see uncommitted work and that updates are not lost. These row-level locks are acquired only for write access; read access to Oracle data does not involve the acquisition of any transaction lock (although it does involve the acquisition of a distributed lock in multiprocessing environments, as discussed earlier).

These two locking mechanisms—distributed locks and row locks—often confuse people initially, so an example may help clarify things. Imagine that instance 1 receives a request to update row N, which resides in block 5 of database file XYZ. Assuming instance 1 does not already have this block in its local cache, it will notify the operating system's distributed lock manager that it wishes to acquire an exclusive distributed lock on this block. Assuming other instances don't hold a distributed lock on the same block (or are willing to release it), instance 1 receives the lock and pages the block from disk into its buffer. (In reality, multiple blocks may be locked if the system was configured such that one distributed lock would "cover" multiple blocks.)

With the necessary block in its cache, instance 1 can acquire a row lock on row N and proceed with the update. After the update transaction has been committed, instance 1 will release its row lock on row N but retain its distributed lock on block 5 until another instance requests it. The presumption here is that subsequent transactions at instance 1 may wish to access other data in block 5, so the block should remain encached and readily available as long as possible.

But the previous scenario can quickly become more complicated. What if instance 2 wants to update block 5 at the same time as instance 1? The update will be permitted, provided it doesn't involve row(s) for which other instances already hold row locks. In the previous example, when instance 1 acquired a row lock on row N, it recorded some information about that lock status with the row. If it receives a request from the distributed lock manager to release its distributed lock (to satisfy another instance's request), instance 1 will write the block back to disk along with information recording that row N is locked. After this write, instance 1 signals that the distributed lock on block 5 can be released (even though the update transaction to row N is still pending). This enables instance 2 to acquire a distributed lock on block 5 and read it in from disk.

At this point, Oracle instance 2 can examine rows in that block, checking to see if the rows it is interested in are still locked by some other process. Updates can proceed on those rows for which no existing transaction locks are held. If instance 2 seeks to update the same row instance 1 is updating, it will have to wait. After instance 1's update is committed and the data is written to disk (complete with the new transaction lock status showing no locks on the row), instance 2 can reread the block from disk and update the row as required. As the reader can imagine, the overhead for acquiring an exclusive distributed lock can become significant if several different instances are trying to concurrently modify the same block(s) managed by a single distributed lock.

Oracle's locking strategy for the Parallel Server is well suited to servicing read-only queries. For read/write applications, performance will be best if each application accesses data rather randomly (instead of most applications requiring access to the same data) or if different applications, executing concurrently, access different data.

As with any parallel processing environment, data partitioning can have a significant influence on performance. Oracle administrators may partition their schemas across different disks (perhaps storing a table and its indexes on different files on different disks).

Parallel Query Option

Oracle7 release 7.1 may be purchased with a parallel query option to enable the server to use multiple processes to execute work on behalf of a single query in parallel. Specifically, Oracle can perform parallel query processing on SELECT statements, subqueries in UPDATE and DELETE statements, and subqueries in INSERT and CREATE TABLE statements. The parallel query option also enables Oracle to process certain index creation activities in parallel, as well as load data in parallel (through the SQL*Loader utility).

Queries are parallelized dynamically when executed, not when statements are parsed. Queries will be parallelized only if they require at least one full table scan, and only if parallel query processing has been enabled through optimizer hints, through the PARALLEL clause of the CREATE TABLE statement, or through appropriate settings of certain initialization parameters. Each of these is discussed later in this section. First, it's important to understand how Oracle implements query parallelism.

Oracle uses multiple server processes to execute certain query work in parallel. One process serves as the *query coordinator*, determining how many additional *query server* processes should be used for the query and how work should be divided among these processes. The query server processes return work to the query coordinator, which may perform additional work (if necessary) before the results are returned to the requesting application.

The number of query server processes that are used indicates the *degree of parallelism* for a given query. As mentioned previously, users influence the degree of parallelism (and, indeed, whether or not parallel query processing is to be used at all) through optimizer hints, the table definition, or initialization parameters. To determine the degree of parallelism used for a given query, the query coordinator checks these three items (in the order previously specified). If none of these items specifies a degree greater than 1, parallel query processing is not used for that query.

The following example illustrates how a query might be written with an optimizer hint to enable parallel query processing. (A more general discussion of optimizer hints was included in the section "Optimizer.") In this case, the user is instructing Oracle to retrieve the names and pricing information for all restaurants included in the RESTAURANT table. The optimizer hint instructs Oracle to perform a full table scan on the table (referenced in the hint by its alias or correlation name, REST), specifying "5" as the degree of parallelism.

```
select /*+ full(rest) parallel(rest, 5) */
    name, pricing
    from restaurant rest;
```

Optionally, users may create or alter tables to enable parallel processing of queries involving these tables. This is achieved through the PARALLEL(DEGREE *n*) clause. Certain initialization parameters can also be used to control the default degree of parallelism supported by a given Oracle instance.

As the reader might suspect, parallel query processing will perrorm better when the files that must be accessed to service a given query are spread across multiple disks. Oracle recommends that users rely on automatic file striping facilities offered by certain operating systems to take advantage of this. If necessary, administrators may manually partition their schemas across multiple disks.

For those users who have both the Parallel Server and parallel query option installed, Oracle enables them to specify both the degree of parallelism (which controls the number of query server processes used to service a single query) and the number of Oracle instances that should be involved. Specifying the number of instances can be achieved through optimizer hints, through the INSTANCES clause of the CREATE TABLE or ALTER TABLE statements, and through initialization parameters. When the parallel query option is installed without the Parallel Server, only one instance is used.

SUMMARY

This chapter described Oracle's Oracle7 DBMS server, the first relational DBMS to be offered commercially and now one of the most widely installed DBMS products. This chapter explained how the product supports key DBMS functions, including lock management, recovery, integrity, and other areas. It also described Oracle's support for contemporary technologies profiled earlier in this book, including distributed database support, replication, parallelism, and middleware.

REFERENCES AND SUGGESTED READINGS

AFSARIFARD, ROSHANAK, and LISA BORDEN. "ORACLE Parallel Server for HACMP/6000 Clusters," *AIXpert*, May 1993, p. 45.

BOBROWSKI, STEVE. "Parallel Oracle 7.1," *DBMS*, December 1993, p. 89.

FERGUSON, MIKE. "Parallel Query and Transaction Processing," *InfoDB*, vol. 7, no. 3, Summer 1993, p. 18.

JACOBS, KEN. "The Oracle Server Story," *ORACLE Magazine*," *January/February 1995, p. 65, and May/June 1995, p. 57.*

"Oracle Gateways Access IBM Data Stores," *ORACLE Magazine,* Summer 1994, p. 21.

The ORACLE Parallel Server, Oracle Corp., 3000103-0291, (no publication date).

ORACLE Parallel Server Administrator's Version 7.0 Developer's Release Documentation, Oracle Corp., 5990-70-0292, May 1992.

ORACLE RDBMS Database Administrator's Guide Volume I Version 7.0 Developer's Release Documentation, Oracle Corp., 6693-70-0292, May 1992.

ORACLE RDBMS Database Administrator's Guide Volume II Version 7.0 Developer's Release Documentation, Oracle Corp., 6694-70-0292, May 1992.

ORACLE RDBMS Database Administrator's Guide Volume III Version 7.0 Beta Draft Documentation, Oracle Corp., 6695-70-0292, February 1992.

ORACLE RDBMS Performance Tuning Guide Version 7.0 Developer's Release Documentation, Oracle Corp., 5317-70-0892, 1992.

ORACLE RDBMS Utilities User's Guide Version 7.0 Developer's Release Documentation, Oracle Corp., 3602-70-0292, May 1992.

Oracle7 Relational Database Management System Feature Summary (including release 7.1), Oracle Corp., A14822, May 1994.

Oracle7 Server Documentation Addendum, Release 7.1, Oracle Corp., A12042-3, 1994.

Oracle7 Symmetric Replication Asynchronous Distributed Technology, Oracle Corp., A13824, September 1993.

PL/SQL Release 2.1 and Oracle Precompilers Release 1.6 Addendum, 1st ed., Oracle Corp., A11828-3, 1994.

PL/SQL User's Guide and Reference Version 2.0 Developer's Release Documentation, Oracle Corp., 800-20-0292, May 1992.

RICHMAN, DAN. "Oracle Pumps Up Its RDBMS," *Open Systems Today,* June 20, 1994, p. 1.

SQL Language Reference Manual Version 7.0 Beta Draft Documentation, Oracle Corp., 778-70-0292, 1992.

SQL*Net V2 Trilogy Beta Draft V2.0.9 Oracle Corp., 6759-20-0392, March 27, 1992.

CHAPTER 15
Sybase's SQL Server

CHAPTER OBJECTIVES

This chapter describes Sybase's SQL Server and a number of related offerings. It discusses major areas of product function, including those that provide for lock management, resource management, backup and recovery, data integrity, security, query support, and performance tuning. Additionally, there is discussion of Sybase technology that supports replication, middleware, distributed databases, and parallelism.

This chapter provides the reader with insight into how a commercial DBMS product has actually implemented the technologies discussed earlier in this book.

OVERVIEW OF DBMS AND RELATED PRODUCTS

Founded in 1984, Sybase released its first product (now known as SQL Server) in 1987. Since its early days, Sybase's DBMS has featured a client/server architecture and certain object-oriented extensions. In the following years, Sybase added various tools and services to round out its product line, as well as established relationships with various hardware and software vendors.

Its DBMS and tools run on a variety of operating systems, including various versions of Unix, OS/2, Netware, VMS, and others. Supported programming languages include Ada, C, COBOL, and FORTRAN. Although the Server and its tools may be installed on a single system, customers typically install the Server on one system and the tools on one or more others. Various network protocols, such as TCP/IP and DECnet, can be used to facilitate communications.

Sybase initially targeted online transaction-processing (OLTP) applications and professional programmers in its marketing efforts but has broadened its focus in more recent years. Through new product offerings, alliances, and acquisitions of other firms, Sybase now offers training and consulting services, application development tools, and decision support tools. A partial list of products Sybase has announced or shipped as of this writing includes:

1. DBMS engine products:
   - SQL Server, the standard Sybase DBMS.
   - Secure Server, a high-security DBMS designed to conform to certain specifications of the Department of Defense.
   - Navigation Server, a parallel database offering currently targeted for the NCR 3600 platform.
2. Connectivity products:
   - Open Client, an application programming interface that enables tools or clients to interface to the Server. This component was formerly known as DB-Library.
   - Open Server, an interface to OEM DBMSs and file systems. This product complements Open Client. It provides Sybase customers with a gateway capability and also enables customers to extend native SQL Server functions.
   - MVS gateway products, which consist of the Open Server for CICS, Open Gateway for DB2, and Net-Gateway. These enable applications on various platforms to access data and services on MVS systems.
   - OmniSQL Gateway, which can be considered a data access middleware product. It provides a common interface to multiple Sybase and non-Sybase data sources.
   - Replication Server, which replicates data and stored procedures across various sites.
3. Tools:
   - Data Workbench, a query/report writer with some facilities for database administrators.
   - SQR, an enhanced report writer.
   - APT Workbench, a forms-based application generator.
   - PowerBuilder, an application development facility.
   - Gain Momentum, a tool for developing multimedia applications
   - SA Companion, a facility for managing local and remote DBMS servers.
   - SQL Monitor, a performance monitor.
   - SQL Debug, a debugger for Transact-SQL (Sybase's implementation of SQL).
   - DEFT, a set of computer-aided software engineering offerings.

Figure 15–1 illustrates how a few of these products might be used together.

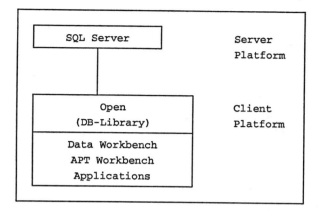

Figure 15–1. Sample SQL Server installation

The remainder of this chapter focuses on functions of SQL Server System 10. When applicable, expected functions in future releases of the SQL Server are also discussed.

Microsoft also provides a DBMS product called SQL Server. For many years, Sybase and Microsoft maintained a technology-sharing agreement, with Microsoft basing its SQL Server DBMS (originally for OS/2 only, and later for Windows NT) on Sybase's code base. In 1994, the vendors modified their technology-sharing agreement to enable them to develop different code bases and compete more directly for relational DBMS sales. The function sets of the two SQL Server lines appear as though they will diverge in the future. This chapter focuses on the Sybase SQL Server product, although a brief summary of expected features and functions in the Microsoft product is included in the section "Microsoft's SQL Server" later in this chapter.

DBMS OVERVIEW

The SQL Server consists of a MASTER database, a temporary database (TEMPDB), a MODEL database, an optionally installed sample database (PUBS2), and optionally created user databases. The MASTER database contains catalogs with systemwide information (configuration parameters, devices, server processes) as well as database-specific information (about objects, dependencies, permissions, and so forth). It is owned by the system administrator. TEMPDB is a temporary work space used by the system to store temporary objects and perform sorting. The MODEL database is a template for all user-created databases; it contains the necessary catalogs and can be tailored to include special permissions and objects that the system administrator wants replicated in each new database. Finally, the PUBS2 database contains sample tables, triggers, stored procedures, rules, and defaults; Sybase tutorials and sample applications reference this database.

Figure 15–2 illustrates how these databases might be configured in an SQL Server system. Note that the databases may span multiple devices and that each

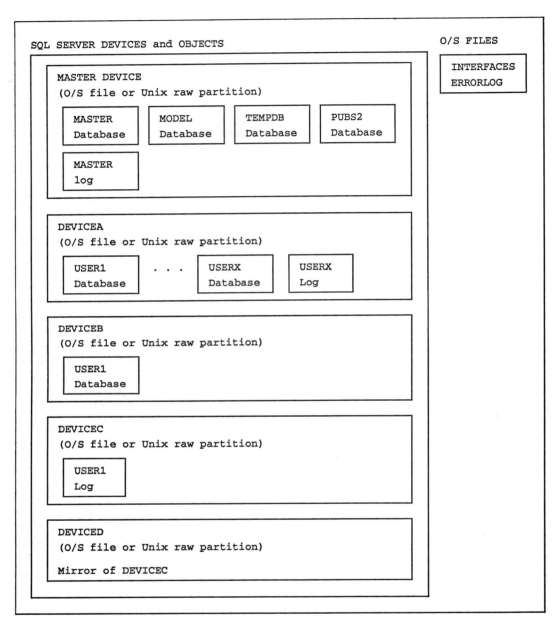

Figure 15–2. Sample structure of an SQL Server system. Note that the USER1 database spans two logical devices and is logged on a third logical device.

device may be mirrored to provide fault tolerance. In addition, logs may reside on separate devices.

SQL Server supports a maximum of 32,767 databases (ranging in size from 2 MB to 2**23 MB).

In addition to databases and catalogs, at least two files are important to the SQL Server administrator: an "interfaces" file, which contains port addresses and logical names for the Server and its clients, and an "errorlog" file, which contains diagnostic information on problems the Server detected during operations, start-up, and shut down.

The SQL Server is multithreaded, enabling a single-server process to service requests from multiple clients concurrently. Sybase's Virtual Server Architecture, which formed the basis for its initial support of parallelism, uses a multi-threaded, multiserver approach to satisfy client requests. Multiple server processes (each of which is multithreaded) can service the needs of various clients. For general information about multiserver architectures, see Chapter 6, "Client/ Server Environments."

DATA MANAGEMENT

When developing a database schema, SQL Server administrators may create a number of objects: tables, views, indexes, stored procedures, triggers, rules, and defaults. In addition, a single SQL Server DBMS can support multiple user-created databases.

Data is stored in databases for which one or more *database devices* have been defined. These devices (created via the *disk init* command) are physical devices or files that have been defined to be usable by SQL Server. Databases may be divided into *segments* to give administrators more control over the placement of tables and indexes for performance reasons. By default, SQL Server creates three segments for each database: a *system* segment (for the catalog), a *logsegment* (for the log), and a *default* segment (for user-created objects).

Administrators may define additional segments for their databases through the *sp_addsegment* stored procedure. Tables, stored procedures, indexes, and other database objects can be created to reside on these additional segments. A single segment may be associated with one or more database devices defined for a particular database.

Careful use of segments can offer performance benefits. For example, segments enable administrators to place nonclustered indexes on devices separate from their tables; this can reduce overall I/O time for certain queries. In addition, a single table may be split across multiple devices, distributing the I/O workload to improve overall read/write times. This is particularly helpful for large, frequently accessed tables. As of this writing, a maximum of 31 segments may be used for each SQL Server database.

Two storage structures are supported in SQL Server: B+ tree indexes (which can eliminate the need to scan entire tables to satisfy the requests of certain queries) and heaps. Page size varies according to hardware platform, but it is generally 2K or 4K. A table's pages are linked together and allocated in *extents*, or contiguous sets of 8 pages. SQL Server System 10 supports 2 billion tables per database and 250 columns per table.

Indexes

SQL Server supports B+ tree indexing to speed access to data. One clustered index is permitted per table, as well as up to 249 nonclustered indexes. Index keys may consist of 1 to 16 columns. Unique indexes can be created to prohibit duplicate key values. Use of indexes, and their impact on performance, is discussed later in the section "Performance."

Data Types

Tables may be defined to contain columns of a variety of data types, including:

- INT, a 32-bit integer (2,147,483,647 to –2,147,483,648).
- SMALLINT, a 16-bit integer (32,767 to –32,768).
- TINYINT, a one-byte integer (0 to 255).
- FLOAT, a four- or eight-byte floating-point number.
- DOUBLE PRECISION, an eight-byte (double precision) floating-point number.
- REAL, a four-byte floating-point number.
- NUMERIC(p, s), 2 to 17 bytes for storing decimal data; p indicates the precision, or the maximum number of decimal digits stored in the column; s indicates the scale, or the maximum number of digits stored to the right of the decimal point.
- DECIMAL(p, s), 2 to 17 bytes for storing decimal data; p indicates the precision, or the maximum number of decimal digits stored in the column; s indicates the scale, or the maximum number of digits stored to the right of the decimal point.
- MONEY, monetary values represented as double-precision floating-point numbers. Values may range between 922,337,203,477.5807 and –922,337,203,685,477.5808.
- SMALLMONEY, monetary values represented as single-precision floating-point numbers. Values may range between 214,748.3647 and –214,748.3648.
- CHAR(n), fixed-length alphanumeric characters of length n; n must be between 1 and 255.
- VARCHAR(n), variable-length characters of length n; n must be between 1 and 255.
- NCHAR(n), similar to *char* but used to support multibyte character sets of certain national languages.
- NVARCHAR(n), similar to *varchar* but used to support multibyte character sets of certain national languages.
- TEXT, variable-length characters of up to 2,147,483,647 bytes.
- BINARY(n), fixed-length binary data (including program code and graphics) of length n; n must be between 1 and 255.

- VARBINARY(*n*), variable-length binary data of length *n*; *n* must be between 1 and 255.
- IMAGE, variable-length binary data of up to 2,147,483,647 bytes.
- DATETIME, two four-byte integers representing the date and time of day. Dates must range from January 1, 1753, to December 31, 9999. Times are accurate to 3.33 milliseconds.
- SMALLDATETIME, two small integers for the date and time of day. Precision is more limited with this data type. Dates range from January 1, 1900, to June 6, 2079; times are accurate to one minute.
- BIT, a single bit (1 or 0).
- TIMESTAMP, instances of *varbinary(8)* data that are automatically updated by SQL Server whenever a row containing a *timestamp* column is updated or inserted.
- SYSNAME, instances of *varchar(30)* data that are used in system (catalog) tables.

Optionally, administrators may create one *identity* column per table; data in these columns will contain system-generated, sequential values that uniquely identify each row within the table. Identity columns must be *numeric* (with a scale of 0) and the keyword "identity" must follow the data type information in the column specification. Nulls are not permitted, and updates may not be made to identity column values.

Sybase was one of the first major relational DBMS vendors to support image and text data types (which can be considered forms of BLOBs or very long fields). The data for these columns is stored in linked lists, and these may reside on a device that is separate from the table's other data. Although image and text data types can be queried and updated through basic SQL statements, Sybase recommends using Open Client calls (and therefore, writing an application) to improve performance.

In addition to the data types previously listed, users may customize system-supplied data types through the use of rules and SQL Server stored procedures. An example of this is provided in the section "Rules."

Integrity

At least three of the objects supported by SQL Server are used for enforcing integrity constraints: triggers, rules, and defaults. All are stored in the appropriate databases, all are tracked by system catalogs, and all are eventually associated with other objects (tables or views) whose characteristics they restrict. They are created through Transact SQL (Sybase's SQL dialect) and through system-supplied stored procedures. Examples of each of these integrity mechanisms should help clarify their use, as well as give readers some idea of the work involved to implement them. Since rules and defaults are easiest to understand, they are discussed first.

It is important to note, however, that many of the integrity constraints that can be enforced through rules, triggers, and defaults can also be defined through new options of the CREATE TABLE statement introduced with System 10. This section also discusses these newer integrity enforcement mechanisms as appropriate.

Rules

Rules specify a range of values (an edit mask) for a column or a user-defined data type. They may include any expressions, arithmetic operators, or relational operators that are valid in the WHERE clause of a SELECT statement, provided they reference only the column to which the rule applies. For example, suppose a table of RESTAURANTs contains a PRICING column that should identify "expensive," "moderate," and "inexpensive" establishments. To implement this rule in the SQL Server, an administrator would use the CREATE RULE statement to specify the constraint and a system-supplied stored procedure (*sp_bindrule*) to bind this rule to a specific column of a specific table. The following example creates a REST_RULE to specify this constraint and binds this rule to the PRICING column of the RESTAURANT table.

```
create rule rest_rule as
    @price in ('expensive', 'moderate', 'inexpensive'
exec sp_bindrule 'rest_rule', 'restaurant.pricing'
```

This syntax may be new to many readers, so some explanation is in order. The first line instructs SQL Server to create a new rule (called "rest_rule" in this example). The second line specifies the conditions for this rule. The "@" symbol can be thought of as identifying a variable, whose contents will later be compared to three subsequent character strings ("expensive," "moderate," and "inexpensive"). The third line associates the new rule (and its "@price" argument) with the PRICING column of the RESTAURANT table. In this way, whenever a user tries to insert or update information in that table, SQL Server will compare the new value for the PRICING column with the three values specified in "rest_rule." If the new value does not match one of these three values, the update or insert operation will not be permitted.

With System 10, SQL Server users also have the option of using the CREATE TABLE or ALTER TABLE statements to define constraints that perform data range checking. Rather than creating the "rest_rule" (shown previously) and binding this rule to the PRICING column of the RESTAURANT table, a System 10 user could specify a CHECK clause when creating the table to ensure that values for the PRICING column are always "expensive," "moderate," or "inexpensive."

```
create table restaurant
   (...
    pricing         char(11)
                    check (pricing in ("expensive", "moderate",
                                        "inexpensive"),
```

As mentioned earlier, rules are frequently used to define new data types. The following example defines a new data type for a San Jose phone number (SJPHONE), which must consist of 10 characters. The first three must specify area code 408. The remaining seven may be numbers or characters (indicated by seven underscore characters).

```
exec sp_addtype 'sjphone', 'char(10)'
create rule sj_rule as
    @phone like '408_____'
exec sp_bindrule sj_rule, sjphone
```

A system-supplied stored procedure (*sp_addtype*) enables an administrator to define this new data type as a fixed-length, 10-character string. The second line creates a rule (named "sj_rule"), which will be used to restrict the data values associated with this new data type. The rule specifies that the first three characters must be "408." The third line invokes another system-supplied stored procedure (*sp_bindrule*) to bind this rule with the "sjphone" data type. Doing so defines the valid data values for this new data type and provides at least partial support for the relational concept of a domain.

Defaults

Creating a default value for a column or user-defined data type is somewhat similar. This example shows how to make the current date the default value for the DATE column in the RATING table.

```
create default date_default as getdate()
exec sp_bindefault date_default, 'rating.date'
```

A new default value is identified to SQL Server ("date_default"), which relies on a Sybase SQL function [*getdate()*] to return the current date. This default is then bound to, or associated with, the DATE column in the RATING table (via the *sp_bindefault* procedure supplied by Sybase).

Optionally, System 10 users may specify defaults through the DEFAULT clause of the CREATE TABLE and ALTER TABLE statements.

Triggers

While rules and defaults are fairly straightforward, triggers and stored procedures can become more complex. Before System 10 was available, SQL Server users relied on triggers to enforce referential integrity constraints. This involved some work and forethought.

For example, imagine that a RATING table contains reviews of restaurants, including an OVERALL score, the DATE of the review, and the employee number of the REVIEWER who conducted the review. The values in RATING. REVIEWER must reference a valid critic; a list of all critics is stored in the CRITIC table, which consists of an ID column for employee numbers, LAST_NAMEs, FIRST_NAMEs, and PHONE numbers. One part of the referential integrity constraint on these tables would require preventing anyone from adding a restaurant review unless it was conducted by a valid critic (or from updating information so that it no longer referenced a valid critic). The following example shows how this might be implemented. The process basically involves comparing the value the user is attempting to insert (tracked in a temporary table, INSERTED) with the values in the parent table (in this case, CRITIC).

```
create trigger rating_update on rating for update, insert as

declare @num_rows int
select @num_rows = @@rowcount
if @num_rows = 0
   return
if @num_rows !=
     (select count(*) from critic, inserted
      where critic.id = inserted.reviewer)
begin
raiserror 35001 'Invalid reviewer. Update not permitted.'
rollback tran
return
end
```

A trigger named "rating_update" is defined for the RATING table and will execute whenever update or insert operations are attempted. A variable ("@num_rows") is declared, and the value associated with a system-supplied global variable ("@@rowcount") is assigned to it. During execution, this global variable will contain the number of rows affected by the attempted UPDATE or INSERT operation at this point. It is this value that is assigned to "@num_rows." A test is made to see if any rows were actually affected. This is necessary because the conditions specified in the WHERE clause of an UPDATE statement might not have been satisfied; therefore, no rows would be affected, and it would be unwise to consume system resources unnecessarily by processing the remainder of the trigger.

Assuming at least one row is affected, a SELECT statement is issued to compare information in the CRITIC table with information the user is trying to update or insert (contained in the temporary table "inserted"). The SELECT statement counts the number of rows in which the new REVIEWER identifier matches a similar identifier in the CRITIC table. That number is then compared to the number of rows that would be affected by the UPDATE or INSERT operation. If the numbers don't match, a referential integrity violation would occur. Therefore, an error is raised, and the update or insert operation is rolled back.

SQL Server enables up to three triggers to be defined per table: one for inserts, one for updates, and one for deletes. In addition, SQL Server supports the notion of nested triggers, or triggers that cause other triggers to execute. This might happen if an update trigger on Table 1 would cause an insert operation to be performed against Table 2, upon which an insert trigger had already been defined. Thus, an update on Table 1 would cause two triggers to fire: the trigger on Table 1, as well as the trigger on Table 2. Nested triggers are supported up to a depth of 16 levels. In addition, SQL Server triggers may be recursive (such that execution of a trigger would cause itself to fire again). Recursive trigger execution may also occur up to 16 times.

Declarative Referential Integrity

System 10 supports declarative referential integrity. This enables users to identify one or more columns of a table to serve as its primary key. Foreign keys can then be identified that reference this primary key, instructing System 10 to automatically enforce the referential integrity constraint. Identifying a primary key through the CREATE TABLE statement implicitly creates an index on this key and ensures that no null values are accepted.

The following example illustrates one way in which a referential integrity constraint might be specified when creating two tables—the CRITIC table, which contains an ID column as its primary key, and the RATING table, which contains a REVIEWER column that serves as a foreign key, referencing the CRITIC table. In this example, the creator of the RATING table is presumed to have proper privileges to reference the CRITIC table.

```
create table critic
    (id int primary key
    ...)

create table rating
    (...
     reviewer int references critic,
    ...)
```

If an update or delete operation involving the primary key would violate the referential integrity constraint, SQL Server will not permit the operation to execute. Users may write triggers to enforce referential integrity if other actions are desired—such as setting dependent rows to null or cascading the delete operation.

SQL Server also enables users to define triggers on tables that were created with declarative referential integrity constraints. In this case, the declarative referential integrity constraints will be checked before any triggers are executed.

ADMINISTRATION

Administering SQL Server is accomplished through Transact-SQL statements (Sybase's SQL implementation), utilities, and Sybase-supplied stored procedures. Together, these facilities enable the system administrator to add devices, create new users and database administrators, monitor and tune performance, load and dump data, and perform a variety of other functions. Unlike some other DBMSs, the SQL Server gives its administrator ultimate power over the system, even allowing him or her to change system catalog tables and rewrite system procedures. However, Sybase does not typically encourage such activities.

Security

Sybase's most secure DBMS offering is its Secure Server product, designed to conform to the Department of Defense's B1- and B2-level security standards. In the standard SQL Server product, users must be granted access to the Server itself, then to individual databases (unless the user simply wants to use those that support "guests," which are discussed shortly), and then to individual objects within those databases. This is shown in Figure 15–3.

Privileges (also called *permissions*) are managed through GRANT and REVOKE statements. Sybase distinguishes between two types of privileges: command-level and object-level. Command-level privileges involve the ability to create a database, table, view, rule, default, or procedure; dump a database (for backup purposes); and dump a transaction log. Object-level privileges involve the ability to select, update, insert, or delete data from a table or view. They also involve the right to execute a stored procedure, even if the user doesn't have the privilege of accessing the view or table referenced within it. A system-supplied stored procedure (*sp_helprotect*) enables administrators to report on the privileges associated with a given database object or user.

Each database administrator has the option of enabling guest users to access the administrator's database. If this feature is implemented, all valid SQL Server users may access that database, performing all functions granted to guests. This feature may be of interest to customers with databases that contain tables or views of general interest to all users or that will be used as a training ground for new users.

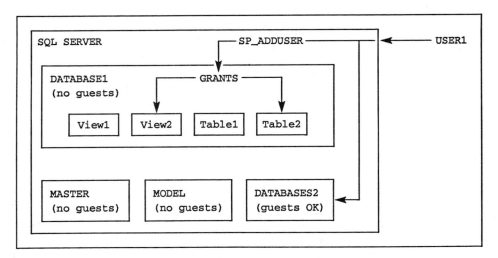

Figure 15–3. Security levels within the SQL Server. User1 is given a valid SQL Server login, then is added as a user of Database1 and GRANTed appropriate privileges. User1 can also access Database2 as a guest user.

Security Groups

Certain privileges are automatically associated with certain groups of users recognized by SQL Server. For example, a systems administrator has all privileges at all times; more precisely, the system administrator operates outside the normal Sybase protection scheme. Database administrators (also called *database owners*) can create most database objects (tables, rules, procedures, views, and defaults) as well as issue certain commands (such as dump a database). Table owners can alter their tables, create indexes and triggers for them, and issue DML statements against them. Anyone (the *public*) can issue transaction control statements (such as begin/end transaction). And other types of users, such as system security officers and system operators, have other predefined sets of privileges.

Note that some members of this *permission hierarchy* do not automatically possess all the privileges of those at lower levels. For example, a database administrator cannot arbitrarily create a trigger on a table owned by another user or read data from a table owned by another user—even if that table was created in the administrator's database. However, *the setuser* command enables the administrator to "impersonate" the table owner and assume all of his or her privileges for that time (including the right to grant table-level privileges to other users, such as the database administrator).

Three of the previously described user types are recognized as *roles* by SQL Server. These are system administrators (who possess the *sa_role*), the system security officers (who possess the *sso_role*), and the system operators (who possess the *oper_role*). The *sp_role* stored procedure is used to grant these roles to individual users. As noted previously, these users will inherently possess certain privileges (because of their roles or user types), but additional privileges may be specifically granted to these roles if desired.

Furthermore, administrators can define their own security groups (through the *sp_addgroup* stored procedure) and assign different users to one or more of these groups (when new users are identified to SQL Server through the *sp_adduser* stored procedure). Privileges can then be granted or revoked to these groups, and group members will automatically inherit any privileges associated with their group.

Audit Trail

System 10 includes support for an audit trail, which enables administrators to track the activities of specific users or monitor overall access patterns. A separate database—the *sybsecurity* database—contains the audit trail (in the *sysaudits* table) and information about global auditing options (in the *sysauditoptions* table). The audit system and its associated database are created as part of the installation process. A system-supplied stored procedure (*sp_auditoption*) is used to enable or disable systemwide auditing.

Various stored procedures can also be invoked to control what events are audited. For example, *sp_auditlogin* enables a security officer to monitor the attempts of any specific user to access any tables or views. Object-level auditing can be enabled by invoking *sp_auditobject*; this enables a security officer to monitor any access attempts involving a specific table or view. Auditing the execution of a particular stored procedure or trigger is accomplished through the use of *sp_auditsproc*.

As mentioned previously, the audit trail is kept in the *sysaudits* table. Access to this table is limited to individual(s) identified to System 10 as system security officer(s). Read-only queries (SELECT statements) may be issued against this table, but read/write queries are not permitted. However, System 10 enables security officers to enter comments into the audit trail through the use of the *sp_addauditrecord* procedure. To prevent the audit trail from growing indefinitely, security officers typically archive old records (perhaps by issuing a SELECT...INTO statement) and then truncate the audit trail's contents (by issuing the TRUNCATE TABLE command).

Concurrency Control

SQL Server provides a number of mechanisms to support concurrency control. This section describes these mechanisms, focusing first on the lock levels and lock modes supported in System 10.

Lock Levels and Lock Modes

SQL Server locks data at the page or table level. In some cases, table-level locks are used with page-level locks to minimize the overhead that might otherwise be associated with lock acquisitions. But before exploring the synergy between page-level and table-level locks, it's important to first understand the types of locks that may be acquired at both the page and table levels.

Page-level locks may be held in one of four modes, described below:

- Shared. This is used only for read operations. Shared locks enable other processes to read data from the same page; however, other transactions may not write to it. By default shared locks are released after the query statement completes.
- Update. This is used during the initial stages of an update operation, in which pages are only being read. During this time, other transactions may read these pages as well. When a page that is subjected to an update lock is about to be changed, the update lock is promoted to an exclusive lock.
- Demand. When it is taking too long to service a write transaction (because multiple read transactions have been acquiring share locks on the resource), SQL Server grants a demand lock to the write transaction. This increases its priority (by moving it to the head of a DBMS-maintained queue) and prevents subsequent read transactions from acquiring shared locks on the resource until the write transaction has completed.
- Exclusive. This is used when modifying data, so that only one process is allowed to access that data at one time. Exclusive locks are held until the end of the transaction.

In addition, various lock modes may be applied to tables. These are:

- Shared. This is the same as shared page-level locks, except that the entire table is affected.
- Demand. This is the same as page-level demand locks, except that the entire table is affected.
- Exclusive. This is the same as exclusive table-level locks, except that the entire table is affected. Generally, exclusive locks involving write operations are acquired at the page level. However, UPDATE and DELETE statements that do not reference indexed columns will cause exclusive table-level locks to be acquired.
- Intent shared. This is used for read operations. After acquiring an intent-shared lock on a table, the owner may try to lock one or more pages to read data. These attempts will succeed as long as those pages are not already locked exclusively by other processes. Intent-shared locks permit other users to read pages within the table as well. Intent-shared locks are acquired for queries that reference both indexed and nonindexed columns.
- Intent exclusive. This is used for write operations. After acquiring an intent-exclusive lock on a table, the owner may try to lock one or more pages to write data. These attempts will succeed as long as those pages are not already locked by other processes. Processes that hold intent-exclusive locks on a table may also try to lock pages in shared mode (for read operations). Intent-exclusive locks are acquired for insert operations; they are also acquired for update or delete operations if these statements reference indexed columns.

As the reader may have determined, there is a synergy between table-level intent locks and some of the previously described page-level locks. Table-level intent locks help SQL Server reduce some locking overhead that typically occurs in production environments. This overhead can occur when the DBMS must determine if a new transaction can be granted the desired locks for reading or writing data. Without table-level intent locks, the DBMS might have to scan the entire page lock queue to see if there would be any conflicts. With table-level intent locks, this scan can be avoided, and the determination can be made more quickly.

Other Lock Issues

SQL Server generally tries to use page-level locks as much as possible to improve concurrency. However, it will try to escalate page locks to a table level if a single statement acquires more than 200 page locks.

Administrators can limit the number of locks used by SQL Server by executing a system-supplied stored procedure to reset the *locks* configuration variable. By default, SQL Server supports 5000 locks. The maximum for System 10 exceeds 2 billion. Sybase recommends that users generally estimate that each concurrent process will acquire approximately 20 locks.

If desired, administrators can monitor lock activity by invoking the *sp_lock* stored procedure. This displays data about locks currently held, reporting on the type of lock, table ID involved, and the ID of the SQL Server process holding the lock.

A holdlock function is used to hold shared locks for a particular table or view until the transaction is completed. When combined with the "set transaction isolation level 3" statement, this offers support for repeatable reads.

SQL Server is capable of detecting deadlocks and resolving them. The process that has consumed the least amount of CPU time is chosen to become the "victim." Its transaction is rolled back, and the resources it was locking are made available to other processes.

Backup and Recovery

Like other DBMSs, SQL Server provides various facilities to support backup and recovery. This section describes System 10's support in these areas, focusing on backup and recovery processes for user databases. Backup and recovery processes for system databases (such as the MASTER database) are generally similar, but there are some differences. Readers interested in this topic are encouraged to consult material cited in "References and suggested Reading."

Backups

SQL Server administrators use the *dump database* command to make backup copies of their databases. This command backs up the entire database and its associated log. Database dumps are performed while the database is online (open and in use); these are sometimes referred to as *dynamic* dumps. If a user tries to update a page that is in the process of being backed up, he or she must wait until that work is completed. Nonetheless, support for online backups helps ensure continuous operations.

The *dump transaction* command is also important to the backup process. This command backs up the log and deletes log records for committed transactions. This command can be executed only when the log resides on a separate device from the database.

While the *dump database* command backs up both the database and the log, it does *not* automatically delete committed log records (as the *dump transaction* command does). Therefore, if administrators simply use *dump database* for their backups, the log will eventually become full and need to be truncated manually (by instructing SQL Server to *dump transaction with truncate_only*. For this reason (and others), administrators are typically encouraged to periodically back up their database and make more frequent backups of their logs, assuming the database and log are stored on separate devices.

On rare occasions, administrators may find themselves in the difficult position of being unable to back up the log because insufficient space exists to log the backup event. This situation can be avoided if log space is monitored closely, if logs are truncated as needed (either manually or through regular backup events, depending on the configuration of the database and its log), or if an appropriate threshold has been set (as is discussed in the section "Setting a Threshold"). However, if this problem arises, an administrator can issue the *dump transaction with no_log* command to truncate the log without logging the backup event. After doing so, the database should be backed up immediately; otherwise, there will be no reliable means to fully recover from errors if necessary.

If desired, administrators may direct their backups to a remote system (running a *Backup Server,* which is supplied as part of System 10). This is accomplished by specifying the desired server name when invoking the appropriate backup command. SQL Server consults its local "interfaces" file to identify the network address for this server and routes the backup to the appropriate location. Similarly, dumps may be restored from remote servers by specifying the appropriate server name when invoking the *load database* or *load transaction* command.

Administrators also have the option of *striping* their backups across multiple dump devices. The Backup Server can write concurrently to as many as 32 devices, dividing the backup into equal portions. Dump striping can reduce the overall time required to back up a database or transaction log.

Logging

Like many other DBMSs, SQL Server maintains a write-ahead log (sometimes called the *transaction log*) that records before- and after-image copies of database work conducted on behalf of transactions. One such log is associated with each database, and logging is always enabled while the database is in use.

Checkpoints are made periodically to synchronize a database and its log. Administrators may influence the frequency of checkpoints by resetting the *recovery interval* configuration variable. This variable specifies the maximum number of minutes needed to complete the recovery process, and SQL Server automatically takes checkpoints at the appropriate frequency to ensure that database recovery will occur within that time period. If desired, administrators may manually force a checkpoint by issuing the *checkpoint* command.

Dual logging is supported through the use of mirrored devices. This mechanism, invoked through the *disk mirror* command, instructs SQL Server to duplicate information on one device onto another device. This can improve overall availability should a device failure occur. However, any disk mirroring activity can impact performance, as I/O activity for write operations is increased.

Recovery

Data can be restored from backup copies with the *load database* command. Similarly, backup copies of logs can be restored with the *load transaction* command. If backups are stored on a remote server or are striped across multiple devices, certain options of these *load* commands must be specified to inform the local SQL Server of appropriate actions it needs to take.

Inaccessible or damaged databases can be recovered by loading the most recent backup copy of the database and subsequent copies of the log (assuming that user data and logs are stored on different devices). If multiple backups of logs were made for a given database, they must be applied in the order made. This brings the database to a consistent state as of the last log backup by reapplying all committed work recorded in the log.

Administrators are encouraged to lock the database (by invoking the *sp_dboption* stored procedure with certain parameters) before loading the database. Among other things, this helps ensure that only the database owner has access to the database during this period. If user access is permitted during the recovery phase, it's possible that some changes may be made to the database between the time the database backup is applied and subsequent log backups are applied. SQL Server detects such cases and causes the *load transaction* activity to fail, as applying the logs may interfere with the new user changes. At this point, an administrator can take appropriate action. This might involve locking the database, reloading the database backup, loading the subsequent log backups, and rerunning the user application(s), if desired.

Setting a Threshold

As mentioned previously, SQL Server enables administrators to set a *threshold* to help them monitor free space left in the log. This is desirable, as it helps ensure that there is always enough free log space to record a backup event (and therefore complete the backup). This mechanism is available to all administrators whose databases and corresponding logs reside on separate devices.

By default, a *last-chance threshold* is automatically established for databases whose logs are stored on separate devices. This last-chance threshold estimates the number of free pages required to back up the log. When this threshold is crossed, SQL Server automatically executes the *sp_thresholdaction* stored procedure. A warning message is displayed and active transactions are suspended until an administrator backs up the transaction log.

However, some administrators may not wish to wait until such a drastic scenario occurs. SQL Server enables administrators to define additional thresholds for their logs. Instead of waiting for free space to nearly run out (and the last-chance threshold to be crossed), an administrator might wish to establish a log threshold when some percentage of the log becomes full (perhaps 50 or 75 percent). When this user-defined threshold is crossed, a user-created stored procedure can be automatically executed to take appropriate action, such as immediately backing up the log.

Establishing a secondary log threshold is accomplished through the *sp_addthreshold* stored procedure. Before invoking this procedure, an administrator would typically query a system catalog table to determine the log's capacity (in pages). Then, the administrator could add a new threshold, specifying the database name, the name of the segment to be monitored, the number of pages at which the threshold is set, and the name of the stored procedure (created by a user) that should be executed whenever this threshold is crossed.

For example, assume that the DINING database has a log segment (LOG-SEGMENT) defined with a maximum capacity of 4096 pages. The following command would add a threshold to this database that would be crossed when the log was 50 percent full (2048 pages). At such time, the DIN_THRES stored procedure would be executed automatically.

```
sp_addthreshold dining, logsegment, 2048, din_thres
```

Nested Transactions

System 10 is somewhat unusual among the relational DBMSs profiled here in that it supports the notion of *nested transactions*. This enables programmers to nest *begin transaction/commit* statements within one another, essentially creating multiple subtransactions. It is important to note, however, that committing a subtransaction has no effect until the outer-most transaction commits. If the outer-most transaction rolls back, all of its subtransactions (even those that have been committed) are also rolled back.

Nested transactions may occur when a single application causes multiple stored procedures or triggers to be executed, each of which may initiate other stored procedures or triggers. These objects may have their own transaction scope (or contain *begin transaction* and *commit* statements), thereby involving nested transactions.

Save Points

Like certain other DBMSs, SQL Server System 10 supports save points. This mechanism enables programmers to selectively roll back portions of a transaction. The *save transaction* statement creates a save point, identifying it by a label. SQL operations included within the scope of that save point can be rolled back, if desired, by issuing a rollback statement that references the save point's label. Save points may be included within applications, stored procedures, or triggers.

Other Issues

Sybase includes more than 80 stored procedures with its SQL Server product, many of which are useful for system administration. While it is beyond the scope of this book to describe all of these procedures, it's worth noting the

kinds of administrative functions for which these procedures are used. They
include establishing and changing members of security groups, displaying and
changing system configuration and database-specific options, obtaining information about remote servers, obtaining information about available database
devices, and reporting on system usage. Customers are free to create their own
stored procedures for administrative purposes, and these procedures can be
made accessible to other users through standard Sybase security mechanisms.

Resource control in SQL Server can be managed through a configuration
variable (*time slice*), which limits the number of milliseconds each user process is
allowed to run. The specified value applies equally to all user processes.

The primary diagnostic mechanisms available to SQL Server administrators
are error messages and records in an error log file (maintained by both SQL Server
and its Backup Server). In addition, SQL Server administrators may use a set of
dbcc commands to check the logical and physical consistency of their databases.
Among other things, this set of commands enables administrators to verify that
internal data pointers and pointers between pages are valid.

Unlike some DBMS products, the Server was designed around the concept
of cooperative processing (or client/server architecture) since its inception.
Therefore, the network must be up and running for Sybase products to be
installed—even if the Server and its front-end tools are all being installed on a
single processor.

QUERY CAPABILITIES

The reader has already been introduced to some Transact-SQL statements in the
previous sections. In addition to the triggers, rules, and defaults Sybase has
implemented, SQL Server also permits procedural logic to be written into stored
procedures. Support for outer joins and updates of views based on joined tables
are among other features supported through Sybase's implementation of SQL.

Stored Procedures

Stored procedures are objects similar to triggers in terms of language constructs.
However, they are typically used for performance gains rather than enforcing
integrity constraints. Stored procedures are a group of SQL statements, often combined with procedural logic, that are invoked with a single database call. They are
stored as database objects for invocation at any time. However, the validation,
optimization, and compilation stages of a procedure's execution need only be
repeated whenever the optimized plan for the procedure is not found in cache.

The following example illustrates a simple stored procedure that returns a
report on restaurants of interest; similarly, this procedure could have been written
to accommodate inserts, updates, or other needs.

```
create proc query_rest
   (@cuisine varchar(30) = null)
as

if @cuisine = null                    /* Help user if no search arg */
   begin
   print "Please specify cuisine at invocation (query_rest 'JAPANESE')"
   return -999
   end

if not exists                         /* Help user if no match found */
   (select cuisine from restaurant where cuisine = @cuisine)
      begin
      print "No restaurants with this cuisine found. Try again."
      return -990
      end

else
   begin
   select name, pricing, phone from restaurant where cuisine = @cuisine
   return 0
   end
```

This example creates a procedure called "query_rest" that expects one input parameter, a character string indicating a type of restaurant cuisine. This parameter will later be used when formulating the SELECT query to specify a search condition. However, the procedure first checks to see if the user forgot to pass in this parameter. If so, it returns an error message and ends. If a type of cuisine was specified, the procedure verifies that at least one row in the table contains an entry for this type of cuisine. If not, it returns an error message and ends. Otherwise, it issues the query and retrieves the desired data, returning without error.

This stored procedure example illustrates how Sybase's Transact-SQL language supports a number of procedural logic constructs (such as if-then-else statements) typical of third-generation programming languages.

Outer Join

Outer joins are supported through the use of the "*=" and "=*" operators. The location of the asterisk ("*") indicates if all rows from the first-named table or the second-named table should be included in the answer set. This example returns all the rows in the RESTAURANT table even if there are no matching rows in RATING (in which case, NULL values are returned):

```
select *
from restaurant, rating
where restaurant.id *= rating.rest_id
```

View Updates

As for updating views based upon joined tables, the Server permits this to a degree. Updates and inserts are allowed only if they pertain to columns derived from the same table. For example, imagine that VIEW1 contains four columns: EMPNO, NAME, SALARY, and DEPTNAME. Furthermore, assume that the first three columns are based on columns in the EMPLOYEE table, while the DEPT-NAME column is based on a column in the DEPT table. Given this, an update or insert would be permitted if it involved EMPNO, NAME and/or SALARY (or, alternately, only DEPTNAME). However, an update attempt on EMPNO, NAME, DEPTNAME would fail. This constraint is Sybase's solution to the problems inherent in updates of views defined on multiple tables, as discussed in Chapter 5, "Introduction to SQL."

Other Issues

SQL Server also permits columns to be defined that may contain null values, although NOT NULL is the default. Nulls are used to represent values that are unknown or inapplicable. In addition, SQL Server also enables table creators to establish default values for columns in tables; if a user inserts a row and neglects to specify a value for the column, SQL Server will record its default value. An example of defaults was included in the earlier section "Integrity."

DISTRIBUTED DATABASE

Distributed database support was an early area of focus for Sybase, as it was one of the first vendors to support two-phase commit processing in a distributed database environment. Sybase continues to offer this support today.

However, SQL Server's support for distributed two-phase commit relies on application programmers to write code to coordinate the commit processing. Multisite updates are not transparent to SQL Server programmers, although they can be transparent to SQL Server end users who execute these applications.

Figures 15–4 through 15–6 depict a sample C application for updating two Servers within a single commit scope. The program identifies the Server named SYBASE to act as the commit coordinator, spawning a separate DBMS process to "oversee" the transaction. Later, the program updates duplicate tables on two different Servers to reclassify all meals listed as "brunch" to "breakfast." For simplicity, minimal error detection logic is included; for readability, the program does not contain any subroutines.

However, SQL Server provides another mechanism to help make multi-site access more transparent for end users. This is achieved through remote procedure calls. Essentially, a programmer could write a procedure on Server1 that calls another procedure stored on Server2, as shown in the following example. How-

```
#include <sybfront.h>
#include <sybdb.h>
#include <syberror.h>
#include <math.h>
main()
{
  DBPROCESS *dbproc;    /* pointer to remote database process */
  DBPROCESS *dbproc2;    /* pointer to local database process */
  DBPROCESS *dbproc_commit;   /* pointer to commit server process */
  LOGINREC *login;    /* current login */
  RETCODE return_code;    /* for remote failures */
  RETCODE return_code2;    /* for local failures */
  int   commitid;    /* transacation identifier */
  char   cmdbuf[256];
  char   xact_string[128];

  login = dblogin();    /* get current login info */
  DBSETLPWD(login, "mypass");
  dbproc = dbopen(login, "SYDEC");    /* start remote process */
  dbproc2 = dbopen(login, "SYBASE");    /* start local process */
  dbproc_commit = open_commit(login, "SYBASE");    /* start commit server */

  if (dbproc == NULL||dbproc2 == NULL||dbproc_commit == NULL)
  {
      printf("Sorry. Couldn't log into all servers. Aborting....\n");
      exit(ERREXIT);    /* abort on error */
  }
  printf("Logged into all servers.\n");
/* set up transaction ID                                      */
  commitid = start_xact(dbproc_commit, "distrib", "test", 2);
  build_xact_string ("test", "Sybase", commitid, xact_string);
  printf("Transaction ID set up.\n");
/* start transaction                                          */
  sprintf(cmdbuf, "BEGIN TRANSACTION %s", xact_string);
  dbcmd(dbproc, cmdbuf);
  dbcmd(dbproc2, cmdbuf);
  dbsqlexec(dbproc);
  dbsqlexec(dbproc2);
  printf("Issued BEGIN TRANSACTION.\n");
/* perform transaction. update data at both sites       */
  sprintf(cmdbuf, "update rating set meal_time = 'breakfast'
      where meal_time = 'brunch'");
  dbcmd(dbproc, cmdbuf);
  dbcmd(dbproc2, cmdbuf);
  return_code = dbsqlexec(dbproc);
  return_code2 = dbsqlexec(dbproc2);
  printf("Sent SQL statements.\n");
```

Figure 15–4. Part 1 of application using distributed two-phase commits

```
/* check for errors. rollback and abort if necessary        */
  if(return_code == FAIL||return_code2 == FAIL)
  {
    printf("Transaction failed at SQL execution. Aborting....\n");
    abort_xact(dbproc_commit,commitid); /* tell commit server of failure */
    sprintf(cmdbuf, "ROLLBACK TRANSACTION");
    dbcmd(dbproc, cmdbuf);
    dbcmd(dbproc2, cmdbuf);
    if dbcmd(dbsqlexec(dbproc) != FAIL)
      remove_xact(dbproc_commit, commitid, 1);
    if dbcmd(dbsqlexec(dbproc2) != FAIL)
      remove_xact(dbproc_commit, commitid, 1);
    dbexit;
    exit(ERREXIT);
  }

/* prepare all servers to commit                            */
  sprintf(cmdbuf, "PREPARE TRANSACTION");
  dbcmd(dbproc, cmdbuf);
  dbcmd(dbproc2, cmdbuf);
  return_code = dbsqlexec(dbproc);
  return_code2 = dbsqlexec(dbproc2);
  printf("Preparing to commit.\n");

/* check for errors. rollback and abort if necessary        */
  if(return_code == FAIL || return_code2 == FAIL)
  {
    printf("Transaction failed at PREPARE COMMIT. Aborting....\n");
    abort_xact(dbproc_commit,commitid); /* tell commit server of failure */
    sprintf(cmdbuf, "ROLLBACK TRANSACTION");
    dbcmd(dbproc, cmdbuf);
  dbcmd(dbproc2, cmdbuf);
  if dbcmd(dbsqlexec(dbproc) != FAIL)
    remove_xact(dbproc_commit, commitid, 1);
  if dbcmd(dbsqlexec(dbproc2) != FAIL)
    remove_xact(dbproc_commit, commitid, 1);
  dbexit;
  exit(ERREXIT);
}
```

Figure 15–5. Part 2 of application using distributed two-phase commits

ever, there is no two-phase commit processing available in this scenario. Each stored procedure is treated as a separate transaction.

```
CREATE PROC proc1...AS
SELECT * FROM table1 WHERE
```

```
/* commit the transaction. rollback & abort if needed. */
  if(commit_xact(dbproc_commit, commitid) == FAIL)
  {
    printf("Commit server failed. Aborting....\n");
    abort_xact(dbproc_commit,commitid); /* tell commit server of failure */
    sprintf(cmdbuf, "ROLLBACK TRANSACTION");
    dbcmd(dbproc, cmdbuf);
    dbcmd(dbproc2, cmdbuf);
    if dbcmd(dbsqlexec(dbproc) != FAIL)
      remove_xact(dbproc_commit, commitid, 1);
    if dbcmd(dbsqlexec(dbproc2) != FAIL)
      remove_xact(dbproc_commit, commitid, 1);
    dbexit;
    exit(ERREXIT);
  }
/* commit preparation succeeded. inform all servers to commit.  */
  sprintf(cmdbuf, "COMMIT TRANSACTION");
  dbcmd(dbproc, cmdbuf);
  dbcmd(dbproc2, cmdbuf);
  if dbcmd(dbsqlexec(dbproc) != FAIL)
    remove_xact(dbproc_commit, commitid, 1);
  if dbcmd(dbsqlexec(dbproc2) != FAIL)
    remove_xact(dbproc_commit, commitid, 1);
/* close connection to commit server  */
  close_commit(dbproc_commit);
  printf("Transaction successfully applied.\n");
  dbexit();
  exit(STDEXIT);
}
```

Figure 15–6. Part 3 of application using distributed two-phase commits

```
EXECUTE sf.db1.user1.rem_proc
              .
              .
              .
  END
```

GATEWAYS AND MIDDLEWARE

Sybase offers a number of products that may loosely be considered data access middleware. Among these are Open Server, Open Gateway for DB2, and OmniSQL Gateway.

Open Server includes a function call library that enables programmers to build interfaces to non-Sybase data sources, trigger external events, and extend the capabilities of an SQL Server DBMS. From a distributed database perspective,

Open Server functions as a tool kit to enable customers to build gateways to foreign data sources not supported by other members of the Sybase product line. In this way, application programmers who are well-versed in Open Client (or DB-Library) calls can use this Sybase API to access non-Sybase data.

Open Server has formed the basis for certain ready-made Sybase gateways, such as Open Gateway for DB2. This product, which uses the companion Open Server for CICS product, enables Open Client programmers to read and update DB2/MVS data via CICS, a popular transaction-processing monitor on MVS. As of this writing, DB2 access is supported at a remote unit-of-work level. (That is, DB2 access is handled in transactions that are separate from those requiring SQL Server access.)

One of Sybase's more recent connectivity offerings is OmniSQL Gateway, which provides a consistent API to multiple data sources, including SQL Server, DB2/MVS, Oracle, Ingres, Unix ISAM files, and DEC RMS files. The product enables programmers to join data from these sources, although updates are currently restricted to one data source per transaction. Future releases of OmniSQL Gateway are expected to support additional data sources.

Programmers may use either Open Client (DB-Library) calls or Open Database Connectivity (ODBC) calls (defined by Microsoft) to access data through OmniSQL Gateway. OmniSQL Gateway includes a global catalog and an optimizer to help ensure reasonable performance. Administrators use system-supplied tools to update information in the global catalog as desired. Customers who purchase the Replication Server (discussed shortly) can use that product to automatically refresh information in the global catalog from other SQL Server DBMSs.

REPLICATION

In recent years, Sybase has begun emphasizing replication or copy management services as a practical alternative to distributed database systems. Sybase provides an asynchronous replication facility that enables customers to maintain multiple copies of their data at various locations.

As shown in Figure 15–7, Sybase captures log records from the primary site and automatically transfers committed transactions to the secondary sites. If a network or other failure prevents the primary site from transferring this information to a secondary site, the primary site will store this information and retry the operation.

The process for configuring a replicated environment is roughly as follows:

1. Create and populate the desired table(s) at the primary site.
2. Create a replicate definition to describe the table(s), specifying the columns, data types, primary key, columns used in the "subscription" WHERE clause, and the location of the primary table.
3. Create an empty table at the replicate site(s).

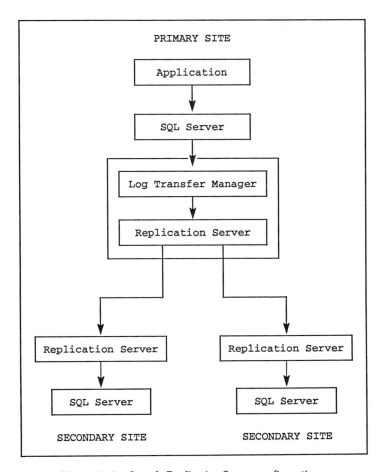

Figure 15–7. Sample Replication Server configuration

4. Create "subscriptions" at the site(s) where the data is to be replicated, such as the one below:

```
create subscription affordable for nyse.stocks at chicago.stock_db where
price >= $20 and price <= $50
```

Replication Server enables any site to accept database changes. However, if a secondary site receives a request to change data in a replicated table, that change is actually redirected to the primary site. After the primary site applies the change, the secondary site is then instructed to apply the change as well.

As of this writing, Replication Server supports SQL Server DBMSs. Sybase has documented interfaces to this product to enable customers to write code that would enable non-Sybase data sources to serve as primary or source sites. This code essentially involves writing the Log Transfer Manager component.

In addition, Sybase has announced its intention to enhance Replication Server to enable it to copy a broader range of data types (including text and image) and to replicate entire databases (instead of individual tables).

PERFORMANCE

SQL Server provides a number of facilities to enable administrators and application programmers to monitor and tune performance. Some of these features have already been mentioned, such as stored procedures and configuration variables. Two important performance considerations that have yet to be discussed are the optimizer and performance-monitoring mechanisms.

Optimizer

The Server's optimizer consults statistics to select an efficient access path. Indexes are used when appropriate to speed data access. However, unless an OR clause is specified in the query, SQL Server will use at most one index per table to satisfy a query's request. A *distribution page* of statistics is maintained for each index, providing the Server with information about how data values are distributed within the table. The *density* of the data, or the average number of duplicates, is also tracked by SQL Server for optimization purposes. Administrators can instruct SQL Server to update its statistics periodically by issuing the *update statistics* command.

SQL Server will dynamically create indexes in certain situations if it determines a cost advantage in so doing. Sometimes referred to as a *reformatting strategy*, this technique is used when no indexes are available or when the available indexes are not useful. Frequent reliance on reformatting (or dynamic index creation) can indicate a need to create new (permanent) indexes to improve system performance.

Finally, the optimizer uses an *index covering* test to determine if all columns referenced in a query are covered in a nonclustered (typically composite) index; if so, the Server never accesses the data pages and retrieves data directly from the index. For example, imagine that a composite index was defined on the ID and NAME columns of the RESTAURANT table. The following query, in which the user wishes to know the name for the restaurant that has an ID of "14356," would not cause any data pages to be accessed because all the necessary information (in this case, the restaurant's name and ID) would be contained in the index pages.

```
select name
from restaurant
where id = '14356'
```

Other optimizer features include the ability to "flatten out" some nested SELECT statements and recognize equivalent join expressions, which perform better than subqueries. The optimizer can also recognize many equivalent SQL expressions (for example, that SALARY BETWEEN 1000 AND 2000 is the same as SALARY >= 1000 and SALARY <= 2000).

In the area of join processing, the Server optimizes queries based upon a maximum of four tables at a time. So, while a join of 16 tables is permitted, the optimizer will split the query into four 4-table joins to select an access path. Join processing is handled through the use of nested loops.

To obtain maximum performance for certain multitable joins, users may need to add additional WHERE clauses because the Sybase optimizer does not make certain logical deductions. This example shows how a query on a three-table join might have to be rewritten for better performance because the optimizer cannot determine that t1.x = t3.z:

```
           Original Query                        Revised Query
select...from t1.x, t2.y, t3.z      select...from t1.x, t2.y, t3.z
   where t1.x = t2.y                   where t1.x = t2.y
   and t2.y = t3.z                     and t2.y = t3.z
                                       and t1.x = t3.z
```

The revised query adds a test for t1.x = t3.z to the WHERE clause. It makes it explicit that if x=y and y=z, then x=z. With this additional knowledge, the optimizer can consider additional access strategies that might result in better performance than any other strategies it has available.

Performance Monitoring

It's unreasonable to expect all programmers to be able to memorize and project optimizer strategies for all given queries. For this reason, SQL Server enables users to view the access plan selected (via *showplan*), the number of physical and logical I/Os required (via *statistics io,* a facility helpful for determining if additional cache is needed), and to "run" a query without actually executing it (via *noexec*) to see what the resulting plan and I/O would be.

The example below shows the way in which SQL Server might process a query involving a join of two tables, neither of which has an index. In this case, the SQL Server has opted to employ a reformatting strategy, which calls for creating an index in a temporary work area at run time.

```
select column_x, column_y
    from table1, table2
    where table1.column_a = table2.column_c

STEP 1
The type of query is INSERT
The update mode is direct
Worktable created for REFORMATTING
FROM TABLE
table2
Nested iteration
Table Scan
TO TABLE
Worktable
```

```
STEP 2
The type of query is SELECT
FROM TABLE
table1
Nested iteration
Table Scan
FROM TABLE
Worktable
Nested iteration
Using Clustered Index
```

Other monitoring facilities include several system-supplied stored procedures. Commonly used stored procedures include *sp_monitor*, which reports on CPU activity and I/Os; *sp_who*, which reports on the activity of user processes; and *sp_lock*, which describes active locks held on tables. Sybase also offers a separate performance-monitoring product, SQL Monitor.

Other Features

A number of other features of SQL Server, some of which have been described previously, can also be used to influence overall system performance.

For example, stored procedures offer performance advantages in a client/server environment. These blocks of SQL code decrease communications overhead between clients and the Server, because they enable multiple SQL statements to be executed through only one call. However, to maximize performance, these procedures must remain in cache.

In addition, configuration variables can be reset to regulate resource consumption and memory usage. This is typically accomplished by executing the *sp_configure* stored procedure, specifying certain parameters. For example, administrators can specify how much memory will be allocated to user connections, the procedure cache, and the disk cache. Tuning the procedure cache can be important, particularly if users frequently invoke stored procedures. The cache should be set to hold a sufficient number of stored procedures to avoid disk I/O and subsequent recompilation of frequently used procedures. Other important considerations include the number of available locks, the maximum number of open database objects, and the size of network packets.

To limit disk contention, the Server supports databases that span multiple devices, as well as separate devices for data, nonclustered indexes, and logs. Administrators can control the frequency of checkpoints to balance these writes with the rest of the system workload. Finally, users may reset a number of query-processing options during their session. Some of these query-processing options can influence overall system performance. For example, a user may issue the *set rowcount N* command to instruct SQL Server to stop query processing after returning the first *N* number of rows.

As of this writing, Sybase has also announced plans to offer an extension to System 10 for improved performance for complex, ad hoc queries. The technology, sometimes referred to as IQ Accelerator, is based on joint development work with Expressway Technologies, which has since been acquired by Sybase. IQ Accelerator is expected to use a different indexing scheme (other than B+ trees) to improve performance for certain types of queries.

PARALLELISM

Sybase supports parallel transaction processing on symmetric multiprocessors through the use of its Virtual Server Architecture (VSA). In addition, Sybase announced its support for parallel query processing through its Navigation Server product, which was not yet generally available as of this writing. This section briefly discusses both capabilities.

Virtual Server Architecture

Sybase's initial support for database parallelism appeared in Version 4.8 of SQL Server in the early 1990s. This support, geared toward exploiting symmetric multiprocessors from DEC, Sequent, and other manufacturers, was based on a Virtual Server Architecture (VSA). Multiple SQL Server engines can be running cooperatively in such an environment, communicating with one another via shared memory. Although multiple SQL Server engines may be running on a single symmetric multiprocessor system (up to one engine per CPU), they all appear to the user as a single SQL Server instance or as a single "virtual server."

Up to 32 SQL Server engines may be supported. One engine performs network management in addition to database management, while the others serve as peers performing database management functions only. Incoming client requests are placed in a "runnable" queue, and an available SQL Server engine attempts to execute the associated task. In this way, multiple transactions may be processed in parallel, with each SQL Server engine working on behalf of a different task.

If an SQL Server engine finds itself blocked (perhaps because it is waiting on I/O activity or a locked resource), it places the blocked task in the "sleeping" queue and begins working on behalf of another task (waiting in the runnable queue). When the blocked task is capable of being executed (perhaps because the I/O completed or the needed lock was acquired), it is placed in the runnable queue and will be serviced accordingly by an available SQL Server engine (although not necessarily the same engine that serviced it previously).

Navigation Server

More recently, Sybase announced a new parallel database offering, Navigation Server, for loosely coupled platforms. The product was jointly developed by AT&T Global Information Solutions and Sybase, and its first offering is expected to ship for NCR 3600 systems. This system is configured in a rather unusual way for the Navigation Server. Each NCR 3600 application processor (AP) node consists of symmetric multiprocessors; multiple such nodes are tied together in a shared-nothing fashion via a communications link (called the Ynet). In this way, the hardware configuration sports a hybrid parallel architecture.

The first release of Navigation Server is not based on SQL Server System 10 (profiled in this chapter); it is based on an earlier SQL Server release. As such, the first release of Navigation Server does not feature certain System 10 capabilities, such as support for declarative referential integrity.

Figure 15–8 illustrates a sample Navigation Server configuration. Each application processor node contains multiple processors. Various Navigation Server components may be configured to run on each node. Overall system components include the:

- Control Server, which processes requests from clients and sends these requests to other appropriate system components. It also returns results back to clients. For any given client request, only one Control Server will be active.
- Data Server, which handles various data manipulation operations. Each Data Server consists of two components:
  - Split Server, which is largely used for processing joins.
  - SQL Server, Sybase's relational DBMS which has already been described in detail.
- DBA Server, which is responsible for coordinating recovery, detecting global deadlocks, interpreting data definition and data control (security) state-

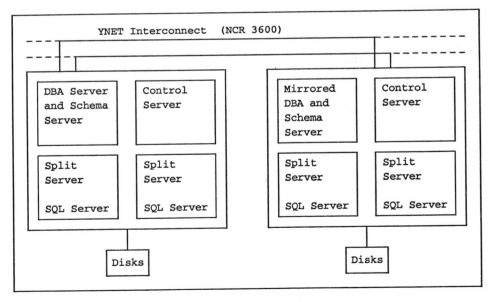

Figure 15–8. Overview of Navigation Server configuration on NCR 3600

ments, compiling data manipulation statements, and performing certain other functions. The DBA Server is actually a Control Server with additional functionality.

Executing on the DBA Server is another component sometimes called the Schema Server, which is responsible for controlling the global directory. The global directory contains system tables and other data needed to run the Navigation Server. Some global directory data is cached in Control Servers and Split Servers to provide performance benefits.

To improve availability, the DBA Server is mirrored on an alternate node and the global directory is also mirrored (by default).

- Administrative Services Server, which provides various facilities for configuration management and modeling, log management, installation, and backup and restore operations.

The Navigation Server is capable of processing database queries (including write operations) in parallel, as well as executing a variety of utility operations in parallel. A companion facility, the Configurator, helps administrators determine the type of partitioning that may be most appropriate for their workloads. Available partitioning options include hash partitioning, range partitioning, and schema partitioning.

Since the architecture of the Navigation Server is likely to be new to the reader, it may be helpful to understand how a given client request might be processed by various components. Imagine that the request involves a join of two or more tables. The request will be handled by a Control Server, which will typically request the services of a Split Server. (Certain join conditions may not require the use of Split Servers, but a discussion of these conditions is beyond the scope of this book.) The selected Split Server may signal other Split Servers to temporarily redistribute data into partitions that can be processed by different nodes. These Split Servers then signal their SQL Servers to process the join, which occurs in parallel. Results are returned to the master Split Server, which passes them to the Control Server for return to the requesting client.

MICROSOFT'S SQL SERVER

Microsoft also offers an SQL Server DBMS for Windows NT (and, in earlier days, supported an OS/2 version). The firm acquired rights to a version of the Sybase SQL Server source code through an earlier agreement, and has announced plans to enhance the product in a number of ways. As of this writing, Microsoft's SQL Server is based on Release 4.2 of Sybase's SQL Server product. A new release derived from the Release 4.2 code base is expected to include support for declarative referential integrity, backward-scrolling cursors, support for symmetric multiprocessors (including parallel query, backup, restore, and load capabilities), and additional administrative tools. It will run on Windows NT.

SUMMARY

This chapter described Sybase's SQL Server, a relational DBMS that runs on a number of operating systems and hardware platforms. The product has enjoyed a growing installation base over the past several years. This chapter explained how Sybase's product supports key DBMS functions, including lock management, recovery, integrity, and other areas. It also described related Sybase products that support contemporary database technologies profiled earlier in this book, including replication, parallelism, and middleware.

REFERENCES AND SUGGESTED READING

BALLOU, MELINDA-CAROL. "Sybase Server Architecture to Support SMP Platforms," *Digital Review,* March 26, 1990, p. 1.

Commands Reference Manual for SYBASE SQL Server for UNIX, Sybase, Inc., Release 4.9.1, Change Level 2, Document ID 32270-01-0491-01, October 1, 1992.

Embedded SQL/C Programmer's Guide, Sybase, Inc., Release 4.0, Document ID 35610-01-0400-02, March 30, 1992.

FERGUSON, MIKE. "Parallel Query and Transaction Processing," *InfoDB,* vol. 7, no. 3, Summer 1993, p. 18.

JOHNSON, STUART J. and KIM S. NASH. "Microsoft SQL Server Seeks to Best Sybase Database," *Computerworld,* June 13, 1994, p. 4.

Navigation Server Product Overview, Sybase, Oct. 31, 1994.

Open Client DB-Library/C Reference Manual, Sybase, Release 4.6.1, Change Level 1, Document ID 32600-01-0461-01, Aug. 1, 1992.

Performance and Tuning Student Guide, Sybase, Oct. 1, 1989.

Replication Server: A Component of SYBASE System 10, Sybase, May 1993.

RICHMAN, DAN. "Microsoft Beefing Up Its NT Version of SQL Server," *Open Systems Today,* June 20, 1994, p. 6.

System Administration Guide for SYBASE SQL Server, Sybase, Release 4.9.1, Change Level 2, Document ID 32500-01-0491-01, Oct. 15, 1992.

SYBASE Navigation Server, Sybase, 1994.

SYBASE Navigation Server: Delivering the Promise of Parallel High Performance, Sybase, Technical Paper Series, 1994.

SYBASE Open Server Server-Library/C Reference Manual, Sybase, Release 2.0, Change Level 3, Document ID 35400-01-0200-03, July 31, 1992.

SYBASE Replication Server, Sybase, May 1993.

SYBASE Products and Services, Sybase, 1992.

SYBASE SQL Server System Administration Guide, Sybase, Release 10.0, Document ID 32500-01-1000-03, May 15, 1994.

SYBASE SQL Server Reference Manual Volume 1: Commands Functions, and Topics, Sybase, Release 10.0, Document ID 32401-01-1000-03, Feb. 1, 1994.

SYBASE SQL Server Reference Manual Volume 2: System Procedures and Catalog Stored Procedures, Sybase, Release 10.0, Document ID 32402-01-1000-03, Feb. 1, 1994.

SYBASE System Management Products, Sybase, April 1993.

SYBASE Troubleshooting Guide, Sybase, Release 4.0.1 through 4.9.1, Change Level 1, Document ID 35900-01-0100-04, Aug. 20, 1993.

SYBASE User Meeting and Training Conference Proceedings, April 25–29, 1993.

Transact-SQL User's Guide for SYBASE SQL Server, Sybase, Release 4.9.1, Change Level 2, Document ID 32300-01-0491-01, Oct. 15, 1992.

Vivoli, Martha L. "Delivering Disparate Data to Users," *SYBASE* magazine, Winter 1994, p. 26.

What's New in SYBASE SQL Server Release 10.0? Sybase, Change Level 2, Document ID 36440-01-1000-04, May 15, 1994.

CHAPTER 16
Computer Associates' CA-OpenIngres

CHAPTER OBJECTIVES

This chapter describes Computer Associates' relational DBMS and a number of related offerings. It discusses major areas of product function, including those that provide for lock management, resource management, backup and recovery, data integrity, security, query support, and performance tuning. Additionally, there is discussion of products that support replication, middleware, distributed databases, and parallelism.

This chapter provides the reader with insight into how a commercial DBMS product has actually implemented the technologies discussed earlier in this book.

OVERVIEW OF DBMS AND RELATED PRODUCTS

Founded in 1980 under the name Relational Technology, Inc., the makers of the Ingres' relational DBMS drew heavily upon research efforts at the University of California at Berkeley to release their first commercial product in 1981. Relational Technology, Inc. later renamed itself Ingres and was acquired by the ASK Group (producers of software applications for the manufacturing industry) in 1990. For some time thereafter, the organization was referred to as "ASK Ingres." In 1994, ASK (and its Ingres division) were acquired by Computer Associates, who had previously acquired manufacturers of two prerelational DBMS products (Cullinet, which made IDMS, and Applied Data Research, which made Datacom/DB). To avoid confusion, the remainder of this chapter refers to the Ingres group within Computer Associates simply as Ingres.

The CA-OpenIngres DBMS (hereafter called Ingres) runs on more than 35 hardware platforms as of this writing, with Unix and VMS platforms accounting for a large portion of its installation base. Ingres' tools for end users and application developers also span multiple platforms, and some can be purchased separately to support non-Ingres DBMSs. Ingres products also support various networking protocols, which contributes to Ingres' ability to support client/server computing and distributed database technologies.

Ingres offers a number of products to address decision support, application development, and connectivity needs. These interface to the base Ingres DBMS. The Knowledge Manager, now shipped with the base DBMS, provides certain integrity and resource control mechanisms. The Object Manager is a separately purchased option that supports user-defined data types and functions. Figure 16–1 provides a sampling of many Ingres offerings.

Ingres is commonly used as a client/server DBMS, with Ingres/Net providing client applications access to remote Ingres servers. The DBMS uses a multithreaded, multiserver architecture.

The remainder of this chapter focuses primarily on R6.4 of Ingres and Ingres/Star. The chapter also describes functions available through extensions to

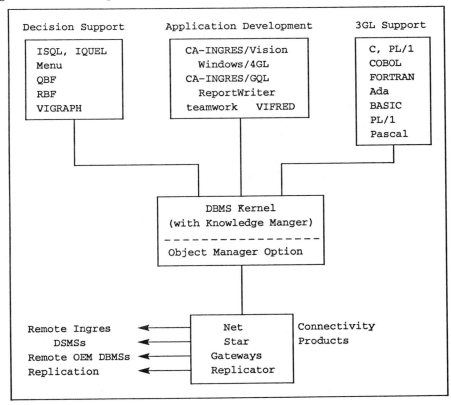

Figure 16–1. Overview of Ingres product line. Additional products are available but not shown.

the base Ingres DBMS (the Knowledge Manager and Object Manager). When applicable, information about expected enhancements in future Ingres releases is also discussed. (Release numbers are expected to change, as the product has been renamed to CA-OpenIngres.)

DATA MANAGEMENT

Ingres supports the basic set of relational data objects—databases, tables, views, and indexes—as well as certain additional objects that lend support for object-oriented functions. These include rules (user-defined integrity constraints) and stored procedures, which are discussed later in the sections "Rules or Triggers" and "Query Capabilities." Other object extensions include support for user-defined types and user-defined functions.

Ingres users may define multiple databases per installation (by invoking the *createdb* command). Each database contains its own catalog tables, user data, and associated files. There is one log file per installation, which logs the work of transactions for recovery purposes. In addition, one master database (*iidbdb*) is automatically created per system; this contains information about all the Ingres databases on that system.

Ingres databases may be defined to use one or more storage devices. In addition, individual tables and indexes within a database may also span storage devices. This is useful for supporting large databases and tables. If desired, databases, tables, and indexes may also be partitioned across different *locations* (or directories) within the same device.

Ingres automatically manages additions to partitioned tables and indexes using a sort of round-robin approach. If a table spans four areas, these additions will be distributed to each area in 16-page portions (approximately 32K). The first 16 pages worth of additions will be directed to the first area, the second 16 pages of additions will directed to the second area, and so on.

Tables within Ingres may contain up to 300 columns, and each row may range up to 2000 bytes. Multiple indexes are permitted per table, and each index may be built upon single or multiple columns (up to a maximum of 32). These indexes may be unique or nonunique. Users may choose the desired storage structure for their tables and indexes, as described in more detail in the section "Storage Structures."

Data Types

Data types supported by Ingres include many of those common to other relational DBMSs. They are:

- FLOAT, double-precision floating point.
- FLOAT(4) or REAL, single-precision floating point.
- INTEGER, four bytes.
- SMALLINT, two bytes.

- INTEGER1, one byte.
- C or CHAR, fixed-length characters.
- VARCHAR, varying-length characters (up to 2000). In comparisons, blanks will be added at the end of the string to make the lengths of both arguments equal.
- TEXT, varying-length characters (up to 2000). In comparisons, blanks will *not* be added to make the lengths of both arguments equal.
- DATE, consisting of year, month, day, hour, minute, and second fields.
- MONEY, consisting of up to 14 digits followed by a decimal point and two addition digits (as in $99999999999999.99)
- Certain logical key values, used to uniquely identify each row of the table.

In addition, the Object Manager in Ingres enables users to create their own data types and related functions. For example, a user might define a data type for managing ordered pairs (X, Y coordinates) and define a slope function that could be computed against this data. To do so, a programmer would use a third-generation language (such as C) to code data type definition routines and data type coercion routines for each new data type. These user-defined data types would then become known to the system and could form the basis for columns in tables.

Code written to support user-defined types and user-defined functions executes in the same address space as the Ingres DBMS itself. Doing so offers maximum performance, but raises some integrity concerns as the user code might possibly modify or somehow corrupt structures used internally by the Ingres DBMS. For this reason, Ingres offers a considerable amount of sample code, as well as consulting services to advise people on the proper use of these functions.

Support for very long fields (sometimes called BLOBs) is expected in a future release of CA-OpenIngres. Very long field support is expected to include LONG VARCHAR and LONG BYTE data types of up to 2 GB each. Users are also expected to be able to define their own large data types (of up to 2 GB each) through the Object Manager extension.

Integrity

Among the Ingres facilities available to support integrity constraints are the CREATE INTEGRITY statement and the CREATE RULE statement. The former enables customers to restrict the valid range of data values for a column, while the latter is a trigger mechanism for supporting user-defined business policies as well as referential integrity constraints. Rules are supported through Knowledge Manager, a separately purchased component.

Data Range Checking

Valid data values for a column may be specified by creating an integrity constraint (specified through the CREATE INTEGRITY command). This ensures that all updates to the base table upon which the integrity constraint has been defined will satisfy the specified condition.

The example below illustrates how two integrity constraints might be defined on two different tables in the DINING database. The first requires that all ID numbers in the CRITIC table range from 1 to 9999; the second requires that PRICING information in the RESTAURANT table be set to "EXPENSIVE," "MODERATE," or "INEXPENSIVE."

```
create integrity on critic is
    id > 0 and id < 10000;

create integrity on restaurant is
    pricing = 'EXPENSIVE' or
    pricing = 'MODERATE' or
    pricing = 'INEXPENSIVE';
```

Because such constraints are associated with tables in the database, their corresponding rules do not need to be specified in user-written applications.

Rules or Triggers

Ingres uses *rules*, or triggers, to support referential integrity and site-specific business policies. Rules are stored as database objects and automatically executed whenever a given database event occurs (such as an attempt to update a particular column of a table). Rules may be defined for updates, inserts, and deletes; an unlimited number of rules may be defined for each table, providing for a modular design. Rules are part of the transaction that caused them to fire, and they fire once for every row that meets the rule condition.

The following example illustrates how a rule might be created to enforce part of a referential integrity constraint. Two tables are involved: the RATING table, which includes reviews of various restaurants, and the RESTAURANT table, which includes the names, phone numbers, and other general data about restaurants. Both tables contain identifying numbers for the restaurants. Under no circumstances should the RATING table contain a review for a restaurant that is not listed in the master RESTAURANT table.

```
create rule rest_rule
    after insert, update(rest_id) of rating
    execute procedure check_rest_id (new_id = new. rest_id)
```

The first line specifies that a new rule (named "rest_rule") be created. The rule will execute whenever someone inserts data into the RATING table or updates the REST_ID column of the RATING table. The rule will invoke a procedure (not yet shown) called "check_rest_id," passing in one parameter. That parameter is the foreign key value for the new restaurant ID in the RATING table (stored in the REST_ID column). The parameter is given the name of "new_id" for use with the stored procedure.

The stored procedure itself is a bit more complex in this case. The code below illustrates one possible means of executing the appropriate constraint checks and taking necessary action.

```
create procedure check_rest_id (new_id integer not null) as
   declare counter integer;
   begin
       select count(*) into :counter
              from restaurant
              where id = :new_id;
       if counter = 1
              return;
       else
              raise error;
              return;
       endif;
   end;
```

The "check_rest_id" procedure expects one integer value ("new_id") to be passed in. This represents the restaurant ID value in the RATING table (the foreign key value). A "counter" variable is declared, which will later be used for test purposes. The procedure begins by counting the number of rows in the master RESTAURANT table that have the same ID as the one someone wishes to change or insert into the RATING table. The result from this SELECT COUNT(*) statement is kept in the "counter" variable. If the foreign key value ("new_id") matched a primary key value (in the ID column of the RESTAURANT table), no referential integrity constraint was violated, and the procedure returns without error. Otherwise, if the foreign key value does not match a primary key value, the procedure raises an error and returns. The rule (previously shown) will automatically detect this error and roll back the update or insert attempt.

A future release of Ingres is expected to support declarative referential integrity.

Ingres enables users to specify update rules for each column in a table. Thus, a given table may have multiple update triggers (or rules) defined for it. In such cases, the order of execution is undetermined. Rules may also cause other rules to fire (depending on the constraints defined in the database). They may be nested up to unlimited levels, subject to available memory.

Other Features

Event alerters are somewhat similar to rules in that both cause certain events to happen automatically when a given condition occurs. However, event alerters notify processes *external* to the DBMS (such as a user application) that an event has occurred, enabling non-DBMS activities to be executed as a result. For example, an event alerter may be created to notify a user application when the price of a certain stock drops below $100 per share. Upon receiving that information, the application can notify the stockbroker or can invoke another program for purchasing additional shares.

Another issue sometimes associated with integrity involves *save points*. Save points can be thought of as markers within a transaction that identify points to which the transaction can be rolled back. This enables applications to incorporate tests within the scope of a transaction, perhaps to back out some or all of the statements that were previously executed. If desired, multiple save points can be defined within a single transaction (each with different names or labels), and programmers can instruct Ingres to roll back the transaction to a given save point.

Storage Structures

Ingres enables administrators to determine the desired storage structures for their tables and indexes. With one exception, all the structures listed below are available for both types of databases objects. Heap is available only for tables.

- Heap: No keys are associated with the table, and data is added at the end of the file. This makes bulk loads go quickly, but can make for poor performance when retrieving data (because the entire table must be scanned to determine which rows satisfy the query).
- Hash: A key is established for the table, and data is assigned to specific page addresses based on a some calculation (automatically performed by Ingres). This provides quick access to queries involving exact matches, but can be slow for queries involving pattern matching ("where name like '%AS%'") or a range of values ("where salary > 50000 and salary < 100000").
- ISAM: Data is sorted by value in the key column, but the index remains static (requiring modification as it grows). It is designed for tables with limited updates and for queries that involve pattern matching or range retrievals.
- B+ tree: Data is sorted by value in the key column, and the index changes dynamically along with the table. This structure is the most versatile, supporting queries with exact matches, pattern matching, and range retrieval. However, it does lock index pages and may require a greater number of index pages than ISAM files. Therefore, it may not be optimal for small, static tables.

Some compression of data is also supported for tables. Character and text fields are compressed, specifically by compressing the trailing blanks and nulls.

Ingres also provides a MODIFY facility to enable administrators to change the storage structure of tables and indexes after they have been populated.

In addition to understanding the various structures of tables and indexes, administrators also would do well to understand the files associated with each database. Each database consists of data files (containing tables, indexes, and the database's catalog), checkpoint files (containing static copies of the entire database), journal files (for journaling), and dump files (containing information about changes occurring during a checkpoint). In addition, each Ingres DBMS also contains a master database, which tracks information about all databases residing at that DBMS.

ADMINISTRATION

Security, concurrency control, and recovery are among the issues of concern to database and system administrators. Like other multiuser DBMSs, Ingres provides mechanisms to support each of these areas.

Security

Like most relational DBMSs, Ingres enables users to GRANT and REVOKE various privileges to other users. These privileges involve operations on tables and views, stored procedures, and databases.

Table- and view-level privileges involve the ability to select, insert, update, and delete data; an "all" privilege may be granted to enable users to perform all of these data manipulation functions. Procedure privileges enable database administrators to permit users to execute specific stored procedures, even if the user does not have authority to directly access the tables referenced in the procedure. In essence, this enables an administrator to restrict users' access to certain tables or views to a very limited set of functions.

Finally, additional database-level privileges are available to users of the Knowledge Manager. These privileges enable administrators to regulate who may create tables and procedures, who may change locking modes for queries, and who may be allocated certain amounts of resources. Lock modes are discussed later in the section "Concurrency Control." Resource allocation is also discussed later, in "Other Issues."

In addition, Ingres enables users to create security groups for different users and to associate privileges with these groups. The product also supports the notion of roles, wherein privileges are associated with applications rather than with the users who invoke them. Both the group and role functions are available through the Knowledge Manager.

The following example shows how a chefs group might be created with various members. Each member will inherit any privileges subsequently granted to the group.

```
create group chefs
    with users = (pepin, puck, child, smith)
```

Similarly, database administrators may wish to grant certain privileges to certain applications. In Ingres, roles are used to accomplish this. To restrict which users may invoke these applications, Ingres enables administrators to optionally specify a password for each role. This example shows how a role is created for the DINER application and how privileges for accessing the RATING and RESTAURANT tables are subsequently granted to this role:

```
create role diner
    with password = 'hungry'

grant select on rating, restaurant
    to role diner
```

An interesting feature of Ingres is its notion of public and private databases. Public databases (which are the type most frequently created) enable any user to work with objects in the database, provided they have been granted the necessary privileges to do so. Private databases permit access only by the database owner, the system administrator (or *superuser*), and other users who have been granted access by the system administrator.

Ingres also supports a means of auditing database operations. The audit facility enables users to extract data from the log for printing or insertion into a user-created table. It is useful for determining what types of DML operations (select, insert, update, and delete) were performed within the database since the last backup copy was made. As of this writing, individual SQL statements are not included in the audit reports. Specific information included in the audit trail is:

- Date and time when the transaction started
- Name (as known to Ingres) of user who performed the operation
- Type of operation (select, insert, update, or delete)
- Transaction identifier
- Table identifier

Release 1.1 of CA-OpenIngres is expected to comply with C2 security levels used by the Department of Defense.

Concurrency Control

To support concurrent data access while preserving transaction integrity, Ingres supports various lock mechanisms. Locking occurs automatically, based on transaction activities, but users can control certain locking functions to tune their systems.

Lock Levels and Lock Modes

Data may be locked at a page or table level. Ingres automatically escalates locks to a coarser level of granularity when it deems it prudent to do so.

Ingres may actually use a combination of page and table locks to service any single request. This is because Ingres uses *intent* locks at the table level that can improve overall concurrency and performance when combined with the more granular page locks. To understand how this works, the reader must first learn about the different modes of locks supported at the page and table levels, and then explore how some of these can be used in synergy.

Page-level locks may be either *shared* (sometimes called *read*) or *exclusive* (sometimes called *write*). Shared locks enable multiple processes to read the same page, but none can write to it. Exclusive locks enable a single process to read and/or write to the page; no one else can access it.

Table-level locks may be *shared, exclusive, intended share, intended exclusive,* or *shared intended exclusive.* The first two types are the same as those described for page locks, except that they affect the entire table. The latter three are *intent* locks that are used with page-level locks to minimize lock overhead associated with supporting concurrent transactions. When a process wants to read data, Ingres will first acquire an intended share lock on the table and then try to acquire a share lock on the page. Similarly, when a process wants to write data, Ingres will first acquire an intended exclusive or shared intended exclusive lock on the table, and then try to acquire an exclusive lock on the page.

Intended share locks are used for read operations. The owner can subsequently try to lock one or more pages to read data. Other processes can read data within the table as well. In addition, other processes can write data, provided the pages are not already locked.

Intended exclusive locks are used for write operations. The owner can subsequently try to lock one or more pages to write data. Other processes may read or write data (provided the required pages are not already locked exclusively).

Shared intended exclusive locks are also used for write operations, but they are more restrictive than intended exclusive locks. Shared intended exclusive locks prohibit all other processes from writing to any page within the table, even if these pages are not currently locked in exclusive mode. Other processes can only attempt to acquire shared locks on pages.

Using table-level intent locks *with* page-level shared or exclusive locks can help improve performance. Consider what must happen when processes make new DBMS requests, which involve the acquisition of locks. Without intent locks, Ingres might have to consult many individual page locks to determine if a new lock could be granted to another process. With intent locks, it can make that determination more quickly because it has some idea of the overall intent of other transactions working with that table.

One other type of lock is also supported in Ingres—a *null* lock—but it is not discussed here as it it used by Ingres for internal purposes only.

User Influence Over Locks

The reader should also note that Ingres users may override Ingres' standard policy of acquiring shared locks for read operations. This promotes concurrency and can reduce the potential for deadlocks, but is not recommended for queries requiring access to stable data. This is because the data that is being read may be inconsistent. Using this mechanism involves issuing this command:

```
set lockmode session where readlock = nolock;
```

The SET LOCKMODE statement also enables users to change the default level of locking (for shared and exclusive locks) from page to table. Another option enables users to control at what point lock escalation should occur. By default, if a transaction locks more than 10 pages within a table, Ingres will try to escalate these to a table lock. The following statement raises the maximum number of page locks permitted for the RATING table to 30:

```
set lockmode on rating where maxlocks = 30;
```

Finally, the SET LOCKMODE statement can also influence how long Ingres will wait on a locked resource before giving up. By default, Ingres will wait indefinitely, which may not always be desirable. The TIMEOUT option enables the user to specify (in seconds) how long Ingres should wait for a lock. If the time expires, the query is rolled back, and an error is returned. However, the transaction itself is *not* rolled back (only the statement for which a lock could not be acquired). For this reason, applications that make use of this option must test for the error and handle the situation as appropriate—perhaps by rolling back the transaction or retrying the statement later.

Other Lock Issues

Ingres supports cursor stability, which ensures that pages are locked only when they are being read. This promotes a high degree of concurrency, although the data may not be the same for the duration of the transaction. The product also supports "dirty reads" (in which transactions may read uncommitted data) and repeatable reads (in which serializability of transactions is guaranteed). The latter is the default.

Ingres also supports deadlock detection. If two transactions are waiting on each other for the same resource, Ingres will choose one of the two to abort (or roll back). Deadlocks are recorded in an error log, which the administrator may consult for tuning purposes.

Backup and Recovery

Support for backup and recovery is a requirement of any multiuser DBMS. Like other DBMSs profiled in this book, Ingres provides mechanisms to support these operations.

The *ckpdb* command enables administrators to create backup copies of a database, which can later be used for recovery purposes. Invoking *chkpd* causes Ingres to take a checkpoint, marking appropriate log entries as inactive and backing up the database to either file or tape. Checkpointing can be done online (while the database is in use) or off-line (while the database is not in use by other processes).

Checkpointing a database that is in use implies that other transactions may be changing the database during this time. The log records for these transactions are placed in the dump file for the database, which will be used later when the *rollforwarddb* command is invoked (to restore the database to its state when the checkpoint began).

Both logging and *journaling* are important to recovery in Ingres environments, so some discussion of each is warranted. The Ingres logging system tracks all database transactions automatically. This system is comprised of:

- A logging facility, which includes the transaction log file
- A recovery process
- An archiver process

The logging facility writes log records for use by the recovery and archiver processes. The recovery process is responsible for online recovery from system failures and user-initiated transaction rollbacks. Ingres records points of consistency in the transaction log file; these records ensure that the database is consistent and facilitates online recovery (when needed).

The archiver process periodically removes records for completed transactions from the log file and writes these records to the database's journal file. Since journaling is optional in Ingres, this occurs only for those tables for which journaling has been enabled (specified by the WITH JOURNALING option of the CREATE TABLE statement). If journaling is not enabled for a particular table, the relevant log records for completed transactions involving this table will be discarded. Therefore, journal files can be thought of as containing a more permanent record of log activities. Each database has its own journal files, which record all changes made to the database since the last checkpoint was taken (if journaling is enabled).

Logging enables Ingres to record before- and after-image copies of the data. As with any DBMS, if log records are not available, administrators will only be able to restore the database to its state as of the last backup. Any subsequent work will be lost. To improve performance of logging operations, Ingres supports group commit processing (discussed in the section "Major Components and Functions").

When a system failure occurs (such as a hardware failure), the recovery process will automatically roll back all appropriate transactions when the system comes back up. Administrators may issue a *rollforwarddb* command to instruct Ingres to recover from certain user errors or a media failure. Assuming that a journaled database is to be recovered and that the database had been previously checkpointed online, Ingres will (1) restore the database to the checkpoint, (2) apply any log records written with the checkpoint (for transactions that were active at that time), and (3) apply any subsequent log records.

Ingres also enables administrators to restrict the point up to which the database will be restored. This can be useful when a serious error occurred at a certain time, and the administrator would like to restore the database to its state immediately before that time. An option of the *rollforwarddb* command supports this, enabling administrators to specify the date and time (down to the second) up until which log records should be applied. A similar option supports the opposite function: it enables administrators to specify that only transactions that started after a certain date and time should be restored.

The following command illustrates how an administrator can instruct Ingres to recover the DINING database up to a specific point in time. In this case, it is assumed that a user made a serious error just after 8:15 A.M. June 19, 1994, and the administrator wants to restore the database to its state at 8:14 A.M.

```
rollforwarddb -v -e19-jun-1994:08:14:00 dining
```

The use of checkpoints (for journaled databases) and *rollforwarddb* offers the most robust level of backup and recovery support. However, two other mechanisms are available for backing up data: *copydb* and *unloaddb*. Both generate scripts that enable users to create backup copies of data and to reload this data into a database (perhaps on a different Ingres system).

The *copydb* command enables Ingres to back up all the tables, views, procedures, and rules owned by the person issuing the command; also backed up are the indexes, column integrity constraints, and security permissions associated with these objects. These can later be restored. Data will be current only up to the point of the backup copy. (No changes since that time will be applied.)

The *unloaddb* enables the administrator to copy an entire database for reloading into a new, empty database. All objects and system catalog tables for the database will be copied. These can later be restored; data will be current only up to the point of the backup copy. (No changes since that time will be applied.)

Other Issues

Restricting the use of DBMS resources may be of concern to administrators. Through its Knowledge Manager component, Ingres enables administrators to limit the amount of I/O permitted per user per query and the amount of rows that can be returned per user per query. When such limits are in place, Ingres' optimizer will estimate the I/O and row retrievals involved for a query. The system will then prevent any queries it believes are too big from ever executing. The example shows how one user might be restricted to receiving no more than 500 rows per query against objects in the DINING database:

```
grant query_row_limit 500
    on database dining to richard;
```

The MODIFY command (mentioned briefly in the section "Storage Structures") provides additional administrative functions. It can be used to specify the minimum and maximum number of pages of a table as well as to regulate the amount of free space (or "fillfactor") initially present in the data pages of a table.

QUERY CAPABILITIES

Unlike other DBMS products profiled in this book, Ingres did not base its original query support around SQL. Early releases of the product offered an alternate query language named QUEL. When SQL became adopted as the industry standard query language for relational DBMSs, Ingres supported SQL as well.

The capabilities of SQL and QUEL are similar in many respects, although QUEL offers certain features not found in SQL. Generally, QUEL is perceived as closer to Codd's relational calculus than SQL but somewhat less user friendly. This example shows how SQL queries for updating and retrieving data might be written in QUEL:

```
SQL                             QUEL

update critic                   range of c is critic
    set last_name = 'CORLEONE'  replace c (last_name = 'CORLEONE')
    where id = 12345                where c. id = 12345

select name from best_bets      range of x is best_bets
    where value = 5             retrieve (x. name)
                                    where value = 5
```

As the reader has seen in previous examples, Ingres also supports the use of nulls to represent missing or inapplicable data.

Today, Ingres has moved beyond base SQL support and extended the language to support rules (triggers) and stored procedures, as discussed earlier.

Procedures in Ingres are written in a manner similar to that of rules: both may involve SQL statements as well as procedural logic statements (such as if-then-else statements). Procedures can be invoked by rules (as shown previously), by applications, or by users of interactive query facilities. They can provide a simple, consistent means for users to access tables and views. The example below illustrates a simple stored procedure that will update the PRICING information associated with a particular restaurant (for example, it would allow someone to note that the restaurant is now "EXPENSIVE" instead of "MODERATE").

```
create procedure price_proc
        (id integer not null, price char(11)) as
begin
    update restaurant
            set pricing = :price
            where id = :id;
    if iirowcount = 1 then
            message 'Pricing has been changed';
            commit;
    else
            message 'No change occurred. Check the restaurant ID number';
            rollback;
            return -1;
end;
```

The procedure is given a name ("price_proc") and is defined to expect two input parameters. The first is "id," an integer that corresponds to the ID column (the primary key) in the RESTAURANT table. The second is "price," which corresponds to the PRICING column in the RESTAURANT table. The procedure begins by attempting to update the pricing information for a particular restaurant.

A test is then conducted to see if any change occurred. Here, "iirowcount" refers to a built-in variable that tracks the number of rows affected by the last-executed SQL statement. It is used here to determine if a row was actually changed as a result of the update attempt. If so, the update is committed and the procedure completes. If no change occurred, an error is raised and the user is asked to verify that the restaurant ID number supplied when invoking the procedure is indeed valid.

In addition, Ingres provides a variety of built-in arithmetic functions. Beyond the basics (addition, subtraction, multiplication, and division), Ingres also supports exponentiation, square root, modulo division, and functions of trigonometry (sine, cosine, arctangent, and so on). With the Object Manager, Ingres also enables users to create new functions for user-defined data types.

Ingres supports dynamic embedded SQL (through their ESQL products). Supported third-generation programming languages include Ada, COBOL, C,

FORTRAN, Pascal, PL/1, and Basic. Ingres also supports Microsoft's ODBC, a call-level interface for Windows. Windows client applications written with ODBC calls can access Ingres data.

DISTRIBUTED DATABASE

Ingres offers different products to support connectivity to remote systems:

- Ingres/Net, which enables applications to access a single, remote Ingres database. This is useful for client/server environments.
- Ingres/Star, which enables users to access multiple databases on a single Ingres system. When combined with Ingres/Net, it supports access to multiple databases on multiple Ingres DBMSs.
- Ingres/Gateways, which enables users to access OEM data. When combined with Ingres/Star and Ingres/Net, these provide access to multiple databases on multiple Ingres and non-Ingres DBMSs.
- Ingres/Replicator, which replicates data between different Ingres systems. When combined with Ingres/Gateways, it can replicate data between Ingres and non-Ingres sysstems. Both Ingres/Net and the Knowledge Manager component are required by Ingres/Replicator. Use of Ingres/Star is optional.

The first two of these products are discussed in this section, while the latter two are discussed in subsequent sections.

Installing Ingres/Net alone enables a user to invoke Ingres tools or an Ingres application on one system and access data in an Ingres database on a remote system. Figure 16–2 illustrates an Ingres/Net configuration.

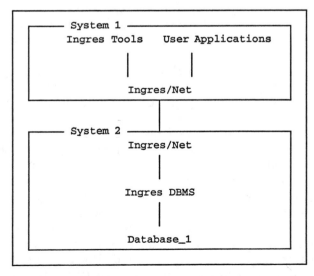

Figure 16–2. Using Ingres/NET to access a remote DBMS

With this configuration, users could connect to a remote database and issue queries to read or write to the database. The example below shows how an application might connect to the DINING database at NEWYORK and query the RESTAURANT table:

```
exec sql
connect newyork::dining

exec sql
select name, phone, cuisine
from restaurant
where pricing = 'MODERATE'
```

A customer wishing to access multiple databases (all on the same system) would install Ingres/Star, as shown in Figure 16–3. Note that, without Ingres/Net, this configuration does not provide access to databases on multiple systems.

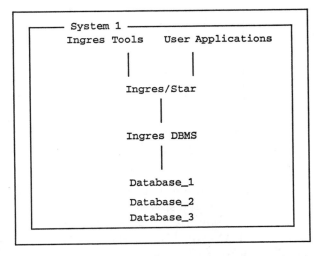

Figure 16–3. Using Ingres/Star to access multiple INGRES databases

But neither of these configurations is what most people have in mind when they discuss distributed databases. Instead, it is the combination of Ingres/Net and Ingres/Star that offers the more robust capability of enabling users to access multiple Ingres databases on multiple nodes within a single application. Figure 16–4 illustrates such a configuration.

Data access is supported at a distributed request level. In other words, a single query statement (such as a join) may involve data in multiple databases on multiple nodes. Furthermore, a single transaction can update multiple databases at multiple sites with automatic two-phase commit processing.

To enable their systems to support this, administrators create a "/star" database and "register" tables residing at remote sites. The registration statement

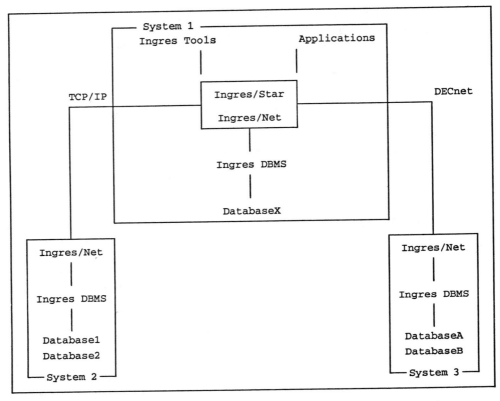

Figure 16–4. Combining Ingres/NET and Ingres/Star. Users can access multiple databases on multiple nodes.

enables administrators to specify a new object name (essentially an alias) to make access to a remote object transparent.

The example below creates an Ingres/Star database (FOOD) consisting of two tables: REVIEWS, which is an alias for the RATING table in the DINING database at the CHICAGO node, and EMPLOYEES, which is an alias for the CRITIC table in the DINING database at the BOSTON node.

```
create food /star
register table reviews as link from rating
    with node=chicago, database=dining
register table employees as link from critic
    with node=boston, database=dining
```

At this point, authorized users may read or write to either of these tables (or both). (Local security constraints are not bypassed by the use of Ingres/Star. Users accessing local or remote databases must previously have been granted appropriate privileges.) A transaction requiring updates to both tables would be supported automatically with system-coordinated two-phase commit processing.

The example below shows how an application might join data from these two tables. In this case, the query will provide a list of all restaurants reviewed in Chicago by one of the roving critics sent from headquarters in Boston.

```
exec sql connect food

exec sql
select rest_id, overall, meal_time, date, last_name, first_name
from reviews, employees
where reviews.reviewer = employees.id
```

To optimize such a query, Ingres/Star maintains a global catalog with statistics about the remote tables. These statistics include information about the sizes of tables, the number of rows per table, and the distribution of data values within a table. Such information is typical of that used by Ingres in nondistributed environments. (More information about Ingres' query optimizer is in the section "Performance.") In addition, Ingres/Star's query optimizer can consider such factors as line cost and remote CPU performance to help it decide if data should be transferred between sites to maximize performance (and, if so, to what site).

GATEWAYS AND MIDDLEWARE

Ingres supports heterogeneous data access through a series of gateway products. As of this writing, Ingres has announced or delivered gateways to IBM's DB2, IMS (a hierarchic DBMS), and VSAM files; DEC's RMS files and Rdb (a relational DBMS); Hewlett-Packard's Allbase (a relational DBMS) and ImageSQL; and Computer Associates' CA-IDMS and CA-Datacom.

Ingres/Gateways to SQL-based systems enable users to access OEM data through the use of a subset of the SQL language (called "Open SQL" statements). These include most of the basic statements, such as CREATE/DROP, SELECT, INSERT, UPDATE, DELETE, COMMIT, ROLLBACK, and DECLARE CURSOR. Static and dynamic SQL are supported. Error message and data type translation services are provided, eliminating the need for programmers to become very familiar with the OEM product.

The gateway to IMS accepts Open SQL statements and supports IMS access through IMS/TM (formerly known as IMS/DC) or through direct connection with IMS/DB (batch and DL/1 programs). The type of connection is set during initialization.

REPLICATION

Ingres offers a data replication product that enables users to automate the process of maintaining copies of tables at multiple sites. Ingres/Replicator supports asynchronous replication of Ingres data to other Ingres systems or to non-Ingres

DBMSs (via Ingres/Gateways). Users may elect to replicate entire tables or a subset of a table. Release 6.4 of Ingres is required (with its Knowledge Manager component), as well as Ingres/Net and support for embedded SQL for C (ESQL).

Figure 16–5 illustrates the overall capabilities of Ingres/Replicator. Ingres classifies its replication services into three broad areas: peer-to-peer, master/slave, and cascade.

Peer-to-peer replication maintains copies of data at multiple sites, with each site able to update the data. Since propagation of updates occurs asynchronously, this has the potential to yield conflicts. How Ingres/Replicator handles such conflicts is discussed shortly.

Master/slave replication is comparable to what many DBMS researchers originally referred to as snapshots. It enables one site to be identified as the primary or source site, and one or more other sites to be identified as the secondary or target sites. Read/write activities are supported at the primary site, and read-only activities are supported at the secondary sites. Master/slave replication can be useful for creating a backup site for disaster recovery.

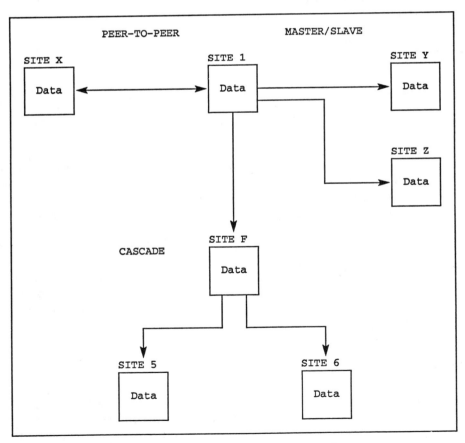

Figure 16–5.   Sample scenarios for Ingres/Replicator

Cascade replication is a variation of master/slave support. One site is identified as primary (with read/write access), and one or more other sites are identified as secondary (with read-only access). However, the secondary sites may, in turn, propagate changes to yet other sites.

Regardless of the type of replication scenario selected, changes to source tables are captured through rules (triggers), which are supported by the Knowledge Manager extension of Ingres. Ingres' replication environment automatically creates the necessary rules on the user's behalf when a table is identified for replication. When a transaction executing against this table commits, the appropriate rule writes some information to a replication input queue, which is actually a table in the source database. This information includes a unique identifier (a replication key), the source table name, and pointers to the data that has been changed.

Information may remain in the input queue for a period of time or may be consulted immediately. This is at the administrator's discretion, who may opt to schedule the job at specific time intervals or identify certain thresholds (perhaps involving the number of rows affected). A rule on the input queue controls when replication occurs.

When replication is scheduled to occur, the Replicator consults the input queue and writes the appropriate table row(s) to a distribution queue, which is another table in the source database. One row will be written for each target database involved. Once the data is in the distribution queue, Ingres/Replicator transfers it to the appropriate targets as soon as possible. Information about the changed data is not removed from the distribution queue until the Replicator receives notice that the remote site committed the work.

Ingres/Replicator also features a Conflict Resolver component, which it uses to cope with update collisions (or conflicting changes). Administrators instruct the Conflict Resolver on how to respond in such situations. Options include giving the initial update priority and rolling back the conflicting transaction, giving the most recent update priority and overwriting the earlier conflicting data, taking some other user-specified action, or halting all replication.

PERFORMANCE

Ingres offers a variety of features to help maximize performance. These include a statistics-based optimizer, a facility for reviewing access path selection, and stored procedures. Defining the proper indexes for tables, as well as selecting an appropriate storage structure, can also enable administrators to improve overall system performance.

Optimizer

Ingres maintains statistics about user data in its catalogs, and its optimizer consults these statistics to determine an efficient means of data access. The *optimizedb* command enables administrators to instruct Ingres to update these statistics as appropriate. As mentioned previously, the use of a global catalog in a distributed database environment enables Ingres to optimize distributed queries and consider such additional factors as line cost and remote CPU performance capabilities.

Ingres offers administrators the option of generating a full set of statistics, or statistics based only on a sampling of the data. The full set collects the most accurate information but is a more costly operation to perform (as more data must be consulted). Sampled statistics may be less accurate than statistics based on the full set, particularly if the specified sample size is too small. However, sampled statistics can be collected in less time and may be quite appropriate for large tables (provided a sufficient sampling size is specified). The example below instructs Ingres to generate statistics for the RATING table in the DINING database, basing these statistics on a random sampling of 2.5 percent of that table:

```
optimizedb -zs2.5 dining rating
```

Other options for gathering statistics include generating information only about the minimum and maximum values of columns or generating information only about values for all indexed columns. In addition, users may create a test file specifying their own statistical information and cause *optimizedb* to update catalog statistics based on this data. This feature can help administrations answer "what if" questions and project how queries will perform in a production environment.

The optimizer can also understand nonuniform distribution of data (such as an unusually high number of employees belonging to department 101) and adjust its access path selection accordingly. Administrators may specify the number of distinct values Ingres will maintain for nonuniform data; the default is 15, but it may range up to 250.

To improve query performance, Ingres' optimizer can "flatten" subqueries into equivalent join operations, which may provide for a more efficient access path. In addition, sort/merge and nested loop join processing is supported.

Query Execution Plan

Ingres also provides a facility for reviewing the query execution plan selected by the optimizer. This can help administrators understand index usage (among other things) and tailor their databases as appropriate.

The example below contains a query involving three columns of a hashed table, with a primary key defined (and an index created) on COL1. "D" indicates the amount of disk I/O, roughly the number of 2K pages to be referenced. The amount shown here is small (one page) because the hashed primary index was used (indicated by "Hashed(col1)" on the final line). A total of 70 pages and 156 rows (tuples) were involved to satisfy this query.

```
SET QEP /G

select col1, col2, col3 from test
   where col1 = 567
   order by col2;
****************************************************************
```

```
QUERY PLAN 3,1, no timeout, of main query

                    Sort on (No Attr)
                    Pages 1 Tups 1
                    D1 C0
          /
          Proj-rest
          Sorted(col1)
          Pages 1 Tups 1
          D1 C0

  /
  test
  Hashed(col1)
  Pages 70 Tups 155
  ************************************************************************
```

Procedures

Stored procedures also help improve performance because they eliminate some of the overhead required to process transactions. A stored procedure may contain multiple SQL statements, but its execution results in a single call over the network to the DBMS. Examples of stored procedures appeared earlier in the sections "Integrity" and "Query Capabilities."

PARALLELISM

Ingres supports parallel transaction processing on certain multiprocessor hardware platforms, including those that support shared-disk environments. This enables multiple Ingres servers (running on different processors) to service the needs of different transactions in parallel. However, the authors have limited information about the Ingres architecture and implementation on multiprocessor platforms and are therefore unable to provide more detailed information.

In addition, Computer Associates recently announced a joint development agreement with ICL to extend Ingres' parallel-processing capabilities.

SUMMARY

This chapter described Computer Associates' CA_OpenIngres (referred to as Ingres in this book), a product originally based on research activities at the University of California at Berkeley. This product is installed on a number of operating systems and hardware platforms. In this chapter, the reader has seen how Ingres supports key DBMS functions, including lock management, recovery, integrity, and other areas. Also discussed were its support for more contemporary database technologies, such as distributed database support, replication, parallelism, and middleware.

REFERENCES AND SUGGESTED READING

ASK INGRES/Replicator, The ASK Group, 902046-001, October 1993.

ASK INGRES/Replicator Technical Background and Competitive Overview, The ASK Group, 902046-001, August 1993.

Distributed INGRES for the UNIX and VMS Operating Systems, Release 6.3, Relational Technology, November 1989.

INGRES Database Administrator's Guide for the VMS Operating Systems, Release 6.3, Ingres Corp., March 1990.

INGRES/NET User's and Administrator's Guide for the UNIX and VMS Operating Systems, Release 6.3, Relational Technology, November 1989.

INGRES Object Management Extension User Guide for the UNIX and VMS Operating Systems, Release 6.3, Relational Technology, November 1989.

INGRES/OpenSQL Reference Manual. Release 6.3, Relational Technology, November 1989.

INGRES/Query Command Summary for the Unix and VMS Operating Systems. Release 6.3, Relational Technology, November 1989.

INGRES/SQL Reference Manual, Release 6.3, Relational Technology, November 1989.

Sequent/INGRES Performance Report: The Silver Bullet Benchmark, Sequent Computer Systems, 1988.

STONEBRAKER, M., E. WONG, P. KREPS, and G. HELD. "The Design and Implementation of INGRES," in *Readings in Database Systems,"* MICHAEL STONEBRAKER, ed., Morgan Kaufmann, 1995.

STONEBRAKER, MICHAEL, ed. *The Ingres Papers: Anatomy of a Relational Database System,* Addison-Wesley, 1986.

WONG, E., and K. YOUSSEFI. "Decomposition—A Strategy for Query Processing," *ACM TODS,* vol. 1, no. 3, September 1976.

PART 4
Object Orientation and Database Management Systems

CHAPTER 17
The Object Database Management System Approach

CHAPTER OBJECTIVES

This chapter introduces the reader to object DBMSs, which differ from relational DBMSs in a number of key respects. Readers will learn basic object-oriented concepts and how they have been applied to the DBMS field. The chapter also provides a sample application using an object DBMS to help the reader understand the way in which many of the object-oriented concepts are actually implemented in a commercial offering. Additionally, there is discussion about the initial target applications of both relational and object DBMSs, so that the reader may more easily compare and contrast these two types of products.

CRITICISMS OF RELATIONAL DBMSS

Until now, this book has focused almost exclusively on relational DBMSs. But in recent years, some consultants and vendors have criticized commercial relational DBMSs as being inadequate for many modern applications. Among the reasons often cited are these:

- Poor support for unconventional data types. Although various primitive types of data are supported (such as integers, floating-point numbers, decimals, and character strings), many other types are supported poorly, or not supported at all (such as voice, documents, video, and image). In addition, users often are not able to define their own types to the DBMS, forcing them to cope with the restrictive type system the vendor chooses to provide.

- Poor support for complex structures. Relational DBMSs require that users view their data in a record-oriented format as simple tables. Doing so may not provide an intuitive or natural means of modeling their data. RDBMSs do not represent data to the user through more complex structures such as linked lists, arrays, hierarchies, and networks.
- Poor performance for applications working with highly interrelated data. Relationships among data often require joins in a relational DBMS environment, and joins are expensive operations. Critics claim that navigational access can provide a more efficient way of traversing relationships between data.
- Lack of programming language integration, which places an extra burden on application programmers. Relational database programmers must learn a separate data access language (SQL) and cope with differences in the data types supported by the DBMS and the data types supported by the programming language. In addition, SQL is a higher-level language than the language used for application development; this can create an awkward and troublesome seam in the languages required to develop applications.

This chapter examines these issues in greater depth, describing how object DBMSs attempt to address them. Chapter 18, "The Extended Relational and Hybrid Approaches" describes how relational DBMS vendors and researchers are also attempting to address some of these issues through different means—by extending existing relational DBMSs or by building new hybrid DBMSs.

BASIC TERMS AND CONCEPTS

In order to understand the functions and overall approach of object DBMSs, the reader must first become familiar with certain terms and concepts associated with various forms of object technology (most often object-oriented programming languages). This section briefly reviews some of these terms and concepts so that readers may better understand how this technology is impacting the DBMS industry.

The reader will note that some object-oriented terms can be language-specific. For example, people with different programming language backgrounds may use the terms *data member* and *attribute* to mean the same (or at least very similar) things. The following sections of this chapter tend to use C++ terminology, as C++ is a programming language widely supported by object DBMSs and much vendor literature makes use of C++ terms. When possible, however, the authors have attempted to introduce equivalent, language-neutral terms in parentheses for those readers who may wish to review more general literature on object-oriented subjects.

Objects

A key goal of object orientation is to enable users to associate more meaning with their data. In an object-oriented environment, data is not perceived apart from the operations that can be performed with the data. An *object* is really thought of as a combination of data and code. In fact, in order to create a new *type* or *class* of object, programmers typically specify both *data members* (or *attributes*) and *member functions* (or *methods*).

The data members describe the structure and characteristics of the object. For example, an "employee" may have data members defined to represent the employee's name, salary, ID number, and so on. The member functions are code that specifies the *behavior* associated with the object, or what objects of this particular type can do. Member functions (or methods) can also be thought of as providing services that are associated with objects. For example, an "employee" class may have member functions defined for issuing a paycheck or changing an employee's compensation package.

Member functions are said to *encapsulate* the underlying data associated with objects. This helps separate the object's interface from its underlying implementation. The idea here is that if an object's implementation must be changed in the future (for example, if a different type of structure needs to be used to represent the object internally), such a change should not impact existing applications. Instead, the interface to the objects should remain the same, and the member functions should be adapted (if necessary) to accommodate the change.

Programmers interface to objects by sending them *messages*. This essentially involves invoking a member function or method, much like programmers working with third-generation programming languages would call a subroutine. The interface to an object consists of the messages one can send it. These messages must be issued according to a certain format, respecting the *signature* of the method (or its name and expected parameters).

By enabling programmers to create their own types or classes, object orientation offers considerable flexibility. This can be important in situations where the real-world entities one is trying to model can't be easily or intuitively represented in a tabular structure.

Class Example

An example might help clarify things. Consider the situation a customer might face when trying to model a report (such as a technical report or an academic report). This is one type of real-life "object" that most people wouldn't normally visualize as a series of rows and columns that constitute a simple (normalized) table. (It could certainly be represented as such, but doing so wouldn't be particularly intuitive.) Most people associate certain characteristics with such reports; they typically expect reports to have an author, a title, a publication date, a body, and perhaps references to other reports. In addition, most people associate certain services or functions with reports. One might say they expect reports to "behave" in a certain way. For example, they may expect to be able to check reports for spelling errors, search reports for certain information, print a report, count the number of words in a report, and so forth.

In an object-oriented environment, a "report" class might be represented as shown in Figure 17–1. Certain data members (or attributes) would be clearly

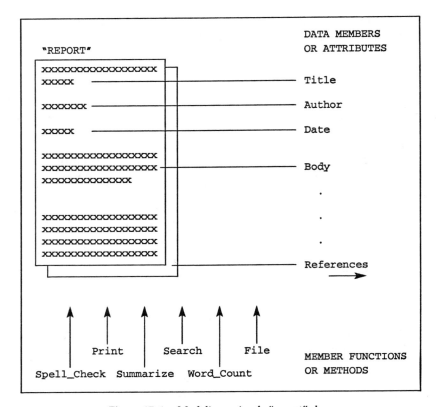

Figure 17–1. Modeling a simple "report" class

defined, as well as the member functions (or methods). More traditional environments might not permit a new type (or class) to be defined at all. Moreover, the member functions representing the object's behaviors (or relevant services) would exist separately, perhaps in a variety of applications.

Object Identity

An important concept associated with the object approach is that each object has an identity that is independent of its state (or data values). In other words, the data values associated with an object are not what is used to uniquely identify each object. Because of this, two objects can have the same data values but still be considered *different* objects (because each has a different identifier).

Hierarchies and Inheritance

In addition to supporting the definition of new classes or types, object-oriented programming languages enable programmers to define *class hierarchies* and take advantage of *inheritance*—two features that are particularly helpful because they enable programmers to reuse previously written code. Hierarchies enable programmers to define new classes or types that are more specialized forms of previously created classes or types. These specialized subclasses or subtypes inherit the data members (or attributes) and member functions (or methods) associated with their parent class(es) or type(s). In this way, the code required to define and implement the parent class(es) is reused, helping to improve programmer productivity. Code reuse is frequently cited as a key benefit of the object-oriented approach.

Again, an example might help clarify this notion. Consider the previous report class, and imagine that it becomes apparent that internal company reports and external (or publicly available) reports need to be treated slightly differently. In an object-oriented environment, two new classes could be defined ("internal_rep" and "external_rep"), each of which is a subclass derived from the original report class. Defining "internal_rep" would require coding only those data members and member functions peculiar to internal reports (such as a security classification and perhaps a new file method to ensure that the data is encrypted before being written to disk). Similarly, defining "external_rep" would require coding only those data members and member functions peculiar to external reports (such as the author's external mailing address and a modified print mechanism that includes the company logo on the bottom of each page).

Figure 17–2 illustrates this class hierarchy.

Overloading

The class hierarchy shown in Figure 17–2 brings up another interesting point associated with object-oriented programming: the ability to *overload* member functions (in this case) so that the same name may be used to perform different operations. At first glance, the reader may think this would serve only to introduce considerable confusion (and perhaps unpredictable results). However, when properly used, overloading can actually simplify the system for programmers.

In Figure 17–2, examples of overloading occurred twice. The print mechanism associated with external reports differs from the print mechanism associated with standard reports; printing an external report will force the company logo to appear on each page, whereas printing a standard (or even an internal) report will not. Nonetheless, "print" is the name given to both of these different member functions. A similar situation occurs with "file." Filing an internal report that carries a certain security classification will cause data encryption to occur before the report is written to disk. This is not the case when filing a standard (or external) report.

In traditional programming languages, programmers would typically create different names for the various print and file functions (such as "print1" for standard reports and "print2" for external reports). Such names may be difficult to learn or remember, and place an added burden on application programmers who would probably prefer that the system resolve the situation for them. Object-oriented programming languages support this. Compilers are usually able to distinguish which print routine should really be executed by checking the type of the object the programmer is working with or by examining the parameters passed when the member function is invoked.

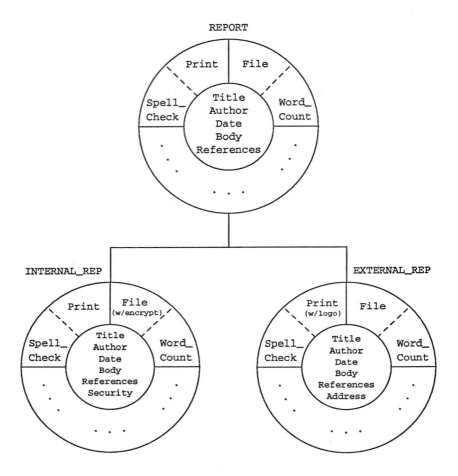

Figure 17–2. A simple class hierarchy

Applying Object Concepts to DBMSs

What does all this have to do with the DBMS community? Object-oriented concepts offer the promise of providing additional flexibility, helping people associate more meaning with their data, promoting code reuse, and helping people model real-world entities more easily. These are useful goals and can be applied to DBMS products in a variety of ways, as this chapter and the next discuss.

KEY DIFFERENCES FROM RELATIONAL DBMSS

Object DBMSs differ from relational DBMSs in a number of areas, as this section describes. These areas include the types of applications these DBMSs initially tried to satisfy, the application programming interfaces (APIs), the underlying system architecture, and even their query interfaces (or lack thereof).

Initial Application Focus of RDBMSs

A significant area of difference between object and relational DBMSs is the type of applications each initially sought to support. While most relational DBMSs focused on supporting traditional business applications in the areas of decision support or online transaction processing, object DBMSs initially focused on supporting different kinds of applications. These applications often involved iterative design work, which is common in computer-aided design, computer-aided publishing, and computer-aided software engineering fields. Because these kinds of applications often imposed drastically different requirements on a database manager, object DBMSs and relational DBMSs differ in a number of functional areas. It may be instructive, then, to briefly review the different requirements associated with relational DBMS and object DBMS applications, exploring how these requirements impacted the features and functions generally incorporated into these two types of products.

Typical business applications—which relational DBMS vendors have traditionally tried to support—often exhibit many or all of the following characteristics:

- Data types tend to be simple, often involving only alphanumeric and numeric data (character strings and numbers).
- Query-based or value-based access is important and may be ad hoc in nature.
- Transactions tend to be short, often completing in subseconds or a few minutes. (Some complex queries are expected to take longer, but not several days or weeks.)
- Concurrency requirements may be high, with dozens, hundreds, or thousands of users requiring access to a single version of the data.
- Robust system management facilities are important, particularly in areas such as recovery, security, availability, and performance tuning.
- Computing environments may range from highly centralized to decentralized environments, spanning portable computers to mainframes and massively parallel processing systems.
- A wide range of tools and applications that interface to the DBMS is important, as is support for many programming languages. Tools required may include products geared toward end users, executives, programmers, and administrators.

Supporting these requirements has caused relational DBMS vendors to implement a number of features. For example, initial releases of these products provided a limited number of data types to support various kinds of numbers and character strings. Some relational DBMSs, as described in Part Three, "Commercial Relational Database Management Systems," have since enhanced their built-in type support, but creating a rich and highly variable type system was not an early design point. The focus on query-based access prompted the development of SQL—a language that is independent of any programming language and that was designed for interactive queries as well as for use in application programs.

Supporting short transactions and high concurrency caused relational DBMS vendors to implement rather strict locking protocols that are sometimes very granular in nature (perhaps locking only a single row of data at a time). Robust system management support forced relational DBMS vendors to implement such features as archive and dual logging, device mirroring, lock escalation and deadlock detection, row- and column-level security mechanisms, system traces, audit trails, and other administrative functions.

In addition, the computing environments available to support most early relational DBMS products were centralized. As relational DBMS vendors ported their products to client/server platforms, they retained largely a server-centric architecture. Processing most of the DBMS workload on the server makes sense for traditional business applications that must support a large number of users who often require a quick means to filter the data they want (via conditions specified in their queries). Finally, successful relational DBMS vendors provide a suite of tools and applications for products, or they have established numerous alliances with third-party vendors to do so.

Initial Application Focus of ODBMSs

Let's contrast this with object DBMSs. Since their initial application focus was not traditional business applications but instead other kinds of applications (such as those involving iterative design work), what requirements did these vendors typically have to satisfy?

- Data types and structures are often complex in nature, incorporating more than simple alphanumeric and numeric data.
- Data is highly interrelated, with much of the processing logic of the application spent traversing these relationships.
- Changes to objects may span hours, days, or even weeks. For example, the process of completing the design for part of a new computer chip or part of a car is expected to take considerably more than a few subseconds or minutes.
- Close integration with an object-oriented programming language (often the language of choice for these types of applications) is important.
- Computing environments tend to involve LAN-based workstations, and the number of concurrent users may be relatively small (ranging from a few coworkers to a few dozen).
- Requirements in areas such as recovery, availability, and security may not be very rigorous.
- Tool support for programmers is a top priority. Tools for end users, executives, and administrators are of lesser importance.

As the reader can see, such requirements are quite different from those that relational DBMSs initially attempted to satisfy. As a result, the features and functions incorporated into object DBMSs are often quite different. For example, object DBMSs rely on the flexible type systems of programming languages such as C++ and Smalltalk to enable customers to create their own classes or types. A single class (or type) may be quite complex, incorporating a number of other types in a structure defined by the programmer. Thus, an employee class written in C++ might contain an integer representing an identification number, an array of characters representing a name, and a pointer to a set of skills (where "skills" is a user-defined type). Furthermore, all employee instances within a single department might be chained together, with each employee containing a pointer to the next employee in the list.

To support data that is highly interrelated and enable individuals to quickly traverse or walk through these relationships, object DBMSs generally focus on supporting navigational access. In relational DBMSs, data relationships are often resolved by joining two or more tables, and join operations tend to be costly to process. Object DBMSs enable programmers to make the relationships between objects explicit; in C++, these are often represented by pointers that can then be traversed quickly. Bill-of-materials processing (in which one wants to determine all the parts and subparts of a given component) can benefit from this kind of support.

The nature of iterative design work dictates that transactions may be quite long by conventional standards. To support these kinds of transactions without locking out other users requires some flexible locking schemes. *Versioning* is one such approach. This enables users to create multiple versions of one or more objects and to work on these independently without impeding other users' access to existing versions. At some later time, different versions of objects can be merged back together (manually) if desired.

Integration with C++, Smalltalk, LISP, or some other object-oriented programming language gives object DBMSs much of the flexibility and power associated with those languages. It also eliminates the *impedance mismatch* between programming languages and SQL, because types and structures implemented in an object-oriented programming language can be supported directly by the object DBMS. Thus, programmers don't need to resolve differences between programming language data types and structures, and the native data types and tabular structure associated with relational DBMSs. However, programming language integration also means that the DBMS has minimal (if any) language independence; this is why most object DBMSs support only a small number of programming languages, mandating that individuals who must access data managed by these systems do so only through one of these languages.

In addition, because object DBMSs premiered in the commercial arena in the late 1980s and focused largely on supporting workgroups, many were designed with a client/server architecture in mind. Their architecture is often client-centric, with much of the processing performed on a client workstation. This is desirable for iterative design applications, where a mechanical engineer trying to revise the design of an automobile engine might want to load all the data associated with the engine into the memory of his client workstation and change or test various configurations.

These features were so different from those incorporated into traditional DBMSs that object DBMS vendors initially placed limited emphasis on system management issues and third-party tools in their initial releases. The applications they sought to satisfy were often somewhat specialized and isolated within certain departments of the company, making certain administrative features (such as strict locking protocols) less critical. As object DBMS vendors have sought to support other types of applications, they are finding that some of these administrative features and accompanying tool sets are mandatory. Some vendors are responding to these additional requirements, although, in general, object DBMSs still lag behind relational DBMSs in these areas as of this writing.

The following chart highlights some of the differences mentioned between the applications initially targeted by relational and object DBMSs.

	OBJECT DBMS PRODUCTS	RELATIONAL DBMS PRODUCTS
Sample application	CAD	Payroll
User environment	Workgroup	Workgroup, corporate
Length of transaction	Minutes, hours. . .	Subseconds, seconds. . .
Concurrency	Flexible	Strict
Data types	User-defined	Alphanumeric, numeric
Data structure	User-defined	Tabular
Data access	Navigational	Query or value based
Programming languages	Smalltalk, C++ (or other OOPL)	Many 3GLs, 4GLs
Tools	Programmer	DBA, programmer, end user

Application Programming Interface (API)

Most object DBMSs do not require the use of a separate database access language (such as SQL) in order to work with *persistent* objects. (Object-oriented environments distinguish between those objects that persist in the database beyond the execution of a program and those transient objects that reside in virtual memory and are not retained for use when a particular program terminates.) Instead, they typically provide classes and member functions (or methods) for languages such as C++ or Smalltalk; programmers can then use these mechanisms to work with the database. In many respects, object DBMSs may be considered extensions of the programming language environment—they enable programmers to define new types and write applications in an object-oriented programming language, providing them with the ability to make the objects they create persistent (and able to be shared with others).

In this way, much of the flexibility and richness of object-oriented programming languages are preserved by object DBMSs. This includes the ability to create new types of objects and implement a data model based on any structure capable of being devised by the programming language. It also means that programmers do not need to resolve differences between their data model and data types, and the predefined model and data types implemented in a more conventional DBMS.

However, this flexibility does come with a price. Someone must create the types desired, which can involve considerable coding, depending on what's required. In addition, associating a certain structure with these objects—such as a linked list—means that the programmer must write the necessary code to implement this structure. Therefore, the start-up costs associated with building an object DBMS application may be high, as programmers must devote a certain amount of time building up a suitable infrastructure. The high costs associated with this start-up have given rise to the production and sale of class libraries containing predefined classes for use in various applications areas. In addition, providing programmers with such flexibility requires them to be quite sensitive to performance issues when designing their classes and structures.

As of this writing, the APIs for object DBMSs vary considerably from product to product. However, most object DBMSs support a C++ interface, and some support Smalltalk as well. A sample object DBMS application coded in C++ is provided later, in the section "Sample Object DBMS Application."

Performance

Performance is often an issue cited as critical in evaluating the suitability of a given DBMS for a given application. Object DBMS vendors often cite performance superiority over relational DBMS vendors for certain workloads. Two engineers at Sun Microsystems—R. G. G. Cattell and J. Skeen—published the results of an engineering database benchmark they devised. This benchmark involved a bill-of-materials application with 20,000 unique parts and 60,000 connections between these parts in total. The performance of four object DBMSs was compared to that of a relational DBMS and Sun's index file system.

Specific DBMS tasks included retrieval, update, and insert operations. In some cases, the object DBMSs performed a given operation more than 10 times faster than the relational DBMS. In extreme cases, performance was more than 50 times faster for a given operation. (For example, one operation took 19 seconds for the relational DBMS to complete, while an object DBMS performed the same task in .03 seconds. For another operation, the relational DBMS took 84 seconds to finish, while two object DBMSs finished in less than 1 second.)

This clearly demonstrated that object DBMSs can provide a much quicker response time for this application than the relational DBMS that was tested. These results are sometimes erroneously used to conclude that object DBMSs simply outperform relational DBMSs for all types of applications. Indeed, researchers rarely make this claim. Rather, many acknowledge that if object DBMSs were to be tested in a benchmark geared toward traditional relational DBMS applications (such as decision support or online transaction processing), object DBMSs would probably not perform as well as relational DBMSs.

More recent benchmark activities have taken place in the object DBMS arena, with the most notable as of this writing probably being the 007 benchmark from the University of Wisconsin-Madison. However, as this benchmark attempted to test performance only of object DBMSs (and not of relational DBMSs), its results are discussed here. Readers are encouraged to consult "References and Suggested Reading" if they are interested in the results of this benchmark.

Client/Server Architecture

Many popular object DBMSs were developed for client/server environments. However, unlike relational DBMSs for client/server environments, object DBMSs tend to have client-centric architectures. Much of the processing is done on the client platform, and the DBMS usually tries to keep server activity to a minimum. This is desirable for many applications involving iterative design work, in which response time can be improved if all objects required by the application are transmitted to the client platform in a single request to the server, so they can be rapidly traversed while in the application memory.

An important issue involves how object DBMSs manage memory at the client and resolve application requests for persistent (database) objects. One approach involves the use of table look-ups. When the DBMS receives a request to access a persistent object, it consults an in-memory table (sometimes called a resident object table, a cached object table, or something similar) to determine if the requested object is already in memory. This table is typically hashed on the object identifier to speed access. If the desired object is already in memory, an entry will appear in this table that points to a descriptor of this object. The descriptor contains the client in-memory address of this object. This approach is illustrated in Figure 17–3.

It's possible that no entry for the requested object will appear in the look-up table; this could occur if the DBMS was recently initialized and the object was being requested for the first time. In such a case, the DBMS will retrieve the object from a database on the server, create a descriptor for it, make an appropriate entry

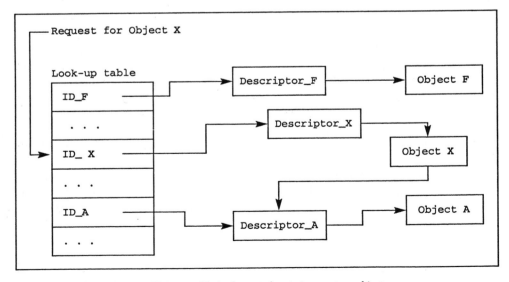

Figure 17–3. Using a table look-up to locate in-memory objects

in the table, and transform the object from its disk representation to its in-memory representation.

It's also possible that objects requested by previous transactions have been swapped out of memory to make room for other objects. In such a case, the look-up table will contain an entry with the object's identifier, but its pointer to the descriptor will be removed. The descriptor itself is also changed, with its pointer to the object set to nil.

As shown in Figure 17–3, pointers from one object to another are resolved through descriptors. For example, if object X was defined to point to object A, its in-memory representation would contain a pointer to the descriptor of object A, which in turn would point to object A itself. This introduces one level of indirection, but it can be beneficial for query processing. Systems that follow this approach to memory management use a set of descriptors for handling the results of a query. The objects themselves are not fetched until demanded, because many times the entire set of objects that satisfy the results of a query are not actually accessed by the client application.

An alternate approach, to date implemented only by one commercial object DBMS vendor, employs a virtual memory mapping architecture that eliminates much of the indirection (including table look-ups) associated with the previous approach. This approach calls for the DBMS to manage a certain region of virtual memory on the client, trapping page faults when an application attempts to reference an object not already in virtual memory. The DBMS then retrieves the appropriate page(s), reads them into the client's virtual memory, and enables the access request to complete. Once the object is in virtual memory, subsequent references can be made at in-memory speeds, without any level of indirection. This is possible, in part, because standard C++ virtual memory pointers can be used for persistent objects rather than a logical object identifier that must be resolved to a specific memory address.

Another important aspect of this approach is that the in-memory representation of objects is the same as the disk representation of objects, which can improve performance in many cases. With this approach, information about the original virtual memory addresses at which persistent objects were created is preserved in the database. Thus, if object 1 contains a pointer to object 2, this pointer will be the virtual memory address at which object 2 was originally created. When these objects are brought back into memory (at the request of some subsequent transaction), the DBMS will try to place them at the same virtual memory locations they occupied at the time of their creation. If this cannot be done, they are relocated and the pointer within object 1 to object 2 is temporarily modified to contain the new location. Note that navigating from object 1 to object 2 involves only a single pointer dereference in this scheme. The approach discussed previously (that uses a look-up table and object descriptors) requires that a descriptor be consulted in order to obtain the memory address.

The two approaches described here differ in another key respect: the unit of data transfer from the server to the client. Systems that use the table look-up approach typically transfer individual objects from the server to the client; such systems are sometimes referred to as *object servers*. As of this writing, the system that uses a virtual memory mapping architecture transfers pages from the server to the client; it is sometimes referred to as a *page server*. The unit of data transfer has performance implications for different kinds of applications, depending on the sizes and number of the objects they reference.

Standards Efforts

Lack of a standard, precisely defined "object database model" and lack of a common interface have caused many potential customers to be skeptical about using object DBMSs. Recognizing this, representatives from a number of object DBMS vendors (including Object Design, Inc. Ontos, O2 Technology, Versant, and Objectivity) formed the Object Database Management Group (ODMG) in an effort to define a standard object model and programming language bindings for object DBMSs. Although not part of a formal standards body (like the International Standards Organization or the American National Standards Institute), the ODMG has drafted an object DBMS standard that it hopes can be used to "jump start" the industry in its effort to provide greater consistency across products so that applications written for various object DBMSs are more portable.

Components of the standard include a definition of a common object model, an object definition language, an object manipulation language, a nonprocedural object query language based partially on SQL, and bindings for Smalltalk and C++. A thorough discussion of this standard is beyond the scope of this book. Readers may consult "References and Suggested Reading" for more information.

SAMPLE OBJECT DBMS APPLICATION

At this point, the reader may wish to understand how one might use some of these features found in object DBMSs (and object-oriented programming languages). It is difficult to provide a generic example, as object DBMS products are relatively new to the industry and lack a single, standard interface or a precisely defined model.

Nonetheless, object DBMSs do share some common characteristics, such as an emphasis on programming language integration. This section shows the reader how a C++ programmer might create a very simple class and write an application that creates persistent instances of this class using the C++ Library Interface provided for the ObjectStore DBMS from Object Design, Inc. To help the reader identify the portions of the code that are specific to ObjectStore, they are highlighted in boldface type.

Creating a Class

The class that will be created provides a simple means of representing pets. Each "pet" is expected to possess an identification number ("petid") and a name ("name"). A simple linked list will be used to provide access to the various pets that will later be created; therefore, each pet instance will also contain a pointer to the next pet in the list.

But, as this chapter noted earlier, classes specify more than just data members (or attributes); they also specify behaviors through the inclusion of member functions (or methods). The member functions for this pet class will be very simple as well. They will include a constructor (for creating new pets), a destructor (for deleting or removing pets), and a show mechanism (for displaying information about pets).

This simple pet class can be defined as shown below.

```
// Header file for simple pets class

// Include necessary header files for I/O and ObjectStore

#include <iostream.h>
#include <ostore/ostore.hh>

class pet {

public:

// Public data members or attributes

int      petid;        // pet number
char     *name;        // pointer to name of pet
pet      *next_pet;    // pointer to next pet

// Public member functions or methods

pet(const int, char*, pet*);    // constructor
~pet();                          // destructor
void show();                     // show pet instance

};
```

With the new pet class declared (usually in a header file, such as the one shown in the previous example), the bodies of the member functions can be written. Most often, this code is included in a separate file, although it could have also been placed in the header file if desired. The following example shows the implementation of the member functions.

```
// Definition of pet class follows.
// The bodies of the methods previously declared are included here.

// Include pet header file
#include "pet.hh"

// Create type specification for ObjectStore.
// Required for all types/classes for which persistent instances
// may be created.
extern os_typespec char_type;
```

```
// Bodies of member functions/methods follow.

// Construct a new pet instance
pet::pet(const int num, char *name, pet *next) {
  petid = num;
  next_pet = next;

  // allocate space for name & copy
  int length = strlen(name)+1;
  this->name = new(os_segment::of(this), length, &char_type)
      char[length];
  strcpy(this->name,name);
}

// Delete pet instance.
pet::~pet() {
  // destroy storage allocated to pet's name
  delete name;
}

// Print pet info to default output device (usually, the screen)
void pet::show() {
  cout << "Pet ID: "<< petid << '\t'
       << "Name: "<< name << endl;
}
```

For those without a C++ programming background, some explanation is in order. The first member function, the constructor, merely assigns two of the three parameters passed (the pet's identification number and the pointer to the next pet in the linked list) to data members declared earlier in the header file ("petid" and "next_pet"). Because the pet's name is represented by a pointer to a character array (a common way of representing character strings in C and C++), the constructor determines the length of the name, allocates appropriate space, and instructs ObjectStore to store this information in the same database segment as the rest of the pet instance. Here, an overloaded form of the C++ "new" operator is used to achieve this.

The second member function is the destructor (signified in C++ by the "~" symbol), which removes a pet instance. The third member function prints information about a given pet to the default output device, which is usually the screen.

Admittedly, such a simple example hardly illustrates the use of complex structures or rich data types that frequently lead people to consider the use of an object-oriented programming language or an object DBMS. But it gives the reader some idea of what's involved in defining a new type or class that will eventually be used to create persistent instances managed by an object DBMS (in this case, ObjectStore).

Creating and Accessing Persistent Objects

With the pet class thus defined, an application can be written that creates new pets and displays the entire list of all pets managed by the DBMS. A simple example follows.

```
// C++ program to use "pet" class
// Create new pets, maintain them in a forward-chained
// linked list, and display the list.
// Use ObjectStore to provide persistence

#include "pet.hh"
os_typespec char_type("char");

main() {

    // Initialize variables.
    pet *head=0;                    // head of linked list of pets
    int number=0;                   // pet ID number
    char pet_name[25];              // pet name
    int total=0;                    // total # of instances to create
    os_database *db1 = 0;           // pointer to a database
    os_database_root *root = 0;     // pointer to a root

    os_typespec pet_type("pet");

    objectstore::initialize();
    db1 = os_database::open("/u/guest/testdb", 0, 0666);

    // prompt for # of pet instances to create
    cout << "Enter number of instances to create: " << endl;
    cin >> total;

    OS_BEGIN_TXN(t1, 0, os_transaction::update)

        root = db1->find_root("pet_root");
        if (!root) root = db1->create_root("pet_root");
        head = (pet*)root->get_value();

        // create the pets
        for (int i=0; i<total; i++) {
          cout << "Enter a pet ID number: " << endl;
          cin >> number;
          cout << "Enter the pet's pet_name: " << endl;
          cin >> pet_name;
          head = new(db1, 1, &pet_type)
              pet(number, pet_name, last_name, head);
          root->set_value(head);
        }

        // Display all pets
        cout << "Here's all the pets: " << endl;
        for(pet* e=head; e; e=e->next_pet)
          e->show();

    OS_END_TXN(t1)
    db1->close();

}
```

Understanding every line of code is not necessary for the purposes of this chapter, but a brief explanation follows. The application begins by declaring and initializing a number of variables. A specific database is opened ("/u/guest/testdb," which conforms to Unix file-naming conventions). The user is prompted to specify how many pets he or she plans to create. An update transaction is then started, and the program checks to see if a database root, or entry point, has been defined for the linked list of pets. If not, one is created.

The user is then prompted to enter the appropriate information for each pet (its identification number and name), and a persistent instance is created for each (by invoking an overloaded form of the C++ "new" operator). Finally, a loop is used to walk through the forward-chained linked list of pets and print the appropriate information for each (by invoking the "show" member function defined previously). The transaction is then closed.

A few points are worth noting here. Object DBMSs typically provide considerable integration with a given object-oriented programming language; had the boldface type not been used in the previous examples, the reader may have had considerable difficulty pinpointing which portions of the code involved the DBMS. Relational DBMSs use a separate application programming interface (usually, SQL) for DBMS access.

Because of their support for object-oriented programming languages, object DBMSs enable customers to create their own types or classes (such as the "pet" class shown here) and define their own structures (such as the linked list used here). Navigational access—pointer dereferencing in C++—is quite common.

Finally, the authors must note that the coding examples shown are extremely simple and do not illustrate many of the features common to object DBMS products, including the use of versioning, collections or containers, error-handling mechanisms, and so forth. The design of the application itself also leaves room for considerable improvement, particularly in the area of performance tuning. But this section was merely intended to give the reader some insight into what it's like to work with an object DBMS—particularly the level of programming language integration that is characteristic of these systems as well as the type of work involved to create a simple class or type.

SUMMARY

Object-oriented technologies have introduced new concepts to the programming and database communities. Chief among these are the close association between data and code, the use of class hierarchies and inheritance, and the ability to overload functions and operators. These features (and others) help object DBMSs cope with real-world objects that are highly interrelated and often have a complex internal structure.

To help the reader compare and contrast object DBMS technology products with relational offerings discussed earlier, this chapter also explored the types of applications each DBMS type initially sought to support and explained how differences in their emphasis have led each to incorporate different product functions. For example, object DBMSs often sought to satisfy applications that supported iterative design work, so a client-centric architecture and client caching are usually supported to improve performance.

To illustrate how persistence can be achieved with an object DBMS, a simple C++ application was included, with sections highlighted to indicate changes to accommodate working with persistent (rather than transient) objects.

REFERENCES AND SUGGESTED READING

AHMED, SHAMIM, ALBERT WONG, DUVVURU SRIRAM, and ROBERT LOGCHER. "Object-Oriented Database Management Systems for Engineering: A Comparison, *Journal of Object-Oriented Programming,* June 1992, p. 27.

ANDREWS, TIMOTHY A. "ONTOS DB: An ODBMS for Distributed AIX Applications," *AIXpert,* May 1992, p. 59.

ATKINSON, MALCOLM, FRANCOIS BANCILHON, DAVID DEWITT, KLAUS DITTRICH, DAVID MAIER, and STANLEY ZDONIK. *The Object-Oriented Database System Manifesto,* July 5, 1989.

ATWOOD, THOMAS. "ODMG-93: The Object DBMS Standard, Part 2," *Object Magazine,* January 1994, p. 32.

BARRY, DOUGLAS K. "ITASCA Distributed ODBMS," *AIXpert,* May 1992, p. 63.

BARRY, DOUGLAS K. "ODBMS Feature Listing," *Object Magazine,* January–February 1993, p. 48.

BUTTERWORTH, PAUL, ALLEN OTIS, and JACOB STEIN. "The Gemstone Object Database Management System," *Communications of the ACM,* vol. 34, no. 10, October 1991, p. 64.

CAREY, MICHAEL J., DEVID J. DEWITT, and JEFFREY F. NAUGHTON. *The 007 Benchmark,* University of Wisconsin-Madison, Computer Sciences Department, Version of April 12, 1993.

CATTELL, R. G. G., and J. SKEEN. *Engineering Database Benchmark,* Sun Microsystems Technical Paper, April 20, 1990.

CATTELL, R. G. G. *Object Data Management,* Addison-Wesley, 1991.

CATTELL, RICK, ed. *Object Databases. The ODMG-93 Standard,* Object Database Management Group, 1993.

DEUX, O., et al. "The O2 System," *Communications of the ACM,* vol. 34, no. 10, October 1991, p. 34.

GOODMAN, NATHAN. "The Object Data Model," *InfoDB,* vol. 6, no. 1, Spring/Summer 1991, p. 2.

KIM, WON. *Introduction to Object-Oriented Databases,* MIT Press, 1990.

LAMB, CHARLES, GORDON LANDIS, JACK ORENSTEIN, and DAN WEINREB. "The ObjectStore Database System," *Communications of the ACM,* vol. 34, no. 10, October 1991, p. 50.

LANDIS, GORDON. "Overview of the ObjectStore ODBMS," *AIXpert,* May 1992, p. 68.

LOOMIS, MARY E. S. "Object and Relational Technologies: Can They Cooperate?" *Object Magazine,* January–February 1993, p. 35.

LOOMIS, MARY E. S. "The VERSANT ODBMS," *AIXpert,* May 1992, p. 73.

Object Data Management Reference Model, ANSI Accredited Standards Committee, X3, Information Processing Systems, Document Number OODB 89-01R8, Sept. 17, 1991.

OTIS, ALLEN, and JACOB STEIN. "The Gemstone Object Database Management System," *AIXpert,* May 1992, p. 54.

SARACCO, CINDY M. "Object and Relational Data Base Management Systems," *Data Management Review,* vol. 3, no. 11, November 1993, p. 8.

SARACCO, CINDY M. "Writing an Object DBMS Application: Part 1," *InfoDB,* vol. 7, no. 4, Winter 1993/1994.

SARACCO, CINDY M. "Writing an Object DBMS Application: Part 2," *InfoDB,* vol. 8, no. 1, Spring 1994.

SOLOVIEV, VALERY. "An Overview of Three Commercial Object-Oriented Database Management Systems: ONTOS, ObjectStore, and O2," *SIGMOD RECORD,* vol. 21, no. 1, March 1992, p. 93.

TAYLOR, DAVID A. *Object-Oriented Technology: A Manager's Guide,* Servio Corp., part number SOOTG1-9/90, 1990.

Understanding the 007 Research Project, Version 1.0, Object Design, April 4, 1993.

CHAPTER 18
The Extended Relational
and Hybrid Approaches

CHAPTER OBJECTIVES

As discussed in Chapter 17, "The Object Database Management System Approach," many of the goals of object technology appeal to a broad range of applications. While some individuals have argued that the best way to realize these objectives in a DBMS environment is to build an object DBMS, others have argued for "marrying" object and relational DBMS technologies or building hybrid or unified systems that attempt to incorporate the best features of each.

Much work is just emerging in this area. Major relational DBMSs have begun incorporating certain object extensions into their products, and a small group of new products has emerged that generally provide more advanced object extensions built largely on a relational base. This chapter explores both of these approaches and describes some of the differences between these approaches and those of object DBMSs.

EARLY RESEARCH EFFORTS

Many of the concepts associated with object technology have engaged relational DBMS researchers for years. For example, Dr. E. F. Codd (who invented the relational database model) published a paper in 1979 that proposed extensions to the relational model that would capture more of the semantics of the data. Among these features and extensions are the use of *surrogates* (DBMS-generated, unique identifiers that are similar in some respects to object identifiers), generalization or type hierarchies, structural inheritance, and new relational algebra operators to exploit the richer semantics associated with these extensions.

In addition, a number of research prototypes were developed that explored ways of implementing certain object-oriented concepts in a relational DBMS context. Two of the more well-known prototypes in this area are POSTGRES (developed at the University of California, Berkeley) and Starburst (developed at the IBM Almaden Research Center). Both were developed in the 1980s.

POSTGRES included components to support *object management* and *knowledge management*, as well as standard data management. Object management involved support for nonstandard data types and structures, while knowledge management involved support for business rules. This prototype has since been upgraded and released as a commercial product called Illustra; that product is discussed briefly later in the section "Illustra."

Starburst was designed to be an extended—as well as extensible—relational DBMS. Like POSTGRES, its features include support for complex structures, unconventional data types, and a rules system for capturing user-defined integrity constraints. Unlike POSTGRES, however, Starburst supports a more client-centric architecture. IBM has incorporated some of the features of Starburst into its commercial relational DBMS product family (the DB2 family).

COMMON RELATIONAL DBMS EXTENSIONS

Varying levels of object support can be found in commercial relational DBMSs and hybrid DBMSs. Among the more common enhancements that can be found in commercial relational DBMSs are:

- Stored procedures
- Triggers
- Constraints
- Very long fields or BLOBs
- User-defined types
- User-defined functions

User-defined functions, stored procedures and triggers most closely approximate the member functions or methods in an object environment, although they are not identical. Very long fields and user-defined types can make for a more flexible data type system, enabling users to store more than just simple character strings and numbers.

Stored Procedures and Triggers

Stored procedures may be thought of as mini-SQL programs that are stored in the DBMS. Essentially, such stored procedures enable customers to write SQL statements with procedural, control-of-flow logic constructs that the vendor has incorporated into its SQL support (such as if-then-else statements and loops). Once these stored procedures have been created, they may be invoked at any time by users who have appropriate access privileges. This promotes code reuse.

A number of relational DBMS vendors support stored procedures of this sort; Oracle, Ingres, and SQL Server are among the products profiled in earlier this book that offer this support. IBM's DB2 Version 2 for AIX and OS/2 also support procedures, although their implementation differs somewhat. Their procedures are written in a third-generation programming language (such as C) with embedded SQL, and they reside outside the DBMS.

In some respects, stored procedures are similar to member functions or methods supported by object DBMSs. Like member functions, stored procedures simplify user access to the underlying data. Those who invoke stored procedures do not need to write the SQL statements (and, perhaps, the procedural logic statements) necessary to execute the query; instead, they merely specify the name of the stored procedure (along with any necessary parameters), and they can reuse the SQL code that constitutes the stored procedure.

However, stored procedures differ from member functions in several respects. Stored procedures are generally not thought of—or defined—as *part* of a table or view. Thus, data and code are still viewed as separate entities. In object DBMSs, member functions exist as part of the overall class definition (even though member functions are stored separately from the class instances in most object DBMSs). In addition, stored procedures are written (at least in part) in SQL. Member functions or methods generally are not; typically, they are coded in C++ or Smalltalk. Finally, stored procedures do not truly support data encapsulation, as tables and views can still be accessed through ad hoc queries and SQL-based applications rather than simply through stored procedures. In an object environment, the underlying data elements of an object can only be accessed through its methods or member functions.

Triggers are often implemented as a special form of a stored procedure. As such, they also bear some similarity to member functions of an object DBMS. Triggers represent a means of enabling customers to instruct the DBMS to enforce their own business rules. They are designed to automatically execute—or fire—when a given database event occurs (perhaps when someone updates a column of a table). Triggers provide a flexible mechanism for enforcing integrity constraints, helping users associate more meaning with the underlying data. They also promote code reuse by eliminating the need for multiple applications to code the same integrity checks.

However, triggers are not identical to member functions, for many of the same reasons that stored procedures are not. They are written in SQL (or "extended" SQL) and are not perceived as being *part* of the table with which they are associated.

Constraints

Like triggers, constraints play a role in enforcing data integrity in a relational DBMS. They are most often written to provide some level of domain support, such as ensuring the valid range of data values for a particular column. This helps associate more meaning with data, so constraints are sometimes broadly considered to be an object extension. (In object DBMSs, such constraints would be coded as part of the class definition.)

Most commercial relational DBMSs enable constraints to perform data range checking but not to restrict the valid operations on a column (which would provide a broader level of domain support). Mechanisms for supporting data range checking include views created with a CHECK option, tables created with a CHECK clause, rules or constraints created separately from tables or views, and user exits. When someone tries to change a table upon which a constraint has been defined, the DBMS automatically verifies that applying the change would not violate the constraint. If no violation would occur, the change is allowed to proceed; if a violation is detected, the DBMS prohibits the attempt and returns an error.

Large Data Types (BLOBs)

Support for very long fields (sometimes called large objects, binary large objects, basic large objects, or BLOBs) adds flexibility to the types of data most relational DBMSs can store. As such, it can be broadly considered an object extension. When commercial relational DBMSs were first released, most supported only those data types most common to traditional business applications: various numeric data types (such as decimal, integer, and floating point) and character data types (such as fixed-length and varying-length character strings). Today, a number of relational vendors offer support for data types that may consume up to 2 GBs of space per row. This enables customers to store less conventional data types in relational DBMSs, including image, text, and voice.

Object DBMSs have usually supported large data types in their initial releases. This is because the application areas they focused on often required support for image and/or text fields. Unlike relational DBMSs, however, object DBMSs enable programmers to define and understand the internal structure of these large fields. (Most relational DBMSs are unaware of the internal structure of BLOB data; this awareness, if required, is usually built into the applications that access the BLOB data.) In some cases, relational DBMSs may place greater restrictions on the use of large fields than do object DBMSs. As with most extensions, support for BLOBs varies from product to product. However, many allow BLOBs to be created by and accessed with SQL, although some restrictions apply.

User-Defined Types and Functions

Other object extensions found in a number of relational DBMSs include support for user-defined data types and user-defined functions. These are less common than some of the other features described previously. As the name implies, user-defined types enable users to define new data types to the DBMS. This improves the overall flexibility of the system and enables users to more closely capture the semantics of their data.

However, in some cases these new types can only be direct derivatives of native system types. For example, a user may be able to define a "part number" data type based on an integer data type, but he or she may not be able to define an "employee" data type that contains a more complex internal structure (such as an integer field for the employee serial number, a character-string field for the employee name, and a set of character strings for the employee's various job skills). Such a restriction is not inherent in object DBMSs, as they were designed to support complex types with a variety of internal structures.

In relational DBMSs, support for user-defined data types may be provided through SQL extensions or through a third-generation language such as C. Specific implementations vary from product to product.

Like user-defined types, user-defined functions also provide for additional flexibility. They enable users to create their own SQL functions to perform operations not supported in a particular vendor's implementation of SQL. For example, a user could write a function to compute the square root of an integer value or to calculate the income tax assessed for a given salary. Once created, these functions can then be incorporated into SQL queries in much the same way that built-in SQL functions can be used.

In some respects, user-defined functions are similar to the methods or member functions of an object-oriented environment. Both represent code that is associated with certain data types, can accept input parameters, and can return parameters as output. However, user-defined functions are usually written in a third-generation programming language (such as C) and do not necessarily encapsulate the data. Access to the data can be achieved outside the function, usually through some series of standard SQL statements. Methods, on the other hand, do provide for data encapsulation and are usually written in a language such as C++ or Smalltalk. In addition, many relational DBMS vendors provide limited, if any, support for overloading built-in SQL functions and operators. Object DBMSs generally support this ability.

COMMON CHARACTERISTICS OF HYBRID DBMSS

Hybrid DBMSs (sometimes called unified DBMSs or object/relational DBMSs) are difficult to define, as these products are relatively new. Although their implementations vary from one another in a number of significant respects, these products generally share a common goal—to provide a high degree of object support while preserving the traditional strengths of relational DBMSs. These strengths include a robust, SQL-based query language and strong system management capabilities.

As such, hybrid DBMSs usually provide the features described earlier in the section "Common Relational DBMS Extensions," as well as a number of others, which the subsequent sections describe. However, they often differ from object DBMSs in several key areas: their architecture is generally server-centric, they generally provide less support for object-oriented programming language integration, and they generally rely heavily on the declarative features of SQL (along with extensions to that language) for data access, rather than the navigational approach to data retrieval and manipulation that is typical of object DBMSs. As of this writing, at least three commercially available products may be viewed as hybrid DBMSs: Illustra from Illustra Information Technology, Inc. (formerly Montage Software), UniSQL/X from UniSQL, Inc., and OpenODB from Hewlett Packard.

Multivalued Columns

Relational DBMSs are sometimes criticized for requiring data to be modeled in a rigid (normalized) table structure, in which only a single value (nondecomposable by the DBMS) can be associated with a single column in any particular row. Some systems, now referred to as object/relational DBMSs, have extended this definition of a table so that a single column of a row can contain multiple values. (Some adherents to the relational approach regard these tables as deviations from the relational model; others maintain that such tables still satisfy the requirements of normalization.)

Table 18–1 illustrates a sample table with multiple values allowed. Here, each employee row contains an employee number, an employee name, and a set of skills associated with the employee.

employee	id	name	skills
	1145783	edward chelini	mvs cics cobol
	4199982	calvin katte	unix c c++ tcp/ip
	8740871	sarah hunter	rdbms cobol

TABLE 18–1

A potential advantage of these tables is improved performance. In a relational DBMS that supports only a traditional table structure, information about employee skills would likely be stored in a separate table from the other employee information. Obtaining a report of all employees and their skills would require a join, which is an expensive operation. With multiple values, the skills information could be stored in the same table as the rest of the employee information, eliminating the need for a join.

Complex Data Types

Hybrid or object/relational systems also support complex data types, sometimes referred to as complex objects. These data types are defined by users and have an internal structure that is understood by the DBMS—a structure that often has multiple fields. In object/relational systems they can be thought of as tables that are nested within other tables.

For example, a department data type could be defined to contain a department number (an integer), a department name (a character string), and a department location (a character string). Once created, this new type could then be used when defining columns for a table. Although the syntax varies for defining new complex data types and for creating tables based on these types, a pseudo-SQL example is written as follows:

```
create type dept
      (dept_no        int,
       name           char(20),
       location       char(20))

create table projects
      (project_id     int,
       title          char(15),
       deadline       date,
       owner          dept)
```

In this example, the OWNER column of the PROJECTS table is defined as containing data of type DEPT. Values appearing in the OWNER column are references to instances of the DEPT data type (which may be considered as rows of the DEPT table). A query of the PROJECTS table (which uses the DEPT data type to identify the owner of a project) might yield a result similar to that shown in Table 18–2.

| | | | | * department * |
| | | | | * data type * |
result	project_id	title	deadline	owner
	14325	lan set-up	12/12/1997	reference_a
	51775	mvs upgrade	10/23/1997	reference_b
	48723	c++ class	06/30/1998	reference_c

TABLE 18–2

The DEPT_NO column values are references to rows in the DEPT table, which itself consists of multiple columns containing data of multiple types. From the standpoint of the object approach, the project table is an object which has as one of its parts another object, namely the DEPT table. And the DEPT table consists of parts of its own.

This support for complex data types is similar to the concepts of classes and types that are common to object-oriented programming languages. However, some hybrid DBMSs place greater restrictions on their support for complex data types than do object-oriented programming languages. For example, the user may not be able to define and manipulate a type that contains a linked list as one of its attributes or data members. An object-oriented programming language, such as C++, supports linked lists that can be manipulated by the application. With C++, programmers can create types of arbitrary complexity and use a variety of data structures (depending on what they may care to code).

Path Expressions

DBMSs that support some of the complex data types described previously often also support path expressions, which enable users to "walk through" the components of a complex type in a single statement. This is somewhat similar to the navigational approach used by object-oriented programmers, although these path expressions do not require users to define and use pointers.

An example may help clarify the use of path expressions. Imagine that the following data types and table have been defined (using pseudo-SQL syntax):

```
create type site
      (site_no        int,
       site_name      char(20))

create type department
      (dept_no        int,
       dept_name      char(20),
       location       site)

create table employee
      (emp_no         int,
       emp_name       char(30),
       salary         int,
       dept           department)
```

A path expression could be used within a query of the employee table to return the name of the site at which employee number 154320 works. Such a query would appear in pseudo-SQL as:

```
select employee.dept.location.site_name
from employee
where emp_no = 154320
```

Inheritance

Inheritance is generally another feature supported by hybrid DBMSs. This enables one type to be derived from one or more other types, creating type hierarchies by inheriting the attributes and behaviors associated with the parent type(s). Subclasses or subtypes are typically defined to the DBMS through SQL, rather than through class or type definitions in languages such as C++ or Smalltalk. Support for inheritance provides greater potential for code reuse and incremental refinements.

COMMERCIAL ACTIVITIES

This section briefly summarizes some of the key functions provided in three commercial DBMS products that can be considered to be hybrid DBMSs: Illustra from Illustra Information Technologies, Inc.; UniSQL/X from UniSQL, Inc.; and Open-ODB from Hewlett Packard. This discussion is simply an attempt to introduce the reader to some of the features and functions supported by commercial hybrid DBMSs. It is not intended to be an exhaustive discussion of their capabilities or a comprehensive list of all hybrid DBMSs.

Illustra

Illustra Information Technologies, Inc. is the producer of the Illustra DBMS (formerly known as the Montage Server), an object/relational DBMS that represents the commercialization of the POSTGRES research prototype described earlier in the section "Early Research Efforts." Unlike the research prototype, which supported POSTQUEL as its query language, Illustra offers an SQL interface. Dr. Michael Stonebraker, who headed the POSTGRES project, the university INGRES project, and who co-founded the firm that produced a commercial version of Ingres, is one of the co-founders of Illustra and its chief technology officer.

The Illustra DBMS enables users to define their own types, functions, operators, and business rules. It also supports multiple inheritance, path expressions, and complex structures.

The product is designed to address the needs of applications that are search-intensive and require the use of complex and/or nontraditional data. An example of such an application is one that requires sophisticated pattern matching, perhaps to scan a number of fingerprints stored electronically and compare them with a particular fingerprint found at a recent crime scene (and subsequently scanned into the system).

Providing an extensible architecture to help improve performance is another design point of this product. Users can define their own access methods, which may provide better performance for their user-defined types. In addition, a number of "DataBlades"—or libraries—are available to handle text, image, spatial, and time-series data. Users and third-party vendors may create their own DataBlades, if desired.

UniSQL/X

UniSQL, Inc., is the producer of UniSQL/X, sometimes referred to as a unified DBMS. The firm was founded by Dr. Won Kim, who worked on the ORION object DBMS project at Microelectronics and Computer Technology Corporation (MCC) and also on database projects at IBM's research division.

UniSQL/X enables users to create their own data types, procedures, complex structures, and hierarchies. Procedures (or methods) may be defined as part of the table (or class); this provides for both behavioral and structural inheritance. Path expressions in queries are also supported.

The product is marketed as supporting traditional business applications as well as more advanced applications, such as those involving office automation, multimedia, and geographic information systems. Since multimedia is an area of emphasis, the vendor provides multimedia classes for the DBMS. These include a generalized large object (GLO) class [similar to a binary large object, described earlier in the section "Large Data Types or BLOBs"], an audio class, an image class, and others. Users and third-party vendors may create their own classes, if desired.

OpenODB

OpenODB, produced by Hewlett Packard, represents a different approach to the development of a hybrid DBMS. The product features an object management layer built on top of a relational DBMS, which is used for data storage, security, recovery, and other traditional DBMS functions. It has been alternately characterized as an object DBMS and as a hybrid DBMS; the authors have chosen to treat it as the latter.

The product supports multiple programming languages (C, C++, COBOL, Fortran, and Pascal) and uses an object-based SQL interface. User-defined types, class hierarchies, multiple inheritance, and overloading are among the object-oriented features supported by OpenODB.

SUMMARY

Many object-oriented concepts are being incorporated into DBMS products outside of the object DBMS arena. Specifically, many vendors have incorporated a number of extensions into commercial relational DBMSs to provide some degree of object support. These extensions include stored procedures, triggers, constraints, very long fields (or BLOBs), user-defined types, and user-defined functions. These extensions provide RDBMSs with a richer data type system (although not one that is as rich as an object DBMS) and help make the DBMS more "active."

A newer class of DBMS products has also become commercially available. Sometimes called hybrid DBMSs, object/relational DBMSs, or unified DBMSs, these products attempt to capitalize on the strengths of both relational and object DBMS products, merging them into a single offering. These products typically provide many of the object extensions discussed earlier in this chapter (that are common to relational DBMSs) but also offer additional functions, such as support for multivalued columns, more complex data types, path expressions in queries, and inheritance. However, they still differ from object DBMSs in a number of key areas; among these is a greater emphasis on query language support and less integration with object-oriented programming languages.

REFERENCES AND SUGGESTED READING

"A New Direction in DBMS," *DBMS*, February 1994, p. 50.

AHAD, RAFIUL, and TU-TING CHENG. "HP OpenODB: An Object-Oriented Database Management System for Commercial Applications, " *Hewlett-Packard Journal*, vol. 44, no. 3, June 1993, p. 20.

BONTEMPO, CHARLES, and CINDY M. SARACCO. "Supporting Objects in a DBMS," *InfoDB*, vol. 7, no. 2, Spring 1993, p. 30.

CHENG, J. M., N. M. MATTOS, D. D. CHAMBERLIN, and L. G. DIMICHIEL. "Extending Relational Database Technology for New Applications," *IBM Systems Journal*, vol. 33, no. 2, 1994, p. 264.

CODD, E. F. "Extending the Database Relational Model to Capture More Meaning," *ACM Transactions on Database Systems*, 4, 4, December 1979.

CODD, E. F. *The Relational Model for Database Management Version 2*, Addison-Wesley, 1990.

HAAS L. M., et al. *Starburst Mid-Flight: As the Dust Clears*, IBM Research Report RJ-7278, January 1990.

HP's Object-Oriented Database Strategy, Hewlett Packard, PRCS4700142, Nov. 23, 1992.

KIM, WON. "UniSQL/X: A Unified Database System," *AIXpert*, May 1993, p. 31.

LOHMAN, GUY M., BRUCE LINDSAY, HAMID PIRAHESH, and K. BERNARD SCHIEFER. "Extensions to Starburst: Objects, Types, Functions, and Rules," *Communications of the ACM*, vol. 34, no. 10, October 1991.

Next-Generation Software Solutions, UniSQL, SBR-CO-0392, 1992.

SARACCO, C. M., and CHARLES J. BONTEMPO. "Applying Object Concepts to the DB2 Family," *IDUG Journal*, vol. 2, no. 1, January 1995, p. 28.

SARACCO, CINDY M. "Object and Relational Data Base Management Systems," *Data Management Review*, vol. 3, no. 11, November 1993, p. 8.

SHARP, BILL. "Open ODB," *HP Professional*, May 1992, p. 26.

STONEBRAKER, MICHAEL, and GREG KEMNITZ. "The POSTGRES Next-Generation Database Management System," *Communications of the ACM*, vol. 34, no. 10, October 1991.

STONEBRAKER, MICHAEL, "Inclusion of New Types in Relational Data Base Systems," in *Readings in Database Systems*, MICHAEL STONEBRAKER, ed., Morgan Kaufmann, 1995.

STONEBRAKER, MICHAEL. *Object-Relational Database Systems*, Illustra Information Technologies, (no publication date).

UniSQL/X Application Program Interface Reference Guide, Release 1.2, UniSQL, 1992.

UniSQL/X User's Manual, Release 1.2, UniSQL, 1991.

INDEX

DATE DUE

GAYLORD

PRINTED IN U.S.A.